Human–Computer Interaction Series

The Human–Computer Interaction Series, launched in 2004, publishes books that advance the science and technology of developing systems which are effective and satisfying for people in a wide variety of contexts. Titles focus on theoretical perspectives (such as formal approaches drawn from a variety of behavioural sciences), practical approaches (such as techniques for effectively integrating user needs in system development), and social issues (such as the determinants of utility, usability and acceptability).

HCI is a multidisciplinary field and focuses on the human aspects in the development of computer technology. As technology becomes increasingly more pervasive the need to take a human-centred approach in the design and development of computer-based systems becomes ever more important.

Titles published within the Human–Computer Interaction Series are included in Thomson Reuters' Book Citation Index, The DBLP Computer Science Bibliography and The HCI Bibliography.

Adam Palmquist · Izabella Jedel · Ole Goethe

Universal Design in Video Games

Active Participation Through Accessible Play

Springer

Adam Palmquist
Faculty of Social Sciences
Nord University
Levanger, Norway

Faculty of Applied IT
University of Gothenburg
Gothenburg, Sweden

Izabella Jedel
Faculty of Education and Arts
Nord University
Levanger, Norway

Ole Goethe
Faculty of Social Sciences
Nord University
Levanger, Norway

ISSN 1571-5035 ISSN 2524-4477 (electronic)
Human–Computer Interaction Series
ISBN 978-3-031-30597-9 ISBN 978-3-031-30595-5 (eBook)
https://doi.org/10.1007/978-3-031-30595-5

This Springer imprint is published by the registered company Springer Nature Switzerland AG
The registered company address is: Gewerbestrasse 11, 6330 Cham, Switzerland

Paper in this product is recyclable.

Preface

While accessibility and inclusiveness might not immediately spring to mind when embarking on a video game design project, they represent critical facets of the design process that can all too often be overlooked. These considerations, seemingly hidden, may only become apparent when an unexpected issue arises. Picture this: you are deep into a game development project when a tester reports they cannot read the text displayed on the screen. As you and your team investigate this anomaly, you discover the player is part of the 8% of the male population globally who are color-blind—unable to distinguish the green font you have used in the game interface.

Such challenges can surface at any stage of a game's lifecycle, resulting from a general lack of awareness or understanding within the development team. This is not typically due to deliberate omissions but rather unintended neglect. Smaller studios, in particular, might sideline these considerations due to resource constraints or the pressure of looming deadlines.

However, it is worth noting that addressing accessibility issues post-launch can often be more resource-intensive than incorporating these considerations from the outset. Although specific data on this within the realm of game development is scant, parallels can be drawn from comparable sectors, and our collective industry experiences strongly suggest a similar trend. Neglecting accessibility can carry a steep price tag, especially in the console game industry. Regions have established forceful accessibility legislation, like the European Accessibility Act, which can result in game companies and studios being embroiled in expensive lawsuits due to this oversight. It is a stark reminder of the developers' responsibility to provide equal access to all users—that also include video game players.

Beyond mere legal compliance—which we view as necessary yet uninspiring—there are many compelling reasons to strive for Universal, Inclusive, and Accessible Design in your games. A universally designed game—an experience thoughtfully crafted to be accessible and enjoyable by players of all abilities and backgrounds—provides a multitude of benefits that extend beyond simply widening the player demographic. Accessibility in video games extends beyond just offering multiple language options, though that is a starting point. By championing inclusivity and accessibility, you invite a diverse array of players into your virtual world, building a broader, more diverse community that, in turn, cultivates a richer, more meaningful player interaction and exchange.

The benefits of Universal Design go beyond mere player numbers. When you create a game that actively embraces all players, regardless of their abilities or background, you send a powerful message about your studio's values. You demonstrate a commitment to inclusivity and accessibility, which enhances your reputation within your player base. Players tend to feel a stronger connection with studios that acknowledge and cater to their individual needs. As a result, this can lead to greater player loyalty, positive word-of-mouth recommendations, and, ultimately, increased longevity of the game within the competitive market.

Moreover, a commitment to Universal Design strengthens your studio's brand, setting you apart in an industry that is increasingly recognizing the importance of accessibility. When your studio becomes synonymous with Accessible and Inclusive Design, you position yourself as a trailblazer—an entity that does not just follow trends but sets them. This unique branding can translate to broader recognition within the industry, attracting not just players but also talented professionals who wish to work in an environment that values inclusivity.

Adopting a Universal Design approach can significantly enhance the status and prestige of your games. Players will likely perceive accessible games as more player-friendly and well-designed, leading to better reviews and higher ratings. Additionally, universally designed games can often qualify for awards and recognition in accessibility and design, providing further visibility and prestige for your studio. Universal Design is not just a question of expanding player appeal—it is a comprehensive strategy to elevate your game, studio, and brand within the vibrant world of video game development.

With *Universal Design in Video Games*, we aim to equip and guide you and your team through the process of integrating Universal Design principles into your work, ensuring your video game designs are as inclusive and accessible as possible. We believe that by prioritizing accessibility and inclusiveness from the outset, you can create a gaming experience that transcends boundaries, providing enjoyment and engagement to various players.

Levanger, Norway/Gothenburg, Sweden — Adam Palmquist
Levanger, Norway — Izabella Jedel
Levanger, Norway — Ole Goethe

Contents

List of Figures

List of Tables

Chapter 1
From Universal Design to Attainable Game Experiences

Abstract Video games constitute an important part of peoples' lives, both from an entertainment perspective and for purposes that go beyond entertainment. For society to become inclusive, video games need to be inclusive. Inclusivity, accessibility, and usability are central concepts of the design of product, services, and experiences. Historically, these terms have been used differently depending on the lens of which one views design. The design lenses of inclusivity all strive toward a more accessible society but differ in terms of the processes underlying how inclusivity is achieved. Viewing video games from a Universal Design lens moves us from a consideration of accessibility in light of disability, toward reaching attainable game experiences for people with various different conditions beyond disability. In Chap. 1, we present the term Universal Design, how it emerged from interrelated design lenses and the key takeaways underlying the term, followed by a presentation of Universal Design in video games. Thereafter the discussion centers around the concept's disability, accessibility, and usability, and how these terms relate to Universal Design in general and Universal Design in video games specifically. Based on the contextualization of Universal Design in the video game space, we propose a definition for Universal Design in video games which centers around promoting an attainable gaming experience (AGE). The objective of the chapter is to provide an overview about historical and current considerations of accessibility and inclusivity to understand how you can approach inclusivity and a Universal Design approach in video games from a more nuanced perspective.

Keywords Universal design · Accessible design · Inclusive design · Design for all · Usability · Accessibility · Video games

1.1 Introduction

Games have been a valued part of peoples' lives throughout history. In the past decades, gameplay has taken the form of video games; games played through the use of electronic devices such as video game consoles, computers, or phones [21].

A. Palmquist et al., *Universal Design in Video Games*, Human–Computer Interaction Series, https://doi.org/10.1007/978-3-031-30595-5_1

The financial market for video gaming has increased significantly during the last few years. Growing from a 44.3 billion market in 2019 to a 60.4 billion market in 2021, it was reported that 66% of the US population played video games for one hour or more per week in 2022 [17]. The rise of video games in society is not surprising. Video games constitute a major part of entertainment [28] and are an essential part of allowing people to connect with each other [11]. Video game play can also positively influence people's well-being, such as contributing to an improved mood, increased emotion regulation, and reduced stress levels [39]. Apart from having entertainment and social value, video games are also to a larger extent being employed in other areas, such as a means of increased learning and exercise [28]. The field of serious games, games used for external purposes beyond entertainment, is growing in research as well as in practice. Video games are consequently becoming an increasingly important part of society as a whole: utilized for both entertainment purposes and purposes that go beyond entertainment [29]. Some of these application areas are discussed in Section III of the book.

The extensive outreach of video games in our society implies potential promising financial benefits for game development. At the same time, the widespread use of video games also infers that accessibility and inclusivity need to be incorporated as a central part of the game design process. For society to be inclusive, people of varying characteristics should have the right to a decent life, enjoyment, and entertainment. The integrated part of video game play in peoples' lives means that for society to be inclusive there is a need to allow as many people as possible, of varying characteristic and in various situations, to be able to participate in video gameplay. Traditionally video games have been viewed as adhering mostly to a homogenous audience consisting of young men. However, recent data has questioned this assumption, showing that video games are played by people of varying demographics and characteristics [17, 29]. Video games can also function as a vessel for inclusivity in themselves. Studies have shown that people who experience conditions that limit them from participating in everyday activities positively relate to video games as they enable them to take part in society on equal terms [11]. Allowing all people to access and enjoy video games is therefore not only a noteworthy goal in itself but can help us create a more inclusive society that benefits us all. Designing for all is one of the key concepts behind Universal Design—a framework that provides the design perspective of creating products and services for all. At its core, Universal Design centers around an understanding of people not consisting of one homogenous group but having varying characteristics that need to be understood and designed for.

Applying the Universal Design lens to the context of video games goes beyond the concept of accessibility. Instead of designing separate games or including assistive technology for players with specific conditions, the lens of Universal Design focuses on designing catered experiences for all that acknowledges that players, as people, are diverse in their characteristics. Apart from benefiting individuals and promoting inclusivity, the Universal Design approach also paves the way for a broader market and offers the potential for commercial success for game developers. In this introductory chapter, we discuss the concept of Universal Design, its application in video games and related concepts.

1.2 The Emergence of Inclusivity

Universal Design, also referred to as *Design For All* [66] and *Inclusive Design* [14], has emerged from several interrelated concepts such as *Barrier-Free Design* and *Accessible Design*. Understanding the meaning and evolution behind Barrier-Free Design, Accessible Design, and Inclusive Design can help distinguish what Universal Design is and what it is not, thus moving us toward how Universal Design can be understood in the context of video games.

1.2.1 From Accessibility to Design for All

Barrier-Free Design is rooted in architecture and environmental design, focusing on the accessibility of buildings. The concept of Barrier-Free Design started emerging in the United States from the 1950s [56]. The movement grew as war veterans returned from the Vietnam war with physical disabilities [56]. National standards were set in the United States, and several assistive technologies were developed in order to allow people with physical disabilities to take part in everyday activities [56]. One example of Barrier-Free Design still present in society is enabling people in wheelchairs to access buildings by including ramps.

The Barrier-Free Design movement opened up for societal changes that allowed broader accessibility, but it also received criticism from people with disabilities since it involved treating people with defined disabilities differently from people without disabilities [40]. Including separate entrances for people with wheelchairs for example implies that people in wheelchairs cannot enter buildings in the same manner as the rest of the population. For people with disabilities to participate in everyday activities in a non excluded way, products and environments needed to be designed and introduced in a way that could be used by all people, and did not treat people with disabilities as special cases [40]. Furthermore, the Barrier-Free Design approach was limited since it focused solely on enabling access based on physical abilities and did not consider cognitive abilities [40].

The introduction of concepts such as Accessible Design and Inclusive Design brought accessibility to a broader range of environments and products, not only involving physical capabilities but also cognitive capacities (Fig. 1.1). Similar to Barrier-Free Design, the Accessible Design approach is rooted in societal changes brought forward by legal requirements and mandates [20]. Accessible Design has been defined as the design of products and services that satisfy legal requirements, mandates, and guidelines, so that accessibility is ensured for people with disabilities [20]. Early approaches to Accessible Design mostly focused on providing adapted features for people with disabilities and were thus criticized for segregating people with disabilities from the rest of society [65]. Accessible Design has evolved over the past year and developed a more nuanced view of disability. However, the focus

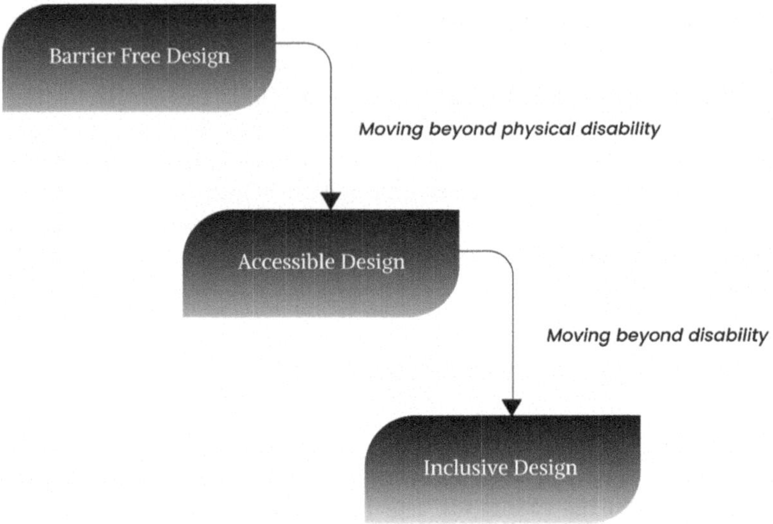

Fig. 1.1 From barrier-free to inclusive design

of Accessible Design still centers around enabling people with defined disabilities to access products and services.

One approach that included people of varying characteristics on a broader scale was Inclusive Design. Inclusive Design was first introduced as making products and environments accessible to as many people as reasonably possible [56]. Compared to Accessible Design, the Inclusive Design movement argued for designing for a broad audience including people with and without disabilities. Instead of focusing on how people with defined disabilities could get access to a service, Inclusive Design focused on allowing as many people as reasonably possible to experience services. The term reasonably in the Inclusive Design definition implied that people with specific abilities could be excluded if deemed too difficult to design for Persson et at. [56], thus introducing the same type of stigmatization earlier approaches had been criticized for. Since the earlier definitions of Inclusive Design, the concept has evolved and is today in many cases used synonymously with Universal Design [14].

The term Universal Design was first coined by Mace [47] in the 1980s as a way to design environments that were both attractive and functional for all people, despite having defined disabilities or not. Mace's view was that Universal Design included a common-sense approach and awareness in the design process to make all products and environments usable by everyone to the greatest extent possible. The Universal Design paradigm's inclusion of all individuals does not solely focus on people with disabilities. It also encompasses other groups marginalized by traditional design standards, including children, seniors, and people of various sizes [30, 46]. The idea underlying the Universal Design concept is that while Universal Design might be necessary to some people, it will at the same time benefit all people interacting with the service, product, or environment. Including features that allow people to interact

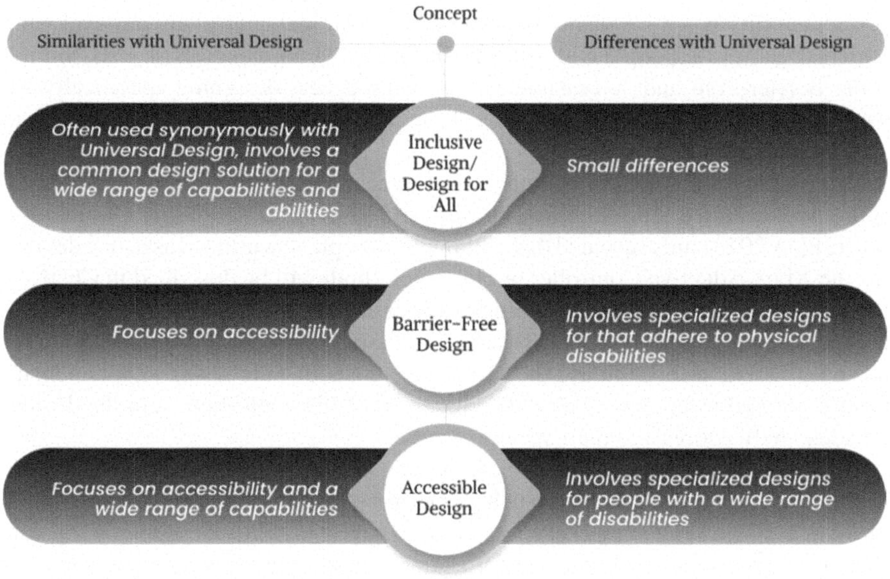

Fig. 1.2 Universal design similarities and differences with related concepts

with a product in various different ways for example does not only allow access for people who could not otherwise interact with the product, but also provide greater choice and flexibility for all.

Universal Design is today often used synonymously with Design For All [66] and Inclusive Design [14], and shares several similarities and differences with Barrier-Free Design and Accessible Design (Fig. 1.2). First, compared to Barrier-Free Design, Universal Design is not limited to physical environments but includes a wider range of capabilities. Capabilities in a Universal Design context refer to the degree to which a person functions, from high ability to extreme impairment, in relation to the interaction with a specific environment [38]. Secondly, compared to Accessible Design, Universal Design is not rooted in legal requirements or mandates [20]. Instead, Universal Design views it advantageous to have an Inclusive Design approach, not only for people with specific disabilities but for all people, no matter the range of their abilities.

1.2.2 From Accessible Games to an Attainable Game Experience

Accessibility in video games has been discussed and applied to an increasing extent over the last decades in research as well as in industry. Early approaches of accessibility in gaming focused on either integrating assistive technologies that allowed for accessibility when it was not possible with traditional controllers or developing particular games for people with specific disabilities Grammenos et al. [28]. Similar to the Barrier-Free and Accessible Design approaches, designing specifically for disability in the context of video games through the two approaches faced criticism from the research field.

The first approach of integrating assistive technologies that allowed for accessibility was criticized for not reaching sufficient levels of accessibility Grammenos et al. [28]. A 2023 study revealed that, although some players utilized assistive devices like the Xbox Adaptive Controller or Quadstick (both will be described in Chap. 4), the majority of players with disabilities did not employ such assistive technologies in their gaming experiences [3]. The study's participants cited several reasons for not using assistive technology: the prohibitive costs of purchasing supplementary devices, limited awareness and knowledge of available controllers, and the devices not adequately addressing their specific needs.

The second approach of developing particular games for people with specific disabilities was also criticized, as such games are often not prioritized commercially due to targeting a limited market space Grammenos et al. [28]. Designing a separate game for visually impaired players for example offers a promising perspective for researchers who study accessibility, but is not as often developed for commercial purposes as game developers want to target a broader audience. The approach of designing games targeting specific disabilities has also been criticized since players with specific disabilities are not a homogenous group [12]. Despite being grouped in the same type of disability, players face various barriers depending on their degree and type of disability in the broader category [12]. For example, some players face complete blindness and can thus not rely on any visual input. Other players face color blindness and can thus not distinguish between certain colors. Designing one game targeting both types of players with a visual impairment might result in an optimal solution for either condition.

Apart from the criticism discussed in relation to early approaches of accessibility in video games, targeting disability specifically in the design of video games also encounters the same stigmatization problem of the Barrier-Free and Accessible Design movements. A Universal Design approach toward inclusivity in video games, in which people with all abilities can participate/play a game, both those with and without defined disabilities could overcome previous limitations associated with Barrier-Free Design and Accessible Design and enable more people to access and enjoy gameplay. Compared to other types of services and products, the main goal of video games is to provide a hedonic yet engaging and aesthetic experience (Schell, [62]). In a video game context, we therefore propose that Universal Design should center around making video game experiences attainable.

1.3 Understanding the Universal Design Lens

According to the Center for Universal Design [72], Universal Design is defined as "the design of facilities, products and services that can be used by people with all abilities, to the greatest extent possible, without adaptation." Unlike its predecessors in Barrier-Free Design and Accessible Design, the definition of Universal Design does not mention disability. Instead, it reflects the concept of people with all abilities. Universal Design does not divide people into two groups, those with and those without disabilities. Neither does it solely focus on promoting usage for people with disabilities. Instead, Universal Design acknowledges that we who interact with products and environments have a diverse set of desires, needs, and abilities [37]. The focal point in Universal Design is thus to see the users as one population with varied abilities and capabilities, designing a solution that can adhere to the population as a whole. Another important aspect in the Universal Design paradigm is that facilities, products, and services should be usable to the greatest extent possible without adaptation. Instead of creating specialized options and alternatives which can lead to segregation and stigmatization, an environment designed from a universal perspective should aim to seamlessly include and integrate features that furnish ease of use for the entire user population [65]. The inclusion of the entire user population in the design space of an artifact implies that Universal Design cannot be introduced as an addition to existing environments or products; it demands to be integrated in the initial phases of the design process [37].

The idea of Universal Design is commendable. At the same time, its feasibility remains a subject of debate. The inclusion of people with all abilities without adaptation helps overcome the stigmatization associated with disabilities over time. However, a discrepancy between *being used by people with all abilities* and *without adaptation* might arise in circumstances in which a product or service simply cannot be made accessible to certain people without using specific adaptations such as assistive technology. In the design of video games for example, including specialized controllers that allow for adapting the way one interacts with the game becomes a necessity for people with specific motor control conditions. In those cases, Universal Design should try to incorporate features that allow for the widest use possible without adaptation, while simultaneously not excluding assistive technologies when necessary. This distinction highlights that designing products and services that are completely universal is often not achievable. In the context of this book, Universal Design should therefore not be viewed as an end goal that can be achieved but as a process toward a desired state. The central discussion of Universal Design should therefore not be <u>if</u> a product or service is universal but rather <u>how</u> to make a product or service more universal.

1.3.1 Relating to Disability in Universal Design

How to relate to the term disability has been a cornerstone in the discussion on Barrier-Free, Accessible, Inclusive, and Universal Design. The term disability has been less emphasized in Universal Design, as the goal is to serve people with all abilities without putting specific emphasis on disability per se. However, neglecting to admit and in-depth understanding of disabilities in the design context might result in an inferior artifact including barriers toward use. As Lid [44] argues, Universal Design centers around designing for people, making it crucial to understand people who face disability as part of their human condition.

The Universal Design perspective considers disability as *relational*, arising from both the person and the environment [44]. In that sense, Universal Design incorporates the social and the medical model of disability [44]. The medical model of disability was the prominent viewpoint of disability before the 1970s, focusing on reducing the problems of people with disabilities through medical prevention, cure, and rehabilitation [64]. The medical model of disability was however criticized for only viewing medical intervention as a strategy for dealing with disability and creating stigmatization around disability [27]. In the 1970s, an alternative model of disability, the social model of disability, arose as a response to the segregation experienced by disabled people [64]. The social model distinguishes impairment, that is, the physical limitation of people, from disability, that is, the social constraints faced due to the environment's design [64]. In other words, disability was not viewed as an individual deficit, but instead a condition that arose when interacting in a society not designed for all types of people. However, while the social model of disability introduced new perspectives and empowerment to people with disabilities, it has also been criticized for neglecting that impairments can negatively impact people's lives beyond accessibility and that societal adaptation will never fully be able to eliminate the disadvantages associated with all impairments [64]. The relational model acknowledges both the medical and social model of disabilities and states that disability emerges in the mismatch or gap between the individual's abilities and the environmental conditions that the individual faces [44]. Similarly, recent guidelines from the World Health Organization [69] define disability as arising from the impairments a person experiences and the effects imposed by the person's environment. To fully understand disability in the context of Universal Design, it is thus important to consider both the impairments that the individual experiences and their consequences in everyday life arising from the design of the surrounding environment.

Following the view of disability as arising in the combination between a person's impairments and the environment one is situated in, disability can take several different forms. People with disabilities are often viewed as one group. In reality, however, people with disabilities are a diverse group of people facing different social and physical barriers in society [69]. Furthermore, disability can arise in different contexts and at several different parts of one's life. A study conducted by Ward et al. [67] concluded that people with disabilities vary between those that report disability as consistent, viewing disability as a personal characteristic, and those that report disability as arising in-consistently over time, viewing disability more as a temporary state. In the intersection of information technology and accessibility, the concept of "situational disability" is emphasized. It underscores the idea that disabilities can manifest when individuals partake in specific activities or find themselves in particular contexts [63]. For instance, being in a noisy environment can diminish one's ability to discern specific sounds, while activities like walking or running might temporarily reduce motor function capabilities.

Based on the complex nature of disability from a Universal Design perspective and the fact that people with disabilities are not a homogenous group, the upcoming chapters focus on conditions rather than disability. Peoples' varying conditions imply that people do not interact with products or services under the same premise but that different causes underlie the ability for people to access, use, and experience products and services. Conditions can for example include temporal or permanent medical impairments such as blindness or limited motor functioning, individual characteristics such as age or body size, or situational disabilities that arise from for example being situated in a noisy environment. Enabling all people to access a product or service therefore requires careful consideration and an in-depth understanding of the varying conditions that people have in different contexts and stages of their lives.

Disabled People or People with Disabilities?

Due to disability arising from interaction with society, when speaking about disabilities proponents for the social model of disabilities view "disabled people" as the correct term instead of the previously used term "people with disabilities" [64]. In this book, we have chosen to stick to the term "people with disabilities" due to adherence with the language used by advocating organizations such as the Convention on the Rights of Persons with Disabilities (CRPD) and the World Health Organization (WHO), as well as due to including the notion of disability being a state that can arise in temporary circumstances.

1.3.2 The Need for Accessibility and Usability

Universal Design centers around accessibility and usability. ISO, the international organization for standardization, defines accessibility in its 2019 norm ISO 9241-210 [35] as the:

> "extent to which products, systems, services, environments and facilities can be used by people from a population with the widest range of user needs, characteristics and capabilities to achieve identified goals in identified contexts of use", and usability as the: "extent to which a system, product or service can be used by specified users to achieve specified goals with effectiveness, efficiency and satisfaction in a specified context of use."

While accessibility is closely related to including people with visual, auditory, motor, and cognitive-related conditions, usability centers around the whole population reaching outcome objectives related to objective performance and subjective measures such as satisfaction [60]. In that sense, accessibility can be viewed as a precondition to usability for the broad population; without being able to access a service or product, a specific person will not be able to find the service or product useful in reaching specific goals.

Accessibility in the context of Universal Design considers that accessibility problems arise from the design of environments that do not consider the full range of human capabilities (Clarkson & Coleman, [15]). In other words, it is not only a person's individual conditions that affect if a service or product is accessible, but rather how such a product or service is designed. Accessibility in Universal Design thus involves matching the design of the physical environment with a person's functional capacity [37]. Designing for accessibility requires an understanding of three main factors [37]:

- The personal component: understanding the functional capacity of the individual or group interacting with the environment.
- The environmental component: understanding which barriers exist in the environment in relation to current norms.
- Accessibility problem: understanding how the personal component and the environmental component align.

To design accessible services or products one therefore needs to understand the target audience who will be interacting with the product or service and specific design aspects that might hinder or enable the users to access the product or service. Accessibility in the context of Universal Design is therefore not only about understanding the conditions people have but about enabling ability through design.

Accessibility can be viewed as a precondition to usability since if a person is not able to access a product, service, or facility, it is by default not usable [20]. Usability extends the concept of accessibility, considering the person-environment encounter, by considering the subjective experience of the person interacting with the environment and the specific activity in the environment [37]. Compared to accessibility, which involves if it is possible to access a product or service, usability involves the experience that arises in the person when interacting with the product or service. It is for example possible for a person to be able to access a service, but if the person is hindered from using the service without a sense of ease and satisfaction, it is not viewed as useful. Apart from considering the personal component, environmental component, and accessibility problem, usability in a Universal Design context therefore also relies on understanding the alignment between the person's capabilities, the specific environment, and the activity [37].

Accessibility and usability in terms of the interaction between a person's capacity and the environment's constraints provide a more nuanced view than focusing solely on disabilities as introduced in early days of Barrier-Free Design, Accessible Design and Inclusive Design. Instead, both the medical model of disability (through the personal component) and the social model of disability (through the interaction between the personal and environmental component) are incorporated to understand the accessibility barriers that can arise in the interaction with a specific environment.

1.4 Toward an Attainable Game Experience

Since the earlier days of Accessible Design, several scholars have addressed perspectives of video game design that align more strongly with the Universal Design lens. Grammenos et al. [28] define Universally Accessible Games as: *"games that are proactively designed to be concurrently accessible to people with a wide range of diverse requirements and/or disabilities"* (p. 3).

Compared to the definition of Universal Design presented by the Center for Universal Design[72], Grammenos et al. [28]'s definition differs in terms of focusing on the proactive design process, emphasizing the need for considering universality early in the design process. This perspective aligns with integrating Universal Design in the initial phases of the design process. Another important consideration with universally accessible game definition is that games should be *concurrently* accessible. Instead of designing specific games for targeted types of defined disabilities, the same game should be playable by people with a diverse set of conditions and abilities. Similar to the idea behind Universal Design, this moves us away from creating catered solutions for specific people and instead strives for a design space that considers that people have differences and can face various barriers in gameplay.

Furthermore, while the definition of Universal Design focuses on allowing usage by all people, the Universally Accessible Design definition includes people with a wide range of diverse requirements. Like Grammenos et al. [28], Yuan et al. [70] argue that designing universal video games needs to consider more than one disability but does not need to include accessibility for people with all types of disabilities. In a sense, the universally accessible game definition therefore focuses on disability and a narrower group of people compared to the Universal Design definition, which includes *people with all abilities.*

As Grammenos et al. [28] states, the main principle of universally designed games should be to allow people to have fun and compete on an equal basis despite having different individual characteristics. Games are at their core meant to be fun and elicit a positive psychological experience. While the goal of Universal Design in video games is to target people with a wide range of requirements, in reality, it might not be possible to create a game that is accessible to all without further adaptation, just as it is not possible to create a game that everyone views as enjoyable. In the Universal Design of video games, the focus should therefore be to consider a broad set of abilities and conditions, include seamlessly integrated features that provide accessibility to the largest extent of the population as possible, and when needed, include additional options for adaptation.

Another distinction between the Universal Design and Universally Accessible Games is that the definition of Universally Accessible Games focuses more on allowing people with disability access. For universally designed video games, the focus should include not only people with disabilities but also people of varying characteristics, such as age and size, to access the game. A younger player could have problems accessing certain game controllers of larger size, which inhibits their ability to interact with the game. For universally designed video games, not only people with specific disabilities should be considered, but also people of several varying conditions.

1.4.1 Cornerstones to an Attainable Game Experience

Just as with Universal Design, accessibility, and usability become a central part of universally designed video games. In video games, people should be able to have fun and compete on an equal basis despite having different individual characteristics [28], which is not possible if video games are not accessible to the person wishing to interact with the game. Accessibility and usability in video games can allow for social benefit in terms of more people being able to partake in and reap the same benefits from gaming, as well as providing financial benefits for game designers in terms of gaining positive publicity and reaching new markets [24].

In accordance with the ISO standard for accessibility [35] for a game to be accessible, it should be possible to use by people from a population with the widest range of needs, characteristics, and capabilities. Game accessibility therefore includes being able to play a game even when functioning under limiting conditions [34]. From the Universal Design perspective, accessibility in video games should involve adapting the environment (the game) to the personal component, allowing people with varying individual characteristics to interact with the game. A Universal Design approach includes incorporating accessibility design features into mainstream products and services [32]. Due to the diverse set of characteristics of different people, it is difficult to find a one-size-fits-all solution. Instead, accessibility in video games often concerns which options to add to allow for an accessible game play for people with disabilities [12] and for people with varying characteristics. Games are in their nature interactive and dynamic which calls for a customizable approach in video game design to allow for higher accessibility, rather than striving to create a "*one-size-fits-all*" solution [49].

In line with the ISO definition for usability [35], usability involves being able to reach a specific goal through a system, product, or service. While usability in a broader software context centers around efficiency, effectiveness, and satisfaction, usability in a game context at its core centers mainly around satisfaction [22]. The reason for which is that efficiency and effectiveness are not always desirable in games since the purpose behind video games is to generate positive user experiences. To reach such experiences most games utilize challenges and barriers that the player needs to overcome to win the game. An overall efficient and effective experience, in which the player can reach the goal without encountering any challenges, would therefore not equate to a positive game experience [22]. Furthermore, usability in games concerns the degree in which a player is able to learn, control, and understand a game [57]. If a player is not able to learn, control, and understand the game, they will not have the chance to attain the positive game experience that can be elicited. Just as accessibility is a precondition for usability in general, the same holds true in the context of video games. If people are not able to access a game, they will not be able to reach the game experience and satisfaction associated with playing the game. Usability in video games from a Universal Design lens should involve understanding the personal component, in terms of the characteristics of the audience, and the alignment between the game and the personal component that generates a specific in-game experience associated with satisfaction. Game usability therefore concerns the degree to which a player is able to attain the game experience.

Three Waves of Accessibility in Video Games

Power et al. [59] describe three waves of accessibility in video games. The first wave of accessibility is about *access*—allowing people to take action, consume information about the state of the game and control the game. People might be excluded in this phase due to a mismatch between the players' capabilities and the game controllers or presentation in the game. Game controllers might for example need to be adapted or buttons remapped to allow some people to access the game. The presentation in the game might need to be adapted for other players, such as alternating the colors or the sizes displayed in the game. The second wave of accessibility presented by Power et al. [59] is about *enablement*; allowing people to face the challenges presented in the game. In the enablement phase, people risk being excluded by not being able to react to the actions in the game and consequently not being able to respond to the challenges. Players with motor impairments for example might risk being excluded in this phase due to not being able to react to the game in a timely manner. To overcome barriers in the enablement phase, the game needs to be adaptable to suit different players while at the same time considering that players can improve over time. The third and final wave of accessibility in video games concerns *experience*: allowing people to take part in the desired experience of the game. The experience phase of accessibility is only achievable if the player can access the game and is enabled but goes beyond the available options to interact with the game and includes what expectations and types of experiences people have while players.

1.4.2 Barriers Toward an Attainable Game Experience

Universal Design in video games concerns usability for people of varying characteristics. The emphasis of Universal Design should, therefore, not only consider people with disabilities. At the same time, understanding individual factors of impairment and the disabilities that can arise when interacting with a product or service becomes crucial to realize Universal Design in practice [44]. As of 2021, the World Health Organization [69] estimated that 1.3 billion people experienced significant disability. The number constitutes approximately 16% of the global population and is expected to rise due to an increasingly aging population [69]. People with disabilities report playing mainstream, commercial games, with similar game preferences to those without disabilities [6]. Not including the perspective of disability in the context of video games as a part of the conditions that people experience would therefore exclude a large part of the potential gaming population, thus not being consistent with the Universal Design approach. A second reason for including the perspective of disability in the context of universally designed video games is that disability can be viewed as a source of innovation, due to the design constraints imposed [32]. The typewriter and the email client are two examples of innovations that were originally designed to allow for visually impaired and auditory impaired people to communicate but are today used universally [32]. Including the perspective of disability in the design process of universal video games could therefore result not only in creating higher accessibility for games but also in new innovations to emerge that can benefit all players.

As stated above, the Universal Design perspective views disability as arising from the combination of a person's capacities and the environment the person interacts with. In a video game context, disability should thus be viewed from the types of individual conditions that affect peoples' ability to partake in gameplay. Video games are demanding, requiring sensor, motor, and cognitive skills to interact with, resulting in video games risking becoming inaccessible to a large percentage of people [28]. Simultaneously, challenge and demand are an integral part of the enjoyment of video games. The goal of video games should therefore not be to remove all obstacles when interacting with a game, but instead to remove the obstacles that hinder the player from accessing the desired in-game experience. The following four main types of conditions are commonly discussed in the context of making video games accessible [2, 7]:

- Visual conditions: conditions that affect vision such as blindness, low vision, and color blindness.
- Auditory conditions: conditions that affect hearing such as deafness or a lack of hearing.
- Mobility/Motor conditions: conditions that affect sensation, coordination, and movement such as paralysis, neurological disorders, or repetitive stress injury.
- Cognitive conditions: conditions that affect mental and social functioning such as learning disabilities, memory loss, or attention deficit disorder.

Based on the view of disability being dependent on the environment, certain types of video games might not result in disability for people despite having individual conditions that cause disability in other circumstances. A person who is in a wheelchair would for example not experience any disability in video games played by everyone in a seated position. The player would however experience disability in contexts that required the player to stand such as specific Virtual Reality (VR) games or Exergames (Discussed further in Section III). The example highlights that disability in video games is contextual and highly dependent on the options that the player has to interact with the game. The same is true with other limiting conditions people face. In the context of temporary or situational disabilities, people can temporarily not be able to play a game due to constraints in the environment, e.g., not being able to perceive sound due to noisy surroundings, software and hardware constraints, e.g., a bad internet connection, or due to gaming skills and preferences [28].

1.4.3 Enablers for Attainable Game Experiences

Several design practices underscore the vital role of language inclusivity in shaping player perceptions and interactions. The terminology and semantics used within the video game's interface can significantly impact its acceptance and comprehension across diverse gaming communities. The terminologies and semantics surrounding design artifacts are crucial in their acceptance and understanding among various communities. Striving toward an attainable game experience requires game designers to be aware of the cultural nuances and norms that can influence how interface elements are received. It emphasizes the designer's understanding of the circumstances and conversations within the discourse, which may often be outside the direct influence of designers. Understanding the broader discourse and societal context—often beyond the direct control of the game developers—is crucial for creating interfaces that resonate with a wide range of players.

For video game design to be genuinely inclusive and accessible, it must be integrated with its surrounding ecosystem, thereby adding value and enhancing the game experience for a broad set of players. For an Inclusive Design to thrive, it must meaningfully relate to its surroundings, enhancing accessibility and value for all stakeholders. In many aspects, the game design process is dissimilar to user experience (UX) and user interface (UI) design—the reasons why will be further explored in Sect. 1.6. The tents in video game design are even more alien to the paradigm of Accessible, Inclusive, and Universal Design.

Perhaps the most obvious difference lies in the function and ease-of-use criteria—a strong drive for designers interested in UX/UI—and the creativity and artistic criteria—which is the primus motor for many game designers and their artifacts (see Figs. 1.2 and 1.3).

The design landscape has long been characterized by diverse approaches that fulfill various human needs and desires. Two dominant paradigms in this regard are hedonic and utilitarian intentions and properties of a devised artifact. For game creators that, in our experience, have extensive knowledge of how to devise hedonic products but rather limited knowledge of utilitarian products, we will shortly delineate the differences between these two and how they function in the context of interaction interface design for video games. The concepts of hedonic and utilitarian attributes, originating from consumer psychology [5, 31], are essential for understanding the foundations

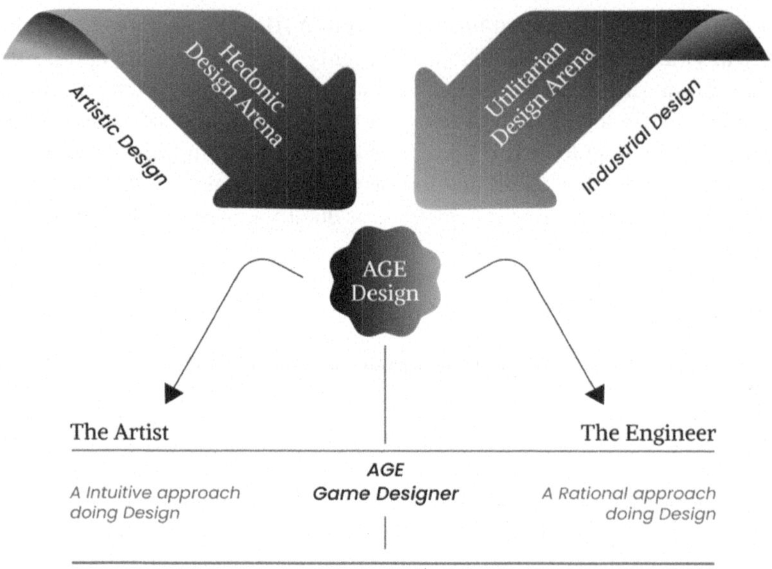

Fig. 1.3 Role of the video game designer when striving for an attainable game experience (modified from Edeholt [18])

of an attainable game experience in a video game's interaction interface. Hedonic and utilitarian attributes assert that audiences' attitudes embody distinct hedonic and utilitarian dimensions, influencing overall attitudes toward diverse product categories to varying degrees. Essentially, when audiences engage with products and services, they perform behaviors driven by two fundamental motivations: hedonic and utilitarian. While both approaches contribute to the overall consumer experience, they prioritize different aspects and, as such, yield distinct results.

Hedonic and utilitarian attributes in technology design represent two functions of a technology artifact [55, 71]. The hedonic design focuses on creating pleasurable and emotionally engaging experiences, like a video game, whereas utilitarian design prioritizes functionality and efficiency, like statistics software.

Hedonic Design Intentions

The hedonic design aims to provide the target audience with experiences rich in emotional engagement, aesthetic appeal, and sensory pleasure. In video game interfaces, this might manifest as visually stunning graphics, compelling storylines, or emotionally resonant music. In video games, a hedonic approach could involve intricate art styles, atmospheric audio, or complex narrative structures. These elements often heighten the audience emotional involvement and generate a sense of immersion, making the game more memorable and personally meaningful.

Utilitarian Design Intentions

Utilitarian design focuses primarily on the functionality and efficiency of a product. In interface design, this equates to intuitive layouts, straightforward navigation, and the quick accessibility of essential features. For video game interfaces, a utilitarian design might be reflected in highly responsive controls, clear and concise menus, and an uncluttered HUD (Head-Up Display). The emphasis is on facilitating smooth and efficient interactions, enabling players to achieve their objectives without unnecessary hindrances.

Better understanding the intentions and properties between these two dimensions is critical in making your video game more attainable, as the player's interplay with the artifact is conducted via an interaction interface—thus, knowing how to devise them functional and practical becomes crucial. For video game creators that aim and strive to provide more attainable gameplay, it must be understood that the interaction interfaces cannot be designed from a sole hedonic perspective; the interfaces must holistically address the functional, instrumental, and pragmatic needs of the players, so that they might participate fully in the game. The video game must provide interaction interfaces that are not only pleasurable and entertaining but functional in regard to the various conditions and circumstances the audience might harbor.

Planned Integration and Good a Balance for an Attainable Game Experience

Hedonic design centers on emotional engagement and aesthetic fulfillment, which may sometimes come at the expense of efficiency or functionality. Utilitarian design, on the other hand, focuses on increasing skill levels and amplifying abilities making it plainer to accomplish certain tasks effectively and rapidly—by potentially sacrificing emotional or aesthetic aspects in the process.

In video games, hedonic elements can significantly enhance player engagement but may introduce complexities that not all players appreciate. Utilitarian elements simplify interactions but could result in a less emotionally engaging experience.

Effective interface design in video games should integrate both hedonic and utilitarian elements to provide an experience that is both emotionally enriching and functionally effective. The key lies in striking a balance that caters to the broadest possible range of user preferences and needs.

While hedonic and utilitarian design intentions serve different purposes, recognizing their unique contributions and limitations can yield a more nuanced and practical design approach. Especially in video game interface design, an integrated approach incorporating both hedonic and utilitarian aspects can lead to more comprehensive and satisfying game experiences.

"You are not the Player"

In addition to the complexities arising from balancing the hedonic and utilitarian design directions, there is a crucial challenge in video game design—particularly when aiming for accessibility and inclusion. This challenge manifests as a paradox often termed "expert blindness." The more intimately the game development team is involved with their game, the more they risk becoming blind to its quirks and imperfections. Over time, this specialized knowledge can evolve into cognitive bias, leading to the emergence of the so-called omnipotent designer phenomenon—a serious pitfall for anyone aiming to create a universally enjoyable gaming experience.

The expert blindness paradox occurs when designers, deeply knowledgeable about their game mechanics, assume that their targeted audiences share the same level of understanding. This assumption can lead to overlooking critical design flaws, which may be glaringly apparent to newcomers. For instance, a game designer might create a player interaction interface that seems intuitive to them simply because they are well-versed in the software's intricacies. Yet, that interface could be bewildering or counterintuitive to a player new to the experience.

To mitigate such issues, when striving to achieve an attainable game experience in your video games, it is imperative to employ data-informed design decisions rather than relying solely on intuitive judgments. Data-informed design approach allows designers to identify potential obstacles and make adjustments proactively, thereby aligning the design more closely with the actual needs and expectations of a broader player demographic. By prioritizing data over intuition, designers not only improve accessibility but also foster a more inclusive and universally enjoyable gaming experience.

Utilitarian design intention primarily focuses on efficiency, often influenced by technological attributes. Nevertheless, efficiency can also bring immense satisfaction when experienced. When every facet of a design is seamlessly integrated, standout creations—those that afterward will be considered "the classics"—discern like they are a natural extension of our senses. They possess a distinct sense of appropriateness, seamlessly fitting into situations and offering a nuanced equilibrium that conveys mastery and control. Distinguishing between pure utility and its inherent significance can be challenging, as they often blend intimately in practice. Indeed, when this occurs, it elevates the artifact to a profound resonance that furnishes meaning.

In various strands within psychology, sociology, and design research, there is like-mindedness that a vital attribute of a devised artifact—whether being a piece of technology, a service, or an activity—should emerge and impress being meaningful to its audience (see, for example [10, 13, 16, 50]).

Not only should the artifact cater to the mundane and functional necessities, but it should also resonate with its audience on a more profound emotional level, evoking a sense of purpose, significance, and meaning among them. Ideally, meaningful artifacts transcend mere utility, becoming integral to our daily lives, shaping how we perceive the world, engage with our surroundings, and understand our circumstance. This intrinsic meaningfulness differentiates exceptional design from the mundane, imbuing it with lasting relevance and value in the eyes of its audience.

According to Krippendorff [42], a valuable criterion for technology artifacts in post-modern society is if its design displays an influential interplay between its audience and the context, if so, there is a high probability that the artifact will have an impact. Artifacts that make sense and appear meaningful convince their audiences that a more desirable future is achievable via technology within a given context [41]. The meaningfulness derived from a design artifact inherently depends on its audience's culture and contexts.

In his seminal work, *The Semantic Turn*, Krippendorff [41] delineates four tenets of meaningful design to consider when attempting to design artifacts that emerge as meaningful and expectantly impact a broader audience: the first tenet revolves around the relevance and perceived benefits of the artifact by its audiences. The second tenet highlights the importance of the design semantics, language, encircling, disseminating, and delivering, ultimately shaping the audience's perceptions of its value. The third tenet is the artifact's recognition of the audience's inherent culture regarding its beliefs, values, sets of standards, encircling norms, opinions, and principles. The fourth tenet accentuates the interconnectedness and compatibility of the novel artifact with those that already exist and thrive in the audience's technology ecosystems.

Even though the level of success of design is always hard to determine due to internal and external factors, Krippendorff [41] proposed tenets of accomplishing a meaningful design artifact: designers must cultivate a substantial acquaintance with their audience regarding their strives, worldviews, conditions, and perspectives of a particular context.

Various audience groupings might derive varied significance and meanings from an artifact [23, 45], such as enhanced personalization features, logical interaction interfaces, or well-calibrated and admiringly responsive input controllers. Trying to please all these strands would only cause you and your team to burn out before your game goes gold and hits the stores. A design artifact's longevity and impact depend on its ability to resonate and cater to the audience's diversified interpretations, significance, and desires. The essence of meaningful artifacts lies in their ability to project and maintain relevance, ensuring that the reasons for their existence and use are apparent and unmistakable. When these pieces fall into place for the audience, the artifact starts to function as a medium that vividly communicates potential desirable futures to its audience, projecting and preserving the meaningfulness and the rationale behind utilizing them in a particular context.

Artifacts that managed to establish communication only with specific segments of their intended audience may inadvertently present some of their features and attributes as unattainable. This can occur in light of the audience's past experiences, current abilities, or the situational conditions within the context. Various external and internal circumstances surrounding design artifacts might impede and hinder segments of an intended audience from fully engaging with an artifact. Depending on the severity of these external and internal circumstances, they could potentially alienate the audiences, causing their conceptualization of the artifact to appear meaningless [36] and devoid of adding value.

For instance, if an interaction interface is incompatible with the player's expectations or experiences, it can lead to the player perceiving the interface, and by extension, the gameplay, as inaccessible or unwelcoming. Therefore, design artifacts, especially interaction interfaces in video games, should strive to communicate their accessibility, inclusivity, and flexibility, consequently conveying a sense that they are making a previously unavailable game experience attainable for the audience. Thus, video game interaction interfaces must be intricately well-crafted and well-informed to stand out as logical, significant, and meaningful to the diverse range of players' conditions, capabilities, and preferences. Hence, the players can derive value and meaning when participating in the game environment. This approach, which in many aspects conceptualizes the raison d'etre of this volume, facilitates a more attainable gaming environment where the interaction interfaces serve as efficacious communicators augmenting the players, amplifying their abilities, and making them, perhaps for the first time, recognize and resemble with the gaming experience—arguably the video games conveyed and inherent properties—and ultimately align with their expectations of full game participation.

Mager and Sung [48] assert that design primarily aims to orchestrate processes and interactions to co-create value for all stakeholders. Recognizing this is essential for any design artifact to be genuinely inclusive and accessible. Each design is inherently context-dependent, requiring designers to continuously iterate and understand their stakeholders' evolving needs and relationships. A video game with attainable experiences should be versatile, benefiting a broad audience in its given context, a meaningful design.

The concept of constructing meaningful design has been pursued in crafting the AGE framework and its four heuristics, which will be explained in more detail in the subsequent chapters. The crux of meaningful design is its ability to project and sustain relevance, ensuring that its purpose and utility are not just needed but highly desirable. By proposing a design framework that strives to increase the production of interactive interfaces that transcend their most basic functionality but oblige making your gameplay experience attainable. We desire to help you construct interaction interfaces that offer enhanced value and become meaningful to your video game audience. The framework prompts your team to consider the broader implications for how the gaming experience might be perceived through your video games arranged and delivered interaction interfaces, thus helping them create added value in your video game for a broader audience.

To frame your video game artifact as being meaningful and furnishing a more significant and desirable future for a more comprehensive audience, it must contain gaming experiences that are attainable for all of them. Accordingly, the game's interaction interface design must convey the available actions and changes, enhancing player understanding and interest and thus fostering credibility. A comprehensive understanding of potential interactions increases the chance of discovering alternative navigation paths [1].

The term "affordances" is applicable here; the term is widely adopted within the HCI and digital design domain. Affordances trace back to ecological psychology, which primarily was established through the works of Gibson [25, 26]. However, its introduction to the technological design domain can be credited to Norman [53]. An object's communicated affordances allow users to discern its explicit practicality and usability. The affordances of an object evolve based on the individuals' understandings, abilities, conditions, and current circumstances. Affordances enable audiences to discern an artifact's features and uses based on their abilities, conditions, and circumstances. According to Norman, affordances are addressing three aspects of an artifact:

- Recognition of the artifact properties.
- Apprehension of how to utilize those properties.
- An estimation of the level of simplicity or complexity of interacting with properties.

Norman's [54] concept of affordances in technology design fundamentally denotes the potential interactions an object or interface suggests. In an interaction interface design, this means developing perceivable cues that signify features that empower the players to participate in the game experience. Your interaction interface must sustain and display affordances that conform to the audience's desires based on their physical and perceptual capabilities. Also, as your interaction interface design aims to address the needs of a more diverse audience for your video games, you should ensure that it presents this undoubtedly. For instance, a game with accentuated features catering to novice and expert players might engage on fair terms; its interfaces should have an apparent focus on how to easily apply them to new players and seasoned players—without making them increase their cognitive effort in gameplay processes. The affordances concept is perhaps even more valuable in augmented reality (AR) and virtual reality (VR) games. In VR gaming, they assure the players that interaction with the game is accomplished by physical gestures, making the locomotion discern meaningful and instinctive. In an augmented reality (AR) mobile game, the affordances reflect the real world as game space, which, based on the player's physical and perceptual capabilities, determines the interaction possibilities, as well as their depth and breadth, for the player. The circumstances surrounding AR mobile games make the concept of affordances crucial; they must convey cues that ensure the audience that the AR gameplay can be experienced fully, independent of their condition or circumstances.

If your video game interaction interface affordances provide universally recognizable cues and interactions, the game experiences appear attainable to a diverse audience with varied experiences and cultural contexts. They should supply the player's insight into how to commit to the video game gameplay experience. Suppose your team is apprehending and starts actively employing the concept of universal affordances in the game interfaces. In that case, you are on the right path to conceiving universally appealing gaming experiences, as they facilitate your transmission of the various functionalities and interaction possibilities within the video game. Furthermore, interaction interfaces that signify and convey its affordances should make sure they are universally recognizable cues to a global gaming audience. They should ensure promoting the inclusive and accessible in your design, accommodating diverse player backgrounds, and enhancing the game's appeal to a broader, more diverse audience. Hence, prolific framing affordances in your interface design can facilitate communication of in-game functionalities, signaling that you are prompting a more attainable gameplay experience environment.

1.5 Principles and Guidelines for Inclusivity

Between 1994 and 1997, the Center for Universal Design at North Carolina State University conducted research, evaluating which characteristics and features could make environments and products as universal as possible, that is as usable by the greatest diversity of people possible Story, [65]. Based on the studies, the Center for Universal Design formulated the following seven principles presented below for Universal Design [72]. The principles were derived to be applicable in various different areas, both in the design of products and environments.

Principle 1: Equitable Use
Making the design useful and marketable to people with diverse abilities. The principle included four different guidelines:

1. To provide the same means of use for all users. When possible, include an equal mean of access to all users, and when not possible, include an equivalent mean of use to all users.
2. To avoid segregating or stigmatizing any user.
3. To provide privacy, security, and safety equally to all users.
4. To make the design appealing to all users.

Principle 2: Flexibility in Use

1. Accommodating the design to a vast range of individual preferences and abilities. The principle included four different guidelines:
2. To provide choice in methods of use.
3. To accommodate right- or left-handed access and use.
4. To facilitate the user's accuracy and precision.
5. To provide adaptability to the user's pace.

Principle 3: Simple and Intuitive Use
Facilitating understanding in the design, for people with different user experience, knowledge, language skills, and concentration level. The principle included five different guidelines:

1. To eliminate unnecessary complexity.
2. To include consistency with users' expectations and intuition.
3. To accommodate a wide range of literacy and language skills.
4. To arrange information in a consistent way with its importance.
5. To provide effective prompting and feedback during and after the completion of tasks.

Principle 4: Perceptible Information
Communicating necessary information effectively to the user in the design, for different ambient conditions and for people with different sensory abilities. The principle included five different guidelines:

1. To include different modes of presentation in terms of illustrations, words, and touch, for conveying important information.
2. To provide sufficient contact between essential information and its surroundings.
3. To maximize the clarity of essential information.
4. To differentiate elements sufficiently to be described.
5. To provide compatibility with a variety of techniques or devices used by people with sensory limitations.

Principle 5: Tolerance for Error
Minimizing hazards and potential adverse consequences of accidents and unintended actions in the design. The principle included four different guidelines:

1. To arrange elements so that hazards and errors are minimized and so that the most used elements are most accessible.
2. To provide warnings of hazards and errors.
3. To provide fail safe features.
4. To discourage unconscious action.

Principle 6: Low Physical Effort
Including efficiency and comfortability in the design so that it can be used with minimum fatigue. The principle included four different guidelines:

1. To allow users to maintain a neutral body position.
2. To use reasonable operating forces.
3. To minimize repetitive actions.
4. To minimize sustained physical effort.

Principle 7: Size and Space for Approach and Use
Including appropriate size and space in the design that allows for reach, manipulation, and use regardless of the body size, posture, or mobility. The principle included four different guidelines:

1. To provide clear line of sight to important elements for any seated or standing user.
2. To make components comfortably reachable for any seated or standing user.
3. To accommodate people with variations in hand and grip size.
4. To provide adequate space for the use of assistive technologies or personal assistance.

1.5.1 Directions for Universally Designed Games

In the context of video games, there has previously not been, to the author's knowledge, any comprehensive set of principles, guidelines, or heuristics that encompass the notion of Universal Design in video games. Instead, most focus has been given to providing specific guidelines for accessible gaming that focus on allowing accessibility to a diverse set of people by considering specific defined disabilities. Examples of the guidelines that have been developed for accessible gaming include:

- Includification by the able gamer's foundation [4].
- Accessibility in Games: Motivation and Approaches [34] by the independent Game Developers Association's (IGDA) special interest group (SIG).

The guidelines offer game developers direction in designing video games that provide higher accessibility. Includification [4] for example provides guidelines in relation to mobility, vision, hearing, and cognition, while IGDA [34] focuses primarily on vision and hearing. While guidelines can assist developers in an increased awareness of accessibility issues and help identify what parts of a game make it more or less accessible to a certain extent [11], solely relying on guidelines is not sufficient to ensure Universal Design in video games. Game design can take on many different forms, resulting in the guidelines not being applicable to all games [70]. While certain features can be added in video games to adhere to existing guidelines, other features need to be adapted to the varied gameplay that is designed for a specific game [8]. Furthermore, with new technologies being developed, there is a need to develop further guidelines to adhere to the new technologies, resulting in the number of guidelines growing over time [11]. Finally, guidelines often do not provide information about how to design the specific accessibility option or if the inclusion of the design options contributes to a positive in-game experience [59]. Accessibility guidelines should therefore be seen as a valuable resource in the context of designing universal videogames, but should not be seen as sufficient in designing universal videogames. In Chap. 2, we instead offer a framework based on design heuristics that can be used in striving toward a more universal game design.

1.5.2 The Eight-Step Process of Universal Design

The process of Universal Design involves an understanding of the population as well as an adherence to accessibility and usability aspects. In the design process, there is therefore a need to include the perspectives of all users, with varying characteristics, who will interact with the product or with the service. Burgstahler [9] describes the following general 8-step process for Universal Design:

Step 1: Identify the application. Specifying to which product, service, or environment in which Universal Design will be applied.
Step 2: Define the universe. Describing the population that will interact with the product, service or environment, and the diverse characteristics of the population such as age, size, and functional limitations.

Step 3: Involve consumers. Involving people with diverse characteristics from the population in all the design phases, including development, implementation, and evaluation. Gaining perspective from experts on accessibility.
Step 4: Adopt guidelines and standards. Selecting or creating Universal Design guidelines or standards and integrating them with other known best practices in the field.
Step 5: Apply guidelines or standards. Applying best practices to the design of the overall application, its subcomponents, and to the operations surrounding the design, to benefit the individuals with a wide variety of characteristics as identified in step 2.
Step 6: Plan for accommodations. Develop processes that provide access to those individuals who do not have access from the design solution, such as assistive technologies.
Step 7: Train and support. Create and provide ongoing support to the stakeholders involved in the design, including diversity and inclusion goals to ensure accessibility and inclusivity.
Step 8: Evaluate. Including measures of Universal Design, collect input from users, and evaluate the design with users that have a diverse set of characteristics and modify the design based on the feedback received.

The 8-step process emphasizes that Universal Design should include an understanding of the end users and their varying characteristics as well as their direct involvement in the design process. Furthermore, the process emphasizes the need for including the stakeholders in the Universal Design process and considering Universal Design early on in the design process. Finally, as previously mentioned, the process also emphasizes guidelines as a valuable part of, but not the entire part of, the process.

1.5.3 Moving Toward Universally Designed Games

Game design is a creative process. Just as it is not possible to provide a step-by-step guide on how to write a best-selling novel, it is not possible to provide a step-by-step guide on how to design a commercially successful game. Instead, as with the writing process, specific skills can be developed and knowledge built over time, through one's own practices or through the inspiration of others. The goal behind designing a good game is however always to deliver an experience. Consequently, the goal behind designing universally designed video games is to ensure that a specific experience can be attained by a large part of the population. Including design options to allow for gameplay to more people should therefore ensure that such options do not disrupt the gameplay experience [11]. The problem behind designing for experience is that it cannot be directly controlled and achieved. In the MDA framework, Hunicke et al. [33] present games as consisting of three main aspects:

- Mechanics: the components of the game including the actions, behaviors, and controls the player can perform within the game world.

- Dynamics: the outcome elicited in the game by the player inputs when interacting with the game.
- Aesthetics: the emotional response experienced by the player when interacting with the game such as challenge or self-discovery.

As Cairns et al. [11] argue, it is not possible to design for a specific experience. Instead, a game can be designed in a manner so that a specific experience is more likely to occur [11]. In other words, from the game designer's perspective, the mechanics of the game can be controlled and to some extent the dynamics that arise. However, the aesthetics of the game only becomes visible in understanding the players' response to the game. For universal game design, it is thus essential to include the third step of the Universal Design process by Burgstahler [9], that is, involving people with vast characteristics to test the game. Involving people with disabilities, or with high awareness of disabilities, for example, can help game designers to prioritize accessibility [58] and ensure that the experience is attainable to as many people as possible. In Chap. 3, we discuss design implications and approaches that can support the process of applying the Universal Design lens in video games by incorporating diverse perspectives from the player community as well as other stakeholders.

1.6 The Universal Design Lens in a Video Game Context

Following the discussion on Universal Design, Universal Design in video games and its related concepts, we move toward a definition of Universal Design in video games. Based on the definition of Universal Design and Universally Accessible Design, Universal Design in video games should include:

- An understanding of players having different conditions which affect their abilities when interacting with the game.
- A design process that includes the perspective of players with varying characteristics and abilities. The characteristics can take many different forms, even within groups of people who have the same defined disability. A core part of understanding players' individual characteristics is therefore to involve the perspectives of players with different characteristics in the game design and development process.
- A design solution that to the greatest degree possible includes seamlessly integrated features that allow as many people as possible to partake in the game without deprioritizing the player experience. Instead of creating catered solutions for specific disabilities, a universally designed game should include several different options and modes of interacting with the game. Furthermore, the experience of the game, moving beyond disability, accessibility, and usability should be at the core of universally designed video games, providing as many people as possible with an attainable game experience.

1.6.1 The Multiple Experiences of Video Games

Many practitioners and scholars use definitions of players, users, gameplay, usability, playability, gaming, game design, UX design, game experience, user experience, or player experience without establishing what such a construct would actually mean. Sometimes, these definitions are also used interchangeably—like game experience and player experiences. To avoid misunderstanding, we will attempt to share some clearance on how we are considering and employing these definitions in the writing of this volume.

Extremely simplified, arguable, game creators typically aim to provide some sort of an approving and memorable experience for their target audience of a game. In the game creation process, there is often an emphasis on the player's holistic experience attained from interacting with the video game. This emphasis encompasses several touchpoints for the player, all with a deliberate objective to make an assertive impression and hopefully create a lasting imprint on the players.

These touchpoints stretch from initial discovery, first introduction, gameplay interactions, playability, interplay, world-building, story, and encounter to post-game reflections. By emphasizing the touchpoints' appearance and what impression and reaction they furnish, the aim is to extrapolate how to immerse the targeted players, engage them emotionally and cognitively, and ensure they derive accomplishment, engagement, satisfaction, action, catharsis, frustration, or other desired emotions. The outcome of this process is the game creator's intended symmetrical or asymmetrical that the player is meant to expect, imagine, sense, conceptualize, perceive, understand, and long for when she takes part in the gaming experience. In this volume, we will call it the game's intended experiences or the game experiences.

We admit that the characteristics and affirmation of a video game's furnished experience are inherently subjective; what one player finds engaging, immersive, and enjoyable, another might not—this is axiomatic in all design forms. However, the axiom does not affect the fact that designers have intentions with their devised artifact's influence and impact on the intended audience.

In the context of this volume, we separate the game's intended experiences from the player's experiences (PX). A complex interplay of various factors shapes a game's holistic PX. Drawing from the arguments of Wiemeyer et al. [68], PX operates on three intertwined psychological, behavioral, and physiological levels. This experience transcends mere playability, accessibility, and game usability. By synthesizing multiple frameworks, Wiemeyer et al. [68] have formed a comprehensive list of variables influencing PX (Table 1.1).

Recognizing that these elements are deeply interconnected, exhibiting complex and layered interactions within the player's experience, is paramount. Each construct does not exist in isolation; rather, they dynamically influence one another, creating a holistic gameplay experience.

Furthermore, there is also a difference between the user experience (UX) and the player experience. Traditional UX testing falls short of a video game PX evaluation, as its standard metrics—like task completion for effectiveness or error rates for

Table 1.1 Variables influencing player experience

PX variables	Definition
Competence	Refers to a player's perceived skill and ability to achieve goals within the game. Games that foster competence typically provide a balance of challenges that are neither too easy nor too hard
Autonomy and control	Relate to a player's sense of agency within the game, where they feel they have meaningful choices, and their actions impact the game world
Immersion	The degree to which players feel "in" the game world. This encompasses: • Spatial Presence: Feeling as though you are "inside" the game world or that it is a tangible place • Social Presence: Sensation of interacting with other real entities, whether they are other players or NPCs (Non-Player Characters) • Flow: A state where players are completely engrossed in the gameplay, challenges match their skill level, and they lose track of time • GameFlow: A model that adapts the concept of flow specifically to game design, considering elements like feedback, challenge, and player skills
Engagement and involvement	Players' long-term commitment and interest in the game, where they repeatedly return to play, are driven by intrinsic and extrinsic factors
Social connections and interactions	Elements of a game that facilitate player interactions, fostering relationships, communication, and collaborative or competitive gameplay
Challenge, tension and curiosity	These three constructs are related to various degrees depending on the game context: • Challenge: Tasks or obstacles that require skill or effort to overcome • Tension: The suspense or emotional intensity experienced by players, often related to uncertainties in gameplay • Curiosity: The intrinsic desire to explore, learn, and discover new aspects of the game world or mechanics
Fantasy and the spectrum of emotions	These three constructs are related to various degrees depending on the game context: • Fantasy: A game's ability to transport players to another realm, allowing them to engage in scenarios outside their daily lives • Spectrum of Emotions: Games can evoke a wide range of emotions in players, from joy and excitement to fear and sadness
Intrinsic motivations	The internal drives that compel players to engage with a game, such as the joy of exploration, the satisfaction of mastery, or the desire for social connection
Feedback mechanisms	Tools or systems within a game provide players with information about their performance, actions, or decisions. This can be in scores, visual or auditory cues, or narrative feedback. Proper feedback helps players understand their progress and adjust their strategies

efficiency—do not directly apply to games [68]. This distinct layering of experience within video games was recognized just a decade ago Nacke et al. [51]. Assessing the playability of a video game is different from evaluating the nuanced experiences of players within that game's environment [19]. Lazzaro [43] emphasizes that the UX and the PX are different. She views UX as the utilization experience—how a system aligns with a task or user expectations. UX designers focus on usability, functionality, ease of use, or other context-dependent and impressionistic indicators of an individual's experience when interacting with a design [61]. PX revolves around the experience of play—how a game caters to the sensation a player seeks when participating in the gameplay.

UX investigates barriers to gameplay, while PX explores obstacles to the sought sensation(s) and delves into the nature of player-game interactions.

Nacke and Drachen [52] explored PX grounded in UX research, highlighting the disparities between games and other software. They emphasize that PX in digital games zeroes in on the emotional, social, and cognitive facets of the interaction between players and games. The distinction has raised awareness of the importance of UX analysis in the game interface while staying consistent with traditional criteria for video game playtesting studies [68].

UX and PX refer to the overall experience of a person interacting with a system or product. They share many principles, but they are distinct in the context in which they are applied and their ultimate goals. While both UX and PX prioritize devising an approving experience and venture for the audience, the context and specifics of that experience differ. UX is broader and applies to any user interaction interface. At the same time, PX is specific to gaming and often involves more emotional and narrative considerations (Table 1.2).

Combining UX and PX poses challenges, primarily because they cater to different facets of human–computer interaction. While they share many principles, the context

Table 1.2 Differences between UX and PX

User experience (UX)	Player experience (PX)
Scope: UX encompasses all user interactions with a product or service. Typically includes websites, apps, software, and, to some extent, physical products	Scope: PX is a subset of UX specific to video games and interactive entertainment. While UX can be applied to any product or service, PX is exclusively concerned with the experience of playing a game
Goal: The primary aim of UX is to ensure that users can achieve their objectives as efficiently, effectively, and enjoyably as possible. Entangles create intuitive, accessible, and user-friendly interfaces	Goal: While UX aims for efficiency and effectiveness, PX often seeks to evoke specific emotions, immerse the player, and ensure they are entertained and engaged. Enjoyment, challenge, frustration (within reason), and immersion can all be intentional parts of the PX
Components: UX involves multiple components, including usability, accessibility, information architecture, visual design, content strategy, and more	Components: PX involves game mechanics, narrative design, audio design, game aesthetics, player agency, and more, in addition to traditional UX components
Feedback and Metrics: In UX, success is often measured by metrics like task completion rate, time on task, user satisfaction surveys, net promoter score, etc	Feedback & Metrics: PX might be measured by player retention, time played, in-game achievements, and player satisfaction, among other metrics

and objectives of their applications differ. Here are some of the difficulties faced when integrating UX and PX:

Different Objectives

- UX: Focuses on ease of use, efficiency, and effectiveness. The primary goal is often to make the user's journey as intuitive and straightforward as possible.
- PX: While usability is essential, the overarching goal is to entertain, engage, and sometimes deliberately challenge the player.

Balancing Usability and Challenge

- Integrating UX practices into game design can sometimes make a game too streamlined or "hand-holding," which may reduce the game's challenge and fun.
- Conversely, adhering strictly to PX might sometimes lead to creating needlessly complex elements from a usability perspective.

Differing Feedback Metrics:

- Traditional UX metrics like task completion rates or time on task might not directly apply to games where objectives can be nonlinear or even purposely obfuscated.
- PX might focus more on emotional feedback, immersion levels, or player engagement over extended periods.

Narrative versus Functionality

- Games often have a vital narrative component. Balancing a compelling story with usability can be tricky. For instance, an essential narrative moment might require an unfamiliar control scheme for the player.

Aesthetics and Immersion

- In PX, the game's look, feel, and ability to immerse players are crucial. Sometimes, this can clash with traditional UX principles. For instance, a minimalist interface might be UX-friendly but not fit a game's aesthetic or thematic elements.

Risk of Homogenization

- Overreliance on established UX patterns could make games feel too similar or formulaic, reducing innovation in game design.

Iterative Testing

- While iterative testing is a staple in UX, it can be more complex in PX due to the multifaceted nature of games. Changing one game mechanic can ripple and affect narrative, balance, and other gameplay elements.

Diverse Player Base

- Games often cater to a broad audience with varying skills and gaming backgrounds. This diversity can make establishing a "one-size-fits-all" UX solution challenging without alienating part of the player base.

Emotional Design

- Games often seek to evoke specific emotions, whether it is fear in horror games or frustration in challenging puzzles. This intentionality can sometimes conflict with UX principles that aim to minimize user frustration or confusion.

Temporal Constraints

- In the gaming world, there is often pressure to release games within specific time frames (e.g., holiday seasons). This can sometimes limit the thoroughness of integrating UX practices into game development.

The focus on humans as part of technology is standard for many approaches within human–computer interaction, so even by labeling them players or users, understanding, and navigating these challenges, developers can enhance the overall experience for players. Despite these challenges, we strongly argue in this volume that video game creators should recognize the importance of integrating various design directives from UX and other strands, making the video game's intended experiences attainable for broader audiences allowing them an elevated, engaging, and immersive game participation.

1.6.2 Universal Design in Video Games—A Definition

As with Universal Design, universally designed video games should be seen as a state that cannot be achieved in totality but should instead be viewed as a process toward a desired state. Based on this notion and the previous definitions for Universal Design and Universally Accessible Games, we define Universal Design in video games as:

> games that are proactively designed so that the game experience is concurrently attainable by people with all abilities, to the greatest extent possible, without adaptation when possible, and with adaptation when necessary.

Firstly, the definition we propose includes the aspect of being proactively designed, that is, considering the entire player population in the initial phases in the design process. Considering the entire player population can take the form of including people of varying characteristics in all the design and development phases, as well as consulting experts on game accessibility. Secondly, the definition we propose also includes that aspect of the game being played concurrently. That is, instead of creating separate games for specific players, players of varying abilities should be able to partake in the same game. Thirdly, instead of solely focusing on accessibility, we include the main goal behind games of designing an attainable game experience. Experience goes beyond allowing players to access and use the game and involves an understanding of what the players experience during gameplay. Fourthly, the definition we propose includes people with all abilities, moving away from the distinction between disability and ability, and considering that people experience disability based on the context they are situated in. One player might experience disability in a certain context of their life but not in another. Designing games that help people overcome the disabilities that would otherwise arise in gameplay consequently becomes the goal for a universally designed video game. Finally, the definition includes that games should be attainable without adaptability when possible, but that in cases when this is not achievable adaptation can be included. This emphasizes that it is better to include special adaptation and assistive technologies when the game experience is not attainable without such adaptation and assistive technologies, rather than excluding certain players.

1.6.3 Introducing a Framework for Attainable Game Experiences

Based on the definition of Universal Design in video games, in the upcoming two chapters we propose a framework and several design implications and processes for an attainable game experience (AGE). The AGE framework (Chap. 2) presents four design heuristics that can be used to design and evaluate video games from a Universal Design lens together with design constraints that form the relative importance between the heuristics in different contexts. The upcoming chapter (Chap. 3) focuses on understanding and incorporating the perspectives of stakeholders in the Universal Design process, a crucial aspect of ensuring inclusivity in your game.

1.7 Conclusion

The present chapter has covered the concept of Universal Design and its application to the context of video games. Universal Design is a term that has emerged over the past decades, taking into account criticism toward earlier approaches such as Barrier-Free and Accessible Design. In the context of video games, Universal Design centers around making game experiences attainable to as many people as possible. At the same time, careful consideration needs to be given to the limiting conditions people face and understand in which circumstances games cause disability and lower accessibility and usability. To implement Universal Design in practice, game developers can be supported by specific principles and guidelines as part of the Universal Design process. While principles and guidelines can offer support, there is also a need to consider the specific context of the video game being developed as well as having an in-depth understanding of the technology and the audiences of the game. Universal Design in video games has the potential to benefit the individuals interacting with the game, the broader society in terms of higher inclusivity, and the game designers who benefit from a larger market space as well as positive publicity.

References

1. Adams, E. W. (2013). *Fundamentals of game design* (3rd ed.). USA.
2. Aguado-Delgado, J., Gutierrez-Martinez, J. M., Hilera, J. R., de-Marcos, L., & Otón, S. (2020). Accessibility in video games: A systematic review. *Universal Access in the Information Society, 19*, 169–193.
3. Baltzar, P., Hassan, L., & Turunen, M. (2023). Assistive technology in gaming: A survey of gamers with disabilities. In *7th International GamiFIN Conference* (pp. 113–118).
4. Barlet, M. C., & Spohn, S. D. (2012). Includification: A practical guide to game accessibility. *Charles Town: The Ablegamers Foundation.*
5. Batra, R., & Ahtola, O. T. (1991). Measuring the hedonic and utilitarian sources of consumer attitudes. *Marketing Letters, 2*, 159–170. https://doi.org/10.1007/BF00436035
6. Beeston, J., Power, C., Cairns, P., & Barlet, M. (2018). Accessible player experiences (APX): The players. In *International Conference on Computers Helping People with Special Needs* (pp. 245–253). Cham: Springer International Publishing.
7. Bierre, K., Chetwynd, J., Ellis, B., Hinn, D. M., Ludi, S., & Westin, T. (2005). Game not over: Accessibility issues in video games. In *Proceeding of the 3rd International Conference on Universal Access in Human-Computer Interaction* (pp. 22–27).
8. Brown, M., & Anderson, S. L. (2021). Designing for disability: Evaluating the state of accessibility design in video games. *Games and Culture, 16*(6), 702–718.
9. Burgstahler, S. (2009). Universal design: Process, principles, and applications. *DO-IT*.
10. Bürdek, B. E. (2005). *Design: History, theory and practice of product design.* De Gruyter.
11. Cairns, P., Power, C., Barlet, M., & Haynes, G. (2019). Future design of accessibility in games: A design vocabulary. *International Journal of Human-Computer Studies, 131*, 64–71.
12. Cairns, P., Power, C., Barlet, M., Haynes, G., Kaufman, C., & Beeston, J. (2021). Enabled players: The value of accessible digital games. *Games and Culture, 16*(2), 262–282.
13. Clark, H. H., & Clark, E. V. (1977). Psychology and language: An introduction to psycholinguistics. Harcourt Brace Jovanovich.
14. Clarkson, P. J., & Coleman, R. (2015). History of inclusive design in the UK. *Applied Ergonomics, 46*, 235–247.
15. Clarkson, J. & Coleman, R. (2010). Inclusive design. *Journal of engineering design, 21*(2–3), 127–129. https://doi.org/10.1080/09544821003693689
16. Csikszentmihalyi, M., & Rochberg-Halton, E., (1981). The meaning of things: Domestic symbols and the self. Cambridge University Press.
17. ESA. (2022). Essential facts About the video game industry. *Entertainment Software Association.*
18. Edeholt, H. (2011). Design, design research and researching design—Exploring methodological diversity. In *Proceeding of Design, Development and Research 2011.*
19. Engl, S., & Nacke, L. E. (2013). Contextual influences on mobile player experience–A game user experience model. *Entertainment Computing, 4*(1), 83–91.
20. Erlandson, R. F. (2007). *Universal and accessible design for products, services, and processes.* CRC Press.
21. Esposito, N. (2005). A short and simple definition of what a videogame is. In *DiGRA Conference.*
22. Federoff, M. A. (2002). *Heuristics and usability guidelines for the creation and evaluation of fun in video games* (Master's Thesis, Indiana University).
23. Friedman, B., Kahn, P. H., Borning, A., & Huldtgren, A. (2013). Value sensitive design and information systems. In P. Zhang, & D. Galletta (Eds.), Human-Computer Interaction in Management Information Systems: Foundation (pp. 55–95). Sharpe. https://doi.org/10.1007/978-94-007-7844-3_4
24. Garber, L. (2013). Game accessibility: Enabling everyone to play. *Computer, 46*(06), 14–18.
25. Gibson, J. J. (1967/1982). Autobiography. In E. Reed, & R. Jones (Eds.), *Reasons for realism: Selected essays of James J. Gibson* (pp. 7–22). Lawrence Erlbaum Associates.

26. Gibson, J. J. (1979/2014). *The ecological approach to visual perception.* Psychology Press. https://doi.org/10.4324/9781315740218
27. Goering, S. (2015). Rethinking disability: The social model of disability and chronic disease. *Current Reviews in Musculoskeletal Medicine, 8,* 134–138.
28. Grammenos, D., Savidis, A., & Stephanidis, C. (2009). Designing universally accessible games. *Computers in Entertainment (CIE), 7*(1), 1–29.
29. Hamari, J., & Keronen, L. (2017). Why do people play games? A meta-analysis. *International Journal of Information Management, 37*(3), 125–141.
30. Hamraie, A. (2016). Universal design and the problem of "post-disability" ideology. *Design and Culture, 8*(3), 285–309.
31. Holbrook, M. B., & Hirschman, E. C. (1982). The experiential aspects of consumption: Consumer fantasies, feelings, and fun. *Journal of Consumer Research, 9*(2), 132–140.
32. Holloway, C. (2019). Disability interaction (dix) a manifesto. *Interactions, 26*(2), 44–49.
33. Hunicke, R., LeBlanc, M., & Zubek, R. (2004). MDA: A formal approach to game design and game research. In *Proceedings of the AAAI Workshop on Challenges in Game AI* (Vol. 4, No. 1, p. 1722).
34. IGDA. (2004). Accessibility in games: Motivations and approaches. White paper. *International Game Developers Association (IGDA).*
35. ISO, I. (2019). 9241-210: 2019 Ergonomics of human-system interaction. *Part 210: Human-Centred Design for Interactive Systems.*
36. Iivari, N., Kinnula, M., & Molin-Juustila, T. (2018). You have to start somewhere—Initial meanings making in a design and making project. In *IDC 2018—Proceedings of the 2018 ACM Conference on Interaction Design and Children* (pp. 80–92). https://doi.org/10.1145/3202185.3202742
37. Iwarsson, S., & Ståhl, A. (2003). Accessibility, usability and universal design—Positioning and definition of concepts describing person-environment relationships. *Disability and Rehabilitation, 25*(2), 57–66.
38. Johnson, D., Clarkson, J., & Huppert, F. (2010). Capability measurement for inclusive design. *Journal of Engineering Design, 21*(2–3), 275–288.
39. Jones, C., Scholes, L., Johnson, D., Katsikitis, M., & Carras, M. C. (2014). Gaming well: Links between videogames and flourishing mental health. *Frontiers in Psychology, 5,* 260.
40. Kose, S. (1998). From barrier-free to universal design: An international perspective. *Assistive Technology, 10*(1), 44–50.
41. Krippendorff, K. (2006). *The semantic turn: A new foundation for design.* CRC/Taylor & Francis.
42. Krippendorff, K. (2021). Design discourse. Design, 333–341. https://doi.org/10.14361/9783839455692-024
43. Lazzaro, N. (2018). "The Four fun Keys." In *Game Usability: Advancing the Player Experience,* edited by Katherine Isbister and Noah Schaffer, 315–344. Boca Raton, FL: CRC Press.
44. Lid, I. M. (2013). Developing the theoretical content in universal design. *Scandinavian Journal of Disability Research, 15*(3), 203–215.
45. Liem, A., & Bonnemaire, G. (2015). Applying design reasoning and seman- tic debate in meaning and identity creation. *Procedia Manufacturing, 3,* 2079–2086. https://doi.org/10.1016/j.promfg.2015.07.257
46. Lusher, R. H., & Mace, R. I. (1989). Design for physical and mental disabilities. *Encyclopedia of Architecture, 3,* 748–763.
47. Mace, R. (1985). Universal design: Barrier free environments for everyone. *Designers West, 33*(1), 147–152.
48. Mager, B., & Sung, T. J. D. (2011). Special issue editorial: Designing for services. *International Journal of Design, 5*(2), 1–3.
49. Mangiron, C. (2021). Game accessibility: Taking inclusion to the next level. In *International Conference on Human-Computer Interaction* (pp. 269-279). Springer International Publishing.
50. Merriam, S. B., & Baumgartner, L. M. (2020). *Learning in adulthood: A comprehensive guide.* John Wiley & Sons.

51. Nacke, L. E., Drachen, A., & Gobel, S. (2010). Methods for evaluating gameplay experience in a serious gaming context. *International Journal of Computer Science in Sport, 9*(2), 1–12.
52. Nacke, L., & Drachen, A. (2011). Towards a framework of player experience research. In *Proceedings of the second international workshop on evaluating player experience in games at FDG* (Vol. 11).
53. Norman, D. (1988). *User centered system design: New perspectives on human-computer interaction*. CRC Press.
54. Norman, D. (2016). *The design of everyday things* (pp. 300–311). https://doi.org/10.15358/9783800648108-300
55. Palmquist, A. (2023). *Plug & Play? Stakeholders' co-meaningmaking of gamification implementations in workplace learning environments* (Dissertation University of Gothenburg Department of Applied Information Technology).
56. Persson, H., Åhman, H., Yngling, A. A., & Gulliksen, J. (2015). Universal design, inclusive design, accessible design, design for all: Different concepts—one goal? On the concept of accessibility—historical, methodological and philosophical aspects. *Universal Access in the Information Society, 14*, 505–526.
57. Pinelle, D., Wong, N., & Stach, T. (2008,). Heuristic evaluation for games: Usability principles for video game design. In *Proceedings of the SIGCHI Conference on Human Factors in Computing Systems* (pp. 1453–1462).
58. Porter, J. R., & Kientz, J. A. (2013). An empirical study of issues and barriers to mainstream video game accessibility. In *Proceedings of the 15th International ACM SIGACCESS Conference on Computers and Accessibility* (pp. 1–8).
59. Power, C., Cairns, P., & Barlet, M. (2018). Inclusion in the third wave: Access to experience. *New Directions in Third Wave Human-Computer Interaction: Volume 1-Technologies*, 163–181.
60. Sauer, J., Sonderegger, A., & Schmutz, S. (2020). Usability, user experience and accessibility: Towards an integrative model. *Ergonomics, 63*(10), 1207–1220.
61. Scapin, D., Senach, B., Trousse, B., & Pallot, M. (2012). User experience: Buzzword or new paradigm? In *ACHI 2012, The Fifth International Conference on Advances in Computer-Human Interactions*.
62. Schell, J. (2019). The Art of Game Design: A Book of Lenses, Third Edition (3rd ed.). A K Peters/CRC Press. https://doi.org/10.1201/b22101
63. Sears, A., Lin, M., Jacko, J., & Xiao, Y. (2003). When computers fade: Pervasive computing and situationally-induced impairments and disabilities. In *HCI international* (Vol. 2, No. 3, pp. 1298–1302).
64. Shakespeare, T. (2006). The social model of disability. *The Disability Studies Reader, 2*, 197–204.
65. Story, M. F. (1998). Maximizing usability: The principles of universal design. *Assistive Technology, 10*(1), 4–12.
66. Waller, S., Bradley, M., Hosking, I., & Clarkson, P. J. (2015). Making the case for inclusive design. *Applied Ergonomics, 46*, 297–303.
67. Ward, B., Myers, A., Wong, J., & Ravesloot, C. (2017). Disability items from the current population survey (2008–2015) and permanent versus temporary disability status. *American Journal of Public Health, 107*(5), 706–708.
68. Wiemeyer, J., Nacke, L., Moser, C., & 'Floyd' Mueller, F. (2016). Player experience. *Serious games: Foundations, concepts and practice*, 243–271.
69. World Health Organization. (2022). *Global report on health equity for persons with disabilities*. World Health Organization.
70. Yuan, B., Folmer, E., & Harris, F. C. (2011). Game accessibility: A survey. *Universal Access in the Information Society, 10*, 81–100.
71. van der Heijden. (2004). User acceptance of hedonic information systems. *MIS Quarterly, 28*(4), 695. https://doi.org/10.2307/25148660
72. Center for Universal Design. (1997). The principles of universal design (Version 2.0). Raleigh: North Carolina State University. https://design.ncsu.edu/research/center-for-universal-design/

Part I
Universal Design Foundations for More Attainable Game Experiences

Accessibility and inclusivity serve as the foundational pillars of Universal Design. In this volume, we make a compelling case that the video game industry, with its wide-reaching influence, should earnestly address these universal tenets to create an equitable and attainable gaming environment where players of diverse abilities can participate to the greatest extent possible. In Chap. 1, we have dove into the myriad design philosophies centered on accessibility and inclusivity in technology. These philosophies serve as the bedrock arguments, underscoring the essentiality of this volume—while this may seem like just another perspective on digital game design at first glance, readers who delve deeper will quickly discern its unique perspective. Building on these foundational promises, the chapter elucidates the journey from Universal Design principles to the specialized domain of AGE. It also reflects the industry's slowly growing commitment to catering to a broader and increasingly diverse audience. The inclusion and accessibility design attributes can serve dual purposes. They can make gaming more inclusive for those with various conditions while expanding the game's adaptability in different contexts, making it more universally enjoyable. This duality emphasizes the importance and broader benefits of integrating accessibility measures into video game design. Part I lays the foundational groundwork for understanding the development and meaning of Attainable Game Experiences (AGE) within the larger framework of Universal Design directions.

Chapter 2 delves into the intricacies of the AGE framework, detailing its four associated heuristics. It succinctly illuminates the directives and constraints that sculpt the design space for universally conceived video games.

Chapter 3 delineates a comprehensive outline of design implications and processes for achieving an AGE design. In this chapter, readers are acquainted with various approaches and design investigations. These investigations are the backbone of AGE, pivotal for deriving robust design implications and making informed decisions in the game creation process. The chapter highlights the paramount importance of design investigation. Drawing informed decisions from accumulated insights is essential to achieve an AGE design. Sole reliance on creator intuition might fall short of producing rational or all-encompassing attainable game experiences.

Collectively, these two chapters aim to create a comprehensive understanding of how various Inclusive, Accessible, and Universal Design directions can be interwoven, applied, and adapted to make today's video games attainable for a broader and more diverse audience.

Chapter 2
The Attainable Game Experience Framework

Abstract Over the past several decades, video games have captured an ever-growing share of public interest, experiencing exponential growth as a form of entertainment. With the burgeoning numbers of gamers globally, the industry has increasingly turned its focus toward improving accessibility and inclusivity. Yet, even as video games capture the imagination of billions, a considerable portion of the populace faces obstacles that prevent full engagement with this medium. These challenges arise from a complex web of factors—ranging from personal circumstances to physical and cognitive conditions. There is, therefore, a pressing need to confront and mitigate these barriers, aiming to make video games universally accessible and inclusive. In Chap. 2, we will conduct a comprehensive design analysis and introduce the Attainable Game Experience Framework—a resource designed to significantly influence your game creation process. Within this framework, we will spotlight four foundational design heuristics and examine their applicability across diverse gaming scenarios. Additionally, we will outline strategies for crafting universally designed video games that can accommodate a wide-ranging audience. Our discussion will be situated within the broader context of the video game design landscape. The primary objective of this chapter is to equip you with critical insights and guidelines that will facilitate your navigation through the complexities of accessibility and inclusivity. Armed with this knowledge, you will be better positioned to develop high-quality video games that resonate with a more extensive and diverse audience.

Keywords Design heuristics · Design directives · Design constraints · Design framework · Attainable game experience · Accessibility · Inclusivity

2.1 Introduction

In 2020, it was estimated that a staggering 3.1 billion people around the globe—equivalent to roughly 40% of the world's population—engaged in video gaming [3]. This statistic underscores the fact that video gaming has transcended its origins as a niche pastime and has become a mainstream cultural phenomenon. However, despite its

A. Palmquist et al., *Universal Design in Video Games*, Human–Computer Interaction Series, https://doi.org/10.1007/978-3-031-30595-5_2

widespread appeal, a significant segment of the population encounters barriers when attempting to participate in gaming activities. These challenges can be attributed to a diverse array of factors, including but not limited to personal circumstances and physical and cognitive conditions [1, 29]. These obstacles are manifold and varied, encompassing everything from physical limitations that impede hand–eye coordination to cognitive issues that affect the comprehension and interpretation of in-game mechanics. Consequently, there is an urgent need to address these barriers in order to make gaming more inclusive and accessible to all.

Throughout the annals of design history, particularly regarding digital artifacts, we have often faced a sprawling and fragmented array of terms that encapsulate various rules, guidelines, conventions, and propositions pertinent to diverse design aspects. In certain fields, these terminologies are even used interchangeably, with the weight of their significance subject to constant renegotiation based on the specific requirements of the artifact, largely dictated by the context [25], and the stakeholder's interests [24]. Locating a comprehensive, universally accepted definition for these terms can be challenging, especially within the multifaceted game design and development sphere [10]. Consequently, in this volume, we lay our groundwork on design terminologies and knowledge explications following the path paved by Fu et al. [12]:

Design Principle: This represents a universally accepted tenet within a particular design domain; it is an axiom so self-evident and firmly rooted that it withstands dispute or debate. These principles are inductively derived from profound understanding and/or empirical explanatory research, serving as blueprints for the game design process, thereby increasing the probability of realizing "good game design."

Design Heuristic: This is a generalized approach built upon extensive experience, sense-making, meaningfulness, and/or preliminary evidence rather than on meticulous measurements or comprehensive research. Although a heuristic does not guarantee an optimal, flawless, or rational solution, it remains invaluable for decision-making and problem-solving within game design.

Design Directive: This guideline, informed by experience, pre-existing solutions in the open market, and/or tacit knowledge, supplies data, inspiration, and preliminary direction to the game design process. It acts as a steppingstone, enhancing the likelihood of securing a successful solution.

Design Constraints: This critical, context-sensitive factor or influence is shaped by the game's purpose, genre-specific preferences, technological constraints, or capabilities, and/or market dynamics. It provides a strategic orientation for the design process, thereby augmenting the possibility of delivering an appealing and significant solution.

2.2 Design Heuristic for a More Universal Gaming Experience

According to Yuan et al. [29], gaming availability issues can manifest in various ways, including but not limited to (1) an inability to receive clear feedback, potentially due to auditory or visual impairments; (2) challenges in discerning in-game reactions, which could be attributed to cognitive difficulties or unclear game design; and (3) limitations in providing inputs using standard gaming peripherals, often faced by individuals with physical disabilities.

Addressing these barriers is essential, not only from an ethical standpoint, to promote inclusivity but also from a practical perspective. By creating more accessible gaming experiences, developers can tap into a wider audience, furthering the reach and impact of their games.

Several principles and guidelines have been derived and presented in the context of Universal Design in general [7] and related to accessible gaming specifically [4, 9, 20]. To derive a practical framework for a more universal gaming experience we embarked on a comprehensive analysis of the most significant guidelines related to Universal Design and accessible video game design. This evaluation process allowed us to distill the most important aspects from a diverse set of sources, which were then amalgamated into what we termed the "synthesized set."

The development of our synthesized set of guidelines achieved a twofold objective. Firstly, it streamlined the process of identifying any latent gaps or incomplete rules within the existing guidelines that we analyzed from pertinent research. Secondly, it illuminated opportunities for enhancing current recommendations. This exercise effectively spotlighted the dimensions of game design where substantial opportunities for refinement and innovation exist. In a subsequent step, we cross-referenced our synthesized set with the foundational principles of Universal Design, as outlined by the Center for Universal Design in 1997 and further elaborated by Story [28]. Simultaneously, we integrated insights from Inclusive Design, which focuses on crafting environments, products, and systems that are intrinsically accessible to individuals of all abilities and circumstances [8]. Moreover, we enriched our framework by incorporating design principles from human–computer interaction (HCI) and interaction design—drawing from seminal works in the fields of user experience (UX) and user interface (UI) design [22–23]. We also considered more nuanced and philosophical perspectives on design artifacts and their various stakeholders [18, 24]. A list of our references and synchronization process is visualized in Fig. 2.1.

By aligning the synthesized set with these principles, we crafted what we have designated as the "Attainable Game Experience Framework." This synchronization process was not merely a merging of two different sets of design rules but rather a thoughtful synthesis aimed at optimizing game design for maximum universal accessibility. Our output, a comprehensive set of design heuristics, is intended to be used as a practical guide for game designers and developers. Our objective is to foster a more profound understanding of enhancing accessibility in video games following the concept of Universal Design, making the gaming experience more inclusive for

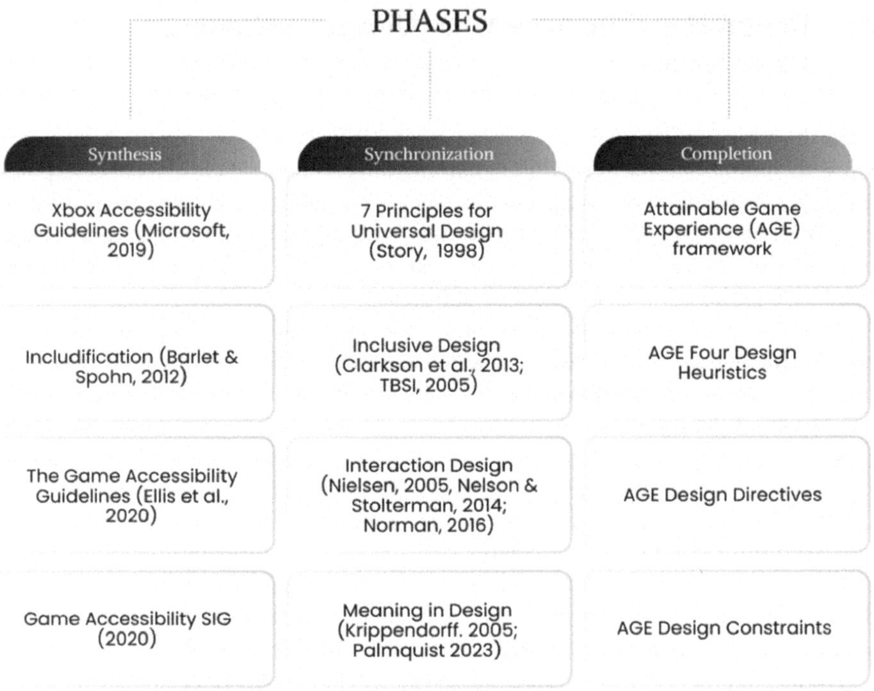

Fig. 2.1 References underlying the AGE Framework

everyone. Through this synthesis, synchronization, and production process, we aim to contribute significantly to the ongoing conversation about accessibility in gaming.

The Attainable Game Experience (AGE) framework is intended to support game designers in realizing Universal Design in video games in practice. Mainly, the AGE framework is based on the definition of Universal Design in video games presented in Chap. 1, specifying Universally Accessible Games as: "*games that are proactively designed so that the game experience is concurrently attainable by people with all abilities, to the greatest extent possible, without adaptation when possible, and with adaptation when necessary.*"

2.2.1 The Four Design Heuristics of AGE

Design heuristics are commonly regarded as practical "rules of thumb" that designers adopt. The legitimacy of heuristics is often derived from exploratory research conducted "in the wild," practitioners' practical experiences, and/or existing solutions that are already prevalent in the open market.

Design heuristics are pragmatic, versatile, and adaptable as necessary to the design, making them subordinate to design principles, which embody widely accepted design fundamentals in a given field that underpin the understanding of what constitutes "good design." Even though not as thoroughly tested, the design heuristics remain an essential aspect, as they typically provide propositions or implications for specific areas in a design, such as a dashboard layout in a strategy game or the heads-up display (HUD) in a first-person shooter, rather than dictating the entire design space and process. Thus, it is crucial to understand that the provided heuristics herein do not encompass the entire game design process. Even more importantly, it should be recognized that the application of our proposed heuristics does not automatically guarantee a successful and widely adopted game. In the contemporary ecosystem that composes the video game industry, numerous other factors need to align, such as successfully identified target groups, release timing, and external communication. To realize Universal Design in practice, there is a need to include people with varying characteristics in the design and development process of the game. In the context of universally designed video games, the presented heuristics can, however, offer a valuable frame of reference about accessibility which can support the process.

The design heuristics we propose in this volume aim to serve as a resource that offers substance to designers' ideas, facilitating critical design decisions and enabling effective communication regarding specific design requirements for the game.

The design heuristics can serve as a vital foundation for constructing design evaluation tools, both before and after a product launch (as presented in Chap. 6). Further, the design heuristics might also function as an interpretive lens, providing a structured approach to decipher both game reviewers' judgments and players' feedback; heuristics might even provide actionable suggestions for addressing their issues with your game masterpiece. Applying such a lens to receive criticism is valuable, as it affords deeper insights into how your design has impacted their behaviors and attitudes through their given perspectives of ease of use, flexibility, and usability. Consequently, the insights gained through this process can assist in identifying design elements in the game that are functioning well, as well as those that require improvement.

Moreover, the benefits of universally designed games are not exclusively limited to individuals with varying disorders or impairments. The concept of "situational disabilities" (see Heilemann et al. [14]) adds a broader context to the discussion. Situational disabilities are circumstances or temporary conditions that may affect an individual's ability to interact with a game effectively.

As put forth by Heilemann et al. [14], a person with a broken arm may encounter difficulty in using typical game controllers, a gamer who is in a loud environment might struggle with audio cues due to background noise interference, a player might have a damaged speaker that renders the game's sound output inaudible. These are all examples of situational disorders or disturbances that could impact a gamer's experience. The significance of Universal Design in digital games is hard to argue against. It is not just about catering to those with permanent disorders but also about accommodating the needs of players who might be temporarily inconvenienced or limited by their circumstances. By doing so, games become more inclusive and adaptable, promoting a more universal gaming experience. This idea has been supported by assorted studies for over two decades [9, 13, 27]. In such research, the importance of situational disabilities in the context of game design is highlighted. In this volume, we propose four game design heuristics for a more attainable gaming experience (AGE):

- Heuristic 1: Fair and Flexible Play.
- Heuristic 2: Adjustable and Equitable Play.
- Heuristic 3: Logical Play.
- Heuristic 4: Error Prevention in Play.

The breadth and depth of the heuristics involved in game design are indeed far too extensive to be entirely encapsulated within a single volume. Nevertheless, we are committed to delivering pivotal insights that pave the way for the acquisition of such knowledge. A multitude of strategies exist to foster a nuanced understanding of universal play in your game. Engaging with relevant literature and enrolling in courses with a focus on Inclusive Design, representation, and accessibility is a worthy starting point.

An additional valuable strategy is to delve into competitive analysis, particularly scrutinizing, so-called, AAA-games. These games, more often than not, showcase some of the most sophisticated design practices in the vast universe of video game development.

By seeking out feedback, performing evaluation, playtesting, and engaging in a free and open dialogue, designers are able to gain a deeper understanding of their audience's needs and preferences. This, in turn, fosters an environment of continuous improvement and refinement, enabling designers to elevate the overall quality of their game design. In this volume, we introduce our proposed Universal Game Design Heuristics for attainable gaming experiences, which emphasize the necessity of crafting experiences tailored to each player's unique characteristics. These include the diversity of player backgrounds and conditions, the range of their behaviors and skills, and the various gaming environments and circumstances they inhabit.

2.2.2 The Granularity of the AGE Framework and Its Design Heuristics

Considering the degree of granularity, the AGE framework and its design heuristics primarily focus on enhancing the attainability of overall game experiences and gameplay features. However, it is crucial to note that the AGE framework does not delve deeply into the specifics of a particular game or its gameplay elements. Digital game design is an intricate, multidisciplinary craft with nuances and complexities that go beyond the surface. It intersects with various disciplines such as programming, narrative design, art direction, sound design, and systems design. Each of these disciplines significantly contributes to players' meaningful experiences with a video game. The involvement and focus of the AGE framework and its heuristics lie more at the macro level of granularity than the micro level. To fulfill the AGE framework's goal of making video game experiences more attainable for a diverse audience, regardless of their individual conditions and circumstances, efforts should concentrate on the game's "interaction interfaces"—the points of contact between players and the video game experiences emerge.

We have employed the term "interaction interfaces" to eloquently convey universally attainable gaming experiences. "Interaction interfaces" refer to points where players engage and interact with the multimodalities of a video game. While the nuances of this term might evolve, its core principle remains: the ways players and games connect and interact. By contemplating how to create robust and inviting "interaction interfaces," we can discuss attainability without delving too deeply into the distinct aspects that often arise in a video game project. By focusing on interaction interfaces, our goal is to shape the perception and direction of game design. This assists creators in laying the groundwork for in-depth, game-specific design considerations without micromanaging or interfering with the game development team's goals and desires. Adopting this interface-centric approach, we believe that we can maintain the scope and focus of our design heuristics. This ensures their applicability across a broad spectrum of gaming contexts without overly intruding into your design space and process.

2.2.3 Heuristic 1: Fair and Flexible Play

The heuristic Fair and Flexible Play is the first of our proposed cornerstones in the AGE framework for a broader audience of participants, irrespective of their unique conditions and abilities. The heuristic strives toward making the game accessible, that is, allowing as many people as possible to play the game [16], even those functioning under limiting conditions [15]. The gameplay is perceived as "Fair" in the sense that people are not hindered from playing the game due to their individual abilities, by integrating higher "Flexibility" in how to interact with and perceive the game.

At its core, this heuristic prioritizes players by recognizing their varied conditions, contexts, and circumstances, and the disabilities that could arise during game play. It involves designing multimodal software interfaces and game controllers in a way that facilitates making interaction between players and the video game possible. The "Fair and Flexible Play" heuristic takes into account and integrates various modalities of interaction, such as visual, audio, and motor, to ensure seamless information transfer between the video game and its participants—consequently, reducing the visual, auditory, motor, and cognitive disabilities that can arise during gameplay [1, 5]. This heuristic caters to players from diverse backgrounds, considering the needs of those with permanent, temporary, situational, or evolving conditions or circumstances that might affect their ability to engage with the game.

By adopting this heuristic, you and your team acknowledge that modern video games should cater to a wide range of players with varying characteristics. As such, designers must put forth the necessary effort to ensure that every player can engage in a game both fairly and flexibly, on their own terms.

The Fair and Flexible Play heuristic also advocates crafting video games that enhance the inclusivity and accessibility of gaming. This can be achieved by designing a game that is flexible, with interfaces that provide adjustable settings, alternative controls, and other accessibility options to meet various players' capabilities. Including these adjustable settings and assistive features allows players with different conditions, disorders, or cognitive abilities to partake in the game. The heuristic aligns with the Universal Design principle of Perceptible Information, by incorporating design features that clarify the information presented [7]. Such design features might include adjustable font sizes, colors, and contrasts, intended for visually impaired players and those who wish to adjust these parameters due to technological constraints or personal preferences. Similarly, design features that provide the option for audio cues and subtitles have a broad reach. These features not only accommodate hearing-impaired players; they also enable non-native speakers by offering clarity to game narratives presented in a foreign language or aiding those trying to distinguish between various audio sources in their multiplayer gaming experience.

AGEs Fair and Flexible Play design heuristic emphasizes the crucial task of examining, evaluating, and refining the gameplay elements that your game intends to feature. This is done with the aim of ensuring their adjustability to enhance the game's accessibility. Meeting these criteria is essential for crafting gaming experiences that invite participation and enjoyment from a diverse and expansive spectrum of players. Apart from considering the accessibility aspect of the game, it is also important to consider inclusivity that goes beyond accessible inclusivity. This includes aspects such as the content and terminology used throughout the game, so that certain players do not experience stigmatization.

Achieving this level of inclusivity necessitates becoming and remaining informed and actively engaging with various strands within the gaming community. In striving to comprehend how your game can further promote an environment where all players within these strands can relish the excitement of gaming, you foster an inclusive, enjoyable, and rewarding experience for all of them.

The Fair and Flexible Play heuristic also encompasses a game design that ensures the gameplay experience can be modified and adapted to better align with a player's preconditions for participation, thereby providing the possibility of enjoyment for a more diverse spectrum of players. Accomplishing this suggests a heightened focus on various game features, exploring how to make them customizable to enhance their inclusivity and versatility, thereby accommodating a wider range of player preferences. In the "Fair and Flexible Design" heuristic, game developers are urged to delve deep into the long-standing philosophical debate on "fairness." Rather than just presenting every player with the same conditions and calling it a day, developers should actively engage with disability communities and advocates. The aim is to craft games that ensure equality of outcome, not just equality of opportunity.

To elucidate this distinction, consider the often-cited metaphor of three individuals wanting to watch a football game over a fence (Fig. 2.2). While two tall, able-bodied adults have no issue viewing the game, the third, who might be a child or uses a

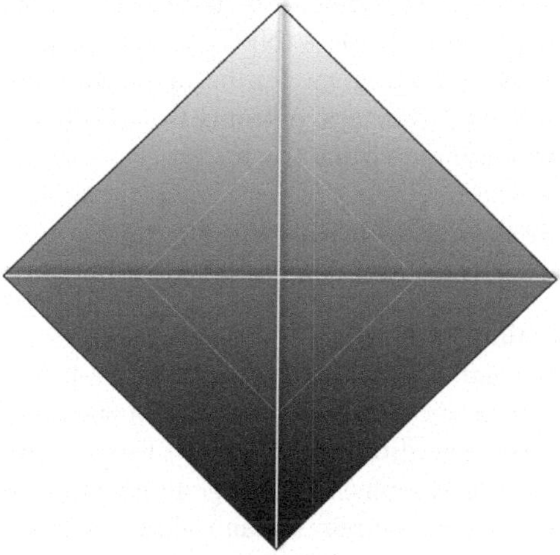

Fig. 2.2 AGE Framework with its four design heuristics. The heuristics are interconnected by four radial lines, centered around a thin mainline in the matrix's core

wheelchair, struggles to see over the barrier. Simply providing equal conditions—level ground, in this instance—leaves the third spectator disadvantaged. On the other hand, offering them a boost, say with a ramp or a box, ensures they enjoy the game just as the others do.

The real challenge for the game developers in adhering to the heuristic of Fair and Flexible Play lies in designing accessibility options that cater to differently abled gamers without compromising on the game challenge. The gameplay experience should be as engaging and rigorous for a person with a disability as it is for a fully able-bodied player. It is imperative to understand that the ongoing discussions about introducing "easy" or "narrative" modes are not mere debates between commercial versus creative goals. Gamers with impairments can possess the same, if not more, fervor as any other player, challenging the conventional notions of what a "core" gamer should be like. As was discussed in Chap. 1, disability arises in relation to the characteristics of an environment, which makes it crucial to understand each player's experience. This heuristic recognizes and underscores that every player deserves a fulfilling and equitable gaming experience.

The Fair and Flexible Play heuristic in your game design also encourages you to be mindful of the localization of your game, as video games are one of the most globally immersive experiences available today. This includes adapting your game's content for new regions, which involves more than mere language translation. It considers associated imagery and cultural elements that influence how your game and its content will be perceived. Depending on the type of game, several different game elements warrant consideration. For instance, this could include interaction interface information such as player stats, location names, item names, map names, and the names of non-player characters (NPCs). Subtitles for in-game dialogue and cut scenes also fall into this category. Furthermore, attention should be given to in-game dialogue between characters, prompts from NPCs, and quest-related text, which steer players through the virtual world.

Design Directives for Fair and Flexible Play
The design directions central to the Fair and Flexible Play heuristic are as follows:

Flexible Participation
Strive to make your game experiences universally attainable through admitting flexible participation in the video game environment and personalization of the interaction interfaces. The directive, based on the statement "If you are forced to play, you cannot play," emphasizes that genuine participation and engagement in gameplay arise from choice rather than obligation. Highlight the significance of autonomy, choice, and genuine interest in transforming a game activity into authentic "play." Introduce an array of adjustable settings, alternative control configurations, and varied accessibility options. Consider players with diverse abilities, physical conditions, and play style preferences. Features should be malleable to suit each player's comfort and requirements, from minute details like adjustable font sizes, color palettes, and contrast levels to larger ones, such as toggle-able audio cues and comprehensive subtitle options.

Fair Gameplay
Endeavor to make your game adaptable to each player's unique circumstances. A fair game does not merely mean setting one standard for all; it means ensuring players can mold the gameplay according to their needs. This could manifest as multiple difficulty levels tailored to varied skill sets, diverse game modes for different play styles, or adaptable control schemes to accommodate physical constraints.

Conscious Localization
When you localize your game, dive deeper than basic language translation. Understand the cultural, historical, and social nuances of the region. Ensure that imagery, symbols, and idiomatic expressions resonate with and are respectful of local customs and values. The aim is not just to make the game understandable, but to make it relatable and respectful to each unique audience.

Community and Audience Commitment
Foster a two-way relationship with the gaming community. Engage in open dialogues with various player groups, ranging from casual players to die-hard

enthusiasts, to disability advocates, and beyond. By staying attuned to their feedback, needs, and evolving preferences, you can continuously refine your game, ensuring it remains both a joy and an inclusive experience for all players.

Attempting to follow these directives, you can work toward creating a game that aligns with the "Fair and Flexible Play" heuristic and fosters an accessible, inclusive, enjoyable, and rewarding experience for all players with your games.

2.2.4 Heuristic 2: Adjustable and Equitable Play

The Adjustable and Equitable Play heuristic underscores the principle that a game should provide features enabling players to tailor and personalize the gameplay experience to their preferences and needs. The heuristic strives to increase the usability of the game, that is, reaching higher satisfaction with the game [11], and a more attainable game experience. The objective is to ensure every player has an equitable chance to enjoy, compete in, and complete the game. This may be reflected in features such as adjustable difficulty settings, input controllers, or game elements that adapt to different play styles. Adjustable and Equitable Play focuses on devising games that accommodate various individual preferences and abilities. Compared to the Fair and Flexible Play heuristic, the Adjustable and Equitable Play heuristic goes beyond being able to access the game and feeling a sense of inclusion and involves the satisfaction with the game and being able to reach the game experience intended. This principle highlights the need to offer multiple ways to customize the gaming experience. Key considerations include support for different input devices, the capacity for remappable controls, and the availability of adjustable gameplay parameters. Developers should provide options for players to adjust game controls, audio and visual settings, difficulty levels, and supportive features designed to cater to differing player tastes and skill sets. Adaptability is central to Adjustable and Equitable Play, with game designers facilitating customizable features that let players modify the game experience as per their needs.

Adjustable and Equitable Play mandates the game developer to provide various means of interaction and access. For instance, support for diverse input devices like mouse, keyboards, gamepads, touch controls, or eye-tracking technology empowers your players to select what input device that best suits them. Design features providing the option of remapping gamepad/keyboard controls and the option to invert the Y-axis cater not only to those with mobility challenges but also to left-handed individuals and those who have grown accustomed to such control setups, having encountered them as default options in their initial gaming experiences. Incorporating a variety of control options and input methods into your game design is beneficial. Doing this empowers players to choose their interaction and play style that best aligns with their priorities and preferences.

Incorporating the Adjustable and Equitable design heuristic in the gameplay settings and assistive features into your game design opens up the experience to players of diverse skill levels and those contending with fluctuating conditions for game participation. These conditions range from temporal and spatial constraints to differing equipment, such as hardware or software. The concept of "situational disabilities" [14] is also covered under this premise. Situational disabilities refer to circumstances or temporary conditions that may impact and impede a player's ability to engage and interact with a game. For instance, a player engrossed in a game on a handheld device during a nighttime flight may deem voice commands unsuitable for guiding their A.I. allies, given the environment. Rather, they may opt for a more discreet and contextually appropriate interaction method, such as touch-screen commands. This choice reflects a trade-off between maintaining the game's immersive quality and the practicality of playing under specific conditions, demonstrating the player's adaptability to their situational constraints.

Recognizing these variable conditions and incorporating adaptable gameplay options into game design are vital strategies to enhance usability and game experience. This approach assures a more inclusive and enjoyable gaming experience tailored to a broad spectrum of players, thus taking into consideration their distinct needs and diverse circumstances.

Moreover, by implementing such design features, designers can allow players to enjoy the game at a pace and under conditions uniquely suited to their individual preferences and participation constraints. This level of customization allows for a more personal, adaptable gaming experience, acknowledging the situational factors that influence game engagement. As such, these considerations contribute to creating an accessible, immersive, and inclusive gaming environment that respects and values player diversity. Using this design strategy not only expands your game's reach and accessibility but also enhances player engagement and satisfaction. It acknowledges that many factors shape every participant's prospect to play and seeks to create an Equitable and adaptable gaming environment. In this way, players can enjoy your game on their terms, contributing to a more personalized, inclusive, and, ultimately, enjoyable gaming experience.

Crafting games with adjustable mechanics tailored to match an array of player inclinations and capabilities allows players to choose the most suitable gameplay approach for their style. Integrating such Equitable into your game design and its interaction interfaces caters to a wider audience, respects players' individuality, and enhances the overall attainability of the game experience. This design strategy facilitates a more personalized gameplay experience and facilitates player comfort and engagement.

Design Directives for Adjustable and Equitable Play

The design directions central to the Adjustable and Equitable Play heuristic are as follows:

Gameplay Attainability through Adjustability

The design directive suggests that an interaction interface catering to a diverse set of player preferences should offer adjustable settings and options to make the intended game experiences more attainable. This directive challenges the traditional "form follows function" mentality and the one-size-fits-all approach, especially given the immense diversity in the gaming community. An adaptable game interface includes various settings, ranging from control configurations for those with motor limitations to options for visually or auditorily impaired players. Features like color palettes for color-blind players, visual cues, and simplified UIs for those with cognitive challenges are essential.

Game Compatibility with Assistive Technologies
As video games gain audiences, there is a growing need to ensure that they are compatible with assistive technologies to cater to the diverse conditions of players. This design directive prompts the game creators to continuously remain updated and be aware of the contemporary and forthcoming assistive applications and devices. Doing this ensures the intended game experiences are attainable to a broader audience. The directive pleads the necessity of being informed of the upcoming input controllers and eye-tracking technologies or other accessibility tools, which can increase the attainability of the video game experiences for players with different abilities. Therefore, game creators need to stay acquainted and well-versed in these technologies to ensure that their games can be enjoyed by everyone, regardless of their level of ability.

Personalizable Interfaces for Enriched Interplay
The design directive argues that the ability to personalize input controls can enhance the gameplay experience as intended by the creators. Recognizing and admitting that players have varied accuracy and precision is crucial. For instance, games requiring precision, like first-person shooters, should offer customizable settings such as aim sensitivity or aim assist. This approach not only boosts players' agency but also makes the game more accessible to a broader range of players. Game interfaces that allow players to adjust and tailor control layouts optimize interactions and increase attainability of the intended game experience. Prioritizing interaction interfaces that allow player personalized controls is a rather low-hanging fruit expediting a broad spectrum of participants' aspirations at the same time increasing the overall satisfaction.

Gameplay Experiences for All Sizes
The gaming community's diversity encompasses demographics, socio-economics, gender, ability, and physical size. An interface embracing this directive provide flexible control schemes, accommodating diverse player sizes offering gameplay adaptations based on the permanent or situational physical condition. The design directive underlines the importance of personalization to warrant that the intended game experiences are attainable for a broader spectrum of the community. It could enclose providing device drivers for third-pert hardware like controllers or handheld gaming devices that accommodating various hand sizes and grips. Moreover, it can concern resizable and repositionable on-screen controller for touch-screen games. In smartphone games, the directive

might reflect the positioning of the interactive game elements verify they are reachable for both right- and left-handed grips or for players with small hands.

By incorporating customizable options, games can become more inclusive and allow players of all abilities to enjoy the experience. This enhances the usability and versatility of the game, accommodating a wider range of player preferences. It is important to make the design accommodating to a wide range of individual preferences and abilities. In the context of XR gaming, the Adjustable and Equitable and Fair and Flexible Play design heuristics are significantly revised due to the XRs medium, which we will discuss and explain more in Chap. 8 on XR gaming experiences.

2.2.5 Heuristic 3: Logical Play

The Logical Play heuristic for game design serves as a pivotal guide for developers, emphasizing the necessity of crafting comprehensible but also intuitive and logical games that make sense and appear meaningful to interact with. This approach places great importance on a player's experience, considering the diverse range of players' skill levels, prior experience, and knowledge. First and foremost, developers are encouraged to create intuitive interfaces that align closely with player' expectations and experiences. Whether it is a navigation menu or a control layout, every interface should be designed to be as intuitive as possible, minimizing the learning curve and allowing players to dive into the gameplay swiftly and effortlessly.

Moreover, clear, easily digestible game tutorials providing player onboarding are a cornerstone in the Logical Play game design heuristic. These tutorials should walk players through the game's mechanics in a step-by-step manner, allowing them to understand the basics and acquire the necessary skills at their own pace.

The Logical Play game design heuristic advises that developers should strive for a streamlined game interface, avoiding unnecessary complexity. This also goes for game mechanics; while complex mechanics can add depth to a game, they should not be at the expense of the overall game logic. Simplicity and complexity must coexist harmoniously in a well-designed game, providing an experience that is easy to pick up and difficult to master.

Logical Play strongly advocates that designers and developers place resources forming logical in-game direction, tooltips, and context-aware assistance. This asset can be a game-changer for participants, helping them overcome hurdles, grasp challenging concepts, and gain mastery over the game mechanics. These tools are not mere add-ons but integral to a supportive and immersive gaming environment. In integrating clear and intuitive game mechanics into the design, developers must ensure that players can quickly and effortlessly understand the game's rules, controls, and objectives. This requires thoughtful design and consistent feedback, ensuring players can navigate and comprehend the game, regardless of their prior expertise or abilities.

Interaction interface and Player Experience are cornerstones of the Logical Play heuristic. Their impact on the player's overall experience and their retention cannot be overstated. The interaction interface encompasses all the on-screen elements that players interact with, including menus, buttons, icons, health bars, maps, inventory systems, and even the in-game cursor. It is the medium through which players interact with the game world, and therefore, it should be clean, instinctive, and responsive. Navigation between different parts of the UI, such as going from the game world to the inventory menu or settings, should be seamless and logical.

Additionally, feedback through the UI, such as highlighting a button when it is clicked or showing damage points when a player hits an enemy, can enhance the sense of interaction and responsiveness. It is also essential to remember that not all players have the same abilities, so accessibility options such as text size adjustment, color-blind modes, or subtitles should be considered during interaction interface design.

The UX, on the other hand, is a broader concept that covers all aspects of a player's interaction with the game. It begins from the moment the game is launched to the player's progression through the game's content. It includes how satisfying the game controls feel, the pacing of the gameplay, the difficulty curve, the balance between challenge and reward, and the emotional engagement elicited by the game's narrative and aesthetics. Respectable interaction interface design makes a game enjoyable and memorable. It ensures that players feel a sense of accomplishment as they progress, that challenges are fair and surmountable with skill and strategy, and that the game world is immersive and consistent. For example, in a role-playing the game, interaction interface design would involve ensuring that the quest structure is engaging, that character progression feels meaningful, and that the game world feels rich and worth exploring.

Good UI/UI in game design aims to make playing the game a pleasant, intuitive, and rewarding experience. It requires understanding the players, including their needs, desires, and potential frustrations. This is often achieved through a combination of design best practices, playtesting, player feedback, and iterative design.

The Logical Play heuristic emphasizes that consistency and adherence to established standards should be seen as fundamental building blocks in crafting a logical game design. This perspective encourages designers and developers to deliver a gaming experience that is intuitive, engaging, and satisfying for the player, minimizing confusion and enhancing overall immersion. Like any interactive medium, it is vital that players are not left in a maze of confusion, wondering if diverse terms, situations, or actions all signify the same outcome. Aligning with platform conventions enhances clarity, fostering a more immersive gaming experience.

For instance, each gaming console carries a set of ingrained player expectations, shaped by years of gameplay on similar platforms. Over time, the gaming industry has cultivated a series of design conventions, akin to those in web and app design, which mold the player's interaction with the game. These expectations, formed and reinforced over time, become instinctive, entwining with the player's muscle memory.

Any deviation from conventional control mappings can noticeably affect the gameplay experience. Players must invest additional time and mental effort to comprehend and adjust to a new control scheme. Simultaneously, they must resist the urge to revert to familiar button presses, increasing the likelihood of in-game errors.

By adhering to industry standards and upholding control consistency, game developers can expedite the player's learning process, encourage more intuitive gameplay, and ensure a seamless and immersive gaming experience overall. The primary objective is to lessen the cognitive burden on the player, enabling them to wholly immerse themselves in the game world rather than grappling with control mechanics.

Finally, the principle of "Chekhov's Gun" functions under this heuristic as well as the direction of aligning with player expectations in the overall game design. Chekhov's Gun is a dramatic principle that states that every element in a story must be necessary, and irrelevant elements should be removed. In other words, if you show a gun in the first act, it must go off in a later act; it must be relevant to the storyline. This principle ensures consistency and relevance, which aligns with players' expectations.

In a game, this could manifest as an item, character, or clue introduced early on that becomes significant later. This use of foreshadowing can align with player expectations because it follows the consistent logic of the game world. Players learn that if something is given attention, it has importance and should be remembered for future gameplay. For example, if players find a unique, seemingly useless key early on in an adventure game, following Chekhov's Gun principle, they expect that key to fit a specific lock later in the game. This aligns with their expectation that each item they encounter has potential significance, and it increases their engagement because they are motivated to find out where and how the key should be used. However, this Chekhov's Gun principle should be used carefully to avoid leading players on unnecessary or frustrating wild goose chases. If the game is full of red herrings that appear significant but are not, it can lead to player dissatisfaction. Similarly, if important items are too hidden or their uses are not sufficiently foreshadowed, players may become stuck or feel that the game is unfairly difficult.

Design Directions for Logical Play

The design directions central to the Logical Play heuristic are as follows:

Emphasize, Expedite, and Sharpen Gameplay Interactions

The design directive contends streamline the process that leads to the actual gameplay, removing unnecessary complexity. It proclaims that the video game interaction interfaces should aid, delineate, and accentuate the core elements that have been decided by the game creator as primary enhancers and enablers of the intended gameplay experience. Doing this will increase its attainability. It also asserts an arrangement of game-related information based on its importance. This approach provides easy access to crucial game details and features, allowing players to locate and understand key information when required quickly.

Expectations Alignment

The design directive underscores the importance of aligning game interaction interface design with player intuition and anticipations. By meticulously crafting game interfaces and interface elements that mirror what players inherently expect, game creators pave the way for a more attainable game experience. The directive argues that by minimizing unwanted friction, the overall attainability of the gameplay experience is elevated, thus allowing players to seamlessly participate in the game without any jarring interruptions. In essence, the directive strives for making the game interaction interface appear like an extension of game itself hopefully leaving a lasting impression on the player.

Logical Feedback and Player Cues

Effective feedback loops are integral to game design. These loops communicate the results of a player's actions, driving adaptations in their future actions. Rewarding successful actions with positive feedback encourages repetition, while negative feedback guides players away from unsuccessful strategies. Both feedback types are essential for a rewarding and educational gaming experience. Ensure the feedback is immediate, specific, and directly related to the player's actions to maximize effectiveness. Moreover, during gameplay and immediately following player achievements or progression, provide effective prompts and engaging cues. Keeping players informed about their progress, rewarding their achievements, and motivating them to continue playing enhances their gaming experience.

Enhancing Experience through Meaningful Tutorials

Games are intricate systems, and complexity can present a learning challenge for players. To enhance the players' understanding of the game mechanics and make the concept more attainable, tutorials play a crucial role. By incorporating well-crafted tutorials, you can display the logic behind the game and help players grasp its mechanics faster. This, in turn, opens possibilities for creating a complex game with multiple layers, stages, and diverse experiences, appealing to a broader player base. These tutorials pave the way for engaging mechanics, problem-solving elements, multiple narratives, and enhanced re-playability.

Logical Interaction Interfaces Amplifying the Player Experiences

The interaction interface includes every part of elements players interact with, demanding a clean, perceptive, and responsive design. On the other hand, UX covers the full spectrum of player interactions with the game, from game controls and pacing to emotional engagement, requiring a careful balance between challenge and reward. Striking a balance in the interaction interfaces of a game is a nuanced task, combining artistry, talent, and precision. When expertly achieved, it enhances the player's experience, making it both accessible and engaging. Achieving this balance requires design consistency, from interaction interface to mechanics, ensuring a logical and dynamic flow through interaction interfaces.

Adherence to consistency and established standards is key to creating a logical game design. It is crucial not to leave players bewildered, wondering if different terms, situations, or actions all lead to the same outcome.

For achieving Logical Play, playtesting is perhaps one of the most crucial things to spend your resources on. By testing the game with a diverse group of players at various stages of development, designers can identify and fix issues with mechanics, difficulty, narrative, and overall attainment of the gaming experiences. The feedback from playtesting is crucial for refining gameplay and ensuring that the final game delivers the intended player experience. The player feedback bleeds into and informs all of our proposed design directives for this heuristic. Therefore, it's highly recommended to conduct playtesting to fine-tune your game.

2.2.6 Heuristic 4: Error Prevention in Play

Our fourth heuristic, "Error Prevention in Play," encourages game developers to look beyond immediate game elements and mechanics. Instead, it invites your team to consider the broader interaction between the game system and the player. Borrowing principles from interaction design, this heuristic advocates for the implementation of mechanisms that prevent players from committing easily avoidable mistakes, thus enhancing the gaming experience.

The Seven Principles for Universal Design, established by the Centre for Excellence in Universal Design in 1997, recommend a design approach that is lenient toward user errors. These established principles advise that errors, when they occur, should be communicated to the users gracefully, in an actionable manner, and with utmost clarity. This approach mitigates user frustration and confusion, thus enhancing the overall UX. However, "Error Prevention in Play" suggests taking the perspective further stresses the importance of proactive error prevention rather than merely graceful error management. In our viewpoint, it is far more beneficial to construct a design framework that precludes players from making errors in the first place—which relates the Error Prevention in Play with Logical Play game design heuristics.

The "Error Prevention in Play" heuristic draws from the synthesized guidelines and on the Seven Principles of Universal Design, especially Principle 5: Tolerance for Error. The heuristic specifically aligns with Nielsen [22] usability heuristics for interface design emphasizing the need to preemptively identify potential pitfalls and implement safeguards that minimize the chance of participants' error. Rather than downplaying the importance of clear and actionable error messages, we suggest a recalibration of the design focus: shifting the paradigm toward preventing unnecessary player error before they materialize in the interaction interface. Thus, we suggest a proactive approach to game design and error management, which is not merely a theoretical proposition; it becomes especially critical in certain genres of video game design.

In the Realm of Serious Games

In the landscape of video game design, there are particular genres, notably Serious Games, XR Games, and Exergames, where the stakes of game development are exceptionally high. Due to stringent legal, regulatory, and safety requirements, developers working in these spaces are mandated to follow a meticulously crafted, predetermined set of rules. Altering or tampering with these guidelines is not merely frowned upon but, in most cases, strictly prohibited by law.

The construction of these games is a delicate balancing act. They are meticulously crafted systems that not only entertain but also aim to instruct, exercise, or simulate real-life scenarios. An inadvertent violation or even casual disregard of the established rules can have far-reaching consequences. The impact extends far beyond mere legal implications, potentially affecting the skill development trajectory of the participants or even posing significant health risks. Serious Games, for instance, aim to impart knowledge or skills development to the participant, often employed in instructional, scientific, or military applications. An error in design or programming could hinder the players' learning process or provide them with inaccurate information. This misdirection could then have a domino effect, impacting their real-world performance or making them misunderstand critical concepts in their line of work.

Similarly, in the realm of XR Games, which combines elements of both virtual and physical realities, safety becomes a paramount concern. If the game's rules are not strictly adhered to, it could disorient the players, causing them to lose their balance or collision with real-world objects, thereby leading to physical harm.

Exergames, on the other hand, are designed to motivate physical activity. A lapse in following the prescribed ruleset could encourage dangerous exercise behaviors or cause the players to injure themselves due to improper workout routines or forms inadvertently—this goes especially for Exergames targeting habilitation or rehabilitation.

In these high-stakes genres of game design, the developer's adherence to the established ruleset is not only a matter of regulatory compliance but also essential for the participants' welfare and optimal skill development. But even when we are not creating games with high-stakes scenarios, it is vital to develop gaming environments that not just tolerate errors and misconceptions but also actively work to prevent them.

In the Realm of Entertainment Games

Even when we are not creating games with high-stakes scenarios, it is crucial to develop gaming environments that do more than just tolerate errors; they should be designed to actively prevent them. In the broader context of game design this could, effective error prevention can significantly enhance a player's experience. It can reduce participant confusion and frustration, improve the flow of gameplay, and keep the player engaged [17].

'Error Prevention in Play' heuristic is broad and might take many forms. For example, when anticipatory cues and alerts are weaved into the game design. These cues are geared toward guiding players and minimizing the chances of error during gameplay; the game could provide warnings just before the execution of high-risk actions or pivotal plot points. Confirmation prompts may be required for significant decisions, such as embarking on a final quest in a game chapter that could potentially influence a majority of other game mechanics.

By including such measures, players are aided in making informed decisions, which helps them steer clear of inadvertent errors. Such elements of design do not merely enhance the overall gaming experience; they also assist players in understanding and mastering game mechanics in a more intuitive and rapid manner. The result is a game system that respects and appreciates the player's time and effort.

Moreover, the use of confirmation dialogs/prompts can prevent players from performing actions that could lead to significant disruptions, sometimes even game-breaking. These prompts offer an additional layer of interaction, ensuring that players truly intend to perform a certain action, such as exiting an avatar customization session without saving changes or leaving a diplomacy interface in a strategy game without confirming decisions. Confirmation prompts are especially crucial for irreversible actions. For instance, before a player exits an in-progress game without saving, a prompt should appear, asking players to confirm their intention to quit. Dialogs and prompts can prevent mishaps caused by accidental button presses or misunderstandings of the game interface.

However, it is important to strike a balance with the use of these dialogs. Overusing them may lead to players habitually agreeing to all prompts to bypass them, diluting their effectiveness. Therefore, the deployment of such prompts should be thoughtful, carefully applied to actions with significant consequences, and sparingly used to maintain their impact.

Another application of the Error Prevention in Play heuristic could be in platform localization, taking into account the inherent limitations of a gamepad's input capabilities. Currently, it is common for console games to assign multiple, context-specific controls to the same buttons—an issue that is seldom encountered when playing with a computer keyboard. Console games' multi-layered utilization of the gamepad significantly increases the game's complexity, imposing a greater "cognitive load" on players than if they had additional input options [2]. Thus, multi-layered control schemes lead to increased player-made errors, which can breed frustration.

In this regard, the Error Prevention in Play heuristic serves as a guideline to minimize the game's cognitive load on players. Thus, context-specific actions and options should be immediately visible or easily retrievable when needed, reducing the requirement for memory recall [26].

To alleviate the player's cognitive load associated with assigning context-specific controls to the gamepad, the use of visual cues and contextual hints could be incorporated. The context-specific control schemes could dynamically appear on the screen as players approach relevant objects or locations. These affordances provide immediate, timely guidance when needed, favoring player recognition over recall.

The Error Prevention in Play heuristic is a strategy in game design that aims to influence the player's overall gaming experience. The central purpose of this heuristic is to foster an uninterrupted, user-friendly environment where players can focus on their main objectives without the hindrance of unnecessary errors.

Design Directives for Error Prevention in Play

The design directions central to the Error Prevention in Play heuristic are as follows:

Player-Friendly Interface Configurations

The interaction interfaces and game controls need to be designed in a manner that the most frequently used actions are within easy reach, thus diminishing the possibility of unintentional errors. For example, if the gameplay frequently necessitates weapon switching, the weapon switch button should be effortlessly accessible. Key actions that could disrupt the game flow, such as exit or restart buttons or the Quick Save/Quick Load buttons, should be spaced adequately on the input controller or in the menus to prevent unintended presses.

Protective Mechanisms Upholding Gameplay

The design directive encourages game developers to incorporate inclusivity features such as auto-saving progress consistently or before crucial events. This helps safeguard against potential losses in the event of a crash or unintentional exit. Adhering to this directive enhances the game's experiences attainability, relieving players from the cognitive burden of manual saving.

Prevent Pitfalls in Crucial Game Scenarios

The design directive wants to raise awareness that in high-stake situations within the video games the interface should be outlined so players must actively choose to proceed deliberately. Such design might involve requiring players to confirm before making significant choices or executing high impact actions—such as selling a rare item or attacking friendly characters. Utilizing visual or auditory alerts can help players avoid making game-altering decisions unknowingly or committing grave errors inadvertently. Designing tasks or challenges that demand active engagement and concentration also helps players remain aware of their actions.

"Recognition" Rather than "Recall" in the Interaction Interfaces

The design directive underscores the importance of minimizing cognitive strain on players by making sure that objects, actions, and options are readily visible or easily reachable. Immediate and context-relevant guidance within the gaming system is paramount. The directive contends that game creators should hone their ability to differentiate between what players need to "recognize" versus "recall" in the interaction interface. Mastering this skill can significantly enhance the audience's attainability of the gameplay intended. Available and clear context-specific guidance for the gaming system is crucial.

Feedback Upholding the Interplay
The design directive encourages the use of positive feedback cues to prevent player slips and errors in the gameplay. Feedback in gaming is a direct communication between the game and the player. Every interaction, from simple jumps to strategic decisions, should offer feedback, be it visual, auditory, or haptic. This immediate response assures players their actions are registered. Visual cues, like damage numbers or character animations, confirm actions. Sound effects, such as clashing swords or victory tunes, enrich the experience. Haptic feedback, through controller vibrations, enhances immersion by engaging touch. In combat, for instance, dwindling enemy health bars, resonating sound effects, and controller vibrations collectively immerse and reassure players of their impact.

Interface Responsiveness Fosters Player Attentiveness
The design directive emphasizes ensuring the interface's responsiveness aligns with swift and accurate reactions to player input. Interfaces that are highly responsive give the game a lively feel, reacting immediately to commands. A lapse in responsiveness disrupts immersion—delays lead to a sluggish gameplay experience and can frustrate players. In contrast, when a game responds with near immediacy, players experience a deep connection, viewing their avatar as a real-time manifestation of their intentions.

By adhering to and incorporating these approaches, game designers can make their games more playable and attainable, while reducing frustration caused by preventable errors. By understanding and adhering to the Error Prevention in Play heuristic during the design phase, you and your team can craft game systems and experiences that are not only more inclusive and accessible but also more satisfying and engaging.

Applying the Error Prevention in Play heuristic is a proactive approach to error prevention, we argue, that will not only enhance player satisfaction and immersion but also streamline the trajectory to attain the intended game experience. Accomplishing this in your interaction interface makes your video game appear more "natural" and seamless—criteria that have increasingly piqued the interest of game critics and players alike [6, 19].

The AGE framework's four design heuristics are rooted in various principles, guidelines, and philosophies from interaction design, user-centered design, or similar approaches the advocates for the integration of elements into the interaction interface, regardless if it's a game or not, that prevent the users from making easily avoidable errors making their intended function more attainable. However, these approaches hold a vast array of potential mechanisms that could further enhance video games beyond mere error prevention. Such mechanisms span a wide spectrum, from well-crafted tutorials and clear, lucid instructions to user-friendly interface designs. Implementing such principles is key to fostering more intuitive, accessible, and enjoyable gaming experiences for all players. We strongly encourage you and your team to delve deeper into the diverse landscape of Information and Communication Technology (ICT) interface design as you continue to refine your game. This exploration will undoubtedly uncover more strategies and tools to elevate your game design and, in turn, increase the chances for a more attainable game experience.

2.3 Design Constraints

The digital game umbrella is vast and has, since the 2000s, undergone exponential growth resulting in new game markets and categories such as Extended Reality Games, Serious Games, or Exergames.

We adhere that diverse game categories are different regarding their purpose, requirements, and given design space. Thus, their implementation of a Universal Game Design approach must vary depending on the category. Therefore, in each category, there may be a distinct set of design constraints that influence and determine the direction of the design space in relation to Universal Game Design, be they enterprise or social benefits or legal requirements. There are several design constraints that establish the boundaries as well as criteria for a video game design space, and they often, but not always, are bound to the following:

The Goal and Purpose of the Game
Universal Game Design must align with the overall and outset goals of participating in the game. For instance, the souls-like game's design intention is to be an exploratory, mysterious, yet unforgiving experience for its players, often resulting in an iterative trial-and-error play style. This approach has been successful in attracting a significant amount of players who fancy this type of game. Thus, this restricts and restrains, but does not forbid, the use of our design heuristic 3: Logical Play. Over-employment of the heuristic in the souls-game may result in a decrease in intended players, who started to reason that the game series has become less attractive due to its increased player aid and lack of complexity.

The Game Technological Constraints/Capabilities
The technology at hand significantly influences design decisions based on its feasibility and resources—emerging technological advancements such as the emerging generative AI models—can pave the way for our design heuristic possibilities, while technology limitations can restrain them. However, these constraints could also spark creativity among designers, prompting them to craft ingenious solutions implementing the universal game design heuristics within these set boundaries.

Requirements of the Game Genre
Depending on the specific domain, certain regulations, standards, or practices may need to be stringently adhered to. These stipulations could significantly impact the extent of implementing the universal game design heuristics in a game product, as compliance with these regulations is crucial—thus determining the form and functionality of the universal game design heuristics in the final product.

The design constraints we have identified are fundamental in defining boundaries and establishing guidelines for the potential application of the AGE Framework's four design heuristics within a game's design space. These lay the groundwork, stipulating what is practicable and feasible within the design purview of the game.

We have pinpointed essential factors that delineate boundaries and set guidelines for integrating the AGE Framework's four design heuristics within a game's design realm. At their core, these criteria provide a foundational blueprint, specifying what is achievable within the game's design scope, as illustrated in the AGE matrix. The matrix's central axis, once subtle, now stands out distinctly, serving as a benchmark for each heuristic in your video game project. Crisp white gridlines divide the design realm into two distinct areas: the inner and outer design spaces. Factors such as game genre or target audience influence these design boundaries, determining which heuristics should be restricted to the inner space or emphasized in the outer space when crafting your game's interaction interface (Fig. 2.3).

Exergame for Stroke Rehabilitation—Illustration of How a Design Space Directive and Constrain Creates Rules for the AGE Heuristics
The crux of developing an effective exergame resides within the parameters of specific design constraints. Several key design constraints exert a considerable influence on this category of exergames. These constraints inform and guide the following design heuristics: Heuristic 2, which addresses Adjustable and Equitable Play, ensures that the exergame can be tailored to require an appropriate level of effort—making it suitable, for example, for patient participation. Alongside this, Heuristic 4, which focuses on Error Prevention in Play, plays a vital role in crafting a secure and beneficial exergame. These heuristics are paramount in ensuring the safety of the participants, particularly those already suffering from impairments due to their health condition.

Stroke rehabilitation, in particular, poses its own unique challenges and demands for the design. The utmost priority must be given to avoid causing any harm to the

Fig. 2.3 Shows the often-cited metaphor of three individuals wanting to watch a game over a fence, a simple yet valuable example that can help your team understand the importance of giving broader audiences a chance to attain your games provided experiences

participants. It is essential to maintain a delicate balance, creating a game that is engaging and therapeutic while also safeguarding the game participants against any potential harm.

On the other hand, these design constraints also necessitate certain restrictions, particularly pertaining to Heuristic 2: Adjustable and Equitable Play. While flexibility is generally encouraged in game design, in the context of exergames, particularly those designed for stroke rehabilitation, it can be a double-edged sword. Excessive or improper use due to too much flexibility could lead to additional injuries in participants.

Therefore, it becomes essential to implement certain safeguards and restraints within the game design. This not only ensures the therapeutic effectiveness of the exergame but also prevents the risk of additional harm due to incorrect or excessive use. The design of the exergame must guide and assist the participants in the correct application, thereby maximizing its rehabilitative potential while minimizing any associated risks. The role of design constraints in the design heuristics is profound in the context of exergames for stroke rehabilitation (Figs. 2.4, 2.5).

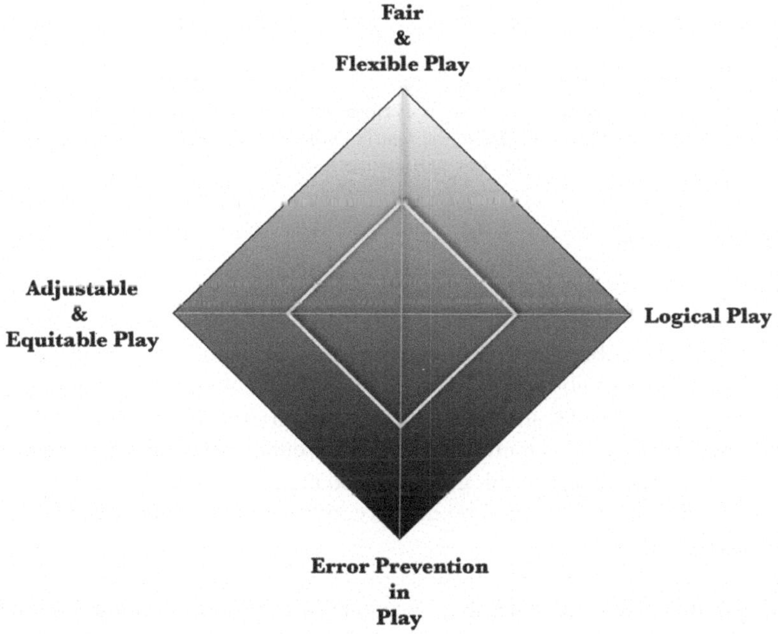

Fig. 2.4 AGE matrix: The central line now prominently marks the baseline for each heuristic. White gridlines define the inner and outer design spaces, influenced by factors like game genre and target audience, guiding the placement of design heuristics in the game's interaction interface

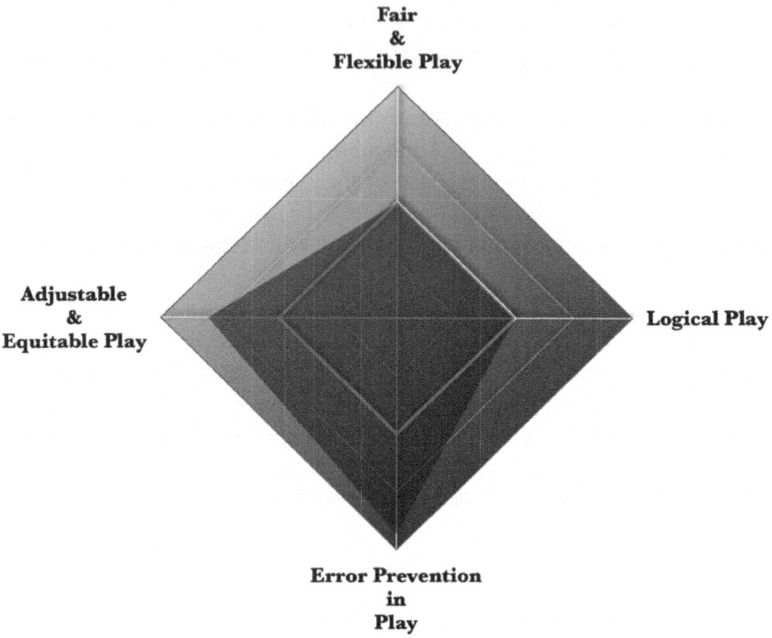

Fig. 2.5 Directives and Constraints for the AGE Heuristics in the Design Space of a Stroke Rehabilitation Exergame. The shaded region in the matrix delineates the design space intended for the interaction interface, defining the limits of AGE heuristics within this context

2.4 Conclusions

In this chapter, we delineated the framework and heuristics aimed at crafting more accessible and enjoyable gameplay experiences. Our central argument posits that Design Constraints are not merely peripheral elements; they hold a seminal role in the landscape of universal game design. These Design Constraints serve as the philosophical underpinnings of a game, shaping its essential mechanics and guiding the development process in a focused, goal-oriented manner. By doing so, they function as a compass that ensures the final product is congruent with the development team's initial vision and objectives.

It is important to dispel any illusions of the game designer as an "omnipotent creator," a notion discussed in depth by Krippendorff [18]. The methodologies, tools, and ideas outlined in this book are not intended to function as a rigid, prescriptive blueprint demanding uncritical compliance. Instead, we offer them as catalysts for discussion and exploration within the unique ecosystem of each game development team.

From our vantage point, imposing a monolithic set of principles as a one-size-fits-all solution would be fundamentally flawed. Such an approach not only risks stifling creativity but also jeopardizes the overarching aim of game design: to produce an experience that is simultaneously engaging, compelling, and imbued with meaningful interactions. Therefore, we recommend employing our framework and heuristics as a flexible toolkit that can be tailored to suit the unique challenges and opportunities presented by each game project.

References

1. Aguado-Delgado, J., Gutiérrez-Martínez, J.-M., Hilera, J. R., de Marcos, L., & Otón, S. (2018). *Accessibility in video games: A systematic review* (Madrid, Spain: Ph.D. thesis, Superior Polytechnic School—University of Alcalá).
2. Ang, C. S., Zaphiris, P., & Mahmood, S. (2007). A model of cognitive loads in massively multiplayer online role playing games. *Interacting with Computers, 19*(2), 167–179.
3. Bankhurst, A. (2020). Three billion people worldwide now play video games new report shows. Available at: https://www.ign.com/articles/three-billionpeople-worldwide-now-play-video-games-new-report-shows. Accessed September 20, 2020.
4. Barlet, M. C., & Spohn, S. D. (2012). Includification: A practical guide to game accessibility. The Ablegamers Foundation.
5. Bierre, K., Chetwynd, J., Ellis, B., Hinn, D. M., Ludi, S., & Westin, T. (2005). Game not over: Accessibility issues in video games. In *Proceeding of the 3rd International Conference on Universal Access in Human-Computer Interaction* (pp. 22–27).
6. Blackler, A., Desai, S., McEwan, M., Popovic, V., & Diefenbach, S. (2019). Perspectives on the nature of intuitive interaction. *Intuitive Interaction: Research and Application* (pp. 19–39).
7. Center for Universal Design. (1997). The principles of universal design (Version 2.0). Raleigh: North Carolina State University. https://design.ncsu.edu/research/center-for-universal-design/
8. Clarkson, P. J., Coleman, R., Keates, S., & Lebbon, C. (2013). *Inclusive design: Design for the whole population.*
9. Ellis, B., Ford-Williams, G., Graham, L., Hamilton, I., Lee, E., Manion, J., et al. (2020). Game accessibility guidelines. Available at: http://gameaccessibilityguidelines.com/. Accessed March 15, 2021.
10. Engström, H. (2020). *Game development research.* University of Skövde.
11. Federoff, M. A. (2002). Heuristics and usability guidelines for the creation and evaluation of fun in video games (Master's Thesis, Indiana University).
12. Fu, K. K., Yang, M. C., & Wood, K. L. (2016). Design principles: Literature review, analysis, and future directions. *Journal of Mechanical Design, 138*(10), 101103.
13. Grammenos, D., Savidis, A., & Stephanidis, C. (2009). Designing universally accessible games. *Computers in Entertainment (CIE), 7*(1), 1–29.
14. Heilemann, F., Zimmermann, G., & Münster, P. (2021). Accessibility guidelines for VR games-A comparison and synthesis of a comprehensive set. *Frontiers in Virtual Reality, 2*, 697504.
15. IGDA. (2004). Accessibility in games: Motivations and approaches. White paper. International Game Developers Association (IGDA).
16. ISO, I. (2019). 9241-210: 2019 Ergonomics of human-system interaction. In *Part 210: Human-Centred Design for Interactive Systems.*
17. Johnson, D., & Wiles, J. (2003). Effective affective user interface design in games. *Ergonomics, 46*(13–14), 1332–1345.
18. Krippendorff, K. (2005). *The semantic turn: A new foundation for design.* CRC Press.
19. McEwan, M. W., Blackler, A. L., Johnson, D. M., & Wyeth, P. A. (2014). Natural mapping and intuitive interaction in videogames. In *Proceedings of the First ACM SIGCHI Annual Symposium on Computer-Human Interaction in Play* (pp. 191–200).

20. Microsoft (2019). Xbox Accessibility. Available at: https://docs.microsoft.com/en-us/gaming/accessibility. Accessed September 29, 2020.
21. Nelson, H. G., & Stolterman, E. (2014). *The design way: Intentional change in an unpredictable world*. MIT press.
22. Nielsen, J. (2005). *Ten usability heuristics.*
23. Norman, D. A. (2016). *Living with complexity*. MIT press.
24. Palmquist, A. (2023). *Plug & Play? Stakeholders' co-meaningmaking of gamification implementations in workplace learning environments* (Dissertation University of Gothenburg Department of Applied Information Technology).
25. Preece, J., Sharp, H., & Rogers, Y. (2015). *Interaction design: Beyond human-computer interaction*. John Wiley & Sons.
26. Sasse, M. A., Brostoff, S., & Weirich, D. (2001). Transforming the 'weakest link'—a human/computer interaction approach to usable and effective security. *BT Technology Journal, 19*(3), 122–131.
27. Sears, A., Lin, M., Jacko, J., & Xiao, Y. (2003). When computers fade: Pervasive computing and situationally-induced impairments and disabilities. In HCI international (Vol. 2, No. 3, pp. 1298–1302).
28. Story, M. F. (1998). Maximizing usability: The principles of universal design. *Assistive Technology, 10*(1), 4–12.
29. Yuan, B., Folmer, E., & Harris, F. C. (2011). Game accessibility: A survey. *Universal Access in the Information Society, 10*, 81–100.

Chapter 3
Design Implications and Processes for an Attainable Game Experience

Abstract This chapter examines the pivotal role of investigating the implications and practices that shape an attainable gaming experience (AGE) design, emphasizing the need for an in-depth understanding of interaction interface design and a comprehensive data collection strategy. The chapter explores informed design philosophies that are instrumental in how they manifest hedonic or utilitarian design intentions. Special focus is placed on achieving a balanced integration of these design philosophies to deliver universally appealing gaming experiences. Detailed guidelines and methodologies are provided for initiating design investigations specifically tailored for AGE-focused projects. This chapter argues that a robust approach concerning the data collection and analysis ensures high-quality interaction interface design and helps advance the principles of inclusivity and accessibility, thereby broadening the appeal and reach of video games to diverse player demographics.

Keywords Design process · Design method · Participatory design · Data collection · Accessibility · Video game

3.1 Implications and Intentions for Interaction Interface Design

When searching for implementing Universal Design in your video game project, it is crucial to recognize that this task cannot alone be accomplished by merely following design intuition. It requires an effort that involves investigating a broad range of sources. This approach is fundamental in ensuring that the resulting video game is accessible and inclusive to a broader audience, regardless of their conditions and circumstances.

By recognizing and incorporating this multifaceted array of perspectives, we move closer to constructing a gaming environment that is not just universally accessible but also enriched by the unique experiences and insights each stakeholder brings. Using such a holistic approach paves the way for video games becoming more inclusive,

A. Palmquist et al., *Universal Design in Video Games*, Human–Computer Interaction Series, https://doi.org/10.1007/978-3-031-30595-5_3

accessible, engrossing, and universally attainable. This process will transpire in the "interaction interfaces" between the players and the video game artifact.

In this book, the term "interaction interfaces" has been chosen to best capture our objective: elucidating the craft of creating more attainable game experiences. "Interaction interfaces" describe the junctions of engagement between two parties—within the AGE context, it is the interplay between the player and the video game. While the term may assume varied nuances as we progress through the book's chapters, at its core, it consistently alludes to the manner in which players and digital game artifacts communicate and engage with each other. With this volume's emphasis on championing an inclusive, accessible, and universally attainable gaming experience, "interaction interfaces" pertain to the myriad ways players immerse themselves in a video game and its gameplay. So, in the context of the volume, interaction interfaces are habitually multimodal and simultaneously encompasses graphical user interfaces (GUIs), command-line interfaces (CLIs), voice interfaces, and touch interfaces, among others.

3.2 Informing the Design

Where to start if you are interested in incorporating AGE in your video game? An axiomatic truth and a natural point-of-departure for the authors is always an AGE investigation. For a video game to be able to achieve more attainable game experiences, the designer needs to be informed, in some cases well-informed, so he/she can make wise and balanced decisions when it comes to the AGE design. The phrase "informing the design" generally refers to the underlying philosophies that guide the creation of a design.

Having the investigation as a starting point for the methodology is logical as AGE's effectiveness and measurement of accomplishment are dependent on its induced influence on the video game project overall as well as the impact of the implemented design insights on the audience, which the game creators have emanated from the multidisciplinary concept of Universal Design. Pursuing constructing video game experiences that are regarded as being attainable for an audience having certain conditions and circumstances, the intuitive and hedonic design approach is not always efficient. For instance, an intuitive design approach cannot, with full accuracy, determine which color patterns that are optimal for players having a dichromatism condition and how it differs from anomalous trichromacy—in such cases, a more practical and functional design approach is preferred. Of course, there are companies, studios, and individual creators that adhere to such ways of working, but far from all.

Therefore, in such matters, a functional and utilitarian approach that relies on investigations should, in certain aspects, be allowed to act as the sovereign method. At the same time, intuitive and hedonic design ways act subordinate—yet it is important that intuitive and hedonic design ways "guide" the functional and utilitarian approach in the video game—reminding you of this because it is all too easy "to throw the baby out with the bathwater."

The importance of reliable, high-quality data for making informed design decisions cannot be overstated. The systematic and consistent collection of data is crucial for the success of any video game project intending to apply AGE. Ensuring that your AGE design has the right prospects and favored conditions of achieving an impact on your video game, thus living up to the expectations from, for example, the audience anticipating that the game experience is attainable or the project team/client that the extra effort/resources was well-spent; it needs to be entrenched. Differing from decisions taken in artistic and creative design. Attention needs to be directed to the specific circumstances and conversations within the discourse, which may often be outside the direct influence of designers.

An AGE design approach draws from design paradigms that stress the importance of making well-informed design decisions based on collected data, such as the design ethnography paradigm (e.g., Müller, [25]; [5, 38]) and user-centered design, which prioritizes the user's needs, tasks, and experience (e.g., Norman, [29, 30]; ISO 9241–10, [14]; [6, 17]).

The inquiries only inform design or create implications for designers to interpret and act upon. The approach aims to enable creators to figure out what artifact the context mandates and give it a concrete shape and means to construct it. It is worth stating that the design discourse of AGE rarely yields a structured creation process, similar to design science research [13, 33]. Furthermore, another similarity with ethnographic design approaches is that the AGE-related investigations should provide in-depth details that might inform the design process or offer actionable insights for prospective enactments.

The AGE design process should be regarded as adaptable, focusing on providing practical investigative approaches that are especially useful for indie game practitioners with too limited resources to dedicate to extensive research. Nevertheless, a project employing AGE design strives beyond merely ticking off boxes in a development checklist; in contrast, it involves a holistic approach that melds the analytical with the creative. Thus, we recommend an integrated, multi-method approach to get a more nuanced and comprehensive understanding of the intended audience's conditions and circumstances that impede and enable them to participate in the gameplay.

Utilizing a diverse and multifaceted investigation approach often offers a more comprehensive understanding of how to commence and engage with the design process of the interaction interface for video games and player engagement. Implementing such an integrated methodology can contribute to the effectiveness of the AGE design process, yielding rich, in-depth insights and broad scope.

By harmonizing these various research strands, designers are better positioned to create gaming experiences that are not only accessible but also deeply engaging for a wide range of players.

We advocate for adopting an AGE design approach for your game's interaction interface during the preliminary phases of the game development process, specifically to gain a nuanced understanding of player circumstances within distinct contexts. For example, this could involve investigating the social dynamics within gaming communities of individuals with disabilities. Such a targeted inquiry, aligned with existing research (see [40]), can yield valuable design implications. These insights could be particularly beneficial for enhancing gaming environments with similar characteristics or challenges, contributing to a more inclusive and accessible gaming experience.

From these in-depth inquiries, a synthesized dataset is generated. This dataset aims to elucidate the needs and circumstances of prospective participants. The ultimate goal is to inform design strategies that make video game experiences universally accessible. Special emphasis is placed on generating reasonable and steadfast findings, as these can serve as actionable insights for an AGE-driven game project or for refining existing video games with AGE heuristics.

AGE lacks a formal assessment process, evaluating if reasonable and steadfast rigorously is imperative. Rigorous scrutiny is essential to assess whether the data is practical and appropriate for exploring issues related to accessibility and inclusivity in video games. This protocol aligns with established design methodologies [27]. A comprehensive and transparent representation is vital in design as such depictions illuminate the key construction processes and designate the generalizability of the determinations [36].

The discourse of AGE design emphasizes understanding and informing the design process through a meticulous analysis of extant knowledge. This can involve conducting individual interviews and focus groups with various stakeholders but may also encompass direct observations of interactions between players and the game.

3.3 Primary and Secondary Investigation Approaches and Records

Primary and Secondary Records aim to inform the AGE design process. Yet, they differ fundamentally in their methodologies and resource requirements. In comparison, primary research involves collecting firsthand data tailored to specific project needs, and secondary research leverages existing studies for new insights. Below, we unpack these approaches in greater detail to understand their nuances, advantages, and limitations.

Source and Nature of the Record
Primary research originates from firsthand investigation, often involving tailored methodologies to collect raw data directly addressing specific research questions. The data is gathered directly from individuals or organizations actively involved in the investigation. In contrast, secondary research relies on data already collected and analyzed in previous studies. This type of research does not involve firsthand data collection but capitalizes on existing datasets and research findings.

Resource Requirements
Primary research tends to be more resource-intensive, both in terms of time and finances. The cost is often justified by the ability to tailor the study's design and methodology to the project's specific needs. Secondary research, on the other hand, is generally less resource-intensive as it involves repurposing existing data. This makes it a more cost-effective option, although it may offer a different level of customization or specificity than primary research.

Data Processing and Adaptability
Primary research typically involves collecting, analyzing, and interpreting raw data, which needs to be rigorously filtered and organized to generate actionable insights for design decisions. Secondary research starts with pre-analyzed data gathered from prior studies. While this data may not require the same level of processing as primary data, it often needs to be adapted or re-contextualized to align with the objectives of the current game development project. This adaptation could alter the original data's intended implications for your AGE design.

While both primary and secondary research methods contribute valuable perspectives to the AGE design process, each comes with its own set of challenges and benefits. Primary research offers the advantage of customization but at a higher resource cost. Secondary research is more cost-efficient but may require modifications to fit the specific context of your game development project. Understanding these distinctions can help researchers and designers make informed choices that best suit their needs, enhancing the likelihood of a successful game development outcome.

3.3.1 A Secondary Investigation Approach and Record

Desk investigations/desk research might prove an invaluable preliminary step for your team to accomplish attainable gaming experiences in your video game. Desk investigation is a commonly employed methodology within practitioner design research and is currently rather "trendy" among UX/UI designers. This approach serves as a conduit for gathering insights from various sources, including existing discussions within the design community, scholarly publications, and previous studies—collectively known as secondary data. While sharing similarities with academic methods like literature reviews and document analysis, desk investigation in a practitioner and development context—especially within small enterprises—is generally less rigorous and strict, making it less resource-intensive.

Engaging in desk investigations is a cost-effective and time-saving strategy. It is a crucial initial step before embarking on more resource-intensive and less controllable research methods, such as stakeholder game prototyping, alpha/beta testing, or gameplay usability testing. If it is well-executed, your desk investigation can significantly facilitate your subsequent actions in the game creation process. By informing your team about game performance, benchmarking against previous releases in the same genre, and projecting potential reception from the gaming community and critics, you make the entire process less resource-demanding. Essentially, by analyzing the past, you prepare your project for its future (Webster & Watson, [46]).

An exhaustive desk investigation can also enhance the efficiency of your game design, development, and innovation process. There is no need to reinvent the wheel for every minor issue; instead, your team can build upon the insights of others. As Isaac Newton once said, you "stand on the shoulders of giants" [28].

Thoroughness in desk investigations equips you and your team with inspirational ideas, constructing profound and entrenched arguments as well as reasonably authorizing and empowering the team to formulate more vigorous design hypotheses—assumptions and propositions that can later be tried and evaluated. Doing so might cause your initial AGE playtest sections to be explanatory instead of exploratory, significantly conserving the project resources—which are often scarce, especially for indie game developers.

Selecting Sources for Desk Investigations

Navigating the digital landscape for information can be challenging, given the plethora of accurate and misleading data. As you conduct desk research to inform your AGE design approach, it is imperative to critically assess the quality and relevance of the sources you consult. Since desk research often incorporates individual insights and findings from external projects that may or may not closely align with your own, due diligence is essential. When utilizing secondary data, special attention must be paid to the ecological validity and transferability of the findings to your specific game development context. Always strive to authenticate these data's factual and objective content while concurrently gauging their applicability to your project's unique requirements.

Industry Analysis

A pragmatic approach to enhancing the AGE design process is rigorously examining video games already available. By studying these existing games through the lens of AGE-related concepts, interactions, and attainable gaming experiences, designers can glean invaluable insights and implications for future design endeavors. Below, we delve into how this assessment strategy can be structured and the benefits it offers. A market analysis of existing games allows designers to understand the current landscape, helping them identify what has been successful and areas requiring improvement. Such investigation can serve as a foundation to construct new and better gaming experiences that leverage best practices and avoid pitfalls observed in other games. Understanding market trends can aid in predicting the future needs and expectations of player communities.

Internal Documentation and Insights from Previous Game Projects
Prior breakdown and analyses—such as project post-mortem documents—conducted within your organization—offer a wealth of information that could serve as a launching pad for your project. Investigate these internal resources, identify key individuals responsible for the data, and engage in direct dialogue with them. Sharing insights can offer a clearer understanding of potential opportunities and challenges, especially when the research is grounded in a similar market context.

Expert Groups and Design Foundations
While the Internet is an abundant reservoir of information, the credibility of sources varies. For example, reputable entities such as the Nielsen Norman Group and the Interaction Design Foundation offer authoritative and comprehensive articles and reports if your research centers on usability. Always vet the reliability of websites, especially when they offer free content.

Libraries
The importance of libraries in an AGE desk investigation is important. Recent academic papers and blogs might be digital; however, valuable breakdowns in the realm of Universal, Accessible, and Inclusive Design were accomplished in the late 1990s and the early 2000s. The authors of these seminal papers have usually written books summarizing their most interesting findings and conclusions; these are often more readable than their journal articles. Therefore, in order to diversify your sources, aim to incorporate the books from the field's founders. Indeed, some of the older works offer insights that stand misplaced in today's society.

Academic Databases
For rigorous scientific research, platforms like ResearchGate and Google Scholar are useful but hard to navigate. Furthermore, while many articles may be behind publisher paywalls, do not hesitate to contact researchers directly to request access to their work. Many academics are willing to share their research findings and outcomes, and asking them to do so might facilitate a deeper understanding of your chosen AGE dimensions.

In conducting desk investigations, adopting a comprehensive and meticulous approach is essential for obtaining high-quality results. This entails carefully selecting, rigorous validation, and strategic utilization of diverse sources. Investing the time and effort to curate and organize these resources meticulously enables the collection of data that robustly underpins the AGE design process. Such due diligence paves the way for a more informed, targeted, and ultimately successful game development journey. A lack of this rigorousness could compromise the quality of the insights gained, thereby impeding the effectiveness of the development process.

Online Forums—In the intersection of primary and secondary investigations

Currently, there are numerous online forums dedicated to specific interests, such as Accessible and Inclusive Design. These include open discussions on Reddit, Discord channels, and specialized LinkedIn groups, which create an information nexus intersecting primary and secondary research.

Depending on the interactional peer-to-peer nature of these platforms might offer more practical insights that are highly interconnected to your situation, which could be beneficial when developing your AGE-designed video game. However, the quality of information gleaned depends on the collective expertise of the forum's participants and the intricate nature of your AGE-related case. Before diving into and adhering to these forums, it is crucial for you and your team to assess, confirm, and agree on whether the community members in the specific online context are adequately competent and trustworthy to assist with your game development inquiries.

Conducting this evaluation collaboratively, possibly also inviting an impartial third party with no vested interest in your project, helps mitigate a range of cognitive biases—such biases might include, but are not limited to, confirmation bias, conformity bias, affinity bias, authority bias, and the halo effect—that could compromise the integrity of your professional assessment and ultimate decision.

Furthermore, suppose your game development is client-driven and financed to meet a client's specific needs. In that case, they may not appreciate your conducting detailed inquiries in open online forums, making it essential to exercise caution when posting detailed inquiries in public forums.

Therefore, make sure that you constantly review the stipulations outlined in your client agreements to avoid inadvertently breaching confidentiality, as seemingly harmless online interactions can become financially and legally perilous.

3.3.2 A Primary Investigation Approach and Record

If you have the chance to do a primary investigation for your AGE-related endeavor, you should always take it. To have firsthand data that considers your own product is frequently better suited to your context than what you mitigate from other cases and generic guides on accessible and inclusive technology design.

Employing a multifaceted strategy that encompasses gamer and gameplay observations, artifact analysis, and methods like interviews, focus groups, surveys, and questionnaires can be employed to inform AGE design. Each method contributes unique insights into different aspects of video games' interface design that can facilitate the intended game experience. Below, we briefly discuss how these methodologies, grounded in academic and practitioner research, can enhance the AGE design process. Be aware that these approaches have been described by many others, and we are just giving them a superficial description.

Gamer and Gameplay Observations
Observing gamers and their interactions with video games provides real-time, authentic insights into user behavior within specific environments. This methodology, supported by Lazar et al. [21] and Preece et al. [35], allows for a nuanced understanding of how gamers engage with game mechanics, dynamics, and aesthetics. It captures the lived experiences of players and offers invaluable data on how they navigate the gaming environment, revealing elements that may need design adjustments.

Artifact Analysis
Artifact analysis involves closely examining pre-existing games to understand how they have successfully—or unsuccessfully—created accessible and engaging experiences. This methodology, cited in the work of Plowright [34], enables designers to deconstruct elements affecting the gameplay and interaction interface arrangements. By studying these artifacts, designers can draw inspiration and gain insights into how to better engage with the varying conditions and circumstances through the AGE design.

Interviews and Focus Groups
Methods like interviews and focus groups can provide an in-depth understanding of player perspectives, shedding light on perceptions of their conditions, circumstances, and reasons for participation. Supported by Norman & Lincoln [31], these methods capture the voices of diverse player groups. This qualitative data can be used to understand player motivations, preferences, and potential barriers to engagement, enriching the overall AGE design process.

Surveys and Questionnaires
Surveys and questionnaires offer another layer of depth to the research mix. These tools not only inform the design process but also serve as a mechanism to statistically validate AGE design theories. By utilizing structured questions and capturing quantitative data, designers can engage in a data-driven design process. This quantitative approach affords a nuanced understanding of player groups, enabling designers to make evidence-based decisions.

3.4 Stakeholder Co-design and Game Community Engagement

Developing a game that aims to provide an attainable experience is a complex task that principally mandates collaboration and thoughtful consideration of various inputs. Emphasizing stakeholder collaboration and fostering meaningful engagement with the gaming community lies at the heart of this approach.

Informing the design is imperative that we actively engage with these diverse groups of stakeholders to ensure that their needs and perspectives are taken into account throughout the design process. By doing so, it is easier to make better-informed design decisions to create a gaming experience that is attainable. This includes players with diverse physical and cognitive abilities and extends to professionals such as game designers, software developers, and interaction interface experts. Moreover, the collaboration does not stop at the technical level; it brings policymakers who can influence regulations, educators who can broaden understanding and training in Accessible Design, and advocates championing the rights of individuals with various conditions and circumstances hindering their game participation. We should now better explore the crucial intersection of co-designing with stakeholders and open development with the gaming community in the context of Universal Design.

Firstly, we will embark on an exploration of the foundational principles and strategies that foster effective co-design. In our discussion, we draw upon the tenets of participatory design, a methodology occasionally viewed as challenging within the game design community; with this approach, we desire to propose a co-design process that centers on creating games that prioritize attainable game experiences for most players.

Secondly, we will delve into the phenomenon of open development and address the game community's instrumental role in propelling and fine-tuning the Universal Design process. We will underscore the necessity of establishing and maintaining continuous feedback loops, enabling gamers of all backgrounds and abilities to actively contribute to shaping a game's development and ongoing refinement.

3.4.1 Participatory Design—A Controversial Practice in Video Games

Participatory design is an overarching design philosophy user-centered approach that involves relevant stakeholders of an artifact in the design process [41]. It invites and includes stakeholders, primarily the intended artifact operators, to express their needs and contribute to the decision-making process. The fundamental principle behind participatory design is the democratization of the creation process. It neglects the design opinions of stakeholders as merely passive bystanders when outlining novel artifacts, thus aiming to engage them in the design journey actively. It aims to empower the stakeholders by acknowledging their ability to contribute valuable insight and ideas. Participatory design is habitually employed to inform the creation process of technological tools and instruments aiming to increase their relevance, usability, and ease of use [35]. Still, the design philosophy generally can be applied to almost any project that includes stakeholders [41].

In video game development, the practice of participatory design is not widespread, yet it exists and is practiced by certain communities. Despite that, academics, as well as the game industry, emphasize iterative design, playtesting, and adhering to community feedback as a success factor [6], the majority of game developers do not embrace stakeholder participation in their game design process [45]. This approach is often attributed to the view of game design as an artistic endeavor. The attitude can be traced to the argument that designing games is primarily an artistic practice—a perspective recognized within the industry and academic circles [3, 9, 43]. The perspective is rooted in the argument that, like other forms of art, games are a medium of expression highlighting design's transformative and tactile artistry [9, 43], underscores the need to have creative freedom prioritizing originality and aesthetic appeal over utilitarian aspects such as functionality or market appeal [3]. In these cases, a game designer's vision, expression, and freedom is preferred over an audience committee informing the design [44, 45]. Positions and perspectives that highlight artistic integrity, creative freedom, and tactile artistry seldom rhyme well with activities harboring terminology such as consensus culture, democratization of creation, and group exercises, which might have contributed to the shallow impact of participatory design in video game projects.[1] Instead, video game designs are generally the result of a single individual's vision, contributing to a somewhat pessimistic viewpoint regarding the application of participatory design within game development [26]. Player and audience involvement in the game design process usually ends at superficial consultation and seldom results in any consequential design decisions [37, 47].

Nevertheless, some strands of game developers effectively incorporate participatory design strategies. For instance, this method has been used in noncommercial gaming contexts [19] examined. The application of participatory design exists within the context of multi-purposed game artifacts such as serious games (e.g., [1, 11, 20]) and gamification (e.g., [4, 32]). As serious games and gamification are designed with aims beyond entertainment, encompassing areas like education, healthcare, and environment, to successfully achieve the intended purpose of these games, necessitates a broader range of skills than a game designer's conventional repertoire, which conceivably makes participatory design a more accepted approach for video game development.

In AGEs design space which stresses the importance of making informed decisions and crafting an interaction interface for the purpose of affording the game experience

[1] Nevertheless, there exist voices that deviate from the excessively artistic emphasis of designing games. For example, Schell [39] offers a blended perspective, suggesting various 'lenses' through which the game design process can be viewed, accentuating that crafting games is a delicate blend of art and science.

to a broader audience. Thus, being reluctant to adopt participatory design—possibly due to fears of sacrificing artistic autonomy by democratizing parts of the process—needs to be reevaluated. Our argument is grounded in reasoning similar to that used for game-based artifacts: the expertise and competencies needed to create universally engaging game experiences often fall outside the habitual skillset of a conventional game designer. These specialized insights vary greatly, hinging on each gaming project's specific genre, platform, purpose, and target audience. This underscores the need for a more nuanced and customized game design and development approach.

In this work, we champion the idea—which we have elaborated in more detail in Chap. 2 concerning the granularity and extent of our four heuristics—that the participatory game design process should shift its focus from gameplay elements and mechanics. Instead, it should prioritize improving accessibility, usability, inclusiveness, and opportunities for personalization within the game. For the sake of simplicity, we optimistically assume that individuals employed as designers for a game project already possess the essential skills for the job. However, they may need guidance to make their envisioned gaming experience more comprehensive, accessible, and appealing to a broader audience.

Better adaptable gaming experiences are the framing of our argument for applying the participatory design approach. We emphasize the importance of including the right contributors in the design process—not just those with strong opinions but organizations and domain experts with the appropriate skills and expertise. This approach ensures that the participatory game design process is both collaborative and informed, leading to more robust and accessible gaming experiences.

3.4.2 Participatory Design Workshops

Participatory design workshops might be crucial in fostering a Universal Design approach for your intended gaming experience. Even if participatory design is relatively uncommon in the domain of game development, game design workshops are not. Game design workshops have been argued to be beneficial instruments for exploring and conceptualizing what excites players in a game or in complex game projects where designers are not likely to understand all the intricacies in the context of game participation [10]. The participatory and the game design workshops have a similar structure and both include exercises and techniques such as brainstorming, mind mapping, prototyping, scenario creation, and role-play to encourage participation and ideation [10, 41].

The distinctions between game design and participatory design workshops lie in their objectives and participant demographics. Game design workshops center around exploring game elements and player motivations, with the ultimate aim of ensuring superior gameplay in the final product. In contrast, participatory design workshops seek to identify and overcome barriers to accessibility, nurture empathy among different stakeholder groups, and devise potential solutions. The overarching goal is to create more universally inclusive gaming experiences.

By actively engaging the intended players in the conceptual design stages, participatory design workshops enhance the potential for a final game that is more accessible and enjoyable to a diverse audience. These workshops transcend the traditional game design approach, embracing a more inclusive and empathetic methodology. They not only accommodate a broader range of player abilities and preferences, but they also foster a more profound understanding among different stakeholder groups, promoting game experiences that are more universally attainable. Online interactive workshops stand out as a remarkable tool for fostering shared understanding and stimulating creative ideation by conveniently connecting stakeholders from all corners of the globe. These workshops transcend geographical barriers and enable real-time brainstorming sessions and insightful discussions using collaborative platforms such as *Miro, Freeform, Mural,* or *Figma.* In these immersive workshops, the participants and the development team collaboratively interpret policies or other forms of aggravated or visualized data, enrich discussions around stakeholder stories, and brainstorm potential solutions. This active and inclusive participation fosters a deeper understanding of the data while stimulating diverse perspectives and innovative thought processes among team members.

Moreover, these digital workshops create an environment of shared ownership and responsibility. This form of collaboration enhances team dynamics and propels team members toward creating inclusive and accessible game designs. As such, online interactive workshops are a powerful platform for facilitating global collaboration and infusing fresh, innovative perspectives into the design process.

When it comes to organizing and executing participatory design workshops, there are a variety of techniques that can be employed. For the purpose of this particular volume, we propose that the process can be boiled down to four fundamental steps.

Stakeholder Selection
The initial step of this process involves the careful identification and recruitment of a diverse ensemble of stakeholders. The selections should encompass players of various abilities, representing a range of experiences and perspectives. Additionally, it is vital to involve game designers, developers, and interface design specialists who can bring a wealth of technical expertise. Furthermore, advocates for disability rights or representatives from accessibility advocacy groups can offer invaluable insights into inclusivity and accessibility standards. Ensuring this diversity will lead to a more holistic, universally designed game product.

Workshop Design
The workshop design should promote an environment that encourages open dialogue, collaboration, and innovative thinking. It can incorporate various activities, such as brainstorming sessions for idea generation and empathy exercises to foster understanding and appreciation of diverse players and their experiences. These co-design activities promote collaboration and shared decision-making, rapid prototyping for immediate feedback, and play testing to validate design choices. A well-structured workshop that caters to these elements will ensure a productive and fruitful co-design session.

Facilitation
Competent facilitators are instrumental in steering the workshop toward its goals. These individuals are tasked with creating an atmosphere that cultivates active participation from all stakeholders. They nurture respect and understanding among participants by setting clear guidelines for respectful discourse and ensuring equal opportunities for all voices to be heard. Additionally, they focus on the workshop objectives and drive the activities toward a constructive conclusion. Strong facilitation is often the backbone of a successful participatory design workshop.

Reflection and Evaluation
After the workshop, it is critical to reflect on the results and evaluate the effectiveness of the design process. This step allows the team to assess the ideas generated, the engagement of the participants, and the overall workshop dynamics. Any feedback gathered from the participants should be analyzed to improve future workshops. Additionally, the designs and prototypes developed during the workshop should be assessed to determine their success in meeting Universal Design principles. This reflective process continually improves the participatory design process, increasing its efficacy in producing universally attainable gaming experiences.

The execution and implementation of participatory design workshops hinge on diverse stakeholder representation, well-planned workshop design, adept facilitation, and insightful reflection and evaluation. By ensuring each of these steps is given attention, it is possible to structure and execute a successful participatory design workshop that is both engaging and productive that enhances the chances of fostering inclusive and universally accessible game designs. The output from a participatory design workshop often ranges from tangible design solutions to more nuanced, subjective insights, which might sometimes seem contradictory or overwhelming. It is crucial to categorize and evaluate these findings to ensure that the final game does not end up muddled or unengaging due to a lack of prioritization.

Evaluating Design Outcomes
Participatory workshops often yield innovative, user-centric design solutions tailored to diverse player needs. The findings could involve fresh features, revisions to existing elements, or inventive approaches to game mechanics. In order to maintain focus in the design and development process, it is essential to evaluate each outcome based on its alignment with the project's goals and its potential to enhance accessibility and engagement for the broadest range of players. In doing this, we strongly recommend using our four game design heuristics as a chart.

Cultural Transformation
Beyond specific design outcomes, these workshops can induce a transformative shift in the culture of the design and development team. The team can develop a deeper understanding of Universal Design's significance and impact by directly engaging with various stakeholders, including players of differing abilities. This

heightened awareness can foster more Inclusive Design practices and nurture a culture of empathy within the team.

Reflective Iteration
Post-workshop, it can be crucial to gather reflections and feedback from participants sometime after the workshop—as their ideas and thoughts might not have been fully developed in the workshop session. Use these insights to fine-tune the future and navigate the ongoing design process. Design process iterations, informed by such developed stakeholders' reflection, help maintain the alignment with the Universal Design heuristics but might also elevate it.

Documentation and Communication
Effective documentation and communication of the process and outcomes of the participatory design workshop are vital. This step ensures that the valuable insights and ideas generated during the workshop are preserved and can be easily shared and referred to by all design and development team members. It also helps track the implementation of the agreed-upon design changes and measure their impact. Furthermore, clear and comprehensive documentation can serve as a helpful resource for future workshops and projects, contributing to the accumulation of knowledge within the organization.

With a definitive focus on inclusive and accessible game design, conducting participatory design workshops in your game project might serve as an arena for diverse stakeholders to collaborate and generate creative solutions. These workshops aim to cultivate empathy and mutual understanding, aligning the perspectives of the design and development team with those of the players. This alignment creates engaging gaming experiences attainable for a more comprehensive and diverse audience.

Participatory design workshops are an indispensable asset in the universal game design toolkit. They empower various stakeholders to directly influence the design process, thereby helping to shape games that cater to a broad spectrum of players. By embodying Universal Design directions, these workshops might become critical in promoting a game development culture that recognizes inclusivity and accessibility as fundamental elements of game development. The resulting gaming experiences resonate with a wide range of players, showcasing the value and impact of a universal game design.

3.4.3 Open Development

In the paradigm of open development, game developers actively adopt a transparent approach, disseminating incomplete versions of their games over extensive periods. This approach to game development places a significant emphasis on the iterative process, involving an ongoing dialogue between the developers and their player communities. The objective of such a transparent model is to cultivate a reciprocal relationship that allows players to actively participate in shaping the games [42].

Within this model of co-designing, players provide constructive feedback, which the developers then use to iterate and refine the game designs, thereby ensuring that the final product caters to the preferences of the participants.

Over the past decade, the open development model has gained considerable traction within the gaming industry. In fact, it has become increasingly prevalent as a strategy for game development and distribution. This trend has been fueled in part by the gaming community's desire for transparency, as well as the growth of digital platforms that facilitate open development.

One platform that has pioneered open development is Steam. In 2013, Steam introduced "Early Access." The Steam platform's Early Access feature facilitates and furnishes the open development model by allowing game creators to give players early admission to games that might be in various stages of development. By doing so, Steam created a means for real-time feedback, allowing creators to polish and fine-tune their games in response to genuine player experiences. The feature has fostered a culture of mutual exchange between game creators and players. As of 2018, Early Access Games accounted for 15% of the games featured on the Steam platform [22]. Lin et al. [22], argue that the 15% can be understood as a widely and rapidly growing acceptance of Early Access Games as well as an interest in open game development within the gaming industry, especially in the indie game scene. Currently, Early Access Games can be found on almost any platform that expedites the commerce of digital games, which provides an opportunity for you and your teams to accumulate implications for the design of your interaction interfaces.

As of today, open development continues to hold its ground as a viable and increasingly preferred model for video game design and distribution. Open development, eliciting player feedback and facilitating game design iteration, embodies a relatively novel approach to player inclusion to refine the game's gaming experience. It leverages innovative communication practices such as the use of in-game feedback widgets [18], live streaming of development work [15], and engaging the audience as designer advocates [42].

Open development can efficiently be utilized as a potent tool for researching the best practices of employing Universal Design heuristics in your game. Open development advocates an approach that employs transparent communication practices that open up the game development process, inviting potential players to participate and give feedback more directly and effectively.

In-game feedback widgets (see [18]) allow players to report issues or provide suggestions from within the game environment itself. This real-time feedback loop enhances the flow of information from audience to the game creators, reducing barriers and facilitating immediate responses.

The act of live streaming development work, as suggested by Ismail [15], creates an unprecedented level of transparency. Game creators can foster trust and collaboration by sharing their progress, challenges, and victories with their audiences. Players, on the other hand, gain a deeper understanding of the design process and can contribute more meaningfully to the development journey. Enlisting players as design advocates, as proposed by Spock [42], bridges the gap between player and creator. These advocates understanding for the players' desires and creators' constraints, enabling more effective communication between the two groups and contributing to a more robust and Universally Accessible Design. In a Universal Design context, these methods shape the player's experience and redefine their relationship with developers. By incorporating player feedback from various strands of the audiences, game creators can iterate their designs to be more universally accessible, aligning with the core principles of Universal Design—to create products usable by all to the greatest extent possible without needing adaptation or specialized configuration.

Therefore, open development necessitates an intertwined relationship between gameplay and communication systems. Interaction with one directly influences experiences with the other. This dynamic feedback loop propels continuous improvements, aligning the game more closely with Universal Design principles and enhancing player satisfaction on a broader scale. In this way, open development contributes to creating inclusive, accessible, and universally enjoyable gaming experiences.

These contemporized communication channels not only promote greater transparency in the development process but also offer developers an opportunity to refine their designs in accordance with diverse player feedback. This feedback, taken from a wide array of player experiences, can influence the broader accessibility of the product, contributing to its universality. Consequently, open development in Universal Design requires integrating gameplay and communication systems. Experience with one directly influences interactions with the other, establishing a dynamic feedback loop that supports Universal Design principles. It ensures that the product or game is usable by everyone to the greatest extent possible, without the need for adaptation or specialized design.

Regarding open development in video games, player functions are essential in conceptualizing the opportunities for player participation in unique design contexts, especially to the collaborative efforts of players to work, run, and evaluate multiple design objects at once. This approach allows for creating responsive ecosystems, enabling players to employ their expertise while having a tangible impact on the game design from their conditions or technologies.

3.5 Striking Right Representation

The success of a universally designed video game relies on the inclusion of a diverse range of perspectives during its development process. A broad spectrum of stakeholders, each bringing unique expertise and perspectives, is vital to this endeavor. The dialogue among these stakeholders can facilitate a deeper understanding of various player needs, industry trends, and the practical aspects of game development. This collaboration not only enhances the quality and accessibility of the game but also ensures its commercial viability and legal compliance. Here, we delve into the critical roles of these stakeholders, highlighting their unique contributions and the methods through which their insights can be harnessed effectively.

3.5.1 *Stakeholder Representation*

In this volume, we propose a categorization of stakeholder representation into primary and secondary tiers (Fig. 3.1). This classification does not imply a hierarchy of importance or value of insights. Instead, it reflects the necessity for game designers and developers to consult certain stakeholder groups more frequently or broadly. For instance, consulting a single player or developer may not provide substantial insights. However, garnering input from a wider array of players or developers can lead to more representative and meaningful data. On the other hand, individual experts such as a professor specializing in human–computer interaction can provide significant, in-depth understanding, hence falling into a different category. This system of classification aims to provide a structured approach to stakeholder consultation in game design projects.

Perspectives from the Players

The players are an integral and vital part of the stakeholder group, as they are the ultimate consumers of the product. The abilities and skills among this group may vastly differ, thereby necessitating a design approach that is truly

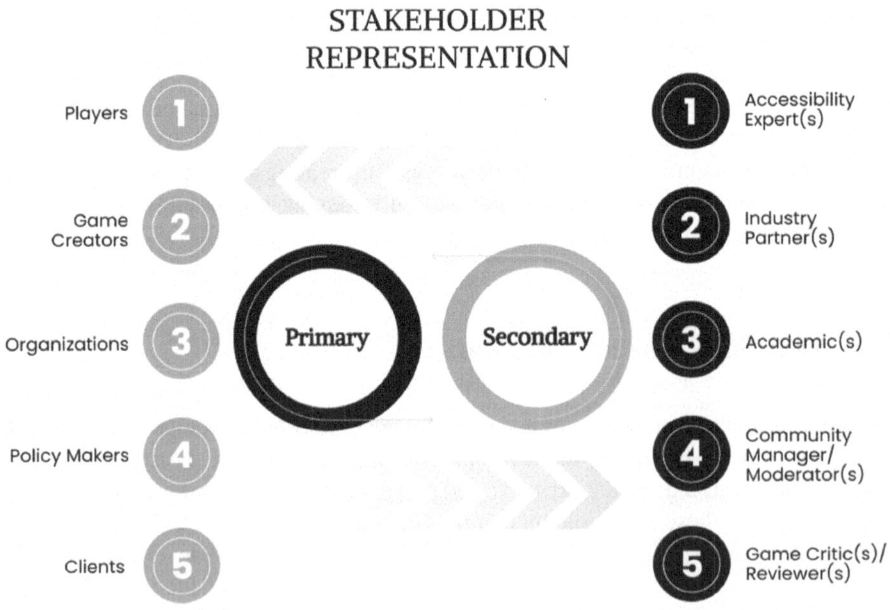

Fig. 3.1 Stakeholder representation consultation

universal. This collective perspective can be effectively gathered through diverse means such as player surveys, one-on-one or group interviews, open development, and active player representation in participatory design workshops. Encouraging active player participation can lead to a deeper understanding of their needs, preferences, and challenges, enabling the creation of more inclusive and enjoyable gaming experiences.

Perspectives from the Developers

Developers are the technical backbone of any game design process. Their knowledge and proficiency form the foundation upon which Universal Design heuristics can be built and actualized in the game you are about to create. It is thus of utmost importance that they possess a comprehensive understanding of these principles. Moreover, they must fully grasp the specific technological requisites and capabilities required to implement these heuristics effectively. Regular training, knowledge-sharing sessions, and discussions about Inclusive and Universal Design practices can foster this comprehension, keeping them updated about the latest trends and techniques in the field.

Perspectives from Organizations and Policy Makers

The voices of organizations for disability rights, health conditions, or impairments as well as policymakers, are particularly significant in guiding a design process aiming for a universal gaming experience. They bring invaluable insights into the legal, ethical, and social dimensions of universally designed video games. These stakeholders can provide guidance to ensure that the design process is not just aesthetically pleasing or technically proficient but is also legally compliant and ethically sound. They can help align the process with legal norms and societal expectations for inclusivity, making games more accessible, fair, and satisfying for everyone, regardless of their abilities or disabilities.

Perspectives from the Clients

In the gaming industry, developers often work on contracts for various clients—critical stakeholders—ranging from established game publishers to media companies owning popular franchises or even individuals without entertainment experience. While the ideal scenario would be to focus solely on player satisfaction, the reality is that client expectations and opinions carry significant weight, especially since they are typically the ones funding the project. According to Schell (2019), there are two kinds of game creators: happy and cranky. The happy ones are good at dealing with the opinions of their clients.

The cranky ones are not good at dealing with the client's opinions. You and your team's ability to build bridges of compromise that delight both you and your client is possibly the most significant indicator of your success as an indie developer. If clients are unsatisfied, they may reduce funding, putting the development team's salaries at risk. In the highly commercial environment that frames the game industry [7], success hinges on a game development team's ability to balance their vision with their client's strong opinions. Therefore, it is crucial to persuasively argue the case for making your game as accessible as possible to a broad audience. Well-presented arguments could win client approval and enrich the project as a whole. Clients may contribute valuable insights or resources on accessibility and Inclusive Design, leveraging their expertise or extended networks.

Furthermore, apart from the stakeholder groups mentioned above, it would be advantageous for your game project team to consider the viewpoints of groups with valuable knowledge and understanding that can enhance and broaden your game project.

Accessibility Expert(s)/Usability Engineers
Experts in accessibility, such as usability engineers, might play a vital role in ensuring that your envisioned game experience is attainable for all players. Usability engineers are typically trained in psychology or UX research and are responsible for evaluating how users interact with assorted products. They have a deep understanding of different conditions and are skilled at identifying potential obstacles, e.g., within game interfaces, that could affect the gaming experience negatively. Their input is vital in creating a game that is adaptable, easy to understand, and navigate, regardless of the player's physical or cognitive abilities. Methods of garnering their insights include consultations, involvement in design meetings, and reviews of game prototypes.

Industry Partner(s)
Sometimes rival industry partners within the gaming industry, the frenemies, possess a keen sense of techniques, resources as well as the commercial aspects of universal game development, especially those who have been acclaimed for having seniority in constructing accessible and inclusive gaming experiences. These can provide insights into the viability of a universal game design, potential strategies, and resources that can support the development process. Engaging them as advisors and inviting them to strategy sessions and discussions can ensure that your game remains commercially viable without compromising its Universal Design goals.

Academic(s)
Researchers and academics in the field of game design, human-computer interaction, applied information technology, and interaction design can provide invaluable evidence-based insights into creating universal gaming experiences. Their understanding of theoretical concepts, awareness of innovative techniques, and familiarity with ongoing research can contribute to a robust, cutting-edge approach to universal game design. Interaction with this group can take place through academic conferences, collaboration on research papers, and direct involvement in the design process.

Game Critic(s) and Reviewer(s)
Game critics and reviewers bring a comprehensive understanding of the gaming industry and an in-depth knowledge of what elements contribute to a successful and engaging game. Their exposure to a multitude of games allows them to identify prevalent trends and effective design practices. Their perspective can be captured through early access reviews, panel discussions, and direct consultations, contributing to a game design that is contemporary, appealing, and relevant.

Community Manager/Moderators
Community managers and moderators interact directly with the game's player base, often making them aware of player needs, preferences, and common issues. Their continuous dialogue with players enables them to offer insights that can enhance player satisfaction and the overall gaming experience. Involving them in regular feedback sessions, design meetings, and post-release reviews can ensure the game design remains responsive to community feedback.

Including these stakeholders in the design process can significantly broaden the scope of perspectives and enrich the design process. By obtaining their insights and feedback, you can gain a more comprehensive understanding of the industry and the community's demands and preferences. Such a collaborative approach can lead to the creation of a more refined and successful game project.

It is essential to recognize that stakeholder perspectives are not static; they can evolve over time due to societal changes, technology, and experiences. Therefore, engaging with stakeholders should be a continuous process, with regular check-ins to understand changing needs and preferences. This dynamic approach can help keep the game design attuned to the current realities of its diverse player base.

When is the Investigation Well Done?
Data saturation is a common concept in scientific research, referring to the point at which collecting additional data no longer contributes meaningful insights for answering the question for your investigation [8, 12]. This serves as an indicator to determine whether the sample size is sufficiently large to understand the topic under investigation. Complex and multifaceted inquiries may necessitate a broader investigation regarding reviewing, a more diverse pool of survey participants, longer interviews, or multi-site observations to arrive at a reliable conclusion.

Whether your investigation employs a primary or secondary research approach, it may not require the same level of rigor as a peer-reviewed paper. However, setting benchmarks for thoroughness and excellence is beneficial. Your indicators for data saturation could, for example, focus on:

- **Similar Information Keeps Appearing:** You have gathered enough data if the information repeatedly conveys comparable insights.
- **Experts Consensus**: Multiple field experts believe you are on the right track and agree that the data you collected is sufficient for your set objective.

- **Checkpoints and Milestones:** Have a few milestones where you check if the data you have so far answers your main question. If it does, you may only need to gather a little.
- **A Distinctive Digit:** To achieve your objective, you can aim to find and analyze five articles or papers on the topic from various sources. You may also collect information from 10 experts in the field or set a strict investigation deadline of 5, 10, or 15 full workdays. It is crucial to refrain from collecting new data after the set deadline, as it may not be helpful in solving your objective within the game project's overarching timeframe.

3.6 Understanding and Applying Diverse Stakeholder Perspectives

In any group of diverse stakeholders, there are bound to be conflicting views and priorities. The game design team must manage these conflicts constructively, potentially using conflict resolution techniques or collaborative problem-solving methods. It is essential to validate all perspectives, even when they differ, and strive to find balanced solutions that respect the needs of various stakeholders. In creating universally designed video games, harnessing the potency of diverse stakeholder perspectives is of utmost importance. As we navigate this process, we immerse ourselves in the confluence of players' desires, developers' expertise, and the broader societal context. We embrace the rich tapestry of these varied viewpoints, analyzing them for recurring themes, contrasts, and unique insights. We then judiciously weave these perspectives into the fabric of the design process, creating a gaming experience that is not only universally accessible but also profoundly resonant with its player base. This approach requires continuous engagement, iterative design, and a commitment to the design heuristics of universal gaming experiences throughout the game's lifecycle.

Collection and Examination of Perspectives
Whether your chosen strategy to achieve a universally designed video game experience relies on Participatory Design or Open Development, the vital first step is gathering and examining the diverse perspectives of stakeholders. Delve into these viewpoints for patterns, unique insights, and points of contrast. By doing so, you will be able to recognize and address player needs effectively. Tools such as thematic analysis or affinity diagrams can facilitate the understanding and categorization of this complex data.

Communicating Stakeholder Insights to the Design Process
After analyzing the stakeholder data, the next step is incorporating these insights into the design process. Translating stakeholder perspectives into actionable design features may require careful negotiation and balancing, as the needs and desires of different stakeholders may diverge. This step, though challenging, is critical for creating a Universally Accessible Game. Regardless of whether you

choose Participatory Design or Open Development, it is essential to maintain a high degree of transparency in the process. Your co-designers should be kept in the loop regarding design decisions and can access detailed information whenever necessary. Doing this not only creates a more Inclusive Design environment but also ensures that the final product truly reflects the needs and preferences of its player base.

Implementing an Iterative Design Process
Adopting an iterative design process is another crucial aspect of universal game design. Stakeholder perspectives should be continually considered throughout each development phase, with modifications made based on the feedback received. This ongoing process of receiving feedback, making necessary adjustments, and refining the product helps ensure that the final game is as universally accessible and enjoyable as possible. Moreover, it emphasizes the idea that design is an evolution, with each iteration bringing the game closer to a form that satisfies a diverse range of player needs.

Maintaining Stakeholder Engagement
Stakeholder engagement should not be a one-off event but a sustained process throughout the game's development cycle. Regular updates, feedback sessions, and open channels for dialogue help maintain stakeholder interest and involvement. This continuous engagement encourages stakeholders to voice their perspectives, thus providing invaluable insights that can enhance the game's accessibility and inclusivity.

Post-release Evaluations and Adjustments
Even after the game's release, the feedback loop should not be closed. Post-release evaluations with various stakeholders offer critical insights into how the game functions in the real world and reveal any unanticipated accessibility issues. These insights allow for further iterations and improvements, reinforcing that Universal Design is an ongoing commitment, not a box to be checked off.

3.7 Four-Step Strategy for Conducting Design Investigations

By tapping into the collective wisdom available, you and your team can make better-informed design decisions in constructing your video game to deliver a highly attainable gaming experience for a broader audience. However, before diving into your desk investigation, it is crucial to take several preparatory steps to ensure your research's quality and efficiency. The following is a step-by-step guide tailored for beginners; feel free to adapt it as your skills develop and your self-confidence grows (Fig. 3.2).

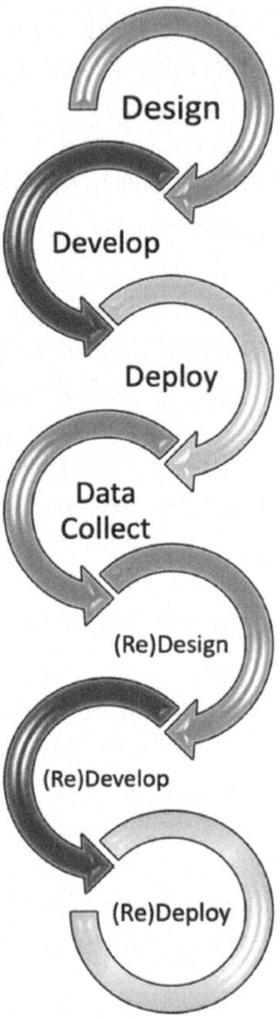

Fig. 3.2 A illustration of the iteration process in the 4-step design investigation

Step 1. Define Your Purpose and Objectives
To commence your inquiry, it is imperative to clearly define the age-related objective of your investigation. This can be segmented into the following components:

- What specific age-related topic are you aiming to understand?
- Why is this distinct purpose significant for your interaction interface in the video game project/could your game project benefit from a different framing of these distinct objectives?
- Which key questions will drive your investigation toward finding significant insights?

In the first step it is important to not jump impulsively into the investigation. Instead, take the time to define your research objectives clearly. A well-crafted problem statement will guide you toward more relevant and actionable insights and help you avoid a shallow or generic analysis. Clear objectives make it easier to discern the relevance of the information you encounter, leading to wasted time and effort. While your primary goal might be to gather evidence that supports your design hypothesis, it is equally important to actively search for information that could challenge or refute your assumptions. This balanced approach ensures a more robust and credible design strategy.

Step 2. Set an Investigation Deadline
Implementing deadlines is a useful tactic for maintaining focus. Decide whether your desk investigation will span hours, days, or weeks. Remember that tasks often expand to fill the time available; setting realistic yet tight deadlines can improve both your productivity and the efficiency of your research.

Step 3. Focus on Your Predetermined Objective of Assembling Your Data
With your goals and deadlines set, you can proceed with your investigation. Be thorough in identifying, collecting, and organizing your data. It could be wise to lay out a couple of inclusion/exclusion benchmarks for your data collection process. Once you commence gathering information, it is advisable to organize it efficiently by summarizing important points, filing it systematically, highlighting significant portions, or resorting to digital storage solutions like a spreadsheet or online whiteboard. This will help you keep track of your data and facilitate easy retrieval whenever necessary. Additionally, consider multiple perspectives to avoid confirmation bias; seek information that challenges and confirms your initial assumptions.

Step 4. Translate the Data Into Actionable Design Implications
One of the most critical phases in your investigation is the analysis. Begin by thoroughly reviewing all gathered information. Compare data from various sources and evaluate their relevance and trustworthiness. Assess whether your research has successfully answered your initial questions and met your objectives. If it has not, you should either revisit your research or reconsider your objectives. The steadfastness of your assembled record is indicated by you and your team's evaluation concerning how reproducible and generalizable they are in a video game design context. There are myriad of approaches for doing this, here follows a superficial assessment suggestion in conducted in two stages: in the first stage, the evaluation could regard a fictive and generic video game creation process that aims to adhere to the AGE philosophy and design heuristics which are informed by your assembled investigation record. Using a generic video game in the first stage gives the record wiggle room, making your teams acquainted with the record and might start understanding how it can be used in a real environment. If the joint evaluation from the stage is regarded as plausible by most of the team, you proceed to the second stage of the evaluation. In the second stage, the steadfastness of the record exclusively concerns its application to the actual video game that you are about to create; important to assess is the record's recognizability of the game genre and game setting, the activities that the players are expected to accomplish in the video game context and how well the assembled record reflects the above. If the record passes the second stage of the evaluation process, commence compiling your investigation record into actionable and applicable design implications fitting for your team's design space.

The provided four-step model is easy to use and adapt; hopefully it will set a clear and focused path for your design investigation, making the process efficient and its outcomes actionable. By adhering to the four-step model, you will follow a structured approach, helping you establish a roadmap—analogue or imaginative—that helps you direct your actions through each step of the investigation.

The four-step approach ensures that your investigation is conducted in a thorough and professional manner, making it less resource-demanding than if an unstructured investigation approach (meaning not having an approach at all) had been used. Hopefully, it will minimize mistakes and oversights while ensuring your findings are actionable and relevant.

Using Generative AIs to Inform the Design of the Interaction Interfaces?

Unless one has been entirely disconnected over the past year, it would be hard to overlook the remarkable rise and application of generative AI language models. As we pen the concluding remarks of this volume, the date reads mid-September 2023. Generative AIs (GenAIs) can support you and your team in several steps in your design investigation, within the data collection step.

Step 3:

- GenAIs help you explore various archives, databases, records, and material.
- GenAIs might also be of assistance in translating websites, articles, and papers that seem interesting for your investigation but are in a foreign language.
- GenAIs can also help you and your team simplify and better understand academic articles that seem valuable but are using too intricate and domain-specific nomenclature.

Step 4:

- At the beginning of the analysis process, GenAIs can support you in organizing, categorizing, and coding the collected data. It can also suggest themes or topics when you are doing the analysis step.
- GenAI might also get help in your final analysis step by asking if there is something you have missed or overlooked and if your analysis is starting to show similarities with other domains that could be of interest to your implications for designing attainable interaction interfaces.

However, if you and your team were planning to use GenAIs as a source informing your AGE design, we advise you to reconsider. GenAIs are periodically pejoratively referred to as "Stochastic Parrots" because, while they can produce convincing text, they often contain errors and include harmful statements [2]. GenAIs only repeat language patterns found in their training data beginning with random ('stochastic') patterns and without understanding their meaning—just as a parrot can mimic sounds without comprehending what it is saying.

The disconnect between GenAI models' appearing to understand the text they use and generate, but the fact is that GenAI does not understand the language nor the "real world," which can lead your team to place a level of trust in the output that it does not warrant.

There must be a consensus in your game creator team that GenAIs do not understand anything. Instead, these tools string words together in common ways from various parts of the Internet. The circumstance poses severe risks to the effectiveness of your interaction interface. GenAI is not informed by observations of the natural world or other critical aspects of either the scientific method or industry investigations, which is common in informing the usability and experience of an interface design, nor is it aligned with human or social values. For these reasons, it cannot generate novel content about the real world, objects, and their relations, such as human-tech or player-game relations. The answers that the GenAI is generated can also be incorrect. You and your team need to be aware that a GenAI does not understand the text it generates providing a probability of incorrect statements—thus a critical stance must be taken to what it generates.

Doing this can be easier said than done; it has been argued that the Chat-like, often friendly, interface of GenAIs provides us with reassurance [16], yet it also distracts us, and to various extent inhibiting our ability to critical evaluation of sources, thus it has been argued that more careful consideration must be accomplished regarding our liabilities and biases that GenAI endows [23], such as generic stereotypes, discrimination against already discriminated groups, or overly normative worldviews [24].

GenAI tends to output only standard answers that assume the values of the owners/creators of the data used to train the models, indeed, if a sequence of words frequently appears in the training data—as is the case with common and uncontroversial topics and mainstream or dominant beliefs.

It is important to be aware that GenAI may have the potential to further marginalize disadvantaged individuals. It is important to recognize that minority voices may be left out due to their lower representation in the training data. It is crucial for you and your team to understand that the text generated by GenAI only represents the most common or dominant worldview from the training data, which may contain problematic or biased content such as stereotypical roles.

Perhaps needless to say, due to the issue that GenAI tends to provide a highly normative output, using such content to inform the design of the interaction interface that shall furnish attainable game experiences in your video game might provide you with overly normative insights, resulting in a skewed and ambiguous design implication. Using skewed implications might result in your interaction interface not assisting in making your video game experiences more attainable, but even worse, an unacquainted designed interaction interface might become a catastrophe, making your video game unattainable for the audience.

While we do not claim comprehensive expertise or a definitive stance on the subject, our engagement with GenAIs is tangible. The authors have an occupational interest in GenAIs, participating in scientific pan-European projects, researching and writing academic papers, and contributing to the scholastic discourse and society's collective understanding of human-AI interaction. Our stance on the matter of using GenAIs to inform design comes from our experience researching and operating them in experimental environments. So, we advise you to proceed using GenAIs for your design investigation with caution.

One thing is for sure: whatever AI predictions for the future we will do at the time of writing, only one thing will be valid for them: they will all be wrong. So, let us put the AI crystal ball away—too many are currently using it anyway.

Instead, let us concentrate on generating our implications from established investigation techniques and previously verified resolutions; this will enable you and your team to make video game interfaces that harbor elevated levels of attainable gaming experiences.

3.8 Conclusion

This chapter has explored the critical role of investigation practices in informing the attainable gaming experience (AGE) design. Constructing a universally engaging video game necessitates gathering a broad spectrum of information and perspectives. It is this rich tapestry of data that lays the foundation for informed, empirically based design decisions.

We have delved into the theoretical underpinnings and philosophies associated with AGE design, examining the distinction between intuitive and data-driven approaches. We also discussed how these methods often yield artifacts that are oriented either toward hedonic or utilitarian intentions. Importantly, we emphasized the necessity of finding a harmonious balance between these competing design intentions to achieve a gaming experience that is both meaningful and universally appealing.

Guidance has been offered on initiating design investigations tailored to inform AGE-oriented projects. Various formats and methodologies for these investigations were explored, providing a roadmap for designers seeking to incorporate inclusive and accessible elements into their games.

By taking a rigorous approach to data collection, designers are equipped with the insights needed to craft experiences that resonate with a wide array of players. This commitment to comprehensive data collection and analysis not only enhances the quality of the end product but also exemplifies the ethos of Inclusive Design, thereby enriching the gaming landscape for players of all backgrounds and abilities.

References

1. Ampatzidou, C., & Gugerell, K. (2019). Participatory game prototyping – Balancing domain content and playability in a serious game design for the energy transition. *CoDesign, 15*(4), 345–360. https://doi.org/10.1080/15710882.2018.1504084
2. Bender, E. M., Gebru, T., McMillan-Major, A., & Shmitchell, S. (2021). On the dangers of stochastic parrots: Can language models be too big? 🦜. In *Proceedings of the 2021 ACM Conference on Fairness, Accountability, and Transparency* (pp. 610–623).
3. Bogost, I. (2007). *Persuasive games: The expressive power of videogames*. MIT Press.
4. Charles, D. K., & McDonough, S. (2015). A participatory design framework for the gamification of rehabilitation systems. In *Recent advances on using virtual reality technologies for rehabilitation* (pp. 2–9). Nova Science Publishers.
5. Crabtree, A., Rouncefield, M., & Tolmie, P. (2012). *Doing design ethnography*. Springer International Publishing. https://doi.org/10.1007/978-1-4471-2726-0
6. Daer, A. J. (2010). This is how we do it: A glimpse at Gamelab's design process. *E-Learning and Digital Media, 7*(1), 108–119. https://doi.org/10.2304/elea.2010.7.1.108
7. Engström, H. (2020). *Game development research*. University of Skövde.
8. Faulkner, S. L., & Trotter, S. P. (2017). Data saturation. *The International Encyclopedia of Communication Research Methods*, 1–2. https://doi.org/10.1002/9781118901731.IECRM0060
9. Flanagan, M. (2009). *Critical play: Radical game design*. MIT press.
10. Fullerton, T. (2019). *Game design workshop: A playcentric approach to creating innovative games* (4th edn). CRC Press.
11. Garzotto, F. (2014). Interactive storytelling for children: A survey. *International Journal of Arts and Technology, 7*(1), 5–16.
12. Hennink, M., & Kaiser, B. N. (2022). Sample sizes for saturation in qualitative research: A systematic review of empirical tests. *Social Science and medicine, 292*, 114523.
13. Hevner, A. R., March, S. T., Park, J., & Ram, S. (2004). Design science in information systems research. *MIS Quarterly: Management Information Systems, 28*(1), 75–105. https://doi.org/10.2307/25148625
14. ISO 9241–210. (2010). Ergonomics of human-system interaction—Part 210: Human-centred design for interactive systems.
15. Ismail, R. (2016). Nuclear throne: Performative game development in hindsight. GDC Vault. GDC Europe 2016, Cologne, Germany. Retrieved from http://www.gdcvault.com/play/1023774/-Nuclear-Throne-Performative-Game
16. Ivarsson, J., & Lindwall, O. (2023). Suspicious minds: The problem of trust and conversational agents. *Computer Supported Cooperative Work (CSCW)*, 1–27.
17. Jacko, J. A. (Ed.). (2012). Human computer interaction handbook: Fundamentals, evolving technologies, and emerging applications.
18. Jeremy, H. (2015). Subnautica feedback system. GDC Vault. Game Developers Conference, San Francisco, CA. Retrieved from http://www.gdcvault.com/play/1022284/Tech
19. Karabinus, A., & Atherton, R. (2019). Communally designed deception: Participatory technical communication practices in an amateur game design community. *Technical Communication, 66*(3), 257–271.
20. Khaled, R., & Vasalou, A. (2014). Bridging serious games and participatory design. *International Journal of Child- Computer Interaction, 2*(2), 93–100. https://doi.org/10.1016/j.ijcci.2014.03.001

21. Lazar, J., Feng, J. H., & Hochheiser, H. (2017). Research methods in human-computer interaction. Morgan Kaufmann.
22. Lin, D., Bezemer, C.-P., & Hassan, A. E. (2018). An empirical study of early access games on the steam platform. *Empirical Software Engineering, 23*(2), 771–799. https://doi.org/10.1007/s10664-017-9531-3
23. Marcus, G. (2022). Hoping for the best as AI Evolves. In *Communications of the ACM* (Vol. 66, No. 4). Association for Computing Machinery. Available at: https://doi.org/10.1145/3583078
24. Metz, C. (2021). Who Is Making Sure the A.I. Machines Aren't Racist? New York, The New York Times. Available at: https://www.nytimes.com/2021/03/15/technology/artificial-intelligence-google-bias.html. Accessed 27 September 2023.
25. Müller, F. (2021). Design ethnography: Epistemology and methodology. Springer Nature.
26. Nardi, B. (2010). *My life as a night elf priest: An anthropological account of World of warcraft*. University of Michigan Press.
27. Nelson, H. G., & Stolterman, E. (2014). *The design way: Intentional change in an unpredictable World*. MIT Press.
28. Newton, I., in Turnbull H. W. & Royal Society (London). (1959). *The correspondence of Isaac Newton*. Cambridge University Press for the Royal Society.
29. Norman, D. (1988). *The psychology of everyday things*. Basic Books.
30. Norman, D. (2016). *The design of everyday things* (pp. 300–311). https://doi.org/10.15358/9783800648108-300
31. Norman, D., & Lincoln, Y. S. (2017). The SAGE Handbook of Qualitative Research (5th ed.). Sage.
32. Palmquist, A. (2023). *Plug & Play? Stakeholders' co-meaningmaking of gamification implementations in workplace learning environments* (Dissertation University of Gothenburg Department of Applied Information Technology).
33. Peffers, K., Tuunanen, T., Rothenberger, M. A., & Chatterjee, S. (2007). A design science research methodology for information systems research. *Journal of Management Information Systems, 24*(3), 45–77. https://doi.org/10.2753/mis0742-1222240302
34. Plowright, D. (2010). Using mixed methods: Frameworks for an integrated methodology. Using Mixed Methods, 1–224.
35. Preece, J., Sharp, H., & Rogers, Y. (2015). *Interaction design: Beyond human-computer interaction*. John Wiley & Sons.
36. Redström, J. (2017). *Making design theory*. MIT Press.
37. Reimer, C. (2017). Dialogic, data-driven design: UX and league of legends. In L. Potts & M. J. Salvo (Eds.), *Rhetoric and experience architecture* (pp. 241–257). Parlor Press.
38. Salvador, T., Bell, G., & Anderson, K. (1999). Design ethnography. *Design Management Review, 10*(4), 35–41. https://doi.org/10.1111/j.1948-7169.1999.tb00274.x
39. Schell, J. (2019). The Art of Game Design: A Book of Lenses, Third Edition (3rd ed.). A K Peters/CRC Press. https://doi.org/10.1201/b22101
40. Shin, J., & Odom, W. (2019). Collective wisdom. In *Proceedings of the 2019 CHI Conference on Human Factors in Computing Systems* (pp. 1–14). https://doi.org/10.1145/3290605.3300546
41. Simonsen, J., & Robertson, T. (Eds.). (2012). *Routledge international handbook of participatory design*. Routledge.
42. Spock, J. (2014). *Bringing the community into the dev team: A look into open development*. GDC Vault. GDC Next 2014, Los Angeles, CA. Retrieved from http://www.gdcvault.com/play/1021475/Bringing-the-Community-into-the
43. Swink, S. (2008). *Game feel: A game designer's guide to virtual sensation*. CRC Press.
44. Taffe, S. (2015). The hybrid designer/end-user: Revealing paradoxes in co-design. *Design Studies, 40*, 39–59. https://doi.org/10.1016/j.destud.2015.06.003
45. Thominet, L. (2021). Open video game development and participatory design. *Technical Communication Quarterly, 30*(4), 359–374. https://doi.org/10.1080/10572252.2020.1866679

46. Webster, J., & Watson, R. T. (2002). Analyzing the past to prepare for the future: Writing a literature review. MIS quarterly, xiii-xxiii.
47. Zimmerman, J. (2014). Psyche and EROS: Rhetorics of secrecy and disclosure in game developer-fan relations. In J. deWinter, & R. M. Moeller (Eds.), *Computer games and technical communication: Critical methods and applications at the intersection* (pp. 141–156). Ashgate.

Part II
Strategies for Enhancing the Attainability of the Video Game Experience

Video game interaction interfaces are intrinsically aligned with the goal of making the gaming experience attainable for all, a foundational aspect of the AGE design concept. To enhance the attainability of a video game, its various interaction interfaces must be meticulously (re)designed and assessed in light of the directives and constraints that mandate accessibility and inclusivity in game technology. Enhancing the attainability of interaction interfaces may also encompass the integration of assistive technologies. These technologies not only enable access to the game experience for players who desire to refine and personalize their gameplay but also for those who rely on technological support to access the video game experience.

In Part II, "Strategies for Enhancing the Attainability of the Video Game Experience," we delve deep into the methods and techniques that game developers can employ to ensure their creations are both accessible and enjoyable for all players, regardless of their unique needs and preferences.

Chapter 4 provides a detailed examination of the cutting-edge tools and devices available to developers, which can be harnessed to cater to a broader range of players. By exploring devices like the Xbox Adaptive Controller and groundbreaking features such as eye-tracking, this chapter underscores how technology can play a pivotal role in making games more attainable.

Chapter 5 focuses on potential design directives and design constraints of the AGE design heuristics. From the layout of the interaction interfaces to the dynamics of in-game localizations, this chapter breaks down the essential components that can make or break the attainability of your video game experience. The information presented will guide developers in crafting spaces and elements that resonate with diverse audiences.

Chapter 6 closes the part with a thorough look at evaluation methods. Even the most well-intentioned designs can miss the mark, which is why it is essential to test and assess games for their attainability. Through real-world examples and a series of best practices, this chapter equips developers with the knowledge to critique their creations constructively and ensure they are hitting the intended mark of inclusivity.

Together, these three chapters form a compass on how to merge the worlds of game technology, interaction interfaces, design, and evaluation in the quest to make your video game more attainable for everyone.

Chapter 4
Assistive Technologies for Attainable Gaming Experiences

Abstract The advent of device-agnostic gaming platforms has revolutionized the industry by enabling seamless cross-platform functionality, thus freeing game developers from the constraints of specific hardware environments. This shift has democratized access to interactive digital experiences, significantly expanding the potential player base. However, challenges such as optimizing for diverse screen sizes and resolutions, ensuring consistent gameplay experiences across devices, and designing innate, responsive control mechanisms remain. These Assistive Technologies can be used in myriad ways to enhance and craft an immersive, distinct gaming experience that transcends the limitations of the platform on which it is played. However, we will explain how to use it to include a broader audience for your video game. This chapter delves into various Assistive Technologies that we and our peers in game development and academia have successfully employed to captivate a broader gaming audience. These technologies are categorized into three overarching dimensions: Visual, Ergonomic, and Audio. Within each category, we highlight exemplary implementations as well as potential obstacles that developers may face when integrating these assistive solutions. We conclude by exploring emerging areas of interest in Assistive Technologies and adaptive Input Controllers, setting the stage for future innovations in accessible and inclusive video gaming.

Keywords Assistive technology · Accessibility · Video games · Game controllers · Adaptive input controllers

4.1 Providing Attainable Gaming Experiences Through Inventive Technologies

In recent years, we have witnessed an exciting progression in digital entertainment, epitomized by the widespread adoption of device agnosticism in video games. This marks a shift, aligning the gaming sector more closely with the broader media landscape by freeing it from the constraints of specific hardware or proprietary formats.

A. Palmquist et al., *Universal Design in Video Games*, Human–Computer Interaction Series, https://doi.org/10.1007/978-3-031-30595-5_4

Device agnosticism, a term initially rooted in the tech industry, refers to the ability of software to function seamlessly across various types of hardware platforms. Previously championed by streaming services like Netflix, this ethos has found its way into interactive entertainment, and its influence has been transformative.

Just as Netflix, HBO, and Amazon Prime allow users to stream movies and TV shows on virtually any device—whether a high-definition smart television, a desktop computer, or a handheld mobile device—the gaming industry is rapidly evolving to offer similar flexibility and convenience. Players can now experience their favorite video games irrespective of the device they have on hand, whether it is a high-powered gaming console, a desktop PC, a mobile device, or even a cloud-based service. The core of this approach is to prioritize the attainability of game experience, providing gamers the liberty to engage with their preferred content at their convenience without the need to invest in specific hardware.

This trend toward device agnosticism in gaming reshapes how games are designed and played and democratizes access to interactive digital experiences. It is lowering the entry barriers, making gaming more accessible to a broader audience, thereby expanding the industry's potential player base.

Thus, the integration of device agnosticism in the gaming industry represents a monumental shift akin to other seismic changes that have shaped the digital media landscape. By breaking away from the restrictions imposed by specific hardware formats, gaming is fast becoming an ever-present part of our digital lives, mirroring the omnipresence of other forms of media entertainment like streaming video and music. While laudable, the progression toward device agnosticism in the gaming industry still needs to be completed. Several areas still need significant attention and development.

Foremost, creating a genuinely device-agnostic gaming experience necessitates overcoming technical limitations and design challenges across multiple platforms. This encompasses optimization for different screen sizes and resolutions, ensuring compatibility across diverse hardware specifications, and dealing with varying input methods from touchscreen interfaces to console controllers.

Another significant challenge lies in the realm of game design itself. While some genres, like strategy and puzzle games, have transitioned well to various devices, others, such as high-fidelity action and adventure games, need help to deliver a consistent experience across all platforms. Maintaining the intended gaming experience can be challenging when a title is being played on a device for which it was not primarily designed. Therefore, designers must continue exploring innovative approaches to create engaging gameplay consistent across different devices.

Creating interaction interfaces that facilitates the intended game experience is another area where improvements must be made. Designing instinctual controls and interfaces that work seamlessly on various devices, from smartphones with touchscreens to gaming consoles with physical buttons, is a notable challenge. Designers must balance different devices' requirements while ensuring the player experience remains uncompromised.

In terms of network capabilities and connectivity, creating a seamless online multiplayer experience that works flawlessly across devices is still a hurdle. Cross-play, or the ability for gamers to use different platforms to play together, has seen strides in recent years but still needs to be ironed out regarding balancing, connectivity, and performance. While the move toward device agnosticism has made gaming more accessible and flexible, much work still needs to be done. From technical aspects to game design and user interface considerations, the industry must continue its innovative efforts to fully realize the potential of device-agnostic gaming. The ultimate goal is to create a gaming landscape that delivers a uniformly high-quality and engaging experience, regardless of the platform used.

Regarding the buzz and emerging trends of Brain-computer interfaces and Electroencephalograms as assistive technology video games

The video game industry has consistently been at the forefront of technological software and hardware advancements. This drive is not just about staying competitive—it is equally about preserving a cutting-edge ambiance, displaying an acquaintance, being up-to-date, and leading in the field. This dedication to progress has created a community and audience that can often be described as technology early adopters rather than latecomers [15].

Increasingly, this innovative spirit is spilling into assistive technologies for gaming. Among the emerging tools are brain-computer interfaces (BCI) and EEG controllers. A striking example is Perri Karval's Twitch stream, where she plays the game Elden Ring using a custom controller. This device interprets electroencephalogram (EEG) signals and translates them into in-game actions. To achieve this, Karval calibrated her EEG headset to detect specific, consistent patterns in BCI that mimic pressing a button on a gamepad or keyboard [12]. She enhanced the setup with headset-mounted accelerometers that replace character and camera movements, making it a complete hands-free gaming experience.

Karval's stream hints at a desirable future for players who experience challenges participating in gameplay that highly depend on hands, such as coordinated motor control of eye movement with hand movement (eye–hand coordination), tasks concerning that the two hands are tightly synchronized (bimanual tasks), hand distortions, or (situational) conditions related to nerves, fractures, blood vessels, and infections. EEG and BCI devices are trending in neurotechnology. With open-source neural hardware and software now more accessible and affordable, hobbyists, engineers, and neuroscience enthusiasts are transitioning tools once limited to academic and medical realms into more casual spaces like video gaming. The fusion of neurotechnology and gaming is not limited to the DIY community. Major game companies and publishers are also delving into this space. Valve, for instance, collaborated with XR company Varjo and neurotech firm OpenBCI to create the Deckard brain-computer interface platform. While no BCI-enabled games from Valve have been released as of now, Gabe Newell, the company's CEO, emphasized the importance of neurotechnology in 2021:

If you're a software developer in 2022 who doesn't have [a BCI headset] in your test lab, you're making a silly mistake. [14]

While there is significant excitement around tailored BCI and EEG applications for gaming, there is a noticeable gap when comparing these with off-the-shelf products. A comprehensive study of consumer-grade EEG devices highlighted several issues, such as BCI illiteracy, where players struggle to produce controllable brain signals.

Moreover, the devices showed inconsistencies in performance and responsiveness to various software, making them less reliable as game controllers [8]. A separate study focused on BCI and EEG in video games acknowledged the gradual increase in the availability of such devices but emphasized consistent performance issues across reviewed consumer devices [6]. This study also pointed to the limited presence of fully-featured games and commercial applications that use BCI and EEG. The inconsistent performance of BCI and EEG devices hampers their utility as reliable game controllers. Compounding this challenge is the steep learning curve associated with using these devices, the issue of setting them up optimally for gameplay, and making the technology more player-friendly. The future trajectory of BCI and EEG in the gaming sector is contingent on technological improvements and their ability to catalyze the mass adoption of this technology in gaming. Since many of these devices have yet to show promising results in independent scientific evaluations, our coverage of BCI as an assistive gaming technology will remain brief.

Our focus, instead, will be on presenting and discussing assistive technologies that have undergone thorough testing, demonstrated efficacy, are affordable, and are readily available to a broad spectrum of gamers. Our chosen technologies also meet criteria like the availability of extensive support, of applicable Software Development Kits (SDK)s for sole game creators and being well-suited for both small and medium-sized game studios.

4.2 Controllers and Accessories

4.2.1 The Anatomy of a D-Pad

As an aspiring or practicing game developer, you must understand the basic construction of traditional gaming controllers. These typically comprise two thumb sticks for movement and camera control, a D-pad for auxiliary movement or menu selection, face buttons for primary in-game actions, shoulder buttons for secondary tasks, and triggers for activities such as shooting or driving. The design of these controllers is built on the presumption that gamers possess specific physical capabilities, such as the ability to hold the controller in both hands, manipulate the thumb sticks and buttons with their thumbs, and engage the shoulder buttons with their index fingers (Fig. 4.1).

Incorporating Better Accessibility in Standard D-Pad Controllers

The game development community, acknowledging the diverse physical capabilities of gamers, has made strides toward integrating specific accessibility features in standard controllers. A key feature is button remapping, allowing players to assign in-game actions to buttons they find comfortable and easy to press. Adjustable input sensitivity settings cater to gamers with varying degrees of motor control, reducing the need for hyper-precise movements. Another feature is haptic feedback or controller vibration, which provides tactile signals corresponding to in-game events, which is especially beneficial for players with auditory impairments. Despite these enhancements, there is a considerable way to go before standard controllers can claim to offer a universally accessible design.

The Mouse and Keyboard—A Manifestation of Traditional Computer-Based Gameplay

Another standard controller, the general input choice among PC gamers, combines a mouse and a keyboard. In this setup, the keyboard serves as the primary input device, offering an array of keys that can be mapped to diverse in-game actions. Alongside this, the mouse, with its precision-driven cursor control and additional buttons, significantly enhances the gameplay experience. Together, they create a dynamic control environment, accommodating a range of gaming genres. Even though the mouse and keyboard are an emblem of traditional computer-based gameplay, surprisingly slight development has occurred for this input controller for digital games.

Fig. 4.1 The design of a D-Pad controller has similar ergonomic configurations, thus having comparable limitations making the game experience attainable for a wide audience

Accessibility Improvements for the Mouse and Keyboard Standard Controller If you and your team aim to acknowledge the vast landscape of gamers, specific improvements can be implemented to make the mouse and keyboard more accessible. For example, Key remapping of both the keyboard and mouse allows players to customize their controls based on their comfort and requirements. Additionally, specific software solutions provide features like sticky or slow keys, helping individuals with motor control difficulties [1]. Provide mouse settings in your game that allow adjustment to cater to the participant's various levels of dexterity and hand–eye coordination.

Despite these improvements, the mouse and keyboard setup have limitations. It assumes a significant degree of fine motor control and manual dexterity, which may not be feasible for all gamers. The static design of standard keyboards can also pose difficulties for individuals with certain physical conditions. Moreover, the reliance on visual feedback for mouse control can create obstacles for visually impaired players (Fig. 4.2).

Today, the differences in controller input between computers and consoles are less distinct than they used to be. Currently, many PC gamers use a D-Pad to experience their games. Additionally, current consoles now come with built-in support for keyboard and mouse usage, which eliminates the need for third-party peripherals.

However, the primary challenge regarding both the mouse and keyboard setup as well as the D-Pad lies in the "one-size-fits-all" approach that they, as standard controllers, tend to adopt. Such a design philosophy often rigidly assumes several conditions, for instance, the use of both hands, a certain level of dexterity, and a

Fig. 4.2 The mouse and keyboard—early icons of computer gameplay

degree of fine motor control that may not align with the physical capabilities of all gamers.

Therefore, as a game developer, your task is twofold. On the one hand, you should take advantage of the accessibility features already available in standard controllers to make your games more inclusive. On the other hand, it is essential to push for further innovation in controller design. Encourage conversations around inclusivity and accessibility in gaming, collaborate with hardware manufacturers, and participate in testing and feedback phases for new controller designs. Always remember that your ultimate goal is to afford and facilitate gaming experiences that as many as possible might attain, regardless of their conditions, abilities, or temporal circumstances.

By understanding the architecture of the more standardized controllers, the D-Pad, the mouse and keyboard setup, and the broad diversity of gamers' abilities and circumstances serve as the foundational stepping stone in facilitating more attainable games. Nevertheless, creating accessible gaming experiences extends beyond merely designing input controllers. It also permeates the realm of game design itself, as seen in elements like the ability to remap controls on the controller. Having such considerations in mind in the game development process assists your game in becoming a further attainable and enjoyable activity for more participants.

However, the drive for inclusivity, personalization, and accessibility is not confined to input controllers alone. A swiftly progressing field lies in the territory of Accessories for Augmenting Accessibility. These innovative tools can provide auxiliary support, enhancing game interaction and making it more accommodating for all players. We will now delve deeper into this exciting field, exploring how it contributes to the further democratization of gaming.

4.2.2 Input Controller Accessories

In the search for more attainable gaming experiences, game accessories extend far beyond mere enhancements to controllers. Accessories are the transformative elements that supplement the limitations of controllers, serving to bridge the gap between a player's physical capabilities and the gaming experience. These accessories become especially essential for individuals with varied conditions and circumstances, playing a crucial role in molding a gaming setup that is uniquely suited to their specific needs and abilities.

For creating a video game that affords attainable gaming experiences, it is vital to acknowledge that the function of gaming accessories extends much further than merely supplementing controller functionality. These devices act as transformational instruments that bridge the gap between a player's physical capabilities and their ability to immerse themselves in a digital gaming world. They are not just helpful but integral for players with diverse abilities, as they allow for the creation of a gaming environment specifically tailored to individual needs. As game developers, our overarching goal is to design engaging, immersive experiences that captivate a broad spectrum of players and keep them coming back for more. This objective extends beyond the confines of the digital realms we create; it also encompasses the physical interfaces—the gaming accessories—that players use to interact with our games. Accessories like joystick extenders, tactile button caps, and controller mounts can significantly enhance a player's experience with your game by improving the functionality of standard controllers.

Take, for instance, joystick extenders; by increasing the lever arm of the joystick, these extenders enhance the grip, facilitating more precise and controlled movements. The colorful options also aid visibility, especially for gamers with visual impairments. This simple addition can substantially improve in-game navigation and action execution, demonstrating the transformative potential of even seemingly minor modifications. Furthermore, the extenders offer an aesthetic appeal that can make the gaming setup more engaging and personalized, adding another layer to the immersive gaming experience.

By encouraging the use of these accessory-enhanced setups, we promote a more inclusive gaming environment where players with a range of physical abilities can partake more fully in the gaming experience. These accessories instruments function to eliminate barriers, create new opportunities, and broaden both who can engage with your game and how they do so.

Therefore, as developers aiming to appeal to a diverse audience, it is critical to understand and incorporate the potential of these gaming accessories within our development strategies. Such an approach reflects our commitment to acknowledging and addressing our players' diverse needs, thereby promoting a more inclusive and accessible gaming environment.

In the fast-paced world of gaming, where developments are swift and relentless, recognizing the significance of gaming accessories is not just advisable but a pressing necessity. By integrating these tools into the design and functionality of our games, we cater to the needs of a more diverse player base, consequently driving the growth of a culture of inclusivity within gaming. It is high time to fully embrace these tools, allowing our games to serve as platforms that invite everyone to partake in the joy of gaming.

Companies in the Game and Technology that Provide Gaming Accessories

In the last couple of years, the market for accessible gaming accessories has expanded and is far from niche; instead, it is a burgeoning space filled with innovative companies dedicated to advancing inclusivity within gaming. Their products enhance the gaming experience and serve as a model for developers aiming to make gaming more universally attainable.

Consider Logitech's Adaptive Gaming Kit, a prime example of this trend. Designed to pair with the Xbox Adaptive Controller, it includes an array of buttons and triggers in varied sizes and shapes. This allows gamers to personalize their gaming setup to their unique requirements, thus extending the adaptability of the Xbox Adaptive Controller (see below).

Companies like AbleNet have also made noteworthy contributions, offering a diverse range of switches, buttons, and mounts to meet a wide variety of needs. Their product line exemplifies flexibility and versatility, ensuring that a broad spectrum of gamers can find a setup that works for them. RAM Mounts, is a company that specializes in providing sturdy and adaptable mounting solutions. These mounts offer flexibility and durability, accommodating a wide range of positioning needs for controllers or switches. These accessories offer more than just a boost to the gaming setup; they empower gamers by providing them with the tools to shape their own gaming experiences, adapting each aspect to their specific needs. This elevated level of customization and adaptability is a testament to the industry's progress in fostering inclusivity. As game developers, it is an inspiring reminder that accessible gaming is not merely an aspiration but a thriving and expanding reality.

Tobii, an eye-tracking technology enterprise, is perhaps better known for applying its technology to sectors beyond gaming. However, the company has begun to carve out a niche in the gaming industry, serving as a supplier of eye-tracking in video games. This technology serves as an assistive tool, making video games more accessible to those whom traditional controllers and keyboards might not accommodate.

Nevertheless, as demonstrated, the scope for enhancing and improving the standardized input controllers accessibility is inherently limited, primarily due to their physical shape and layout. Due to this, the accessories for input controllers can only provide restricted assistance.

As such, we will now venture into the domain of specialized game controllers, exploring their contemporary adoption barriers prospects and how you and your team might integrate them into your game development process to accommodate a more comprehensive array of player needs.

4.2.3 Specialized Controllers

Interactive entertainment has witnessed a profound metamorphosis with the emergence of specialized game controllers. Far from mere variations of traditional models, these innovative devices are uniquely designed, boasting features tailored to various gaming scenarios. As per specific sources, the rise of esports has contributed significantly to the evolution and popularization of these specialized controllers [21]. The increasing mainstream acceptance of esports catalyzed the demand for these distinctive devices, given their potential to confer advantages in specialized esports arenas [21].

However, the use of specialized controllers in competitive gaming environments is a subject of ongoing debate. On one side of the argument, these controllers present an opportunity to level the playing field for players with physical disabilities. Conversely, the advantage some controllers might provide introduces questions concerning fairness in competitive gaming.

Although this topic merits extensive discussion, it falls outside the scope of this book. Here, we focus on exploring specialized game controllers conceived from an empathetic and inclusive perspective, acknowledging the diversity of gamers' physical abilities and the pursuit of immersive gaming experiences. Specialized controllers range widely in their design and functionality. Some offer multiple switches for complex command sequences, precision-calibrated analogue sticks for nuanced movement, foot pedals to replicate the driving experience, and even devices operable by mouth or eyes. Notable among these are the Xbox Adaptive Controller [10] and the QuadStick [2]. The former reimagines the traditional gaming controllers architecture, offering sizable programmable buttons and an array of ports for various external devices. The QuadStick [2], on the other hand, is a mouth-operated joystick designed to provide gaming interaction for quadriplegic individuals. These examples underscore the industry's drive to ensure gaming is accessible and enjoyable for everyone.

Despite the progress in hardware development, a significant challenge regarding game compatibility with these specialized controllers still needs to be addressed. Often, developers prioritize designing games compatible with mainstream consoles and standard controllers, inadvertently overlooking the need to ensure compatibility with these advanced devices. This issue can arise due to the perceived complexity of supporting various devices, a misconception of the audience for specialized controllers, or traditional development practices primarily focusing on standard input devices.

This oversight not only restricts the gaming experience for players with specialized controllers but also limits developers' ability to fully utilize these advanced devices' potential. By failing to support specialized hardware, developers miss opportunities to offer more immersive, affluent, and inclusive gaming experiences that could widen their audience base.

There is a pressing need for a shift in development practices to rectify this. Developers should consider hardware compatibility from the earliest stages of the game design process. By incorporating diverse controller capabilities into their design, they can not only enhance gameplay for a broader range of players but also foster innovation, pushing the boundaries of what is possible in interactive entertainment.

In addition to developers, other stakeholders have a role to play. Industry standards should evolve to encourage support for a broader range of controllers. Hardware and software manufacturers should collaborate to ensure seamless integration between their products. Furthermore, educating players about compatible controllers and their effective utilization is crucial. Clear, accessible information can help gamers make informed choices and fully utilize their hardware's capabilities.

The rise of specialized controllers signifies a vital evolution in gaming. By catering to the diverse physical capabilities of gamers and offering personalized, accessible gaming experiences, these devices have the potential to democratize the gaming world. They represent a shift in the industry's perspective, recognizing the wide-ranging demographic of gamers and asserting that everyone should have the chance to engage with and enjoy the interactive gaming world.

Examples of Implementations of Specialized Controllers in Video Games
Arguing for the application and benefits of specialized controllers is conceivably best accomplished through concrete examples, shedding light on how inclusive design can significantly impact the gaming industry. Thus, here are some major ones, but we

implore you to look beyond these as many more might be more valuable in informing your design and development process.

Microsoft's Xbox has made commendable strides in accessibility by incorporating compatibility with the Xbox Adaptive Controller. Recognizing the need for a more inclusive gaming experience, in 2017, Microsoft created the Xbox Adaptive Controller. This innovation was not simply tailored for a particular disability. Instead, it was conceived as a versatile foundation that synchronizes effortlessly with a myriad of existing peripherals, fostering a more accessible gaming environment across platforms—both on PC and Xbox consoles. The objective was to accommodate and actively enable gamers, regardless of their specific conditions and circumstances. The extensive array of adaptive features the Xbox Adaptive Controller facilitated allowed a more considerable number of players to engage in the world of gaming on a more equitable and fairer level.

The Xbox Adaptive Controller offers large programmable buttons and multiple ports for various external devices, allowing gamers with various levels of mobility to customize their gaming experience. Microsoft's compatibility efforts have garnered positive feedback from the community, setting an inspiring precedent for other platforms. Specific games have also excelled in supporting specialized controllers, offering enhanced gaming experiences for players with varying physical capabilities. A prime example is the racing game "Forza Horizon 4" [22], widely praised for its extensive customization options. The game's settings allow it to be compatible with an array of specialized controllers, making it accessible to various gamers.

Similarly, "The Last of Us Part II" [16], an action-adventure game developed by Naughty Dog, has earned acclaim for its comprehensive suite of accessibility features. These features extend beyond controller customization to include options like text-to-speech, high contrast mode, and remappable controls, representing an integrated approach to accessibility that considers diverse gamer needs.

Mobile gaming, a rapidly growing sector, has also seen examples of successful implementation. For example, "Superbrothers: Sword and Sworcery EP" [20] is a mobile game praised for its unique gameplay mechanics that can be easily adapted to different control schemes. This has allowed it to be enjoyed by players using specialized controllers tailored to their individual needs.

By embracing specialized controllers, you can significantly broaden your game's appeal and player base. The above examples should serve as guides for developers looking to incorporate similar features and send a clear signal to gamers about which titles are designed with their needs in mind. Such steps in the game design contribute not only to an attainable gaming experience but also to a more diversified gaming community of your game and promote an industry culture that values and caters to gamers of all abilities and conditions.

Possible Obstacles and Ethical Considerations that Hinder Participant Adoption of Specialized Controllers

For game creators seeking to incorporate specialized controllers into their titles better, understanding the potential barriers to their adoption is vital.

The first barrier is Affordability. Specialized controllers, due to their intricate design and advanced technology, often carry a higher price tag compared to standard controllers. This can dissuade a portion of your potential player base, particularly those who might benefit most from these devices but lack the resources to afford them. Addressing affordability, consider how your game can still offer an inclusive and engaging experience for those who might not be able to afford specialized controllers. Additionally, explore partnerships with manufacturers and non-profit organizations to develop programs that can subsidize the cost of these devices for players who need them.

The second barrier is Availability. Specialized controllers may not be easily accessible in all regions, limiting the audience that can take advantage of these devices. As a developer, understanding these geographic constraints can guide your design process and the partnerships you form. Availability can be facilitated by working with hardware manufacturers and global distributors to ensure your players have access to the necessary specialized controllers wherever they are located. Your support in advocating for wider distribution can make a significant difference.

The third barrier is Adaptability. Many players, especially those accustomed to traditional controllers, may struggle to acclimate to the unique control schemes of specialized controllers. This could deter players from trying games that require these devices, even if they offer a superior experience. In managing this barrier make sure to develop your games with flexible control schemes that the player can easily customize. Providing in-game tutorials that guide players on how to make the most of their specialized controllers makes the transition more manageable.

The fourth and last barrier we term is, Technological compatibility. Ensuring the technological compatibility of your game can be challenging. This is because there is a wide range of games, platforms, and specialized controllers that need to be fully compatible. It can be a complex task to achieve this. Therefore, we recommend you to reach out and start collaborating with hardware manufacturers to ensure your game is compatible with their devices. This can involve using the manufacturer's SDKs, evaluating your game extensively with different controllers, and offering robust support to help players troubleshoot any issues they encounter (Fig. 4.3).

As you and your team are looking to incorporate better and include specialized controllers into your gaming ecosystems, it is essential to understand the potential regulatory and ethical aspects associated with these devices.

When enhancing accessibility through specialized controllers, you may encounter questions of fairness. For instance, controllers that are designed to make gaming more accessible for some individuals could potentially provide an unfair advantage to others, especially in competitive scenarios. Balancing the need for accessibility with fairness in gameplay is a delicate task. Another issue to consider is how your game design affects competition. You need to ensure that your game, especially if it involves competitive elements, remains fair and balanced for all players, regardless of the type of controller they use. This becomes even more critical regarding professional esports events with high stakes. To navigate these challenges, we propose the following approaches:

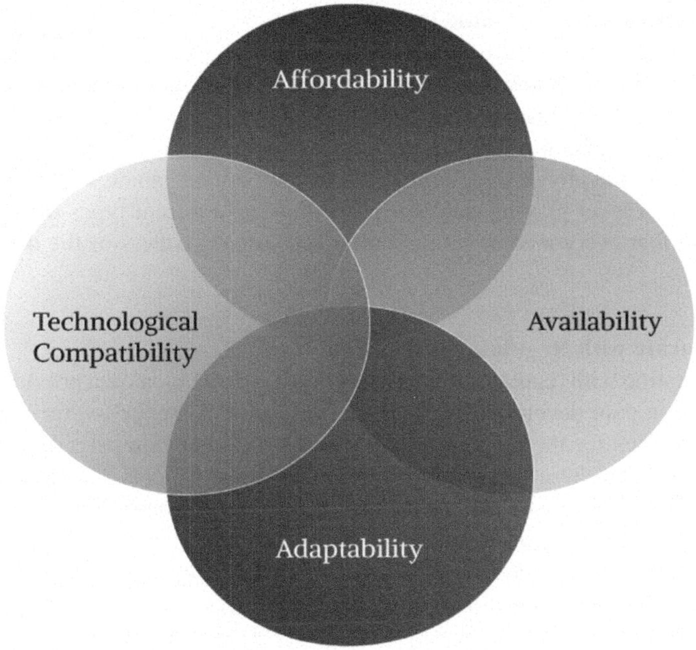

Fig. 4.3 Complications and contemplations for game creators to consider when seeking to incorporate specialized input controllers

Understanding the Regulations

As developers, staying abreast of the various regulations and standards related to accessibility in gaming is vital. This knowledge not only facilitates compliance with essential guidelines but also aids in averting potential legal issues. Regularly check for updates and changes in legislation and consider partnering with legal experts who specialize in accessibility law to ensure you fully understand and adhere to these guidelines. By doing so, you can build accessible games with confidence and contribute to making the gaming landscape more inclusive.

Open Discussions

Foster and engage in robust dialogues about accessibility and specialized controllers within the gaming communities and industry forums. These platforms can serve as invaluable avenues for gaining insights into the player experience, understanding the challenges players face, and exploring potential solutions. By actively participating in these conversations, you can stay at the forefront of developments and incorporate player feedback into your game design process to better cater to the needs of all players.

Seek Fairness in Your Game Design
Game design should prioritize fairness and equality, ensuring that game mechanics do not disproportionately favor any one type of controller. This involves continually testing and adjusting your game mechanics to ensure they work well with different types of controllers. Implement strategies that focus on player skill and strategy over the physical input method. In competitive games, consider how you can create a level playing field for players using different types of controllers, ensuring that everyone has a fair shot at success, regardless of the devices they use.

Collaborate with Regulators and Organizations
Collaboration with regulators and accessibility organizations can provide valuable guidance in your development process. These entities are well-versed in creating fair guidelines for the use of specialized controllers in competitive gaming. By partnering with these organizations, you can glean insights into best practices, leverage their expertise to shape the use of specialized controllers in your games, and help establish industry standards that benefit all players. This collaborative approach can lead to innovations that enhance the gaming experience for everyone, making it more enjoyable, inclusive, and equitable.

Remember that our ambition behind incorporating specialized controllers is to help you sculpt a gaming ecosystem where every player, irrespective of their abilities, conditions, and circumstances, can attain the envisioned gaming experience. As you confront this endeavor's regulatory and ethical complexities, remember that your contributions are crucial in fostering a more equitable and diverse gaming landscape.

Navigating toward this inclusivity may be filled with challenges, but always keep in mind that the ultimate goal is to facilitate a gaming experience accessible to a broader audience. Overcoming these obstacles not only enhances the experiences of your players but also potentially expands your player base. This approach cultivates an inclusive gaming culture that values the diversity of its players. Pursuing this mission attests to the potential of gaming as a universal language that transcends several barriers.

As we witness the rapid evolution of technology, coupled with a growing emphasis on player personalization, game accessibility, and inclusive participation, we stand on the cusp of a new era. The emergence of advanced, specialized input controllers in the gaming industry seems imminent. This state of flux underscores the vital need for game developers to stay informed and adaptable, not just in the research phase of a game project but throughout its entire lifecycle. Refrain from keeping abreast of the latest developments could be a costly misstep, especially when a novel input controller could bring significant advancements in the gaming experience.

4.3 Eye-Tracking and Motion Control for Attainable Gaming Experience

4.3.1 Eye-Tracking Technology Functionalities in Games

Eye-tracking technology is a rapidly advancing area that records and analyzes where and when we focus our gaze. The technology works by illuminating the eye with infrared light to generate reflections from various parts of the eye. These reflections are then captured by high-resolution cameras and processed by complex algorithms to calculate the point of gaze, where exactly the player is looking.

In a gaming context, eye-tracking provides a natural, intuitive way of interacting with digital environments. It enables developers to create games that respond to the player's gaze direction, eye focus, and eye-lid blinks [17]. Eye-tracking technology can be employed to enhance immersion, creating dynamic lighting and depth-of-field effects that change as players look around. Eye-tracking technology can be a potent asset for enhancing both the competitive edge and accessibility in gaming. For instance, in a first-person shooter (FPS) game, an eye tracker might be employed as a novelty and a tactical tool, potentially offering players a distinctive advantage in competitive gameplay [4]. In the heat of battle, the ability to rapidly acquire targets merely with a glance can streamline gameplay, offering an immediacy of response that conventional controls might not be able to match. This capacity can provide players with an invaluable edge, particularly in the split-second encounters typical of FPS games.

However, the utility of eye-tracking technology extends beyond the competitive sphere. It serves as a powerful tool to augment accessibility, providing an alternative or supplementary input method for gamers who may find traditional controllers challenging to use.

Picture this, the same FPS game, but this time, the player's avatar moves through the three-dimensional game space solely based on their eye movements. Enabling such an input design would drastically reduce the reliance on conventional control schemes, opening up the gaming experience to a broader audience. Such a feature could potentially significantly alter how games are played and perceived, thereby making gaming more inclusive and diverse.

Thus, the implementation of eye-tracking technology in gaming is twofold. While it can undoubtedly enhance gameplay dynamics and provide a competitive edge, its value as a tool for increasing accessibility and promoting inclusivity in gaming is equally, if not more, significant.

History and Evolution of Eye-Tracking in Gaming

The journey of eye-tracking technology in gaming has been a transformative one. While eye-tracking has been used for decades in fields like psychology and medical research, its application in gaming is relatively recent, spurred on by advances in technology and growing recognition of the need for more accessible gaming experiences.

Early attempts at incorporating eye-tracking in gaming were often hampered by cumbersome equipment, low accuracy, and excessive costs. However, since eye-tracking technology has recently taken some serious steps forward, eye-tracking devices have become smaller, more accurate, and more affordable, leading to their increased adoption in the gaming industry as well as its audience.

In the late 2000s and early 2010s, companies began exploring the possibilities of eye-tracking in gaming in earnest. Tobii Tech began to release affordable, consumer-friendly eye-tracking devices devised for gaming, and game developers started to integrate eye-tracking functionality into their games.

Over the past decade, eye-tracking technology has continued to mature and gain acceptance. An increasing number of games now support eye-tracking, and the technology has been incorporated into various gaming platforms. As developers have gained experience with eye-tracking, they have found innovative ways to leverage the technology, creating games that are more immersive, intuitive, and accessible.

The evolution of eye-tracking in gaming exemplifies the industry's ongoing commitment to leveraging technology to create more inclusive and immersive experiences. As digital technology continues to advance, it is clear that eye-tracking will play an increasingly prominent role in shaping the future of gaming.

Implementing Support for Eye-Tracking Can Improve Gameplay for a Wide Range of Players

Integrating eye-tracking technology into gaming applications has the potential to elevate gameplay for a more extensive demographic than one might initially anticipate. It is not just a feature that enriches the gaming experience for players with physical limitations—although this aspect is paramount and should not be undervalued—it is an enhancement that can redefine the entire gaming experience for all players, regardless of their physical abilities.

Eye-tracking provides an alternative input mechanism for gamers with certain conditions or circumstantial limitations that can make video games more accessible and interactive. It opens up a world of possibilities, allowing these gamers to engage in a medium that might otherwise have been challenging to access with traditional controllers.

However, the benefits of eye-tracking extend well beyond accessibility. The technology adds a new dimension of immersion and interactivity to gaming that all gamers can appreciate. For instance, in an action-adventure game, a player's on-screen character could react to whatever the player is looking at instead of being limited to pre-defined interactions. The game can adapt and respond to the player in real time, creating a gaming experience that's more dynamic, immersive, and engaging. Moreover, the technology also offers competitive advantages in specific gaming genres. In strategy games or player-vs-player combat scenarios, eye-tracking could provide players with quicker response times, more precise controls, and a heightened sense of awareness.

In the world of game development, these capabilities could change how games are designed and played. The use of eye-tracking can potentially transform games from being simply visually appealing experiences into environments that interact with players in a more intimate and personalized way. Eye-tracking technology support could enhance gameplay for a broader audience than initially expected, leading to more inclusive, engaging, and immersive gaming experiences.

Besides the accessibility aspects, an eye tracker is also a technology capable of monitoring both head and eye movements concurrently, unlocking the potential for profoundly personalized gaming experiences. By tracking the player's gaze and head orientation, this tool can create an interactive layer that responds to a player's natural behaviors, paving the way for a gaming experience that is as unique as the individual.

Games that implement eye-tracking respond to more than just button presses or joystick movements—they react to where the player is looking. It enables the personalization of in-game elements based on the user's gaze. For instance, game characters might react to direct eye contact, or the game environment could change based on where the player's attention is directed. These personalized interactions create a gameplay experience that is not just immersive but genuinely individualized.

Integrating head-tracking in tandem with eye-tracking further enhances personalization. The eye tracker can accurately interpret the player's intended point of interest by detecting head movements, even if their gaze and head are moving independently. This nuanced interpretation of player behavior allows for a more natural, intuitive interaction, mirroring the complexity of real-world experiences within the digital realm.

Eye-tracking extends the possibility of customization beyond the game mechanics and into the accessibility realm. Eye-tracking can be an alternative or supplementary control method for gamers who may find standard controllers challenging due to physical restrictions. This ability to customize the mode of interaction means the game experience can be personalized to the player's physical capabilities, further broadening the appeal and accessibility of gaming.

The dual functionality of eye trackers brings unprecedented personalization to video games. It allows for a more intimate connection between the player and the game, offering a dynamic, engaging, and highly personalized gaming experience that can be tailored to accommodate the needs and capabilities of a diverse range of players.

4.4 Motion Controls

4.4.1 Overview of Motion Control Technology

Motion control technology refers to systems that track, interpret, and respond to player movements, translating them into on-screen actions or game mechanics. These technologies often involve accelerometers, gyroscopes, infrared sensors, and cameras to capture motion data. The Nintendo Wii, for example, popularized the use of motion controllers in gaming with the introduction of the Wii Remote, but the trend has expanded far beyond that console.

As technology has evolved, so has the accuracy and sensitivity of motion control. Advanced systems like the "PlayStation Move" [18], the "Xbox Kinect" [9], and virtual reality controllers like the "Oculus Touch" [13] or the "Vive controller" [19] offer more immersive experiences, with precise motion tracking and a wide range of movement interpretation.

At its core, this technology captures, analyzes, and translates player movements into corresponding actions within a digital interface or game environment.

Foundational Elements

Sensors and Components

- Accelerometers: Measure changes in velocity, aiding in determining directional movements.
- Gyroscopes: Detect angular rotation, providing insights into orientation and tilt.
- Infrared Sensors: Employ infrared light to detect motion, which is particularly useful for determining distances or relative positioning.
- Cameras: These tools play a dual role by visualizing movements and aiding in spatial recognition.

Evolving Precision and Sensitivity

- *Advanced Implementations*: With platforms like PlayStation Move and Xbox Kinect, motion control delved deeper into capturing a broader range of human movements. These systems could track everything from a player's full-body dance routines to the subtle nuances of hand gestures.
- *Virtual Reality (VR)*: VR controllers, like the Oculus Touch or Vive controllers, have brought motion control into 3D spatial interaction. These devices track movement and provide haptic feedback, heightening immersion by simulating touch and interaction within virtual environments.

The evolution of motion control has been remarkable. It has transcended beyond being a mere gaming trend and has demonstrated the incredible potential of fusing human natural motion with digital experiences. This integration has revolutionized interactive entertainment, enabling developers to push the boundaries of what was previously thought to be impossible. The future of motion control technology is exciting, and we can expect to see even more innovative advancements in the coming years.

4.4.2 Enablers and Barriers of Motion Controls in Video Games

Incorporating drivers for using assistive technology for video games, it is imperative to thoroughly examine the advantages and disadvantages of motion controllers regarding your team's desired video game experiences. These devices undoubtedly provide numerous benefits, such as facilitating intuitive and engaging interactions with digital content. However, it is equally important to acknowledge the potential drawbacks that motion controllers may pose. For instance, some players may experience physical discomfort or difficulty using these devices due to their design or sensitivity. As such, it is crucial to carefully weigh the pros and cons of motion controllers when determining their suitability for specific assistive technology applications. By doing so, one can make informed decisions that prioritize player safety, comfort, and satisfaction—reflecting the AGE design heuristics Error Prevention in Play as well as Flexible and Fair Play (Figs. 4.4 and 4.5).

Incorporating motion controls into gaming can offer a distinctive and imaginative gaming experience. However, it is essential to strike a balance that meets the diverse preferences of the gaming community. Doing so can create a more inclusive and enjoyable gaming environment for all. Considering the varying levels of physical abilities and personal preferences of gamers, game developers should strive to provide options that cater to both motion-controlled and traditional gameplay styles. This approach will encourage more players to engage with the game and ensure that the gaming experience is not exclusive to a specific group of individuals. Finding a middle ground in motion-controlled gaming will lead to a more diverse and welcoming community where everyone can enjoy the games they treasure.

4.4.3 Examples of Games that Utilize Motion Control in an Accessible Way

Wii Sports (Nintendo Wii)
"Wii Sports" [11] bundles together a collection of sports games—tennis, baseball, bowling, golf, and boxing. Wii Sports is a classic example; Wii Sports offers simple, intuitive controls for games like tennis and bowling. Its ease of use made it popular among players of all ages and abilities.

Accessibility Features
The game offers an intuitive design where the player's movements with the Wii Remote correspond directly to actions on-screen. The minimalistic and straightforward approach to controls, coupled with a forgiving gameplay mechanic, ensures that players of varying skill levels can engage without feeling overwhelmed. Visual and auditory cues further aid in making gameplay more inclusive.

Dance Central (Xbox Kinect)
"Dance Central" [3] challenges players to mimic on-screen dance moves, scoring based on accuracy. Dance Central is a dance game accessible to many, not necessarily because it was easy, but because it allowed players to engage at their comfort level. The game also provided feedback on accuracy without punishing players too harshly for mistakes.

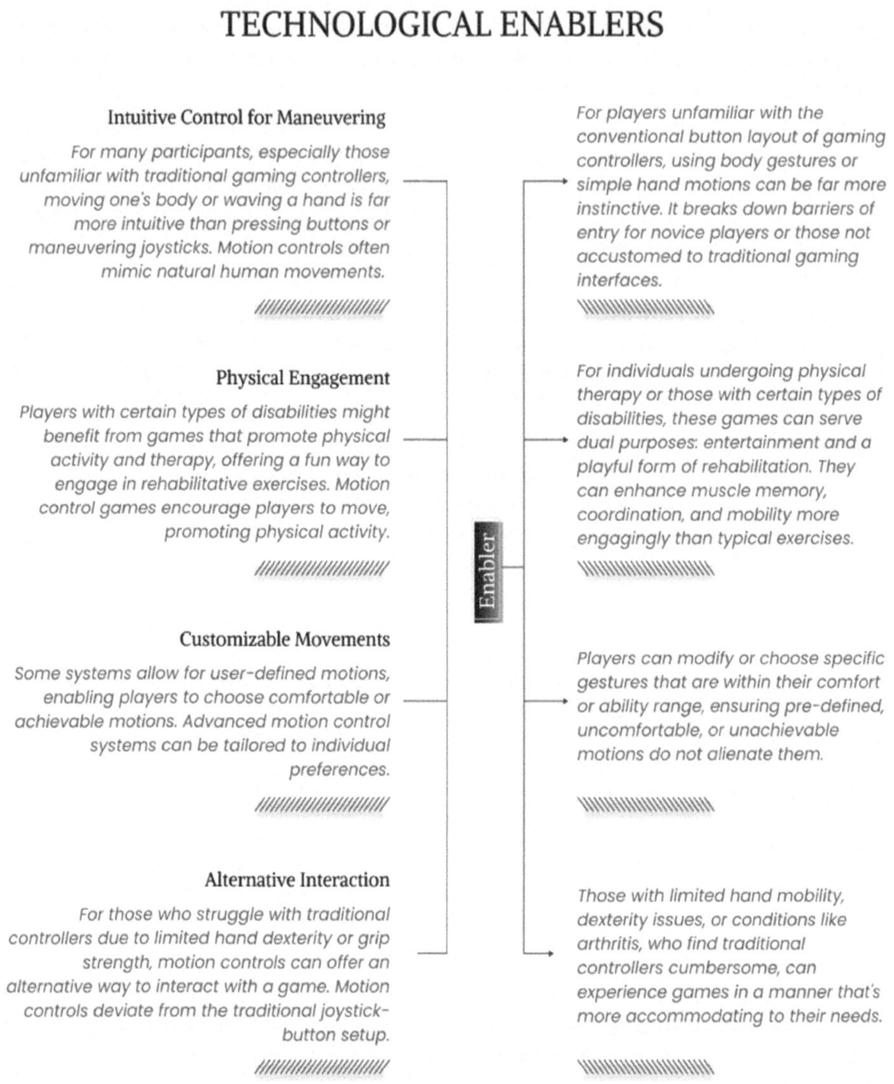

Fig. 4.4 Various interaction interface features might harbour potential to enable the intended gameplay experience to a broader audience

Accessibility Features

With a diverse array of songs and dance routines, players can choose the intensity and complexity of their experience. Real-time feedback helps players understand their performance without being overly punitive. Moreover, the Kinect's ability to capture full-body motion means that handheld controllers do not restrict players, allowing for a more fluid and natural movement experience.

Fig. 4.5 Correspondingly, features in the interaction interface might impede the intended gameplay experience for specific game audience groups

Beat Saber (VR)
Set in a neon-lit environment, players use virtual lightsabers to slash through blocks in rhythm to the music. "Beat Saber" [5] is a rhythm game where players slash at blocks with lightsabers; Beat Saber's simple concept and customizable difficulty levels allow for a broad range of player abilities to engage and enjoy.

Accessibility Features
Beat Saber offers a range of difficulty levels, ensuring that novices and seasoned players can find a comfortable challenge. The game's inherent design focuses on

hand-eye coordination rather than full-body movement, making it more accessible to players with mobility constraints. Custom song support and modding communities have also enabled a broader range of experiences tailored to dissimilar needs.

Journey for Elysium (VR)
"Journey for Elysium" [7] is an adventure game inspired by Greek mythology, players navigate the underworld in a quest to reach Elysium. This VR title uses a unique rowing mechanic, making navigation and interaction simple and more physically immersive without demanding overly complex motions from the player.

Accessibility Features
The game's primary interaction mechanic, rowing, offers a smooth and immersive way of navigating the virtual environment. This eliminates the need for complex button combinations or intricate gestures. The serene pace and clear visual cues ensure the player is not rushed, allowing them to engage at their preferred speed.

Recognizing the potential of motion controls is vital in paving the way for more inclusive gaming. The examples provided above underscore the advancements in the realm of accessible motion control, but the ever-evolving landscape of technology and game design opens doors for developers to create even more accessible experiences. Prioritizing the needs of a diverse player base not only enriches the essence of gaming but also positions it as a universally cherished form of entertainment. To harness the full potential of motion controls in bridging accessibility challenges, developers must remain attuned to the varying needs of players. The ultimate aim is to cultivate a gaming environment where every individual can partake in the wonder of interactive play.

4.5 Speech Recognition and Voice Control

4.5.1 Speech Recognition

Speech recognition is a fundamental technology that enables the conversion of spoken language into written text, or the execution of commands based on recognized phrases. The process involves recording audio, applying preprocessing techniques, extracting relevant features, and then matching them against stored patterns or templates in a database. In modern times, this technology depends on the utilization of machine learning and deep learning algorithms to improve its accuracy and efficiency. Speech recognition technology translates spoken words into digital commands or transcribes them into written form. It is a blend of acoustics, linguistics, and computer science, converging to understand human language in real time. The fundamental steps involve:

- Audio Capture: This is the initial phase, where spoken words are recorded using a microphone.
- Preprocessing: The recorded audio undergoes filtering to eliminate background noises and enhance speech clarity.
- Feature Extraction: Salient features of the preprocessed audio, like pitch and tone, are extracted for further analysis.
- Pattern Matching: The extracted features are compared with a vast database of speech patterns or templates.
- Machine Learning and AI: Contemporary systems utilize machine learning and profound learning algorithms to refine recognition capabilities continuously. Over time, they adapt to a user's speech nuances, improving accuracy and responsiveness.

Speech Recognition and Its Incorporation Into Gaming

Within gaming, the concept of early integration can be observed in titles such as "Hey You, Pikachu!" exclusively on the Nintendo 64 platform. With the progression and maturation of technology, voice commands were subsequently incorporated to complement the gameplay experience, amplifying both immersion and accessibility for the player. Modern Implementations for voice commands in video games transitioned from mere gimmicks to crucial gameplay elements. Titles across platforms began to harness speech recognition for more immersive experiences, allowing players to communicate with in-game characters, issue strategic commands, or even navigate game menus using voice. Additionally, voice control began playing a pivotal role in making games more accessible to those with mobility challenges. The integration of speech recognition promises an even more intuitive and immersive experience. The fusion of voice with gameplay showcases the endless possibilities of human–machine synergy.

4.5.2 Advantages of Voice Control in Gaming

Inclusivity Through Hands-Free Gameplay: Empowering Players with Physical Conditions

When it comes to gaming, some players may face difficulties due to physical disabilities. One such challenge is posed by traditional controllers, which can require intricate hand–eye coordination and make gameplay difficult for those with mobility challenges. However, there is a solution that can help open the world of digital exploration and competition to these players. By utilizing voice commands, they can enjoy hands-free gameplay that allows them to experience and enjoy gaming without barriers. This is an excellent solution for those who may have difficulty using traditional controllers and opens a new world of possibilities for gaming enthusiasts with physical disabilities.

- Barrier Elimination: For many players facing mobility challenges, the intricate designs of traditional gaming controllers can prove to be a hindrance. The dependence on precise hand–eye coordination can exclude a segment of gamers.
- Voice as a Bridge: Voice-controlled gameplay offers an alternative. By vocalizing commands, players can immerse themselves in the virtual world, making games more inclusive. This bridges the gap between physical limitations and the vast universe of digital gaming, ensuring that everyone has a seat at the table of interactive entertainment.

Enhancing the Depth of Gameplay Experience

To enhance the overall gameplay experience, players are now able to issue voice commands while simultaneously managing in-game controls. This means that players can engage in richer multitasking without feeling overwhelmed by excessive button combinations. Additionally, as games continue to grow in complexity, navigating through menus or selecting from a myriad of options can become cumbersome. However, with the integration of natural language processing, gamers are now able to state their desires in a more intuitive manner, streamlining interactions and allowing for a more seamless gameplay experience.

- Simultaneous Interactions: Voice control, combined with traditional controls, creates a layered gameplay experience. Gamers can execute voice commands while still employing hand controllers, adding depth and dimension to actions.
- Reduced Cognitive Load: Instead of remembering convoluted button combinations, players can vocally express actions. This eases the cognitive burden, allowing players to focus on strategy, narrative, and enjoyment.

Seamless Interface Navigation with Natural Language Processing

As the video game industry evolves and the industry products increasingly become elaborate, players may find it challenging to navigate through menus or make selections from a vast array of options. However, with the implementation of natural language processing, gamers can now verbally express their desires and streamline their interactions with ease. This technology enables players to communicate with the game using natural language, making gameplay more intuitive and enjoyable.

- Game Complexity: Modern games often come packed with dense menus, intricate settings, and an array of options. Navigating these can become a tedious task, detracting from the immersive experience.
- Streamlined Interactions: With the integration of natural language processing, games can understand and act upon vocalized intentions. Players can simply express their wishes, such as "Open inventory" or "Show map," reducing the steps needed to execute common tasks. This more intuitive interaction method paves the way for smoother, uninterrupted gameplay.

The incorporation of voice control into the realm of gaming signifies the harmonization of technological advancements with human intuition. As the proficiency of voice recognition systems continues to progress, they possess the potential to revolutionize the gaming industry, rendering it more convenient, player-friendly, and stimulating. Nevertheless, there are also certain obstacles associated with this technology.

4.5.3 Challenges of Implementing Voice Control

Achieving recognition accuracy and diversity is challenging, especially when accounting for the multitude of accents, speech patterns, and individual quirks. This task becomes even more arduous when we consider additional factors such as speech impediments or background noise. Indeed, ensuring accurate recognition under such circumstances requires significant effort and attention to detail.

Latency Issues

In fast-paced games, real-time feedback and action are crucial for the gameplay experience. However, delays in recognizing speech and translating it into in-game action can significantly hamper the responsiveness of the game. This can be particularly problematic in real-time games where every millisecond counts, as it can impact the player's ability to react quickly and make timely decisions. Therefore, it is essential to ensure that the speech recognition and translation processes are optimized to minimize any potential delays and ensure a smooth and enjoyable gaming experience for all players.

- The Need for Speed: Especially in fast-paced games, where split-second decisions can alter outcomes, delays in speech recognition and subsequent in-game execution can be detrimental. Achieving a seamless transition from spoken command to in-game action is imperative to maintain gameplay fluidity and player immersion.
- Vast Vocal Landscape: The realm of human speech is astonishingly diverse, comprising a plethora of accents, dialects, and individual nuances. Recognizing and accurately interpreting such a vast array of speech patterns is a daunting challenge for developers.
- Additional Complicating Factors: The task is further complicated by speech impediments, varying intonation, background noises, or even the emotional tone of speech. Ensuring impeccable recognition in such varied scenarios necessitates rigorous testing, advanced algorithms, and adaptive learning systems.

Integration Challenges

Incorporating voice commands into traditional controller-based gameplay can significantly enhance the gaming experience. However, this integration must be skillfully executed to avoid any potential confusion or chaos for the player. Thoughtful game design is necessary to ensure a harmonious blend between voice commands and traditional control schemes. By doing so, players can seamlessly switch between different modes of control, resulting in a more immersive and engaging gaming experience.

- Balanced Gameplay Experience: The interplay between voice commands and conventional control schemes is delicate. Game designers must meticulously craft the experience to ensure voice inputs complement, rather than disrupt, the flow of gameplay.
- Avoiding Overwhelming Stimuli and Commands: Implementing too many voice commands or integrating them haphazardly can risk overwhelming or confusing the player. Thoughtful design ensures that voice control augments the experience rather than making it cumbersome.

As the use of voice control in gaming becomes more prevalent, it is essential to address the challenges that come with it. Successfully overcoming these obstacles can lead to a new level of interactivity, which has the potential to enhance the immersive and inclusive nature of gaming significantly.

Examples of Games and Platforms Utilizing Voice Control in Gameplay
Voice control has evolved from a novelty into a compelling interaction method in modern gaming, providing immersive experiences and accessibility features. A few standout titles have experimented with this technology and successfully integrated it into gameplay, either as a core mechanic or as a supplementary feature.

Video Game titles that have experimented with this technology and successfully integrated it into gameplay, either as a core mechanic or as a supplementary feature. Games such as "Tom Clancy's EndWar," "Mass Effect 3," and "Skyrim" exemplify this trend, each in unique ways that cater to different genres and audiences.

> **"Tom Clancy's EndWar"**, pushed the real-time strategy genre forward by implementing voice commands as an essential gameplay element. This approach allows players to direct units and execute complex strategies without cumbersome menu navigation, making the experience more fluid and engaging. This feature can also assist players with various conditions, enabling their participation.
> In **"Mass Effect 3"**, voice control was an auxiliary feature to enhance gameplay, but it can also aid players with various conditions and circumstances for participation. In the gameplay, players can issue verbal commands to squad members, enabling quicker and more efficient tactical decisions during combat. This feature enriches the role-playing experience by deepening player engagement and adding a layer of realism.
> **"Skyrim"**, while primarily an action RPG, saw its gameplay elevated through platform-specific voice integration features. Players can use verbal commands on consoles with voice capabilities to access items, navigate menus, and even cast spells, thus reducing the need to pause the game and break immersion. Equally, this feature can be employed to afford players with cognitive or ergonomic conditions facilitating their participation.

The utilization of voice control in gaming has been showcased through various titles, highlighting the diverse and extensive possibilities it brings to the table.

These three titles presented above serve as a testament to the potential of this technology, providing a glimpse into the future of more immersive and engaging gaming experiences in a variety of genres.

Platforms and Software That Support Voice-Controlled Gaming
Numerous gaming platforms have incorporated voice control as an essential feature to enhance user experience. The Xbox platform, equipped with its cutting-edge Kinect technology, provides gamers with seamless voice control to navigate and interact with their games. Likewise, the PlayStation platform offers camera accessories to enable voice control capabilities for gamers. In addition to these platform-specific solutions, software giants like Google and IBM have also introduced their Voice API and Watson software solutions, respectively, that have been utilized to develop advanced voice control functionalities for gaming applications.

4.5.4 Some Prospects of Speech Recognition Technology in the Gaming Industry

The gaming industry is in a highly transformative era, as advances in Artificial Intelligence and speech recognition technologies open up novel avenues for interaction and immersion within virtual environments, making the game more accessible. The prospects range from enabling lifelike conversations with Non-Playable Characters (NPCs) to facilitating complete voice-controlled gameplay and enhancing Augmented and Virtual Reality experiences.

The Potential of Elevated Interaction Design in Video Gaming
The latest advancements in AI technology have paved the way for enhanced interaction between players and NPCs in gaming. With improved speech recognition capabilities, players can engage in more lifelike and nuanced conversations with NPCs, resulting in a more immersive gaming experience. This development has the potential to transform scripted gaming experiences into dynamic and engaging conversational adventures, allowing players to fully immerse themselves in the game world and interact with its inhabitants in a more meaningful way.

The Potential for Full Voice-Controlled Games or Hybrid Gameplay Styles
With the advancement of technology, we expect to witness the emergence of games where voice is not just an additional feature but a central gameplay mechanic. These games will likely incorporate voice recognition software that allows players to control their characters and interact with the game world using voice commands. Additionally, we may see the development of hybrid games that seamlessly combine traditional controls with voice commands, creating a unique and immersive gaming experience. This exciting evolution in gaming technology promises to bring a new level of interactivity and engagement to the gaming community.

The Potential of Integration with AR/VR Gaming for Attainable Gameplay Experiences
The integration of voice control technology into Augmented and Virtual Reality games has the potential to enhance the overall gaming experience significantly. With hands-free interaction, players can become more fully immersed in their digital environments, allowing for a more seamless and natural interaction with the game world. This adds an extra layer of interactivity and engagement and offers a more accessible gameplay experience for individuals with physical limitations or disabilities. By leveraging the power of voice controls, game developers can unlock new possibilities and create more engaging and immersive gaming experiences for their audiences.

The incorporation of speech recognition technology in the realm of gaming is set to fundamentally transform the way we engage with interactive entertainment. The possibilities are interesting and range from the augmentation of non-player character dialogues to the development of innovative voice-centric gameplay mechanics and the advancement of cutting-edge augmented and virtual reality experiences. Speech recognition technology serves as a driver of this transformation of attainable gaming experiences.

4.6 Conclusion

As we journey further into the evolving landscape of technology, the future of specialized controllers unfurls with boundless potential. One can anticipate the emergence of more advanced, innovative devices designed to cater to an ever-expanding gaming environment. Virtual Reality (VR) and Augmented Reality (AR), which have been making significant inroads into the gaming industry, are prime examples of such advances. We can foresee the creation of controllers that are specifically designed for these immersive experiences. These could be equipped with advanced motion-tracking capabilities, offering greater precision in capturing hand movements, thereby enhancing the in-game interaction. In addition, introducing nuanced haptic feedback technology could allow gamers to "feel" the game elements, blurring the lines between the virtual and real world and amplifying the level of immersion.

Beyond these advancements, we stand on the precipice of even more disruptive technological breakthroughs. Consider, for example, the potential of brain-computer interfaces in gaming. These high-tech devices could provide entirely new interaction methods, bypassing the need for traditional or even specialized controllers. Such interfaces could detect and translate neural activity into in-game actions, offering a direct, seamless channel for gamers to interact with the virtual world. The speed at which technology advances implies that such innovations could be closer than we think. The future of gaming promises to be more inclusive, immersive, and interactive, and developers will play a crucial role in shaping this exciting frontier.

References

1. Brown, M., & Anderson, S. L. (2021). Designing for disability: Evaluating the state of accessibility design in video games. *Games and Culture, 16*(6), 702–718.
2. Davidsson & Yankelevitz. (2014). *QuadStick* [Hardware]. QuadStick.
3. Harmonix Music Systems. (2010). *Dance Central* [Video game]. Microsoft Game.
4. Isokoski, P., & Martin, B. (2006). Eye tracker input in first-person shooter games. In *Proceedings of the 2nd Conference on Communication by Gaze Interaction: Communication by Gaze Interaction-COGAIN 2006: Gazing into the Future* (pp. 78–81).
5. Ilavský, J., & Hrinčár, V. (2018). *Beat Saber* [Video game]. Beat Games.
6. Kerous, B., Skola, F., & Liarokapis, F. (2018). EEG-based BCI and video games: A progress report. *Virtual Reality, 22*, 119–135. https://doi.org/10.1007/s10055-017-0328-x
7. Mantis Games. (2019). *Journey for Elysium* [Virtual Reality game]. Cronos Interactive.
8. Maskeliunas, R., Damasevicius, R., Martisius, I., & Vasiljevas, M. (2016). Consumer-grade EEG devices: Are they usable for control tasks? *PeerJ, 4*, e1746. https://doi.org/10.7717/peerj.1746
9. Microsoft. (2010). *Xbox Kinect* [Motion-sensing input device]. Microsoft.
10. Microsoft. (2018). *Xbox Adaptive Controller* [Hardware]. Microsoft.
11. Nintendo. (2006). *Wii Sports* [Video game]. Nintendo.
12. Nolan, M. (2023) This gamer turned EEG tech into a game controller. In *IEEE Spectrum*. Accessed the 2023-09-31.
13. Oculus, V. R., LLC. (2016). *Oculus Touch* [Virtual Reality controller]. Oculus VR, LLC.
14. Oloman, J. (2021). What Valve's Gabe Newell Thinks Brain-Computer Interfaces Will Do For Gaming IGINordic Accessed the 2023-09-31.
15. Rogers, E. (1995). *Diffusion of innovations* (4th edn). The Free Press.
16. Schatz, E., Cambier, R., & Cambier, R. (2020), *The last of us Part II*. Naughty Dog.
17. Smith, J. D., & Graham, T. N. (2006). Use of eye movements for video game control. In *Proceedings of the 2006 ACM SIGCHI International Conference on Advances in Computer Entertainment Technology*.
18. Sony Computer Entertainment. (2010). *PlayStation Move* [Motion controller]. Sony.
19. Studios. HTC Corporation & Valve Corporation. (2015). *Vive Controller* [Virtual Reality controller]. HTC Corporation & Valve Corporation.
20. Superbrothers, Games, C., & Guthrie, J. (2011). *Superbrothers: Sword & Sworcery EP* [Video game]. Capybara Games.
21. Tjønndal, A. (Ed.). (2022). *Social issues in Esports*. Taylor & Francis.
22. Turn 10 Studios. (2018). *Forza Horizon 4* [Video game]. Microsoft Studios.

Chapter 5
Design Elements and Design Spaces for Attainable Game Experiences

Abstract This chapter focuses on the design directives and design constraints within the four heuristics of AGE and the critical need to balance them for accomplishing the development of universally accessible and inclusive video games. It argues that AGE heuristics serve not merely as guidelines but as a dynamic scaffold that provides foundational insights for informed design decisions. This chapter explores how such a balanced approach transcends conventional accessibility, leading to the creation of games that are deeply responsive to the diverse needs of a wide player base. Through this balance, the chapter underscores the industry's ongoing commitment to Universal Design principles, advocating for a gaming landscape where players of all abilities can engage and participate.

Keywords Design space · Design heuristics · Design directives · Attainable game experience · Accessibility · Inclusivity · Video game

5.1 Navigating the AGE Framework

The operation process of the AGE framework is pivotal when mapping the positions of various options in the framework. The reliability and accuracy of the outcomes hinge significantly on the method adopted for data collection. When evaluating this dimension, it is essential to consider the ecological validity: how well the data gathered (from playtests, literature reviews, observations, focus groups, and so on) mirrors and predicts the behavior of your video game in real-world scenarios—see the works by Kihlstrom [14], Salkind [32], and Palmquist [26] for deeper insights. It is crucial to ensure that the data can be utilized to reflect authentic conditions for your game to offer you and your team a diverse and holistic representation. Additionally, the experience and understanding of the person implementing the framework in each context plays a vital role in determining the quality of the outcomes.

The AGE framework is a hybrid framework designed to position the four heuristic attributions in a video game and what the game creators need to enhance to make it attainable without overwhelming the participant, e.g., their cognitive load. While

A. Palmquist et al., *Universal Design in Video Games*, Human–Computer Interaction Series, https://doi.org/10.1007/978-3-031-30595-5_5

there are many methods to proceed with this in video games (see Chap. 3), the outline provided below is intended as a foundational, step-by-step guide. Nevertheless, it is imperative to understand that the most suitable methods and strategies will invariably depend on the unique context and objectives of the particular video game, as well as the demographics and preferences of its participants.

Clarify the Objective of the Video Game
Begin by understanding and articulating the primary motive behind implementing AGE in your video game. What specific gameplay experience are you trying to make more attainable? How does this particular experience shape or influence the broader gaming journey? Delving into these questions will provide a clear roadmap for your AGE process, ensuring you focus on elements that truly matter.

Highlight the Pivotal Gameplay Experiences
It is essential to maintain a deep understanding of those gameplay moments that hold significant importance. These moments can make or break a player's experience and impact their perception of the game. Recognizing these pivotal gameplay experiences is crucial as they form the backbone of the narratives you will collect and play a central role in gauging players' attitudes toward various game constructs.

Engage with Relevant Investigations Records to Aid Your AGE
To accomplish your AGE design well, it is imperative that you involve and carefully scrutinize the investigation records that are relevant to your project. By doing so, you will be able to inform your design comprehensively, enabling it to be deeply integrated into the core of the design process. This will ultimately lead to a more effective and efficient outcome, benefiting all parties involved. Therefore, take the time to thoroughly review and analyze the relevant records before proceeding with your project.

Assess Your Narratives
Once you have collected the narratives, employ the AGE Heuristic Matrix to dissect and understand them. Place each critical stakeholder within the context of your video game, ensuring you have a clear perspective on their position and influence.

Map the Design Interdependencies
Develop a visual model that illustrates the relationships for your design. Highlight any trade-offs, dependencies, or synergies that exist between them. This representation can assist you in understanding the intricate web of relationships and potential points of contention or collaboration.

Delve Deep into Your Collected Research Records and Conducted Analysis Embark on thoroughly examining the AGE Heuristic matrix, pinpointing stakeholders' distinct meaning attributions tied to gameplay experiences. Dedicate time to reflect upon these attributions and draw conclusions from them. Be particularly observant of the dynamics among different groups: note where their interpretations of gameplay experiences converge, where they diverge, and how they potentially influence one another.

5.2 Directives and Constraints Designing Attainable Game Experience

A particularly compelling topic in this volume, we believe, centers on the methodology behind crafting video games in line with the AGE design heuristics. What foundational principles underpin well-designed games that foster accessible gaming experiences? What do the authors define as "exemplary video design" in this context? While each of the three authors has distinct preferences and cherished projects pertaining to universally designed video games, we are poised to outline some guiding directives. Engaging your target audience or other potential gaming communities in open game development or hosting participatory design workshops with key stakeholders is a strategy we unanimously endorse.

Our goal in the ensuing passages is to provide clarity through industry examples that have adeptly tailored their games for broader inclusivity. These entities might not explicitly reference or even be familiar with the AGE framework, but their undertakings align with its ethos. The subsequent segment will delve into the four design heuristics of the AGE framework juxtaposed with the corresponding design directives and constraints that was kaleidoscopic viewed in Chap. 2. It is important to note that the design directives and constraints presented are merely elucidative, as their vast possibilities and application areas are too expansive to fit within a single volume. While the applicability, stringency, and efficacy of both the design directives and constraints for crafting attainable gaming experiences—whether taken from this book or discovered through your own design investigation—are context-specific, they should also be recognized as highly adaptable and reusable. Metaphorically, it could be described that the directives and constraints do not repeat themselves in every video game interaction interface, but they often rhyme. This means that while details change, circumstances change, settings change, and audiences change, similar events affecting directives and constraints' applicability, stringency, and efficacy will essentially recycle showing striking similarities.

As we delve into each of the four heuristic sets of directives and constraints, it is essential to note that we do not provide a step-by-step approach for integrating them with your video game design and development process. Due to the unique nature of each game and its genre, no quick, one-size-fits-all solution exists. The design process for interaction interfaces must be tailored to suit specific video game scenarios and your team's design and development process.

While the volume does not outline a specific game design method or process, we want to emphasize that the authors have utilized various game design techniques to craft more attainable gameplay experiences. These techniques echo the detailed methodologies found in widely recognized and esteemed works, such as Schell [35], Salen and Zimmerman [33], Hunicke et al. [13], and Fullerton [11]. Nevertheless, we have also employed practices from sources that might be less frequently mentioned nowadays but are no less vital, such as Elias et al. [7] and Costikyan [5]. Whether used individually or in combination, these game design approaches align well with the idea of the four AGE heuristics that direct the design of video game interaction interfaces. Each volume mentioned above focuses on game attributes, design principles, and the creative journey behind game concepts. They offer profound insights into the intricacies of game development and serve as invaluable resources. Nevertheless, it is essential to recognize that the content within these books resembles an artistic game design approach to various degrees, and perhaps they do not consider the design investigations for informing the interface outline as crucial as the AGE framework does.

When it comes to game design, aside from the pronounced similarities between UCD and Design Ethnography (see Chap. 3), the AGE framework—particularly its four heuristic directives and constraints—echoes the concept of game design patterns delineated by Björk and Holopainen [2]. Inspired by architectural principles, Björk and Holopainen's approach seeks to identify recurrent design patterns across multiple games. A primary objective of this endeavor is to establish a unified terminology for discussing game design elements. Additionally, these identified patterns aim to serve as templates for crafting innovative and attractive game experiences. We reason that the directives and constraints identified in your design investigation and analyzed through the AGE framework could function similarly to game design patterns but focus on game interaction interfaces.

The design directives and their real-world video game examples presented in this chapter are somewhat superficial and one-dimensional. Their value here lies in serving as guiding inspiration for you and your team. Customization is essential to tackle the unique challenges of making your game experience more accessible to a wider audience. Many design elements in a game interaction interface are crafted with a specific purpose in mind. Relying exclusively on the interpretations of other game creators and adapting their elements to your needs can pose issues. Remember that you might not be fully aware of the original context of the creation of a particular interface element nor the designer's primary intention for it.

5.2.1 Fair and Flexible Play

The design directives that constitute Fair and Flexible Play originate from design traditions that stress inclusivity and accessibility is essential in the design of an artifact. In this section, we will explore the different directives that can be included in the Fair and Flexible Play design heuristic (Fig. 5.1), with the aim to give an idea

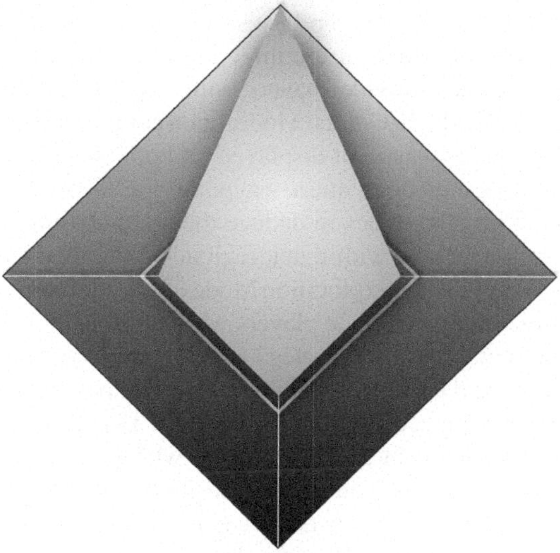

Fig. 5.1 The design space for the fair and flexible play heuristic

of the potential directives involved to improve your understanding of this vital aspect of the AGE design. However, it should be noted that numerous others exist and may vary depending on your game genre, participants playing circumstances, conditions, and context.

Flexible Participation

The authors of this volume hold true that the video gaming world today is made more exciting by the diverse backgrounds and experiences that players bring. This amalgamation of diversity is a testament to gaming's universal appeal. Catering to this vast player base, therefore, mandates a game design as varied as its audience.

For instance, a two-child parent working full time has limited playtime, yet s/he might cherish brief gaming sessions at the end of the day as a way to unwind. Such players might prefer a "casual mode" that offers digestible story snippets or challenges that can be completed in shorter periods. On the other hand, a college student on break might relish the opportunity to delve deep into expansive game worlds, spending hours uncovering secrets and embarking on elaborate quests.

Consider the role-playing game (RPG), "The Witcher 3" (2016), in recognizing the varied preferences of its player base, integrated multiple difficulty settings to accommodate a range of gaming experiences for their most casual players or those mainly interested in the story, they could opt for the "Just the Story!" mode, which lowers combat difficulty and allows for a smoother narrative experience. Conversely, their hardcore gamers who were seeking a test of their gameplay skills could challenge themselves with the "Death March!" difficulty, turning most combat encounters into a demanding test of strategy and reflexes.

Similar features can be found in the three latest installments of the Assassin's Creed series. These games provide players with two navigation options: Guided Mode and Exploration Mode. In Guided Mode, upon completing tasks, the player will receive an automatic quest waypoint displayed on both HUD and map. In contrast, Exploration Mode does not offer quest waypoints on the HUD or map. Instead, players must rely on in-game clues to deduce their destination, narrowing it down to a specific region and an area within that region, which is indicated on your map. Perhaps, needless to say, but the Exploration Mode offers, and consequently demands, more play time, which might exclude players with a limited time to play.

Furthermore, in digital real-time strategy (RTS) games, pausing or slowing down the tempo and activity and issuing commands are often favored features, particularly when the RTS game is played on a console with a D-pad instead of a computer with a mouse and keyboard. In an RTS setting, while the D-pad may be seen as less agile compared to the swift and versatile mouse and keyboard, introducing features like game pausing or slowing down can level the playing field, ensuring that all players can strategize effectively, regardless of their input controllers or game platform preference. Thus the pausing/slowing down features make the gameplay experiences attainable for console players with D-pad as well.

Moreover, the pausing/slowing down feature might also prove valuable for those who get overwhelmed by the relentless pace of the RTS game's more intense scenarios or for those who just wish to play at a more contemplative pace. In this regard, adding the pausing/slowing down features facilitates, affords, and encourages broader player participation in the RTS gameplay irrespective of their real-time decision-making skills.

Meanwhile, some types of sandbox games like "Stardew Valley" [1], "Graveyard Keeper" [16], and "My Time in Portia" [28] provide a protean gameplay blend, and by doing so, it allows players to decide the pace for themselves; engage in intense farming, base building and/or combat activities while granting serene intervals where they can fish, stroll the local village, and interact with its inhabitants without any pressing time constraints. In those games mentioned above, but also others, management simulation video games, the pace is largely tailored to a player's unique playstyle preferences, which can vary across different game sessions. By integrating features that resonate with this adaptability, developers are championing attainable gaming experiences. Game creators striving to personalize and customize gameplay pacing and modes do not just enhance their chances for delivering attainable gaming experience for a broader audience; they also show that they respect and acknowledge their players' diverse lives, schedules, and circumstances, thus having a solid opportunity of forging a deeper connection between themselves and their games audience—which is a strategic effort for succeeding the game industry.

Fair Gameplay

Based on the author's combined experience in game teaching and creation, we believe that to design a good video game, the pursuit of fairness is not about "leveling the playing field" by imposing a singular standard on all participants. Instead, it is about recognizing the varied challenges, abilities, and desires of the players and providing avenues for them to tailor the game experience to their needs. At its core, fair gameplay celebrates the spirit of inclusivity and adaptability, ensuring that no player feels left out or disadvantaged.

The concept of fairness extends beyond just competitive balance. It is about crafting a game environment where players can engage with content at their comfort level while still feeling the thrill and challenge that games provide. By introducing multiple difficulty levels, developers acknowledge that players come with a spectrum of skill levels, ensuring both newcomers and veterans can find a sweet spot of challenge and enjoyment. Offering diverse game modes allows players to select a play style that resonates most with their gaming preferences, be it a casual experience, a narrative-driven one, or an adrenaline-pumping challenge. Additionally, having adaptable control schemes ensures that players with physical constraints are not barred from the experience but are instead provided with a means to enjoy the game just as anyone else would.

For instance, "Celeste," [38], a critically acclaimed platformer game, brilliantly embodies the principles of fair gameplay. At first glance, it is a challenging game that tests precision and timing. However, its "Assist Mode" allows players to modify the game's difficulty in various ways, such as slowing down the game speed, granting invincibility, or providing infinite air-dashes. This not only makes the game more accessible to those who might find the standard difficulty too challenging but also allows players to adjust the gameplay according to their comfort and skill level. It is a fair approach that respects both the player's desire for challenge and their need for accessibility, ensuring that every player's experience is uniquely tailored to them.

Conscious Localization

The globalization of the gaming industry has underscored the importance of localization, a process that goes beyond mere language conversion. Truly localizing a game is an art of bridging cultural divides, demonstrating an awareness and appreciation for the distinct characteristics of diverse audiences. A well-localized game captures the essence of its original design while also weaving in the tapestry of cultural, historical, and social values of the region it is being adapted for.

Awareness in game localization means more than just preventing potential faux pas; it is about actively engaging with a culture's unique attributes. It is crucial to consider every element—from character costumes, narratives, and in-game holidays to how gestures, symbols, and even colors are perceived within a particular culture. Additionally, if translated verbatim, idiomatic expressions can often lose meaning or even take on unintended connotations. Therefore, adapting such phrases to align with local sayings or sentiments is pivotal.

An illustrative example of aware game localization is seen in the game "Final Fantasy XV [37]". The English version mentions a tomato risotto dish in one of its side quests. However, in the Japanese version, the dish is a classic rice and egg bowl. The developers recognized that a rice and egg bowl is more familiar and comforting as a local Japanese dish, while tomato risotto has a broader appeal to the Western audience. Another subtle but notable example is from "The Legend of Zelda: Breath of the Wild [10]," where a character's gesture was altered between the Japanese and Western releases to ensure it was understood and not seen as inappropriate or confusing by different audiences.

Such nuances in localization do not just make games more accessible; they also enhance a player's immersion by making the game world feel authentic, familiar, and respectful of their cultural background.

Community and Audience Commitment

A video game's success and lifecycle are not measured nor determined merely by its sales or reviews but also by the depth and vibrancy of its player community. This community, diverse in its composition and vast in its experiences, holds invaluable insights that can elevate a game from being just "good" to "exceptional."

Building and nurturing a two-way relationship with the gaming community is more than a strategic move; it is a commitment to understanding and valuing player perspectives. Regularly hosting Q&A sessions, engaging in community forums, initiating feedback polls, and even participating in gaming conventions can help developers to bridge the gap between creation and consumption.

Moreover, consider beta-testing phases that involve a wide range of players. Such phases offer a hands-on experience to players and provide developers with real-time feedback. Active engagement demonstrates transparency, building trust between the developers and the community.

One instance of effective community engagement is the development of "Minecraft" [29]. In their early days, Mojang, the game studio behind the game, constantly contacted its community, gathering feedback and implementing suggested features. They would often release early versions of updates to a select group of players, allowing them to spot bugs, suggest improvements, and even develop new content ideas. This iterative process, rooted in community feedback, helped mold "Minecraft" [29] into the global phenomenon it is today.

5.2.2 Design Constraints for Fair and Flexible Play

The design heuristic "Fair and Flexible Play" is a crucial consideration when developing video games with AGE that are easy to use and can be tailored to the players' preferences without requiring any modifications. While the primary objective is to provide a high level of flexibility, it is important to acknowledge that there may be potential challenges to be mindful of if this principle is implemented too strictly in your video game project. Thus, it is essential to strike a balance between flexibility and feasibility to ensure that the video game is both able to personalize and yet is functional without cannibalizing each other.

Gameplay Quality Assurance Challenges
The more complex a game becomes regarding flexible use, the harder it is to test all the possible permutations to ensure they are bug-free, well-balanced, and enjoyable. Designing for fairness and flexibility often requires additional development resources for alternate game modes, control schemes, and accessibility features. In multiplayer settings, ensuring "Fair and Flexible Use" can become a balancing nightmare, potentially leading to a meta-game that is less fun, competitive, or skill-based. Too much flexibility can make it challenging to ensure that all players are on a level playing field, thus affecting the competitive integrity of the game.

Risk of Oversimplification
The drive to make video game interaction interfaces fair and flexible could lead to oversimplification, which may rob experienced participants of the complex and challenging experience they seek. For example, puzzle games meant to challenge the player's abilities in specific ways may lose their core appeal if adapted to be too flexible. Thus, in an attempt to make your video game more universally attainable, there is a risk of oversimplifying gameplay or narrative elements, which may disappoint players looking for a more profound or more challenging experience.

Compromised Game Integrity
Certain games are built around specific mechanics or skill levels that could be compromised if made too flexible. For example, in competitive esports titles, too much flexibility in terms of game mechanics could lead to an unbalanced playing field.

Community Segmentation
Providing numerous options for gameplay may result in a division within the player community. This can lead to difficulties in establishing shared strategies and norms finding opponents or collaborators with similar playing styles. This could ultimately harm the game's longevity by hindering shared experiences, discussions, and multiplayer matchups.

Competitive Balance and Potential for Exploitation
In multiplayer settings, ensuring "Fair and Flexible Play" can become a balancing nightmare, potentially leading to a meta-game that is less fun, competitive, or skill-based. Too much flexibility can make it challenging to ensure that all players are on a level playing field, thus affecting the competitive integrity of the game. If a video game is too flexible in its rules or mechanics, some players may exploit this flexibility to gain an unfair advantage, undermining your video game's competitive integrity.

The "Fair and Flexible Play" heuristic can make video games more accessible and potentially expand their audience; these considerations suggest that it is crucial not

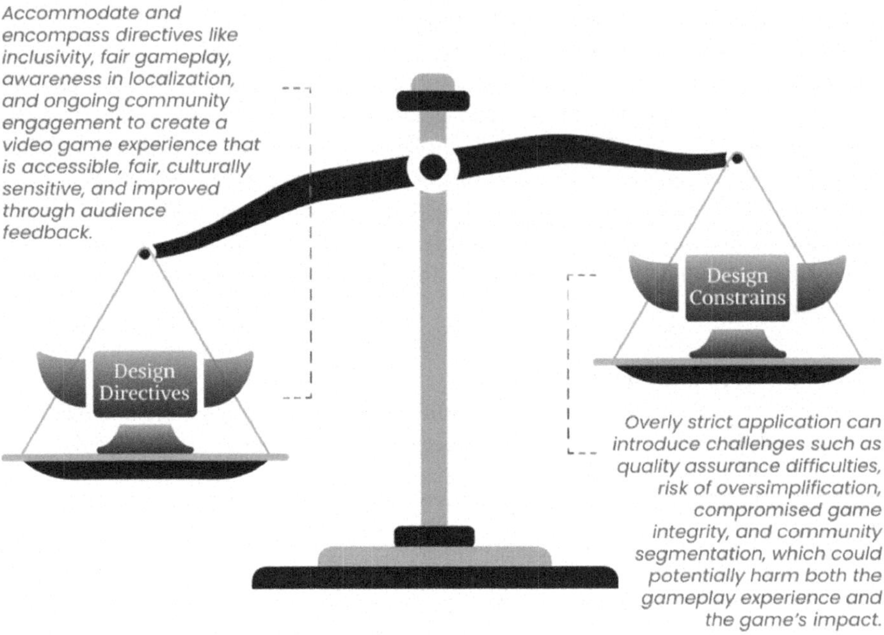

Fig. 5.2 Balancing directives and constraints in the "Fair and Flexible Play" heuristic for your interaction interface design

just to include it "by default" in every aspect; an overly strict application in your video games might introduce various challenges and compromises that developers must consider carefully (Fig. 5.2).

5.2.3 Adjustable and Equitable Play

Approaching the design directive in the design space for Adjustable and Equitable Play, the appropriate lens to employ is the comprehensive personalization of the game experiences. Hereon, we will be taking a closer look at the factors that influence the design of the Adjustable and Equitable Play heuristic (Fig. 5.3).

Communities subscribing to the Adjustable and Equitable Play design perspective emphasize a multifaceted approach to creating adjustable and equitable gameplay experiences. These methods include employing ethnographic design techniques in analogue and digital realms. In the analogue context, this involves observing individuals as they engage in gaming activities, while the digital aspect entails active participation in the games themselves. Additionally, involving stakeholders at various stages of game development is another strategy that aligns closely with participatory design principles.

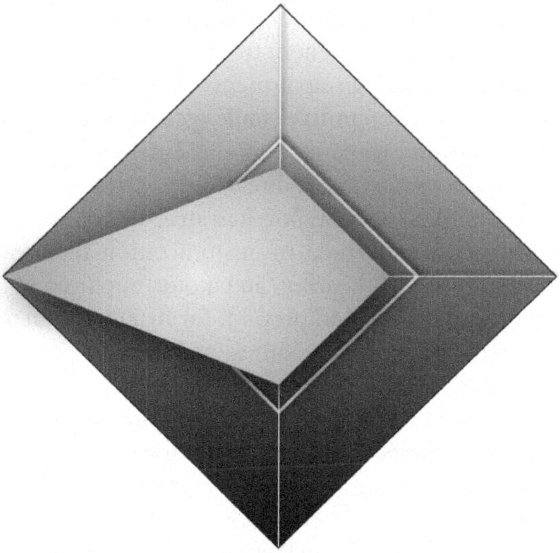

Fig. 5.3 A design space focusing on "Adjustable and Equitable Play" heuristic

When focusing on the Adjustable and Equitable Play heuristic, open development is a transparent approach that facilitates continuous dialogue with diverse communities. These communities range from the game's target audience and organizations advocating for ethical and inclusive gaming culture to groups focused on disability inclusion within the gaming industry.

Moreover, it is essential to consider input from communities that may not be directly linked to the gaming world but still have a stake and influence in it. This includes sectors like the tech industry, which often has to anticipate and adapt to broader design trends before they become pervasive in the gaming community. By embracing such a comprehensive approach, designers can stay one step ahead and create gaming experiences that are both adjustable and equitable for all players.

Gameplay Attainability Through Adjustability

Ensure your game is available to a wide variety of players by including adjustable settings, alternative controls, and other accessibility options. Players with different abilities, conditions, or preferences should be able to customize the game to their comfort level. It is about acknowledging that a one-size-fits-all approach is no longer viable in a world teeming with diversity.

An adaptable games interaction interface is one that offers a rich tapestry of adjustable settings. From alternative control configurations that can cater to someone with limited motor skills to varied accessibility options that help those with visual or auditory impairments, the scope for inclusivity is vast.

Taking into account the diverse range of players is fundamental. Some might have color vision deficiencies and would benefit from adjustable color palettes or contrast settings. Others might have hearing impairments, making subtitle options and visual cues crucial. Others might have cognitive challenges that make more straightforward graphical interface layouts and game instructions essential.

A widely recognized example of this directive in action is the game "The Last of Us Part II" [30, 34]. The post-apocalyptic narrative-driven action-adventure game has been recognized for its multitude of customization features [17] as it offers around 60 settings to aid visually, hearing, and motor-impaired players [30]—or just for personalization. Visually impaired players, for instance, can use a high-contrast mode that color-codes the environment, allies, and enemies, making navigation and combat more manageable.

Additionally, audio cues can be used to guide players toward items or objectives. For those with motor disabilities, the game allows for fully remappable controls and even a setting where players can play entirely using the joystick. Such attention to detail underscores the significance of comprehensive inclusivity, ensuring that every player's experience is catered to and celebrated. Thus, it is up to you to make sure that various game features can be customized to enhance inclusivity, accessibility, and retainability—this could range from adjustable font sizes, colors, and contrasts to optional audio cues and subtitles.

Game Compatibility with Assistive Technologies

The directive upholds that developing video games with Assistive Technologies in mind providing options that make using such devices easier can improve accessibility. Upholding and striving for better attainability in your game products is not just a smart strategy, it is a crucial statement, an acknowledgment of the diverse community of players that populate, enrich, and enliven the industry. Contemporary, it is almost indisputable that assistive technologies have been game-changers, literally. For many players with disabilities, specialized controllers provide the bridge to immersive gaming experiences. To assist and accommodate this audience, various hardware companies and game platform suppliers have provided the gaming industry with controllers that have interchangeable parts to modify grip sizes or button positions. Additionally, specific assistive technologies have made game participation easier, opening up opportunities for new segments of gaming audiences. The aim of design directives in this context is to raise awareness among game creators. This encourages them to develop more accessible and compatible digital game artifacts, providing updated device drivers that ensure ease-of-use even for players with limited software or hardware skills. A notable example is the Xbox Adaptive Controller developed by Microsoft (see further Chap. 4). This device was uniquely designed to meet players' limited mobility needs, allowing them to customize their controller setup with peripherals that suit their specific needs. With its large programmable buttons and multiple USB ports for external devices, the controller brings a level of adaptability previously unseen in the gaming industry.

Eye-tracking technology is another technology that could be used to overcome barriers and make your game more attainable. Games that integrate this eye-tracking feature, like "Assassin's Creed: Origins", allow players to navigate and interact with the game environment using only their gaze [39]. Such advancements provide an accessible gaming experience for those who might find traditional controls cumbersome or impossible.

Moreover, the importance of customizable in-game settings must be stressed more. Some players may use assistive devices to play games, including specially designed controllers, eye-tracking systems, or voice control software. Developing games with these systems in mind or providing options that make using such devices easier can improve accessibility. For example, providing robust key binding options can make it easier to set up specialized controllers, and designing games with clear, high-contrast visuals can enhance the experience of players using eye-tracking systems. The option to rebind keys or controls means that players can tailor the game interface to their personal comfort, making games like "Overwatch" (2016) or "Fortnite" (2017) more accessible to a broader audience. When a game offers high-contrast visuals or settings that enhance visibility, it becomes easier for players using eye-tracking systems or those with visual impairments to engage with the content.

However, the drive for inclusivity should not stop at the digital frontier. In the realm of real-life gaming events, the push for accessible spaces is just as vital. For instance, events like the Evolution Championship Series (Evo), a premier fighting game tournament, should ensure not just digital but also physical inclusivity. From ramps and wheelchair-accessible viewing areas to spaces allocated for assistive devices and personal aides, these measures ensure that every fan, regardless of their physical capabilities, can be part of the exhilarating atmosphere.

Recognizing and catering to the community's diverse needs is not just good game design; it is an affirmation of the gaming world's commitment to its players, ensuring that everyone, regardless of their challenges, can find joy, camaraderie, and adventure in the digital realm.

Personalizable Interfaces for Enriched Interplay

Discovering ways to personalize input controls is a valuable method to enhance players' experience. By tailoring input controls to the players' desires and preferences, you can create a more personalized experience that will increase player satisfaction. Personalization can be achieved through various methods, such as allowing players to customize input control settings, providing suggestions based on past player behavior, and adapting to player input patterns. By prioritizing personalization in your input controls, you can create a more engaging and player-friendly experience that will keep players coming back.

The most distinguished game experiences celebrated by various players often devise from its controls' responsiveness and nuances. When controls become second nature to players, immersion in the game world is elevated. Central to this experience is ergonomics, which ensures players can comfortably and efficiently interact with the game without strain or discomfort.

For instance, in PC gaming, the default "WASD" control scheme has become a staple. It is no coincidence that many primary in-game actions are associated with keys immediately adjacent to this setup, such as the "E" or "Q" keys. The first-person shooter "Counter-Strike—Global Offensive" [4] uses the "E" key for important interactions, knowing that players can easily reach it while navigating with the "WASD" keys.

When we transition to consoles, the importance of thumb-centric design becomes evident. Controllers for systems like the PlayStation or Xbox are crafted with the understanding that the thumbs are the primary digits in play. Critical actions are often assigned to the face buttons or analogue sticks, ensuring players can execute them swiftly. An example of this is the "Dark Souls" series (2011, 2014, 2016), where dodging—an essential maneuver—is mapped to the easily accessible "circle" or "B" button. On the mobile game front, with the proliferation of touch-screen games, there is a delicate balance to maintain. Thus, Mobile Game developers must ensure that on-screen buttons are neither too cluttered nor overly simplistic. The battle royal game "PUBG Mobile" [18] demonstrates this rather well, allowing players to customize their control layouts, moving fire buttons or aiming toggles to their preferred screen locations.

Gameplay Experiences for All Sizes

The diversity within the gaming community is vast, spanning not only demographics, socio-economics, gender, and ability but also physical size. Recognizing and addressing this broad array of needs and preferences will increment the attainability of the intended gameplay experience for more players.

Another significant influence of heuristic design directive in interaction interface design is attentiveness to provide possibilities for miscellaneous gameplay control remapping that are easy to use without diminishing the intended game experience. By allowing players to reassign in-game actions to their preferred keys, buttons, or motions within the game interaction interface, game creators can cater to a diverse range of players. In the case of touch-screen games, the multiplayer online battle arena (MOBA) title "Vainglory" [36] has adopted movable on-screen controls, allowing players to reposition their combat abilities as they prefer. Recognizing the variety in players' handedness, some games, like the first-person RPG "Skyrim" [12], allow players to choose their character's "sword hand." Whether one is a left-handed archer or a right-handed swordsman, the game ensures a natural-feeling gameplay experience. Similarly, games, especially those using mouse and keyboard controllers, frequently offer key binding options. This ensures that both left-handed and right-handed players can create an optimal control scheme for their preferences.

In the VR game "Until You Fall" (2020), players are given a straightforward choice before each play session: to play standing up or seated. This choice automatically adjusts the relevant interaction interface. By posing this simple question at the start of "Until You Fall" (2020), the game creators cater not only to players with permanent physical conditions but also to those with situational conditions who still wish to engage in gameplay.

The design directive emphasizes player personalization and tailored customization considering their sizes. Game creators recognizing the directive better warrant that their intended game experiences are attainable for a vast segment of the gaming community.

5.2.4 Design Constraints for Adjustable and Equitable Play

The AGE heuristic of "Adjustable and Equitable Play" is aimed at making games and their settings accessible to as many people as possible, regardless of age, ability, or situation. While this heuristic has many virtues, there are arguments against its strict application in video games, especially in domains that blend the interaction interface design with the actual game design.

More Complexity = More Development
Making a video game adjustable for equitable use often involves adding multiple modes, settings, and control schemes, among other features. This increases the game's complexity, potentially leading to more bugs and possible crashes. Resources on making the game universally adjustable and equitable should be spent wisely so it improves the attainability of the gameplay experience for broader audiences.

Overwhelming Customization
Providing numerous adjustable options could make the different interaction interfaces complex and overwhelming, especially for casual players. This could detract from the game's accessibility and usability.

Game Genre Focus
Video Games often aim to deliver a specific experience, targeting a particular audience. Adjusting a game to everyone's needs may dilute this focus, resulting in a game that tries to be everything to everyone but excels at nothing. The result could be a less cohesive and engaging experience for the genre's target audience.

Teams Artistic Vision
Video Games are not just utilitarian design products but also a form of art—hedonistic artifacts. The artistic vision might involve creating a specific experience that challenges the player in particular ways. For example, a game designed to be brutal and unforgiving—like From Software titles such as the "Dark Souls" series—may lose its essence if adjusted for more accessible and equitable use.

Dilution of Unique Game Mechanics
Video games often have unique mechanics or challenges designed to be experienced in a specific way. If these mechanics can be widely adjusted, it could dilute the game's uniqueness, making it feel overly generic.

Oversimplification Risks
Developers might oversimplify game mechanics or narrative elements to make a game adjustable and equitable. This could result in a loss of depth or complexity that disappoints players seeking a rich and fulfilling experience. Moreover, if a game is devised to be too adjustable, it may rob players of the satisfaction that comes from overcoming obstacles through skill and ingenuity. Certain games rely on a carefully curated pace that could be disrupted if players have too much control over adjusting the game to their liking.

While the heuristic of "Adjustable and Equitable Play" is crucial for making more inclusive and accessible environments in many contexts, its strict application in video games can lead to various issues. These include a loss of focus, higher complexity regarding development and maintenance, and a potential compromise of the artistic vision of the video game. As such, game developers often need to carefully weigh the benefits and drawbacks of this design principle within the specific context of their project (Fig. 5.4).

5.2.5 Logical Play

Approaching the design constraints in the design space for Logical Play in your game, the appropriate lens to use is the overall logic of the game interface as well as the player flow. Hereon, we will be taking a closer look at the factors that influence the design of the Logical Play heuristic (Fig. 5.5).

Prioritize, Facilitate, and Refine
Strive to streamline the process that leads to the actual gameplay, removing unnecessary complexity. Preserve the core elements that enhance the joy and engagement of the gameplay experience. When participants reach crucial gameplay loops, ensure they can easily navigate past barriers that are not essential to the gameplay. One effective method is skillfully arranging game-related information based on its importance. This approach provides players quick and easy access to crucial game details and features, allowing them to locate and understand key information whenever needed. By doing so, the game optimizes player engagement and maintains a seamless and immersive experience.

Examples of potential game-disrupting distractions to avoid could include imposing a narrative on the players during a scenario that already taxes their cognitive resources, such as an intense gunfight. Avoid providing extraneous yet pointless spaces in the level design that suggest progress or exploration but are merely empty

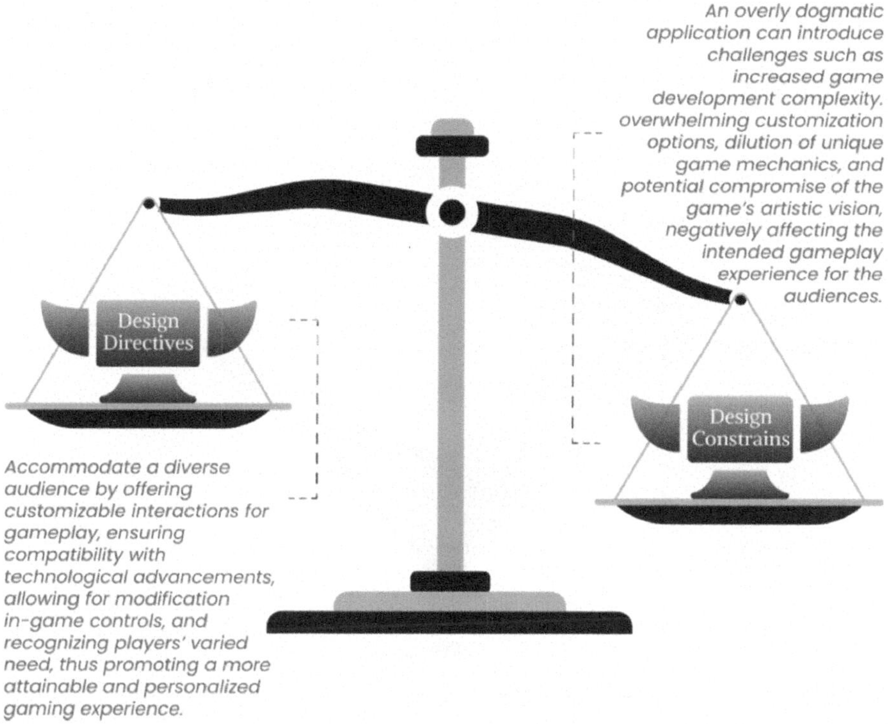

Fig. 5.4 To achieve an applicable interaction interface design, the adjustable and equitable play heuristic's directives and constraints must be carefully balanced to prevent undue incomprehensiveness in the interaction interfaces

areas. Also, avoid prompting the players to engage in unhealthy monitoring of statistics or comparisons between player stats—is it a game or a spreadsheet simulator? Furthermore, occasionally constraining the open-ended nature of the game experience can help prevent overwhelming distractions for the players. Providing clear boundaries and understandable limitations can stimulate participant creativity [23].

Expectation Alignment

Confirm that the game design consistently corresponds with player intuition and expectations. Create an environment that feels natural and intuitive, enhancing the overall gaming experience by minimizing friction. For instance, Players expect the game world to follow specific "rules" consistently. For example, if a type of tree in the mystical forest is shown to be flammable in one situation, players will expect it to be flammable in other similar situations. Thus, the game design alignment: Ensure that the game world is consistent. If a tree catches fire in one situation, the same type of tree should catch fire under similar conditions elsewhere in the game. This consistency supports the player's intuition and makes the game world more immersive and natural. Players typically anticipate that any items or elements introduced in a game,

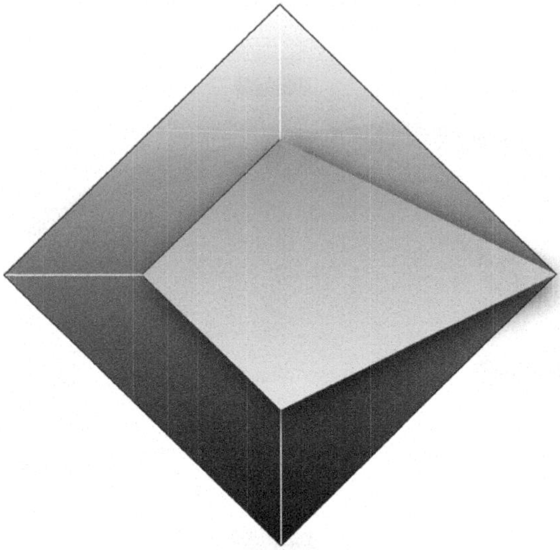

Fig. 5.5 A design space focusing the logical play heuristic

especially those that are unique or emphasized, will serve a purpose or function as the game progresses. By both attentively and skillfully incorporating "Chekhov's Gun" [3, 25] into your design, you can introduce an element or mechanic early in the game that not only evolves and gains significance but also appears intuitive and coherent within the overarching design, thus establishing a logical connection. On the other hand, a less adept implementation might involve the introduction of an element or mechanic that contradicts the overarching design and remains unexplained or unresolved throughout the gameplay. This can result in a seemingly illogical component that could potentially frustrate players or disrupt the game's coherence.

Logical Feedback and Player Cues

Effective feedback loops are integral to game design. These loops communicate the results of a player's actions, driving adaptations in their future actions. Rewarding successful actions with positive feedback encourages repetition, while negative feedback guides players away from unsuccessful strategies. Both feedback types are essential for a rewarding and educational gaming experience. Ensure the feedback is immediate, specific, and directly related to the player's actions to maximize effectiveness. Moreover, during gameplay and immediately following player achievements or progression, provide effective prompts and engaging cues. Keeping players informed about their progress, rewarding their achievements, and motivating them to continue playing enhance their gaming experience.

For instance, in our game "Inter-Galactic Endless-Quest," we have constructed feedback loops, prompts, and cues to enhance the player experience. After completing the introductory tutorial, players embark on a space adventure, facing various challenges and making critical decisions. When players succeed in overcoming obstacles, we provide immediate and specific positive feedback, such as visual effects, celebratory sounds, and congratulatory messages. This positive reinforcement encourages players to repeat successful actions, boosting their confidence and motivation. Conversely, when players make mistakes or fail to achieve their objectives, the game offers constructive negative feedback. This may include visual cues indicating failure, accompanied by helpful hints or advice on improving their approach. By guiding players away from unsuccessful strategies, we create a learning experience that promotes adaptation and growth.

Ensure that the feedback loops are tightly connected to the player's actions throughout the game. Whether it is completing a challenging puzzle or defeating a formidable enemy, the feedback is directly related to their achievements or setbacks, reinforcing the cause-and-effect relationship.

Moreover, we provide effective prompts and engaging cues as players progress through the game or achieve significant milestones. For example, when players level up, they receive a pop-up notification displaying the new abilities or rewards they have unlocked. Additionally, after completing a major quest, we display a cinematic cut-scene to celebrate their achievements, further immersing them in the game world.

By constructing these explicit feedback loops, prompts, and cues, we aim to keep players informed about their progress and successes, rewarding their accomplishments, and motivating them to continue their Galactic Quest. This approach enhances the gaming experience, making it rewarding and engaging throughout the journey.

Enhancing Experience Through Meaningful Tutorials

Games are intricate systems, and complexity can present a learning challenge for players. Tutorials play a crucial role in enhancing the players' understanding of the game mechanics and making the concept more attainable. By incorporating well-crafted tutorials, you can display the logic behind the game and help players grasp its mechanics faster. This, in turn, opens up possibilities for creating a complex game with multiple layers, stages, and diverse experiences, appealing to a broader player base. These tutorials pave the way for engaging mechanics, problem-solving elements, multiple narratives, and enhanced re-playability.

One prime example of enhancing the player experience with well-designed tutorials can be seen in the critically acclaimed game, "The Legend of Zelda: Breath of the Wild" [10]. This game utilizes a comprehensive tutorial in its beginning stages, known as the "Great Plateau" section. Here, players are introduced to fundamental game mechanics such as combat, puzzle-solving, climbing, cooking, and utilizing magical abilities. The tutorial is integrated seamlessly into the storyline. It does not feel like a separate, didactic segment but rather an explorative adventure. By doing this, the developers keep the players engaged while still providing them with the necessary skills and knowledge to progress in the game.

In the "Great Plateau" section, the game does not force the player to follow a strict path but encourages exploration and interaction with the environment. This approach allows the players to learn at their own pace, experiment with different strategies, and gain confidence before moving on to more challenging areas.

After the Breath of the Wilds tutorial, players are well-prepared to face the game's intricate and diverse challenges. They are equipped to deal with different combat scenarios, understand the utility of cooking and gathering resources, and use their various magical abilities to solve complex puzzles.

Logical Interaction Interfaces Amplifying the Player Experiences
The design directive sustains that the interaction interfaces as well as Player Experience (PX) are crucial aspects of Logical Play heuristic. In the plot of this directive the game interaction interfaces should include only the necessary elements at a given time providing the players instinctive and responsive interaction. On the other hand, PX covers the full spectrum of player interactions with the game, from game controls and pacing to emotional engagement, requiring a careful balance between challenge and reward. For instance, the first iteration of Super Mario Bros. [19] could be argued as having a perceptive graphical interface and interaction design. In relations to its graphical interface the game screen shows valuable information such as the score, number of lives, and timer, placed where they are easily visible but do not obstruct the gameplay. The action buttons are easy to use, and the response time is excellent, resulting in smooth controls. The design is clean and intuitive; for instance, power-ups are presented distinctly, and enemies are visually differentiated.

For instance, the logic Super Mario Bros. [19] is well thought-out. The game's complexity gradually increases, introducing new challenges at a manageable rate. The controls are straightforward, with jumps and movements directly corresponding to button actions, minimizing the learning curve. Moreover, emotional engagement is fostered through a balanced reward system. Players feel a sense of accomplishment when they clear a level, collect power-ups, or defeat enemies. However, failure is not overly punitive, as players simply restart the level, maintaining a balance between challenge and reward. Super Mario Bros. [19] is a clear example of Logical Play game design, where both UI and UX play crucial roles in creating an intuitive, engaging, and rewarding game.

5.2.6 Design Constraints for Logical Play

The Logical Play heuristic in video game design seeks to ensure that interface elements and game mechanics operate in a way that is intuitive and logical for players. However, the application of this heuristic is shaped by various design constraints and impeding factors. Below is an expanded discussion on these:

Innovation and Originality
Adhering strictly to logical or intuitive video game elements can stifle creative ingenuity. Game developers might refrain from experimenting with unique, unorthodox mechanics to avoid confusing players. This is particularly significant given that some of the most memorable video games in history have succeeded precisely because they offered something unconventional, breaking the norms of "logical."

Learning Curve and Hand-Holding
A game with challenges and a learning curve can offer a more rewarding experience. Over-reliance on the Logical Play heuristic can result in a game that spells everything out for the player, thus taking away the joy of discovery and mastery. This phenomenon is often referred to as "hand-holding," and can make a game feel overly simplified or dumbed down. The absence of an element of surprise or challenge in how game mechanics are used can rob players of the delight of unraveling a game system's intricacies on their own terms.

Genre-Specific Requirements and Thematic Dissonance
Different game genres have different requirements for player engagement. Puzzle games, mysteries, or games that involve complex strategic thinking might rely on non-linear, illogical elements to create challenges. Enforcing Logical Play in such cases would dilute the intended experience. Furthermore, games set in inherently fantastical, surreal, or abstract environments might suffer from thematic dissonance if every element adheres strictly to real-world logic.

Cultural Contrasts
It is worth noting that logic cannot be deemed a universal constant, as cultural perspectives frequently influence it. Video game elements like a symbol in the interface that appears intuitive and straightforward in one culture may be perceived as illogical or puzzling in another. This can inadvertently lead to the exclusion of specific player demographics or make localization efforts more challenging. Therefore, it is essential to consider cultural differences when designing game mechanics and to be mindful of potential barriers that may prevent players from fully engaging with the game.

Subjectivity and Resource Constraints
The notion of what is logical can be highly subjective, varying from player to player based on personal experiences and perspectives. Striving for a universally logical gameplay experience could result in a design that aims to satisfy the "lowest common denominator" and fails to engage any particular group. Additionally, conducting rigorous testing to ensure logical coherence across all elements could require significant time and resources, which might not be feasible for smaller development teams with budget and time constraints.

Although the Logical Play heuristic is a valuable approach to video game design, some games may have better choices. Focusing exclusively on the Logical Play heuristic could result in overlooking other AGE heuristics, such as Fair and Flexible Play, which may hold greater significance depending on the game's objectives. Therefore, you and your game developers must consider these factors when deciding whether to integrate the Logical Play heuristic into their design strategy. By taking a comprehensive logical approach to your interaction interface design process, it will become easier for you and your team to make well-informed decisions that align with the video game's objectives and end goal, generating a more satisfactory playability and accessible game usability consequently increasing the attainability of the intended game experience.

5.2.7 Error Prevention in Play

Avoiding factors that influence the prevention of unintentional errors during gameplay, it is essential for the game creator to consider the high stakes and stressful situations that may arise from menus, interface, mini-games, and in-game player choices. In this section, we will explore the factors that can affect the Error Prevention in Play heuristic (Fig. 5.6), which design directives enforce, and the design constraints that are liable for restricting it. We aim to give an idea of the potential factors involved to improve your understanding of this vital aspect of the AGE Framework. However, it should be noted that numerous others exist and may vary depending on your game genre, participants playing circumstances, conditions, and context (Fig. 5.7).

Player-Friendly Interface Configurations

The design and arrangement of the interaction interfaces are focal in establishing the player's trajectory assisting them attaining the intended game experience. Crafting this experience around ease of use is essential, emphasizing actions players will perform regularly. By ensuring that frequently used controls and commands are prominently and intuitively positioned, developers can significantly reduce the chances of players making inadvertent mistakes. Consider a game where players often need to change weapons. In such scenarios, the control mechanism for weapon toggling becomes a frequently accessed function. Positioning this control or command in a location where players can instinctively find and use it ensures smoother gameplay. It also minimizes the instances where players might mistakenly press the wrong button or command, which can be especially crucial in high-pressure game situations.

Additionally, some game functions can significantly affect the gameplay experience if activated unintentionally. Commands like "exit," and "restart," or features like "Quick Save/Quick Load" can dramatically alter the progress or flow of a game if triggered accidentally. Such controls, therefore, demand a careful placement strategy.

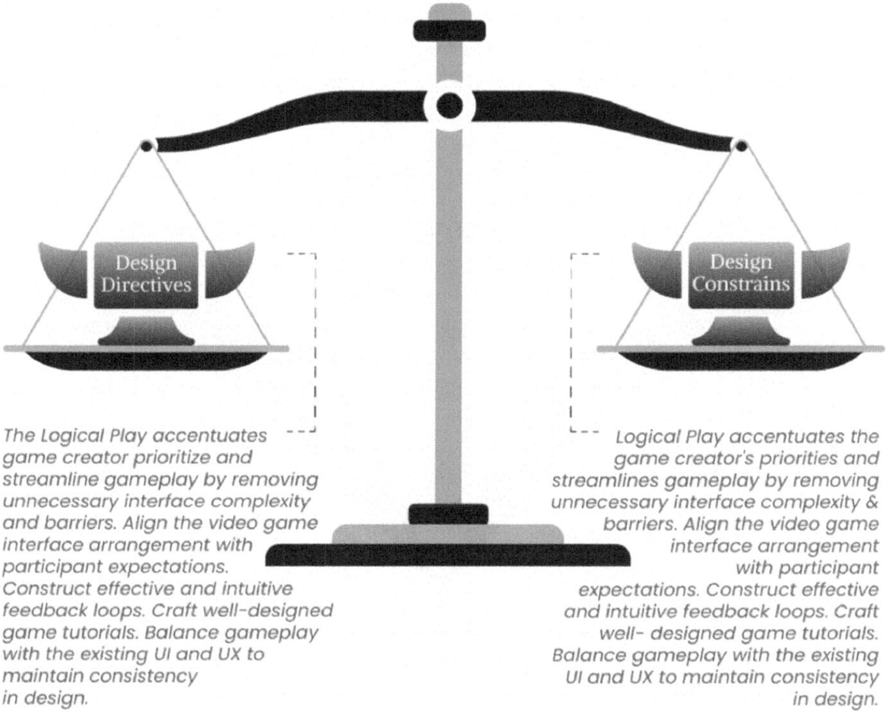

Fig. 5.6 Harmonizing directives and constraints in the "Logical Play" heuristic for interface designs within the AGE framework

Whether positioning them farther away from frequently accessed buttons on a physical controller or placing them in a nested menu within the game's interface, these commands should be safeguarded against accidental activations.

An optimally arranged interaction interfaces is not just about aesthetics or functionality—it is about understanding the player's journey, anticipating their needs and actions, and then designing an interface that facilitates a seamless and error-free gaming experience. By prioritizing the positioning, pacing, and arrangement of the interface components, creators might increase their provided gameplay attainability.

Correspondingly, in line with the ideas presented in Chap. 3, it has been suggested that allowing game participants to remap their input controller can significantly reduce the chances of errors occurring during gameplay. This approach can go a long way in ensuring that a wider audience enjoys a positive gaming experience. By affording greater control over the gaming process, players can customize their experience to suit their unique needs and preferences. By doing this you can provide more engaging and immersive gaming experiences, which might ultimately result in higher levels of satisfaction for all involved.

Fig. 5.7 The design space error prevention in play heuristic

Protective Mechanisms Upholding Gameplay

As video games evolve in complexity, the need for reliable safety nets becomes increasingly paramount. A robust fail-safe system acts as this safety net, ensuring players' hard-earned progress is not lost due to unpredictable disruptions.

A key component of such a system is the auto-save functionality. Autonomously saving the player's progress at regular intervals or crucial junctures within the game, auto-save acts as a silent guardian, capturing and storing players' achievements and advancements. Imagine a player navigating a particularly challenging segment of a game, only to have their console or PC crash. Without an auto-save in place, they would potentially be forced to revisit and replay extensive sections, leading to heightened frustration and even potential disengagement from the game. However, with consistent auto-save checkpoints, the sting of such unforeseen challenges can be significantly lessened. It is not just about having an auto-save feature; it is about tailoring it to the player's needs. Different players have varying playstyles and tolerances. Some might prefer frequent saves to ensure every minor achievement is captured, while others might lean toward less frequent saves for a more challenging experience.

By providing gamers with the ability to customize their auto-save settings, developers are essentially offering them a personalized safety net. This flexibility lets players choose how risk-averse or risk-tolerant they wish to be, fostering a more tailored and individualized gaming experience.

Integrating thorough fail-safe mechanisms is more than just a technical necessity; it is a gesture of respect toward the player's time and effort. It demonstrates a developer's commitment to providing not just an engaging gaming experience but also a reliable and customizable one where players feel both challenged and secure.

Prevent Pitfalls in Crucial Game Scenarios

In video gaming, certain moments can define a player's experience trajectory. Whether it is a pivotal boss battle or a significant storyline decision, these high-stakes situations often require precision and intent. During these intense segments, a player's decision, whether intentional or accidental, can drastically influence the outcome. Hence, it becomes essential for developers to implement controls that facilitate deliberate choices, minimizing the likelihood of inadvertent blunders.

One effective measure is the introduction of confirmation steps. Think of it as a second line of defense, a momentary pause, asking players, "Are you sure?" This brief interruption can prove invaluable, especially when a player is on the verge of making a game-altering decision, like trading a unique artifact or accidentally engaging in a skirmish with a friendly character. Such a seemingly simple prompt can mean the difference between an exhilarating victory and a regrettable mistake.

To amplify this safeguarding effect, visual and auditory cues can be harnessed. Bright flashing indicators, distinct sound alerts, or even vibrating feedback on a controller can serve as immediate and unmistakable signals, drawing a player's attention to the gravity of their impending action. These multisensory alerts can snap players out of a potentially automatic response mode, urging them to consider their decisions with heightened attention

It is also beneficial to design challenges that demand sustained concentration. Problems that necessitate meticulous planning, combat scenarios that require tactical strategy, or storyline branches with significant repercussions can all keep a player's mind actively engaged. When players are deeply immersed and focused, they are less likely to make careless oversights.

The gaming experience is as much about immersion and challenge as it is about guidance and protection. By safeguarding players from inadvertent actions in critical situations, developers can strike a balance, offering a gaming landscape that is both thrilling and forgiving, allowing players to navigate high-pressure moments with confidence and intent.

"Recognition" Rather Than "Recall" in the Interaction Interfaces

When outlining the arrangements of various interfaces in the video game, the developer's ability to distinguish between what the player needs to "recognize" or "recall" can profoundly influence player engagement and satisfaction. The concept of "Recognition and Recall" is often used as interface design principles in human–computer interaction [6] and interaction design [31]. Recognition identifies an event or piece of information as familiar, while recall refers to retrieving related details from memory. In the video game context, "Recognition" refers to the ease with which players can identify familiar elements, whereas "Recall" demands that players remember details from past experiences. Game creators can create a more intuitive and player-friendly environment by prioritizing recognition in gameplay mechanics.

Independently from the participant's conditions or playing circumstances when engrossed in a game, they are juggling a plethora of cognitive tasks, such as managing resources, strategizing moves, or immersing themselves in a storyline. Adding the burden of memory recall can become overwhelming and potentially hamper their enjoyment. Instead, a system that leverages recognition eases this cognitive demand, presenting players with readily identifiable cues, symbols, and options.

For instance, consider an inventory system in an RPG. Rather than expecting players to remember the properties of each item, a recognition-based system might showcase items with distinct icons, colors, or tooltips. Incorporating this approach means that players are instantly shown its purpose and benefits when they hover over an item, aiding decision-making on the spot.

Furthermore, context-aware instructions or hints can be invaluable. Players might need to remember specific controls or game mechanics in a fast-paced game scenario. Instead of forcing players to dig through extensive manuals or tutorials, providing context-sensitive tips can be a game-changer. Imagine a player approaching a locked door in an adventure game; a timely hint reminding them of a recently acquired key can enhance fluidity and maintain immersion.

Advocating for "Recognition Over Recall" is about respecting the participants' circumstances and cognitive resources devoted to play. By foregrounding familiar cues and providing context-driven guidance, developers can curate an experience that feels both intuitive and rewarding. It is a subtle yet powerful approach to design that, while often overlooked, can significantly elevate the overall player experience.

Feedback Upholding the Interplay

As a game developer, you understand that the feedback provided by a game is its way of communicating with the player. Whenever a player interacts with the game, whether it is a basic action like jumping or a more intricate strategy move, they are engaging in a conversation with the game. Thus, important interaction within a game, whether it is an input command, or a decision made, should provide some form of feedback to the player. This feedback can be visual (e.g., a flashing button), auditory (a confirming sound), haptic (a vibration in the controller), or a combination of these. Immediate feedback ensures the player that their action has been registered and executed. For instance, Visual feedback, such as a character's animation, damage numbers floating off an enemy, or even subtle interaction interfaces changes, gives players instant visual confirmation of their actions. Auditory feedback, like the clash of swords or the triumphant tune of a completed quest, adds depth and richness to the gaming experience, often amplifying the emotional impact of player actions. Haptic feedback felt through vibrations in the controller or other tactile interfaces, offers a more visceral, tangible acknowledgment, adding a layer of immersion by engaging the player's sense of touch.

For example, consider a player engaged in a heated combat scenario. As they deploy their attacks, the enemy reacts—health bars diminish, impactful sound effects resonate, and the controller vibrates with every successful hit. This multisensory feedback not only reassures players of their effectiveness but also deeply immerses them in the moment, making every decision feel weighty and consequential.

Interface Responsiveness Foster Player Attentiveness
While feedback tells players the outcome of their actions, responsiveness assures them that the game is always attentively listening. Responsiveness, on the other hand, refers to the game's ability to react to a player's input quickly and accurately, ensuring that gameplay feels fluid and reactive. It is the difference between pressing a button and witnessing an immediate reaction versus experiencing a noticeable delay. A game that boasts high responsiveness feels agile, immediate, and alive, reacting seamlessly to every player's input.

When a game fails to be responsive, it breaks immersion. A delayed jump, a slow-to-react character, or an ability that activates seconds after being triggered can make the game feel sluggish, often leading to player frustration. On the other hand, when every command results in an almost instantaneous in-game reaction, players feel a deeper connection with the game world. Their avatar becomes an extension of their will, moving and acting in real-time synchrony with their commands.

Feedback and Responsiveness are the unsung heroes of game design—but they are also essential in providing error prevention within the gameplay. They work behind the scenes, shaping the player's experience, building trust, and ensuring that the virtual worlds feel as alive and reactive as the real ones. By prioritizing these elements, game developers can craft games that are not just interactive but also engaging and facilitate attainable gaming experiences for a broader audience.

5.2.8 Design Constraints for Error Prevention in Play

The heuristic Error Prevention in Play is a cornerstone in the AGE framework; it has roots in Nielsen's *Ten usability heuristics of effective user interface design* [24]. Error prevention is employed across many applications in many industries, ranging from healthcare to e-commerce; minimizing the chance of user error is often paramount. However, the unique landscape of video gaming offers a counterpoint to Nielsen's [24] heuristics, especially when error prevention overlaps and transpires into the actual gameplay. Below are some arguments against the unbridled application of Error Prevention in Play in video game design.

Challenge and Complexity
Video games often thrive on the degree of challenge and complexity they offer. A well-designed game entices players with increasingly difficult obstacles, encouraging them to hone their skills to progress further. Implementing stringent error prevention measures can neutralize these challenges, rendering the gameplay bland and uninspiring. By eradicating all potential mistakes, designers might inadvertently strip away the thrill of overcoming difficult challenges or solving intricate puzzles.

Learning Through Failure/Inquiry

One of the unique educational virtues of video gaming is its capacity to encourage learning through failure. Players who make mistakes are often presented with immediate feedback, allowing them to adapt and improve. An overzealous implementation of error prevention would stifle these dynamic learning opportunities, depriving players of valuable lessons from failure. This is overly important in the context of creating game-based products.

Player Creativity, Autonomy, and Interactivity

Video games are a medium defined by interactivity, allowing players significant autonomy to explore and engage with virtual worlds. Over-applying error prevention measures can curtail this freedom, fostering a more passive gaming experience. Gamers are often more satisfied when they are allowed the autonomy to figure things out independently rather than being led through a sequence of predetermined actions. Furthermore, such limitations on player choices can stifle creativity, removing the freedom to experiment and discover unique solutions to challenges.

Community and Social Interaction

Specific game creators like From Software and Archangel Studios have made their mark by producing purposefully complex and unforgiving games. Some games even go as far as removing the pause functionality during combat to heighten tension and challenge. While seemingly counter-intuitive from an error prevention standpoint, these design choices have galvanized a dedicated fan base and active community.[1] Moreover, "Speedruns" are an illustrative example of how game errors or glitches can enrich gameplay. Players often exploit these glitches for faster completion times, creating an entirely new subculture within the gaming community.

Exploration and Discovery

An essential aspect of many games is the thrill of exploration and the joy of discovery. Whether it is the location of a hidden Easter egg, or a secret room filled with treasures, these features are often made intentionally complicated to find or access. Over-application of error prevention can undermine the allure of these elements and prevent players from the fulfilling experience of taking risks and making serendipitous discoveries.

Lastly, the focus on eliminating potential player errors could result in a labyrinthine system that becomes difficult to manage or update. This over-engineering could consume disproportionate development resources and introduce new complications

[1] However, these communities have been noted for fostering toxic behavior against accessibility and inclusion, so exercise caution when deciding whom you and your game are courting. For a deeper understanding, see the comprehensive discussions by Fahey [8] and Parlock [27]. Further research on this topic is available in studies by Kowert [15] and Frommel et al. [23].

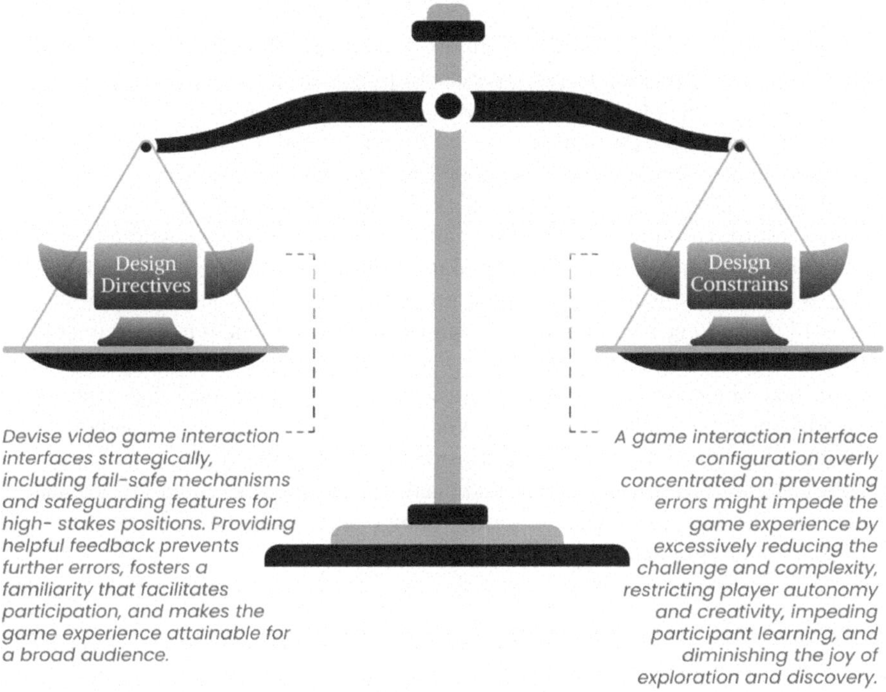

Fig. 5.8 Harmonizing directives and constraints in the "Error Prevention in Play" interaction interface design

that manifest as unforeseen errors or bugs, defeating the purpose of error prevention in the first place. While the heuristic of Error Prevention in Play undeniably enhances the usability and accessibility of software applications, the idiosyncratic nature of video gaming challenges the universal applicability of this heuristic. By considering this medium's unique demands and virtues, developers can strike a more nuanced balance that enriches rather than dilutes the gaming experience (Fig. 5.8).

Feature Creep—A Double-Edged Sword

Feature creep, defined as an excessive accumulation or uncontrolled addition of features to a video game and its interaction interfaces, is a common mistake in the indie industry. While adding more features may initially enhance a game, it can inadvertently distance the game from its core objectives and goals, harming its overall gameplay experiences and decreasing its attainability. An over-complicated game interface can be daunting for players, especially those new to gaming. Instead of creating an engaging experience, feature creep might alienate potential players by overwhelming them with options and complexities. Also, overfilling your video game with excessive features can lead to software bloat, making the game sluggish, and exhibiting inconsistencies in its overall performance, responsiveness to player action, feedback loops, or other latency-related issues. Likewise, too many game features increase the cognitive load of the participants, which might be fatal for their adoption of it or lower their overall performance (See Further Chaps. 7 and 8).

In the context of the AGE framework, feature creep functions as a double-edged sword. Cramming your video game interaction interface with as many accessibility components possible, making them adjustable, optional, and flexible will, besides making your game project extremely resource-demanding, most likely become a liability in making your game experiences more attainable for a broader audience.

Instead, in your design investigation (Chap. 3), make sure that you are prioritizing what matters in making your interaction interfaces a conduit for attainability in your video game. Ensure that the game remains approachable and interesting for a wider audience. So, be mindful, plan ahead, and consider the benefits of added interface components against the potential risks of problematizing the attainable gameplay experience.

5.3 Conclusions

In the quest to develop universally accessible and inclusive video games, the role of the Attainable Gaming Experience's four design heuristics as both enablers and boundaries cannot be underestimated. In this chapter, we have outlined how these interwoven heuristics might offer a structured design framework, serving as a repository of valuable insights that inform our design decisions. If used properly, the consequence is more than just the creation of accessible and inclusive video games; it is the development of gaming experiences that are deeply attuned to the diverse needs of a wide range of players. Such games offer not just accessibility but an enriching, engaging, and compelling experience that holds universal appeal for a broad audience.

As we advance in this volume, this insight is essential, as our focus remains steadfast on attainable gaming experiences via the interaction interface design. We continue to be guided by a vision of a gaming landscape where every individual—irrespective of their abilities—can find satisfaction, excitement, and immersive experiences. Balancing the enablers and barriers within the AGE framework ensures that this vision becomes not just an ideal but a tangible reality, further enriching the tapestry of gaming experiences available to participants from all walks of life.

References

1. Barone, E. (2016). *Stardew Valley*, Chuckelfish
2. Björk, S., & Holopainen, J. (2005). *Patterns in game design* (1st ed.). Charles River Media.
3. Chekhov, A. (2008) [1887–1904]. *Five plays. Ivanov, The Seagull, Uncle Vanya, Three Sisters, and The Cherry Orchard*. Oxford University Press.
4. Cliffe, J. (2012), *Counter-strike—Global offensive*. Valve Corporation.
5. Costikyan, G. (1994). *"I Have No Words and I Must Design." Interactive fantasy 2*. Hogshead Publishing.
6. Dix, A. (2003). *Human-computer interaction*. Pearson Education.
7. Elias, G. S., Garfield, R., & Gutschera, K. R. (2012). *Characteristics of games*. MIT Press.
8. Fahey, R. (2019). *"Accessibility" and "difficulty" aren't the same thing*. Opinion Gamesindustry.biz Published on April 12, 2019. Reviewed 15, September, 2023
9. Frommel, J., Johnson, D., & Mandryk, R. L. (2023). How perceived toxicity of gaming communities is associated with social capital, satisfaction of relatedness, and loneliness. *Computers in Human Behavior Reports, 10*, 100302.
10. Fujibayashi, H. (2017). *The Legend of Zelda*. Breath of the Wild, Nintendo
11. Fullerton, T. (2019). Game design workshop: a play centric approach to creating innovative games. 4th edition CRC Press.
12. Howard. T (2011) *Skyrim*, Bethesda Game Studios
13. Hunicke, R., LeBlanc, M., & Zubek, R. (2004, July). MDA: A formal approach to game design and game research. In *Proceedings of the AAAI Workshop on Challenges in Game AI* (Vol. 4, No. 1, p. 1722).
14. Kihlstrom, J. F. (2021). Ecological validity and "Ecological Validity." *Perspectives on Psychological Science, 16*(2), 466–471.
15. Kowert, R. (2020). Dark participation in games. *Frontiers in Psychology, 11*, 2969.
16. Lazy Bear Games. (2018) *Graveyard keeper*. tinyBuild.
17. Leite, P. d. S., & Almeida, L. D. A. (2021). Extended analysis procedure for inclusive game elements: Accessibility features in the last of us Part 2. In: M. Antona & C. Stephanidis (Eds.), *Universal access in human-computer interaction. design methods and user experience. HCII 2021. Lecture notes in computer science* (Vol. 12768). Springer. https://doi.org/10.1007/978-3-030-78092-0_11
18. LightSpeed & Quantum Studio. (2018). *PUBG mobile*. Krafton, Tencent and VNG Games.
19. Miyamoto, S., Yamauchi, H., & Tezuka, T. (1985). *Super Mario Bros*. Nintendo Entertainment System. Nintendo.
20. Miyazaki, H., Zin, N., Ishizaki, J., Kimijima, Y., Hirai, S., & Yoshida, H. (2011). *Dark Soul I*. From Software.
21. Miyazaki, H., Zin, N., Ishizaki, J., Kimijima, Y., Hirai, S., & Yoshida, H. (2014). *Dark Soul II*. From Software.
22. Miyazaki, H., Zin, N., Ishizaki, J., Kimijima, Y., Hirai, S., & Yoshida, H. (2016). *Dark Soul III*. From Software.
23. Moreau, C. P., & Dahl, D. W. (2005). Designing the solution: The impact of constraints on consumers' creativity. *Journal of Consumer Research, 32*(1), 13–22.
24. Nielsen, J. (2005). Ten usability heuristics.
25. Pan, J. Y. (2021). Chekhov's guns: Technology, design, and intention in narrative fiction.
26. Palmquist, A. (2023). *Plug & Play? Stakeholders' co-meaning making of gamification implementations in workplace learning environments* (Dissertation University of Gothenburg Department of Applied Information Technology)
27. Parlock, J. (2019). *The biggest hurdle of accessible games may be the community, not developers*. Opinion Polygon Published on Dec 23, 2019. Reviewed 15, September, 2023
28. Pathea Games (2019), *My Time in Portia*, Team 17.
29. Persson, M., & Bergensten, J. (2009). *Minecraft*. Mojang.
30. PlayStation. (2020). Accessibility options for The Last of Us Part II. https://www.playstation.com/en-us/games/the-last-of-us-part-ii/accessibility/. Reviewed 28, September, 2023

31. Preece, J., Sharp, H., & Rogers, Y. (2015). *Interaction design: Beyond human-computer interaction.* Wiley.
32. Salkind, N. J. (Ed.). (2010). *Encyclopedia of research design* (Vol. 1). SAGE.
33. Salen, K. & Zimmerman, E. (2003). *Rules of play: Game design fundamentals.* MIT Press.
34. Schatz, E., Cambier, R., & Cambier, R. (2020), *The last of us Part II*. Naughty Dog.
35. Schell, J. (2019). *The art of game design.* CRC Press.
36. Super Evil Megacorp. (2014). *Vainglory*. Super Evil Megacorp & Rogue Games Inc.
37. Tabata, H. (2016). *Final fantasy XV*. Square Enix.
38. Thorson, M. & Berry, N. (2018). *Celeste.* Maddy Makes Games.
39. Tobii Gaming. (2017) *7 eye tracking features in Assassin's Creed ® origins.* Tobii https://www.tobii.com/blog/revealed-7-eye-tracking-features-in-assassin-s-creed-origins. Reviewed September 28, 2023.

Chapter 6
Assessing the Attainability of Video Game Experiences

Abstract This chapter delves into the methodology for conducting an Attainable Gaming Experience (AGE) design assessment, applicable to video game artifacts at various stages of development—from inception to completion. The chapter explores the advantages and disadvantages of adopting a multimodal approach for evaluating AGE design, aiming to ensure that the game experience is accessible to a diverse audience. It further contrasts the effectiveness of expert testers with specialized knowledge against employing community testers who represent a range of physical, sensory, or cognitive conditions. Additionally, the chapter provides a comprehensive outline of crucial considerations within these assessments, guided by the four core AGE design heuristics.

Keywords Evaluation · Multimodal design artifacts · Game testing · Assessment · Video game

6.1 A Multimodal Approach

In the 2000s, the rapidly progressing game industries and the increasing culture of video games [8] demanded the development of pristine approaches and processes to analyze the participants and their experience engaging and interacting within the game frame and comprehend the relationship between games and participants (see [1, 2, 9]).

The rapidly growing game domain and novel approaches and processes resulted in an ongoing discussion throughout the 2000s and 2010s in mostly game studies but sometimes bleed into the industry [8]. The debate stood between primary ludologists, who focus on game mechanics and rules, and narratologists, who concentrate on games' storytelling and narrative aspects of games. At present, it is widely acknowledged that gameplay and narrative hold equal value in the gaming experience. The ongoing debate acknowledges that these two aspects are not separate but are interconnected and equally important. This approach considers that games offer unique experiences and interactions while still being able to tell stories—resulting

A. Palmquist et al., *Universal Design in Video Games*, Human–Computer Interaction Series, https://doi.org/10.1007/978-3-031-30595-5_6

in a blended and interactive characteristic that traditional narrative mediums cannot reproduce [24]. As explained in Chap. 2, the granularity of the AGE framework does not delve profoundly into the specifics of either gameplay or narrative elements. Instead, it focuses on how its four heuristics can make the elements of gameplay and narrative more attainable for a broader audience. Thus, our lens and approach toward video games, as a design artifact, in this volume was determined to be multimodal in nature.

The use of a multimodal approach in video games is not uncommon and has been implemented in many domains and contexts [4, 13, 31]. One of the most comprehensive and detailed frameworks for understanding players' game experiences is the *Ludonarrative framework* [35]. Toh's framework places significant emphasis on the multimodality of games. Multimodality is demonstrated in games through their incorporation of various forms of interaction, feedback, and sensory inputs. This includes visual, auditory, and haptic feedback, along with diverse forms of control such as gestures, voice commands, or traditional gamepad input.

6.1.1 Multimodal Design Artifacts

Within the realm of gaming, the term "multimodal" typically describes games that offer varied modes of player interaction or engagement. This variety encompasses a wide array of sensory inputs, such as visual, auditory, and haptic feedback, alongside diverse control methods ranging from gestures and voice commands to traditional gamepad input. Furthermore, the game might feature multiple gameplay modes or strategies. Specifically concerning video games, a game is viewed as multimodal if it integrates an assortment of gameplay elements or interactive modes. For instance, a game might weave together action sequences, puzzle-solving, dialogue-driven character interactions, and exploration, each demanding unique skill sets or strategies from the player. With the progression of technology, the sphere of game design has broadened to encompass distinct experiential modes such as virtual reality (VR), augmented reality (AR), and mixed reality (MR), all of which offer an individual and immersive gaming experience, further reinforcing the concept of multimodality. It is noteworthy that multimodal game design is frequently employed to enhance the depth and richness of the gaming experience, catering to various styles of player engagement and thus attracting a wider audience.

6.1.2 Multimodal Design Artifacts Require Multimodal Assessments

When designing and developing a video game, it is nearly impossible to consider all the different ways a player might interact with a game. As individuals have engaged in games for millennials, and through that, a multitude of factors has come to influence the ways we play games [7, 19, 30]. These factors can be discussed and argued endlessly, but for the sake of the scope of this volume, we broadly divide them into three classifications: player-specific factors, game-specific factors, and environmental factors.

6.1.3 Multimodal Video Game Assessments Mandate Multifarious Skillset and/or Experiences

Designing video games for accessibility and inclusion, ergo striving for an AGE, predicament might emerge. A rather fascinating paradox exists for all designers; the more the game development team plays their game, the more they grow to comprehensively understand how the game functions and begins to, unintentionally, overlook its oddities and flaws, in the end making it very challenging to foresee issues the intended participants might encounter [12]. The paradox of "expert blindness" happens when people are deeply knowledgeable about their subject, and they often assume that others share their understanding. Expert blindness can lead to overlooking design flaws that may be obvious to those without the same level of expertise. The understanding can inadvertently create a cognitive bias, preventing the anticipation of issues faced by participants—which, in the end, might cause the birth of the "omnipotent designer" (see further Krippendorff [15]), a direct hazard for creating games that aspire to harbor a universal game experience. For example, game creators might devise an interaction interface that makes perfect sense to them because they know the software or the product inside and out. However, to a novel player, the interface might be confusing or unintuitive. Given the multifaceted nature of multimodal game testing, a wide range of skills is required. Therefore, the evaluation approach for the AGE framework is firmly rooted in the HCI bricolage method of *Cognitive walkthrough* [18] and adopts two principal approaches: the specialist method and the stakeholder method.

The Specialist Method involves the expertise of diverse gaming professionals (for a more detailed explanation, refer to Chap. 3). This method employs a two-step sequential explanatory heuristic evaluation process.

The initial phase is a directed quantitative analysis, which provides specific numerical data about the game's design and usability. This is followed by an unrestricted qualitative evaluation, and a deeper dive into the experiences, perceptions, and responses of the players. The aim here is to supplement the "what" obtained from the quantitative results with the "why" and "how to"—why these results are so and how they can be addressed effectively.

The Specialist Method is a rigorous, systematic examination of the AGE heuristic, examining how these principles can be seamlessly integrated into the game design. Its purpose is to detect and diagnose recurring usability and accessibility issues in video games. By leveraging the extensive knowledge and experience of industry professionals, this method can highlight potential areas of concern that could potentially hamper the fluidity of the gaming experience. This strategy is designed to utilize industry expertise to its maximum potential, ensuring that the end product offers an enjoyable and immersive experience to all players.

In contrast, the Stakeholder group/Game community Method encompasses the active involvement of larger groups who have vested interests in the final game product. Their engagement might occur during the AGE development and/or evaluation process, during a predefined period. Such groups might consist of targeted audiences, community members representing gamers with conditions, fellow game developers, or individuals who have a financial or emotional investment in the game's success. This approach relies on a singular quantitative heuristic evaluation procedure. The nature of this process can be highly diverse: it might be tightly directed and operated under strict time limitations or be undirected, allowing adaptability with respect to time.

Upon gathering the quantitative data, the game's development team scrutinizes the collected input from the involved stakeholder group(s). These evaluations usually appear as responses on either a 4- or 8-step Likert scale. In situations where multiple stakeholder groups have conducted different types of data analysis—such as statistical or cluster analyses—their results are also integrated into the overall consideration.

The Stakeholders/community method is rooted in the principle of "strength in numbers"—the belief that a more extensive and more diverse group of evaluators can provide a broader range of insights. However, the effectiveness of this method hinges on carefully selecting the right stakeholders to ensure relevant and meaningful feedback. It is crucial that the invited stakeholders have a clear understanding and interest in the game's design, gameplay, and overall objectives.

By harnessing the strengths of both methods, game developers can attain a holistic understanding of the game's usability, accessibility, and overall player experience. This insight serves as a critical asset in refining and optimizing the game, ensuring it meets and surpasses the players' expectations. Both methods can, with some modification, be used for developing new games and/or updating existing games. In this sense, video games inherently offer a multimodal experience by integrating visual graphics, sounds, music, spoken or written language, and interactive elements.

6.2 Game Testing—A Short Tutorial

Testing and assessing if a video game sufficiently facilitates its gameplay experience by making it more attainable for a broader audience is inextricably tied to usability testing, the primary distinction being the tester's identity. Whereas usability testing can be conducted by individuals familiar with the game, accessibility testing requires a diverse range of testers, specifically those with various physical, sensory, or cognitive limitations, to ensure the game is universally playable. Thus, the essence of the difference lies not in the testing process itself but in the unique perspectives brought by those conducting the tests.

Accessibility testing of a design artifact is often likened to technology usability testing due to its similarities; however, a key distinction lies in who conducts the tests. This evaluation method has long been established within the broader software industry, and the game industry has followed suit in recent years. Many major game publishers have established internal divisions dedicated solely to conducting usability testing for their games. Usability tests are typically carried out in specialized labs by usability experts—a resource we strongly advocate utilizing if available to you or the publisher of your game.

Professional usability labs often have state-of-the-art recording equipment that captures an in-depth view of the user experience. The lab monitors various aspects affecting the experiences, including a close-up shot of the participant's hand movements on the controls—a keyboard, mouse, or game console controller—in the context of the main interface. In some cases, additional cameras may be deployed to record the participant's facial reactions, providing a more comprehensive understanding of the user's experience.

Moreover, participants' thoughts are recorded as they verbally express their cognitive process while navigating the product. This valuable feedback is recorded over the product's sound, capturing real-time insights into the user's mindset and potential areas of improvement.

The testing session is typically conducted from behind one-way glass, where researchers and the product's designers and producers observe. Communication with the participant is maintained through an intercom, fostering an environment that encourages candid feedback. A test script, prepared before the session, directs the participant's actions. It prompts the participant to explore various areas within the product or complete a set of tasks, allowing the team to observe and analyze user behavior in various scenarios.

Following the session, data on participants' success in completing the tasks, alongside an evaluation of how any findings might impact the final product, are compiled into a comprehensive report. This report is a crucial tool for understanding player experiences and making necessary adjustments to the design of your game interaction interfaces, but perhaps also—if unlucky—the overall video game design due its low game usability or lack of playability.

In essence, when carried out effectively, playtests concerning game usability and playability can be a powerful instrument in video game development, helping to furnish more straightforward and attainable gameplay experiences for a wide range of players.

To assess the attainability of your intended game experiences, you can conduct a "non-specialist's playability" test that includes a diverse set of individuals who have not previously played your video game. Remember, even if you have conducted numerous playtests with various individuals, they are disqualified for this accessibility test due to their prior exposure to your game. The ideal candidates for your test should:

- Represent a cross-section of your target audience, embodying a variety of abilities, age groups, and backgrounds to ensure a universal design perspective.
- Be objective participants—do not use coworkers, friends, or relatives to avoid bias.
- Be unfamiliar and inexperienced regarding your video game interfaces.

To ensure a robust testing process, strive for a group that to the best possible represents your diverse target audience. When it comes to amount it is always tricky to give a decent rule of thumb, a higher amount gives more data, which also gives you more analysis work to do. We recommend using a segmented approach with a smaller number of participants in the beginning, then while progressing in the AGE design and development iteration cycle you scale up. Thus, aiming for three to five individuals from each segment of your target audience is a good starting point, but securing about eight participants is ideal.

To derive the most value from these sessions, identify the most critical areas in your game from a universal design standpoint. This list should cover aspects like game startup, critical choices, and features that impact accessibility and inclusivity within the game. Upon identifying these critical areas, create a script to guide participants through them, providing tasks that yield insights about their interactions with the game.

Keep the script straightforward. Its principal function is maintaining the structure during testing, reducing potential confusion, and ensuring every crucial step is noticed. The participants must focus on your game's inclusivity and accessibility features rather than the game mechanics themselves. By facilitating a testing environment that prioritizes a universal design approach, you will gather invaluable feedback that will ultimately improve the accessibility, inclusivity, and overall usability of your game.

Playtesting is a cornerstone in the process of video game development, offering invaluable insights into player interactions, interface usability, and overall product reception. While the methodologies for playtesting can vary considerably, the underlying objective remains consistent: to gather data from real players on pre-release features and functionalities. We will now outline the most commonly employed playtesting approaches used across both independent and enterprise-level game companies. A standard playtest session aims to collect a diverse array of data from the gaming community, providing an empirical basis for refining game mechanics, interactions, and interfaces. The standard session may employ one or several of the following approaches:

Group Playtest
Description: A collaborative evaluation of the game involving multiple playtesters in a group setting. Applicable to both single-player and multiplayer games.
Data Collection: Feedback is typically collected via surveys administered at intervals throughout the session.
Duration and Setting: Sessions may last from one hour to five days and can be conducted either virtually or in-person.

Individual Playtest
Description: This one-on-one format allows for a deep dive into the player's experience.
Data Collection: Discussions with the participant cover their experiences, preferences, and other pertinent topics.
Duration and Setting: Sessions usually last from 30 to 120 minutes and can be conducted either virtually or in-person.

Extended Playtest
Description: Designed to collect long-term player feedback, this format allows developers to observe gameplay over an extended period.
Data Collection: Continuous monitoring and interaction, usually online.
Duration: These playtests typically extend over several weeks.

Playtester Survey
Description: A quantitative approach aimed at gathering opinions from a large sample size.
Data Collection: Surveys may vary in length and complexity and are usually administered online.
Duration: These playtests can last for half a day or extend over several weeks.

Focus Group
Description: A moderated discussion involving 6–10 playtesters, aimed at collecting qualitative data.
Data Collection: The researcher or moderator guides the conversation, prompting each group member to share their thoughts.
Duration and Setting: Sessions generally last between 60 and 90 minutes and may be conducted online or on-site.

Community Playtest
Description: Allows the broader gaming community to assess the game remotely, focusing primarily on metrics related to the AGE heuristics.
Data Collection: Post-playtest surveys are generally employed to collect feedback.
Notes: Games used in these sessions should be pre-final versions, as the main goal is to identify bugs or crashes.
Duration and Setting: For an indie game the tests typically span 1–3 months depending on the development phase and the intricacy of the interaction interface features under scrutiny. The playtest is executed online and is supplemented with follow-up surveys, interviews, and behavioral data analysis, etc. fitted to the specific objectives of the test.

Choosing the appropriate playtesting tactic depends primarily on what you and your team want to be more informed about in the context of attainable game experiences, here various factors such as the type of data needed, the development stage of the game, and the available resources come into consideration. By understanding the nuances of each method, game developers can make informed decisions that substantially impact the game's success post-launch.

6.3 Assessing the Attainability of Gaming Experiences Using AGE Design Heuristics

Video games provide a rich and immersive multisensory experience that utilizes a combination of visual graphics, high-quality sound, captivating music, intricate language, and interactive gameplay, providing a unique combination of elements that allows gamers to fully engage their senses and transport themselves into a virtual world, creating an unforgettable and engaging experience, their interaction interface can be hard to evaluate. Therefore, let us exemplify how to evaluate these artifacts from the AGE perspective. However, be mindful that these are merely assessment examples; for your game project, they will probably differ. As all video game projects are unique, this chapter provides only a tentative and rather generic outline of how these assessments and analyses can be conducted, reflecting AGE four design heuristics. We strongly recommend that you and your team modify these to fit your AGE purpose. Furthermore, the real-world examples in this chapter serve as inspiration—a benchmark against which you can measure your interaction interface or video games. Keep in mind that numerous design elements in a game's interaction interface are specifically tailored for a particular purpose. Borrowing ideas solely based on other game creators' interpretations and adjusting their elements for your use can lead to challenges. It is important to recognize that you may not completely understand the initial context or the original intent behind a given interface element.

6.3.1 Fair and Flexible Play

Evaluating Flexible Participation

Within the contemporary gaming landscape, individuals hailing from myriad circumstances are drawn to the immersive experience of video games. With this diverse array of players comes an equally diverse set of perspectives and limitations, each adding to the richness and universality of the medium. In order for AGE design to succeed, it must be flexible enough to appeal to and accommodate this diverse audience. Remember, if the participants feel forced to play in a certain way, they will most likely not be playing for long, thus ensuring valuing if the game does force a certain type of player behavior on their participant, that might appear harmless but can have consequences for certain strands in the audience.

Encouraging Flexible Gameplay Experiences
Evaluation Task: A successful employment of an AGE design in a video game interaction interface, should prove to be flexible and adaptable to its potentially diverse audience's needs and preferences for engaging in game participation.
Evaluation Criteria: The game interaction interface ensures:

- An equal experience for every player, irrespective of their preferences and needs.
- A broader appeal than games offering only specific gameplay modes (like Story/Narrative modes).
- Can players modify the frequency of prompts or hints within the interaction interface?
- Does the gameplay interaction interface allow for personalization of stances, audio, and lighting settings?

Inclusion of Flexible Gameplay Features
Evaluation Task: Incorporating the AGE design into a video game should enhance gameplay flexibility to cater to a wide range of player styles among diverse audiences.
Evaluation Criteria: For instance, assess if the gameplay incorporate:

- Players can pause or slow down gameplay, aiding players with cognitive conditions as well as in strategic planning for inexperienced players.
- Do such Flexible features level the playing field between diverse platforms (e.g., console vs. computer) by affording or impeding fairness in gameplay?

Flexibility in Game Modes
Evaluation Task: Evaluate if the game seems considering the diverse gameplay preferences of its (intended) audience. For example, "The Witcher 3: Wild Hunt" [5] offers various modes: "Just the Story!," catering to those who prioritize story over combat challenges, while "Death March!" for those seeking intense combat challenges.
Evaluation Criteria: Examine if the game offers:

- Modes suitable for players looking for short, digestible gaming sessions, like those with limited gaming time.
- Extended modes for players who desire in-depth exploration and longer gameplay durations.

Adapting to Different Paces
Evaluation Task: The games "Stardew Valley" [3], "Graveyard Keeper" [16], and "My Time in Portia" [27] allow players to set their game pace, balancing intense activities with calmer, relaxed intervals. The approach has been prized and valued. Evaluate if the video game seems considering the possibility of adjusting game pace.

Evaluation Criteria: Assess if the game provide:

- Players having cognitive conditions or otherwise are overwhelmed by fast-paced scenarios, providing an option for more reflective gameplay?
- Players who wish to enjoy the game without the pressure of real-time decisions.
- Interaction interface assistants
- Afford players autonomy over their gameplay style or game mode.
- Does the video game deliver a comparable gameplay quality in all offered game modes, settings, and interaction interfaces?

The significance of personalization in gameplay cannot be understated. When developers introduce options for customizable pacing and modes, it not only demonstrates an understanding and appreciation for the diverse lifestyles, timings, and challenges of their players, but it also fosters a deeper connection between them and the gaming community. This strengthened bond often becomes a foundational element for achieving success within the gaming industry. When assessing a game's customizable gameplay pacing and modes, it is important to prioritize how well it caters to its player community's various needs, preferences, and limitations. A well-designed game should be inclusive, adaptable, and flexible to ensure all players feel valued and accommodated.

Evaluating Fair Gameplay

A one-size-fits-all approach does not achieve gameplay fairness (as indicated across the Chaps. 2, 3, and 5). It requires acknowledging players' diverse challenges, abilities, and desires and offering them opportunities to customize the game experience based on their individual needs. Fairness in a video game's AGE design ensures equal chances and caters to various player abilities, challenges, and preferences. A fair game allows players to customize their experience according to their individual needs, promoting inclusivity and adaptability.

Recognizing the Audience View of Fairness

Evaluation Task: An incorporated AGE design strives to encourage equitable game participation by addressing the diverse values, motivations, and desires of players.

Evaluation Criteria: Evaluate if the game:

- Offers multiple difficulty levels catering to both new and experienced players.
- It provides a variety of game modes, allowing players to choose an experience that aligns with their preferences, be it casual, story-driven, or high-intensity gameplay.
- Includes adjustable control schemes to accommodate players with physical constraints, ensuring they can enjoy the game just like anyone else.

Prioritizing Fair and Just Participation

Evaluation Task: Fair gameplay goes beyond just balancing player skills and competition. It also emphasizes creating a positive and equitable gaming environment, prioritizing both fairness and justice within the game's context.

Evaluation Criteria: Check if the game fosters such an environment by:

- Players can interact with content at their comfort level and playstyle in a fair manner.
- They can still experience the excitement and challenges inherent to gaming.

Honoring Player Autonomy and Experience
Evaluation Task: One of the critical aspects of the AGE approach is to prioritize player autonomy and game experience. The players should be free to make their own choices and decisions regarding fair gameplay.
Evaluation Criteria: Evaluate if the AGE provides and let participants choose if they, e.g., desire to have a golden trail showing the way or if they do not wish to have a map at all—when all is said and done, their personal game experience is what matters. Evaluate if the AGE provides a seamlessly integrated fairness without disrupting the flow or feeling of gameplay authenticity. Assess if the video game:

- Recognizes players' diverse skill levels.
- Respect their individual gaming preferences.
- Allow them to adjust interaction interfaces or gameplay elements to match their comfort and skill level.

Real-world Illustration of Fair Gameplay:
Remind and refer to renowned examples to benchmark fairness in gameplay in your evaluation effort:

- Maddy Makes Games [34] serves as a representative illustration of how fairness can be integrated into gameplay. At its core, Celeste is a challenging platformer designed to test the skills and reflexes of the player. However, it also includes an "Assist Mode," a feature that respects the player's desire for a challenge and their individual accessibility requirements. In Assist Mode, players can adjust various elements of the game's difficulty to suit their needs. Options include altering the game speed, enabling invincibility, or providing additional air-dashes. This ensures that the game can be tailored to the player's comfort level, allowing them to engage with the content without feeling overwhelmed or under-challenged.
- Similarly, Mario Kart [26] for the Nintendo Switch incorporates an accessibility feature known as "Auto-Steer" or "Smart Steering," colloquially referred to as "radio car mode." This function assists players by automatically correcting their course, helping them to stay on track during races. Like Celeste's Assist Mode, Mario Kart's Auto-Steer respects players' differing skill levels and accessibility needs. It allows newcomers or those with limited dexterity to participate and enjoy the game without detracting from the challenge for more experienced players, who can turn off this feature.

- Celeste and Mario Kart demonstrate how inclusivity and fairness can seamlessly integrate into game design. These features act not merely as "easy modes" but as nuanced tools that give players the autonomy to customize their gaming experience. They show that fairness in gameplay is not just about leveling the playing field but about creating a flexible environment where players of all abilities can find engagement, challenge, and fun.

In evaluating fair gameplay, it is crucial to recognize and respect players' diverse challenges, abilities, and desires. The game experience must be tailored to meet their unique needs. As an evaluator, you must ask yourself if the game allows modifications to accommodate specific preconditions for participation. Evaluating the fairness of a game means assessing the different possibilities for adjustment, alternate game modes, or flexible control options.

Evaluating Conscious Localization

The gaming industry's globalization highlights the significance of localization, which involves more than just translating the language. Proper localization involves bridging cultural barriers and showing an understanding and respect for the unique qualities of different audiences. A successfully localized game should maintain the essence of its original design while also incorporating the cultural, historical, and social values of the region it is being adapted for. Game localization is more than just translating text. It is the art of making a game universally accessible while respecting and embracing cultural differences. Effective localization maintains the original game's essence and incorporates the target audience's cultural, historical, and social values.

In-Depth Understanding of Cultural and Local Customs

Evaluation Task: An effectively localized game transcends mere avoidance of cultural pitfalls. It seamlessly integrates and resonates with the distinct attributes of the target culture. One of the hallmarks of successful localization that has been argued is enhanced player immersion [14]. An authentically localized game feels familiar and respectful to a player's cultural background, making them feel deeply connected to the game world.

Evaluation Criteria: Examine the video games AGE directive based on the following parameters:

- Evasion of cultural stereotypes.
- Thoughtful portrayal of characters, including their attire and backgrounds.
- Decent representation and authenticity of in-game events and traditions.
- Accurate interpretations of gestures, symbols, and colors within the cultural context of the game.
- Check if idiomatic phrases, which can quickly lose or distort their meaning during translation, are adjusted to resonate with local idioms and sentiments.

Analyzing Real-World Video Game Examples
Once again, we consider it advisable to use established and prosperous localized games as a standard for assessing the effectiveness of localization efforts in video games that have incorporated AGE in their design.

- Final Fantasy XV [32]: In Final Fantasy XV, attention to cultural nuance extends beyond mere language translation and into the fabric of the in-game universe, including its culinary offerings. One striking example of this cultural attunement is the game's treatment of cuisine in its side quests. In the Western release, one of these quests prominently features a tomato risotto—a dish that resonates as comfort food with many Western audiences. By contrast, the Japanese version opts for a rice and egg bowl, tapping into a similar sense of culinary nostalgia in its home country. The localized approach to cuisine is more than a superficial change; it serves as an inclusive strategy aimed at creating a deeper connection between the game and its players. By featuring food items that resonate with regional comfort and familiarity, the game effectively bridges the gap between fantasy and reality, thereby enhancing the immersive experience for players from diverse cultural backgrounds.
- The Legend of Zelda: Breath of the Wild [11]: The Legend of Zelda: Breath of the Wild offers another compelling example of cultural adaptation in game design, particularly in how it approaches character gestures. The game developers undertook the careful task of tailoring these non-verbal cues to match the cultural expectations and norms of the various regions where the game was released. For instance, a gesture that might be considered friendly or neutral in one cultural context could potentially be construed as disrespectful or offensive in another. This level of detail underscores the developer's commitment to creating an inclusive gaming experience. By adopting gestures to meet regional norms, the game ensures that its characters remain relatable and understandable, regardless of the player's cultural background.
- The devil is in the details; in both Final Fantasy XV and The Legend of Zelda: Breath of the Wild, these efforts represent a broader commitment to culturally sensitive game design. The attention to detail in localized cuisine and adapted character gestures enhances the overall player experience and fosters a sense of inclusivity and respect for cultural diversity. These adaptations demonstrate that video game design can—and should—consider the rich tapestry of its global player base, striving for universal appeal while honoring local nuances.

When evaluating this design directive in the Fair and Flexible Play heuristic, it is crucial to assess the appropriate elements. In evaluating the localization of a video game, it is crucial to possess a thorough understanding of the cultural nuances that come with it. Not only that, but it is equally essential to ensure that the game is accessible to everyone while still managing to resonate deeply with players from a wide range of backgrounds. This requires a great deal of sensitivity and attention to detail, as even the slightest misstep in localization can lead to a game that feels out of place or even offensive to specific audiences. Ultimately, achieving successful game localization requires carefully balancing between universality and cultural awareness. The goal is not only to make the game easy to comprehend but also to make it culturally appropriate and sensitive.

Evaluating Community and Audience Commitment

Predicting a video game's impact, monetization, and lifecycle can be challenging, both in advance and retrospectively. Nevertheless, the vibrancy of its player community often provides vital clues. Assessing this design directive presents inherent challenges, primarily due to the multifaceted backgrounds and preferences of the intended gaming audience. This evaluation extends beyond just the video game artifact, encompassing various channels of communication, including email correspondence, social media interactions, and other information sources. Another crucial dimension of this assessment pertains to how adeptly the developers have integrated feedback from the community into the game's evolution. However, such an assessment can offer invaluable insights, deepening our understanding of a game's reception, impact, and monetization potential.

Recognizing the Value of the Gaming Community

The engagement and vitality of a player community often reflect the resonance and sustainability of a game created by game developers. Moreover, a strong community can provide transformative insights that elevate a game from satisfactory to outstanding.

Listening and Recognizing the Community

Evaluation Task: Assess if the creators have been listening and recognizing their gaming community.

Evaluation Criteria: Potential probing questions to be asked are:

- Have the game creators adhered to the community, offering transformative insights that might have made the game experiences more attainable?
- Has the attention and vitality of the player community, as monitored by the game developers, reflected and resonated manifestations of (conceivable) impact, commercial indication, or potential lifecycle span of the video game?
- Why so?

Evaluate the Communication with Community and Other Stakeholders

Evaluation Task: Genuine engagement with the gaming community requires hard work, emphasizing a sort of two-way communication.

Evaluation Criteria: Evaluate the game creators:

- Regularity of community interactions, e.g., through giving Q&A sessions.
- Active participation in community forums and discussions.
- Regularly conducting feedback polls to gauge player sentiment.
- Showed representation at gaming conventions to foster personal connections.

Evaluate Leveraging on Player Testing for Community Opinion
Evaluation Task: An active, ongoing relationship with the community fosters trust, demonstrating that developers are receptive to feedback and committed to enhancing the gaming experience based on player input.
Evaluation Criteria: Consider if the creator's game development process:

- Incorporates beta-testing stages that include diverse player groups.
- Utilizes these phases to allow players a firsthand experience, inviting feedback to polish and refine the game.
- Values transparency by informing players of development processes, changes, and updates.
- Has done or does actively integrate community suggestions into game updates and improvements.
- There is a visible acknowledgment of the contributions of the community in the game's development process and patches.

Real-World Benchmarking of Community Engagement
As always, using well-known real-world examples can shed light on how effective community engagement can be executed. Minecraft [28]: Mojang Studios might function as a benchmark, known for its early approach to community engagement. This engagement is not confined to superficial interactions but encompasses a full spectrum of community involvement that directly influences the game's ongoing development.

Regular Interaction with Player Base
Building the early Minecraft Mojang understood the importance of maintaining an open communication channel with, it is at first just intended, players. The company kept players in the loop through forums, social media, developer diaries, or live Q&A sessions. This regular interaction served a dual purpose: it kept the community engaged, ensured they felt heard and valued, and gave the development team a real-time pulse on player sentiment and needs.

Early Update Releases
One particularly effective strategy Mojang employed was release of early update versions, often called "snapshots" or "pre-releases," depending on their state of readiness. These early releases served as a testing ground, allowing players to experiment with new features, mechanics, and changes before they are officially incorporated into the game. These helped build excitement and anticipation and allowed Mojang to gather critical feedback during Minecraft development.

Thorough Consideration, Evaluation, and Response to the Provided Feedback by the Community
Importantly, Mojang did not just collect player feedback; they actively integrated it into their development cycle. Whether it was fine-tuning gameplay mechanics,

squashing bugs, or even reconsidering the addition of particular features, the community's voice is a direct influence. It is still not uncommon for certain features to be revised or even entirely reworked based on the collective wisdom and insight of the player base.

Community Insights for Elevating the Game Experiences
Mojang's proactive approach to community engagement resulted in a game that almost appeared co-created by its community. Minecraft has undergone substantial changes and improvements over the years, many catalyzed by community suggestions or criticisms. This process creates a sense of ownership and investment among players, reinforcing Minecraft's position as not just a game but a collaborative platform for creativity. Mojang's strategy with Minecraft set a standard for how community engagement can and should be integrated into game development. The game's ongoing refinement and evolution are testimonies to what can be achieved when developers treat their player base not as mere consumers but as active participants in the game's journey. This ethos of community-centric development elevates the game itself and sets a precedent for the industry.

When evaluating a game creator's interactions with its player community during game development or post-release, it is vital to determine if they have maintained an open and consistent line of communication. Engaging with the targeted community is not just about active participation; it is about acknowledging the community's invaluable insights. Furthermore, it is essential to check if the creators have genuinely ensured a two-way communication channel with their audience. Has there been a genuine effort to facilitate a productive exchange of information and feedback to enhance the gaming experience? Or has it merely been a narcissistic, ego-serving initiative on the part of the game creators?

6.3.2 Adjustable and Equitable Play

Evaluating Gameplay Attainability Through Adjustability
To make a game accessible for all players, adjustable settings, alternative controls, and other accessibility options should be provided. This allows players with different abilities, conditions, or preferences to customize and personalize the game according to their condition or comfort level. It is essential to recognize that a one-size-fits-all approach is not appropriate in a world that's full of diversity. The gaming world is diverse when aiming to conduct an AGE design; the game should reflect this by moving beyond the one-size-fits-all idea. It should be designed to cater to a wide range of players, each with unique needs and preferences. Here are some suggestions on how to accomplish this.

Assessing the Interaction Interface Adjustability Options
Evaluation Task: Allowing players with different conditions to customize the game to their liking ensures that the broader audience can enjoy it comfortably and equally. In verifying the interaction interface catering to the diverse conditions within the gaming community, make sure it fosters an inclusive balance and not overemphasizes one condition at the cost of another.

Evaluation Criteria: Certify that the video game system offers an ample range of:

- Adjustable interface settings
- Alternative control schemes and technologies
- Comprehensiveness of accessibility options

Evaluate the depth and breadth of the game's settings adaptability by considering if the system attends audience equally regarding their:

- Physique/mobility conditions
  - For instance, does the interaction interface afford varying assistive technologies or customizable input controllers?
- Visual conditions
  - For instance, does the interaction interface have varying color contrasts, customizable palettes, or adjustable fonts and font size?
- Auditory conditions
  - For instance, does the interaction interface afford subtitles of varying languages, visual cues, or succinct INTERACTION INTERFACE arrangements independent of audio?
- cognitive conditions
  - For instance, does the interaction interface afford customizable settings to accommodate players with different cognitive needs?

Ensure that the game accessibility options regarding participants' conditions are comprehensive and adequately catered; it is imperative to create accommodating accessibility options without discrimination.

Evaluating the Granularity and Detail of the Availability Options
The options and alternatives' usability, richness, and detail are paramount. A video game that provides Accessibility Options with no or limited impact might get an **A** for effort. Still, in the long run, it is a waste of resources and an embarrassment.
Evaluation Task: A practical way to determine the effectiveness of such options is by checking if they provide meticulous details.

Evaluation Criteria: For instance, you can check the granularity of the video game option:

- Offers changeable fonts, adjustable font colors, and font sizes.
- Provides the spectrum of the standard color contrasts and palettes.
- Includes optional audio cues, subtitles, and alternative control methods.

While it may be commendable for a game to offer Accessibility Options, ensuring they have a significant impact is essential. Otherwise, it will only be a waste of resources and may reflect poorly on the game's overall quality.

Utilize Real-World Benchmarks for Your Evaluation Protocol
To ensure that your evaluation of inclusive and accessible game design is accurate and effective, utilizing acclaimed and trendsetting examples as benchmarks is highly recommended. These examples can serve as valuable references for identifying successful strategies and techniques implemented in the industry. By analyzing and comparing these examples with your design, you can better understand how to improve your game's inclusivity and accessibility. Ultimately, this approach can lead to a more enjoyable and fulfilling gaming experience for all players, regardless of their abilities or backgrounds. For instance, The Last of Us Part II [29] is a trailblazer of accessibility settings, offering over 60 accessibility options for players with various conditions. Features such as high-contrast modes for visually impaired players and remappable controls for those with motor disabilities exemplify thoughtful design. Using The Last of Us Part II as a benchmark might appear tough, yet we recommend that you always measure against the finest out there; then, the game creators have something to strive toward regardless of how many of the 60 options they accomplish to incorporate in the video game.

Assessing the flexibility and customization of a video game interaction interfaces it is crucial to thoroughly examine its ability to be modified to fit a diverse range of demands. This is to ensure that not only are all participants' experiences accommodated but that they are also elevated to their fullest potential. A video game with a well-incorporated AGE design should be able to adjust its mechanics and features to cater to various playstyles and preferences, resulting in a more inclusive and enjoyable gaming experience for everyone involved.

Evaluating the Game Compatibility with Assistive Technologies
By prioritizing player personalization and tailoring customization, game creators can ensure that their games afford attainable gaming experiences that are affordable and enjoyable for a more sizable portion of the gaming community's audiences. The gaming arena is constantly metamorphosing due to rapid technological evolutions. Successful game developers should be agile in adapting to these changes, ensuring their games are both innovative and accessible across various platforms. Consider how games leverage modern technology to enhance playability. The true essence of forward-thinking design lies in blending innovation with accessibility, ensuring a wider reach and inclusivity. The quality AGE design acknowledges its vast and

varied player base. This affirmation is strategic and a nod to the enriched community that propels the industry forward.

Embracing Assistive Technologies
Evaluation Task: A video game employing an AGE design accommodates and utilizes assistive tools.
Evaluation Criteria: Examine the game's adaptability and compatibility with assistive tools by considering examples such as:

- Integration with the Xbox Adaptive Controller by Microsoft, a tool crafted to serve players with limited mobility.
- Incorporation of eye-tracking functionalities enables players to navigate the game world using only their gaze, which is particularly beneficial for individuals who might struggle with conventional controls.
- Compatibility with speech recognition software, allowing players to use voice commands as an alternative to traditional input methods, aiding those who might have dexterity challenges.
- Support for haptic feedback devices that provide tactile sensations, enhancing gameplay immersion and assisting players who benefit from sensory cues as gameplay indicators.

Level of Adjustability in Video Game Settings
Evaluation Task: Examine the degree of customization available in the game settings to assess how well the game caters to diverse player needs and preferences, ensuring a more inclusive and comfortable player experience when engaging in the gameplay.
Evaluation Criteria: When evaluating the game, focus on the following key features:

- The capability to rebind keys or customize control configurations, which is essential to accommodate varying player requirements and enhance personal comfort.
- Availability of high-contrast visuals and settings designed to improve visibility, vital for players using eye-tracking systems or those with visual impairments.
- Audio customization options, such as volume sliders for individual sound categories, to aid players with hearing sensitivities or those using assistive audio devices.
- Inclusion of various gameplay speed or difficulty settings to ensure that players of different skill levels and cognitive needs feel catered to.
- Review the ability of players to adjust the interaction interface elements, such as visual placement and dimensions, audio volume, magnitude of haptic feedback enabling a more tailored, player-friendly, and easier attainable game experience for all players.

Holistic Inclusivity via the AGE Design
Evaluation Task: An AGE interactions interface design aims for comprehensive inclusivity, striving to ensure every player feels acknowledged, appreciated, and accommodated. This involves not just digital aspects but also the physical interaction elements. Rather than being a secondary consideration, inclusivity should permeate the core of the design, ensuring that every player, irrespective of their challenges, can immerse themselves in the gaming experience.
Evaluation Criteria: To ascertain the level of inclusivity within the game, examine the following:

- Are there sufficient options allowing players to tailor their experience according to their needs, preferences, or limitations? Does the game offer features such as voice commands, screen readers, or haptic feedback mechanisms to aid those with specific challenges?
- Does the game showcase a wide array of characters, backgrounds, and narratives, ensuring representation across different ethnicities, genders, and abilities?
- Does the game support various control methods, accommodating players with mobility restrictions or those using assistive devices?
- Is there a mechanism for players to provide quick feedback, suggesting improvements or highlighting areas where inclusivity could be further enhanced?
- Does the game provide ample warnings for content that might be triggering or sensitive to certain player groups, allowing them to make informed decisions?

Ultimately, assessing the design directive of the AGE heuristics that concern adjustability and equitability in play, try to consider whether the game system is rigged and capable for adjustability by, for instance, seeing if it contains a mod-support in its current or foreseeable configurations. Furthermore, try to determine the level of video game's creators' longstanding commitment to supporting technological adaptability, assistive tools integration, and their affirmation and commitment toward its diverse player base. It is one thing to talk the talk, another to walk the walk.

Evaluating the Personalizable Interfaces for Enriched Interplay
Personalization, Accessibility, and Inclusion is fast starting to become buzzwords for game entrepreneurs, startups, and indie studios, while they actually address such topics rather poorly. A serious game creator that incorporates AGE will simultaneously merge attainability with good gameplay design, and with their video games not only deliver a vast experience but also champion a gaming world where everyone has a seat.

Evaluating Personalization Prospect of the Game Controls
Evaluation Task: A game's ability to enhance player engagement and satisfaction is often linked to how well it supports personalized input controls. Players place significant value on being able to adapt controls to resonate with their unique playstyle and comfort levels. Personalized adaptabilities ensure that every player,

irrespective of their preferences or physical challenges, can have a tailored and immersive gaming experience.
Evaluation Criteria: To assess the extent of personalization in the game's input controls, consider the following:

- Does the game allow players to save and switch between multiple control profiles, facilitating varied play styles or shared game environments?
- Can players modify the sensitivity of analogue sticks, mouse movements, or touchpad controls, ensuring precision and responsiveness tailored to their needs?
- Are there options to choose between different preset control layouts catering to diverse gaming backgrounds or hand configurations?
- Can players adjust the intensity and frequency of vibration or tactile feedback mechanisms to enhance their immersion or comfort?
- Are there features such as sticky keys, toggle instead of hold actions, or single-hand modes to cater to players with specific requirements?
- When modifying controls, are there real-time visual or auditory indicators that help players understand the changes being made?
- Does the game offer a safe or isolated environment for players to test and get accustomed to their personalized control settings before diving into the main gameplay?

Adaptive Personalization Recommendations
Evaluation Task: A game's ability to offer adaptive personalization based on the player's history and observed input patterns is a testament to its forward-thinking design approach. This proactive adaptability not only streamlines the gameplay experience but also makes the game more intuitive and responsive to the player's evolving needs and preferences over time.
Evaluation Criteria: To assess the depth of adaptive personalization in the game, consider the following:

- Does the game recommend control adjustments or configurations based on frequently used commands or observed struggles in the player's input patterns?
- Based on a player's performance, does the game suggest difficulty modifications, either by elevating the challenge or simplifying certain sections, ensuring a balanced gameplay experience?
- Does the game analyze the player's choices and preferences to suggest relevant options?
- Are there adaptive tutorials that respond to the player's demonstrated skills and learning pace, offering guidance in areas where they might need more assistance?
- Does the game incorporate feedback loops where player reactions or feedback to certain events can influence future gameplay scenarios or challenges?
- Does the game adjust its visual or auditory settings based on the player's commonly selected preferences or evident sensitivities?

- Does the game identify and suggest accessibility features, like subtitles or high-contrast visuals, based on observed patterns or inferred preferences?

Ergonomic Considerations
Evaluation Task: Examine the game's interface and control schemes to determine the ease and comfort with which players can interact, aiming to minimize physical strain and enhance player experience.
Evaluation Criteria: Assess if the video game provides ergonomic gameplay attainability:

- PC Gaming: Does the design prioritize the arrangement of crucial controls around the standard "WASD" configuration to ensure comfortable hand positioning and minimize stretching?
- Console Gaming: Are the primary in-game actions assigned to easily reachable areas of the controller, particularly focusing on thumb accessibility, given the layout of conventional controllers?
- Mobile Gaming: Does the game's touch interface maintain a balance between spaced-out controls to avoid accidental taps and yet ensure the essential functionalities are accessible?
- Adjustability of the Default Control: Is there an option for players to modify the default control scheme to suit individual comfort levels?
- Rest Intervals: Are there reminders or suggestions for players to take breaks, especially during prolonged gaming sessions, to reduce physical fatigue?

Real-World Benchmarking Examples
Reflect upon successful implementations in the industry for inspiration and benchmarks:

- PC games, like "Counter-Strike: GO" [6], position primary interactions within easy reach of the standard navigation keys.
- Console titles, like "Blood Bourne" [10], place essential functions within immediate thumb access.
- Mobile games, such as "PUBG Mobile" [17], empower players to dictate their on-screen button layouts.

Ensure that control designs and customization options are suited to the platform's unique characteristics. Whether it is PC, console, or mobile, recognize and optimize for each platform's inherent strengths and limitations. When evaluating a game's commitment to control personalization, focus on its adaptability, ergonomic design, and responsiveness to platform-specific nuances. A video game that scores well on these fronts indicates that the interaction interfaces, as well as a creator's dedication, delivering an attainable gameplay experience for its players.

Evaluating the Gameplay Experiences for All Sizes
Customization of the video game interaction interfaces should be effortless, intuitive and user-centered. It should be easygoing for players to amend the control schemes,

recalibrate for their preferred body position for participating, incorporate assistive technology, and alter the proprioception settings. One goal of an AGE interaction interface is that it should ensure being accessible and consequentially attainable for a broad player-base as possible. Thus, apprise if the current game interaction interface facilitates intuitive and dynamic customization and if it accommodates its targeted audience as well as current player base's diverse knowledge, shapes, and sizes. Recognizing that the gaming community comprises individuals with diverse physical characteristics, such as varied sizes, grip preferences, and motor control, is essential.

Hardware Customization
Evaluation Task: Check for the availability of customizable hardware.
Evaluation Criteria: Assess if:

- Gaming devices like controllers have swappable components for grips and hand sizes.
- There are accessible products in the market, like the Xbox Elite Wireless Controller, which permits players to change grip sizes or button placements as per comfort.

Adjustability Allowing Player Diverse Preferences
Evaluation Task: The Adjustable and Equitable game design tenet recognizes players' diverse preferences in their play.
Evaluation Criteria: To evaluate if the video game contains this;

- Examine if the video game, especially those allowing mouse and keyboard as input devices in the gaming platforms, offers (re)binding options. Ensure this feature is well-developed so it affords an equitable outlook for an attainable gameplay experience attracting a broader player base.
- For touch-based games, look for features like "Vainglory" [33] that allow players to relocate on-screen controls, ensuring the game interface feels natural and intuitive.

When assessing whether a game is welcoming to people of all sizes and preferences, it is essential to look at its hardware customization options, software flexibility, consideration of handedness, and how easy it is to tailor the gaming experience. Moreover, a video game modality interface devised with attainable gameplay in mind is a statement that displays the game creator's commitment to serving a more diverse game audience. Thus, inspecting how these customization features are framed and communicated when evaluating this design directive might be worthwhile. If no one has identified or apprehended these features' functions, they might not be used. Then, the resources spent on developing and incorporating them will be wasted.

6.3.3 Logical Play

For evaluating the design constraints in the design space for Logical Play in your game, the appropriate lens to use is the overall logic of the game interface as well the flow. Hereon, we will be taking a closer look at the factors that influence the design of the Logical Play heuristic from the drive examples in Chapter 2. Guidelines of how to evaluate a Logical Video Game interaction interface.

Simplify to Amplify
Game interface designs should prioritize eliminating unnecessary hurdles that stand between the player and the core gameplay. The video game's interaction interface should emphasize delivering an uncomplicated, direct route to the main gameplay, allowing players to dive in without distraction.

Retain the Essence
Evaluate how the game preserves its fundamental elements that uplift the fun and involvement of the gameplay. Maintaining the primary features that define the game's unique character and draw players in is vital.

Seamless Navigation
Assess the game's ability to let players bypass non-essential obstacles seamlessly. The game should ensure that players are necessarily held up by barriers irrelevant to the central gameplay experience.

Organized Game Information
Examine how the game presents its in-game information. It should be laid out in a manner that ranks it by relevance and urgency. This ensures players can effortlessly find and comprehend critical data when required, contributing to a smoother gameplay experience.

Minimize Distractions
Look out for the presence of potential interruptions, such as:

- Empty sections in the game environment that misleadingly indicate progress or exploration.
- Excessive emphasis on statistics tracking or player comparisons, which can distract from the central gameplay.

Creative Frames and Boundaries
While open-ended experiences can be engaging, they can sometimes lead to overwhelming choices for players. An effectively designed game might occasionally impose limitations to guide players and foster creativity within set boundaries [25].

Evaluate Player Experience
Check if the game prioritizes making the gameplay experience further attainable for broader audience. A well-designed interaction interface in any video game should strive for an uninterrupted, immersive environment where players can engage fully without being sidetracked by superfluous elements.

Appraising video game's interaction interface design based on the "Prioritize, Facilitate, and Refine" design directive focuses on the ability of the game to deliver a streamlined, distraction-free environment that keeps players engaged and immersed. The essence lies in offering an uninterrupted, core gameplay experience without unnecessary complexities.

Evaluating the Expectation Alignment
Consistency in the video games interaction interfaces is preferable, it should mirror player expectations consistently. When assessing a game, check if it maintains regularity in its world and mechanics. For instance, if a specific environmental feature behaves in a particular way at one point, it should act similarly throughout the game to preserve player intuition and world immersion.

Logical Game World Interactions
Ensure that the interactions within the game world align with established logic. For example, if a specific tree type is flammable in one game segment, it should consistently exhibit that trait throughout. Such logical congruence solidifies the player's trust in the game world's predictability.

Significance of Introduced Elements in the Interface
Players anticipate that prominently introduced or unique items in a game will have a defined purpose as they proceed. Evaluate how effectively the game integrates the principle of Chekhov's Gun: any element introduced early on should evolve and gain importance in a manner that feels organic to the player and ties neatly into the overall narrative and gameplay.

Coherence and Purpose
Check for the presence of any interface elements that might feel out of place or without clear intent. The introduction of interaction elements in the interface that contradict the broader design or that are left unexplained or unresolved can detract from the game's coherence. Such anomalies can lead to player frustration and disrupt the immersive experience.

A Unified Design in the Interaction Interfaces
A well-aligned game design ensures an intuitive experience, allowing players to predict or understand outcomes based on prior knowledge or established game logic. Assess if the game facilitates this intuition and sustains player immersion without any jarring inconsistencies.

Estimating the "Expectation alignment" in a video game interaction interface, it is crucial to pay close attention to the consistency, predictability, and purpose of the various elements introduced throughout the gameplay. A well-crafted expectation alignment in a video game will align and integrate with player intuition without coming forth as a predictable, cliché, or bleak carbon copy of an already-released title. Assessing the video game's cohesiveness and alignment with our meaning should result in an immersive, sense-making, and captivating experience that is devoid of inconsistencies. By ensuring that all aspects of the game are aligned with the players' expectations, developers can create a cohesive and enjoyable gameplay experience that keeps players coming back for more. The success of any video game hinges on the ability of its design to meet and exceed the expectations of its target audience, providing a seamless and fulfilling gaming experience that leaves players feeling satisfied and engaged.

Evaluating the Logical Feedback and Player Cues

The effectiveness of feedback mechanisms in a game is pivotal. Feedback mechanisms denote a game's ability to relay to the player the consequences of their actions, fostering both learning and adaptability. Positive reinforcements for the right decisions and corrective insights for mistakes ensure a balanced and informative gameplay. Evaluating this design directive requires the evaluators to ensure that video games provide feedback is:

- **Immediate:** Feedback should follow swiftly after a player's action, cementing the cause-and-effect relationship.
- **Specific:** Feedback should be precise, letting players know exactly what they did right or wrong.
- **Relevant:** Ensure the feedback is directly tied to the player's recent action, making it pertinent and useful.

Beyond the above, evaluate if the video games' provided player cues and prompts are understandable and coherent. Lastly, inspect if the player's game progress is clearly outlined, comprehensible to follow, and does contribute to an immersive experience via direct milestones or juiciness. Milestones effectiveness can be assessed based on:

- **Relevance**: Their function as indicators should be relevant to the player's achievements or progress, ensuring players are aware of their journey and growth.
- **Engagement**: Their ability should capture players' attention, making them more invested in the game.

To illustrate feedback a bit further, consider the following example of the made-up game "Inter-Galactic Endless-Quest." We have designed it with an emphasis on enhancing the player experience through feedback. Post the initial tutorial, as players venture into their space odyssey, they encounter challenges and make decisions. The aftermath of these decisions is communicated through:

- **Positive Reinforcement:** On successful navigation of challenges, the game offers instant, specific positive feedback. This might be in the form of graphics, sounds, or messages, nudging players to maintain successful strategies.
- **Constructive Feedback:** On less successful ventures, instead of mere notifications of failure, the game offers constructive insights or hints. This ensures players not only realize their mistakes but also learn from them, fostering adaptability.

The correlation between player actions and feedback is maintained consistently. Whether they solve a complex puzzle or conquer an adversary, the feedback mirrors their direct actions. Further, as players traverse the game, they are met with apt indicators and signals, highlighting their progress. For instance, leveling up is paired with a clear notification of unlocked abilities or items. After a significant achievement, players are treated to an immersive cut-scene, deepening their connection to the game world.

The yardstick for estimating the effectiveness of feedback loops, prompts, and cues rests on their immediacy, relevance, specificity, and overall engagement. Implementing these enhances gameplay, making it a blend of rewarding, educational, and thoroughly captivating experiences.

Evaluating the Enhancing Experience Through Meaningful Tutorials

Understanding game mechanics and overall logic is a primary concern for players as they embark on a new gaming experience. The tutorial's function is to bridge the knowledge gap, enabling players to quickly grasp the game's mechanics and dive deeper into its complexities. Efficiently executed tutorials not only elucidate game mechanisms but also set the stage for sophisticated gameplay, nuanced challenges, and multi-layered experiences that cater to a broad spectrum of players.

In-Game Tutorials

Tutorials should foster a rich gameplay filled with engaging mechanisms, narrative twists, problem-solving sequences, and heightened replay value. Let us illustrate this with two real-world game examples: Our first example is "The Legend of Zelda: Breath of the Wild." The "Great Plateau" section serves as a foundational tutorial for players. It gracefully introduces players to the core mechanics of the game. Similarly, "Dark Souls" [21–23] offers a well-crafted tutorial design with its "Undead Asylum" segment. Unlike conventional hand-holding tutorials, "Dark Souls" introduces players to its unforgiving world by providing minimal guidance. Players learn through trial and error, noticing enemy patterns and understanding the importance of timing in combat. What both the "Dark Souls" and "Zelda: Breath of the Wild" tutorials achieve are:

- **Narrative Integration**: Rather than compartmentalizing the tutorial as a distinct and pedagogic segment, it is ingeniously woven into the game's narrative. Such integration ensures players remain invested in the game's storyline while acquiring essential skills.

- **Player Autonomy**: Both tutorials promote exploration and environmental interaction, empowering players to learn and adapt at a pace that aligns with their preferences. Here, the "Great Plateau" is the most distinct. Instead of constraining players with rigid pathways, it encourages in-game inquiry with a high amount of interaction with the game elements constituting Breath of the Wild. A high amount of freedom is provided but within a restricted area—which is important for becoming overwhelmed early in the game. This approach empowers players to learn and adapt at a pace that aligns with their preferences, fostering experimentation and confidence-building.
- **Player Skill Readiness**: Post-tutorial, players emerge adeptly equipped to tackle the myriad challenges awaiting them in the larger game context. The player toolkit now comprises diverse combat strategies, an understanding of resource management, and a grasp of the PC abilities pivotal for navigating the complex and intricate games that are "Zelda: Breath of the Wild" and "Dark Souls."

Thus, to evaluate an in-game tutorial's logic and efficacy, one might focus on assessing:

- **Seamlessness**: Is the tutorial effortlessly incorporated into the game such as its narrative or world-building?
- **Flexibility**: Does the tutorial offer players the autonomy to explore, experiment, and learn at their own pace?
- **Skill Transfer**: After completing the tutorial, are players competently prepared to engage with the game's deeper complexities?

An essential criterion for in-game tutorials is their logical structure. It's vital to ensure that the tutorials are relevant to all potential gameplay styles. For example, would a Half-Orc Barbarian character benefit from learning advanced spell casting? Or should an Elven Mage be taught how to expertly sever limbs with a battle-ax during a berserk rage? Probably not that particular play-through, but the next?

In the assessment of a video games attainability via its presented interaction interface, ensure that its in-game tutorials are efficient and relevant, providing an intuitive and logical feel for the players. Also control how they impact the game's pacing, increasing/decreasing player feelings such as confusion, frustration, and understanding, and if they provide or enhance opportunities for adding game complexity. As the purpose of implementing an in-game tutorial is to equip players with the fundamental skills and knowledge required to successfully overcome challenges, make sure that you assess its practicality. Also, consider if the tutorial has the potential to enhance player engagement and satisfaction and increase the overall appeal of the game. A well-designed tutorial provides players with a sense of accomplishment and confidence, leading to a more enjoyable and immersive gaming experience.

Logical Interaction Interfaces Amplifying the Player Experiences
Interaction interfaces designed with the PX in mind are foundational elements in the Logical Play design philosophy. Evaluating their influence on the game's aesthetic appeal, functional significance, and projection of the player's perceived desirable future is essential to gauge its overall quality and resonance with players.

Interaction Interfaces
Encompasses the modality elements that players interact with in the various interfaces of the game. Evaluating this might involve the following:

- **Clarity and Intuitiveness**: Is important information like score, lives, and timers easily visible and strategically placed? They should be readily accessible without impeding the actual gameplay.
- **Responsiveness**: Do the action buttons respond quickly to player inputs, ensuring fluid controls?
- **Design Coherence**: All game elements, from power-ups to adversaries, should be distinguishably designed in the interaction interfaces. This helps in intuitive recognition and strategy formation for the player. For example, Super Mario Bros. (1985) showcased power-ups and enemies with clear visual differences, aiding in quick player decisions.

Playability
This is a holistic perspective encompassing a player's complete interaction journey with the game, from controls to emotional attachment. Key areas to evaluate might include:

- Interface Complexity Pacing: The complexity of the games interfaces should scale progressively, offering new challenges at a digestible rate. A player should feel the complexity increasing without being overwhelmed.
- Control Simplicity: The controls should be straightforward, and their effects (like character jumps and movements) should map intuitively to the corresponding button inputs, ensuring minimal friction in the learning phase.
- Players play well, if they know how: Depending on the game genre, the interaction interface should prioritize positive feedback over negative to bolster player engagement. While consequences for failures are integral, they should not be excessively severe. Games that adopt this mindset allow players to restart from a point near where they faltered, rather than compelling them to replay the entire level. The approach introduces logical challenges without leading to disproportionate player frustration.

Using the benchmarks, one can comprehensively evaluate any game's adherence to the Logical Play design directive, where its playability forges an intuitive, captivating, and gratifying gaming experience. When finely tuned, it elevates the player's experience, rendering the game both accessible and captivating. To ensure a rigorous and comprehensive evaluation of the interaction interface supporting the gameplay, consider the following aspects:

Complexity Scaling
Evaluation Task: Assess the game's challenges to ensure equity among its elements. A well-balanced game presents challenges that are stimulating without overwhelming. Does progressively increased complexity as players advance?
Evaluation Criteria: Analyze how challenges evolve throughout the game and whether they align with player progression.

Feedback Elements in the Interface
Evaluation Task: Immediate and clear feedback for player actions.
Evaluation Criteria: Check if the game provides immediate feedback when players decide to act.

Mechanics Consistency
Evaluation Task: Uniform video game interaction interfaces throughout different scenarios. Familiar design paradigms offer players a sense of comfort, which can amplify their overall enjoyment.
Evaluation Criteria: Investigate any anomalies or changes in game mechanics that might disrupt the player's understanding.

Interface Predictability
Evaluation Task: From elements to controls and mechanics, maintain a coherent and predictable game interface. Consistent and intuitive interaction interface elements.
Evaluation Criteria: Review the placement, design, and functionality of interaction interface elements for coherence and cohesive experiences.

Control Responsiveness
Evaluation Task: Controls that respond accurately and promptly to player input.
Evaluation Criteria: Test controls under various scenarios to gauge their reliability and precision.

Adherence to Genre Conventions
Evaluation Task: Incorporation of accepted and proven design principles from the game's genre. A clear and consistent design dispels potential confusion, allowing players to immerse fully.
Evaluation Criteria: Compare game elements to other successful titles in the same genre to ensure alignment.

By methodically appraising these aspects, you can ascertain the effectiveness of the gameplay balance and design consistency, ensuring a memorable and enjoyable gaming experience for all players. A balanced and consistent game enables players to concentrate on honing skills and strategizing rather than grappling with unpredictable mechanics and design anomalies—consider the things that matter.

6.3.4 Error Prevention in Play

When assessing the factors that influence the prevention of unintentional errors during gameplay, it is essential for the evaluator to take into account the high stakes and stressful situations that may arise from menus, interface, mini-games, and in-game player choices. In this section, we will explore some of the factors that may affect the Error Prevention in Play heuristic design constraints, as presented in Chap. 2. However, it should be noted that numerous others exist and may vary depending on your game genre, participants playing circumstances, conditions, and context.

Evaluating the Player-Friendly Interface Configurations
The arrangement of game interaction interfaces, menus, and controls is a paramount factor shaping a player's journey and experience within the digital realm. Such configurations can enhance or hinder gameplay, making their strategic design a top priority. Below are guidelines how to evaluate this design directive:

> **Emphasis on Common Actions**
> **Evaluation Task**: Ensure that controls and commands used regularly are easily accessible and intuitively positioned.
> **Evaluation Criteria**: Analyze if players can effortlessly access frequently used actions without diving deep into menus. For instance, in a combat-oriented game, if weapon-switching is frequent, its control should be effortlessly accessible.

> **Error Prevention**
> **Evaluation Task**: Place potentially disruptive commands like "exit" and "restart" in areas where they are less likely to be triggered accidentally.
> **Evaluation Criteria**: Assess if these game-changing commands are distanced from primary action buttons or nested in sub-menus to prevent unintended activations.

> **Consistency in the Video Game Interface Design**
> **Evaluation Task**: Maintain a consistent layout and design across various menus and interfaces.
> **Evaluation Criteria**: Ensure that similar actions and commands retain consistent placement and appearance throughout different game sections.

Adaptive Design for Diverse Players
Evaluation Task: Allow players the option to customize and remap their input controls.
Evaluation Criteria: Check if the game provides players with the flexibility to modify controls to align with their play style and preferences, ensuring an inclusive experience for a wider audience.

Optimized Aesthetics with Functionality
Evaluation Task: A well-arranged interface should meld both attractiveness and usability.
Evaluation Criteria: Examine if the interface aesthetics sacrifices functionality and vice versa. The visuals should complement, not complicate, the player's attainment of the game experience.

Player-Centric Design in the Game Interaction Interface
Evaluation Task: Determine how effectively the game's interface has been crafted with the foresight of player behavior, preferences, and potential actions.
Evaluation Criteria: Utilizing insights from player feedback and test sessions, assess the video game based on:

- Does the interface naturally align with the player's expected behavior patterns without necessitating a steep learning curve?
- Does the interface react swiftly and appropriately to player inputs, facilitating smooth gameplay?
- Does the game preemptively address common player needs, offering solutions or options before they become apparent pain points?
- Adaptive Features: Does the game learn from repeated player behaviors, subtly refining the interface over time to better cater to individual play styles?

When assessing the interaction interface organization in games, it is fundamental to recognize its integral role in shaping gameplay experiences. An interface that prioritizes user needs and aligns with intuitive player behaviors not only enhances gameplay but also broadens the game's appeal to a diverse audience. The suggested evaluation aspects for this design directive are rooted in the various modalities described in Chap. 3, with a focus on creating engaging and satisfactory gaming sessions for the participants by minimizing the frustration and helplessness that might appear from doing an unintentional mistake due to high cognitive load or inferior design interfaces.

Protective Mechanisms Upholding Gameplay
The intricacies of modern video games necessitate advanced fail-safe mechanisms. These systems play a pivotal role in safeguarding a player's progress and efforts against unforeseen disruptions, ensuring a seamless and frustration-free gaming experience.

Presence of Auto-Save Feature
Evaluation Task: Ascertain that the game has an auto-save function that regularly captures a player's progress.
Evaluation Criteria: Examine the game for regular or milestone-based auto-save points. For example, does the game save after critical events, boss fights, or upon completing specific tasks?

Adaptability of the Auto-Save function
Evaluation Task: The auto-save feature should cater to different play styles and preferences by being customizable.
Evaluation Criteria: Can players adjust the frequency of auto-saves? Investigate whether the game allows for customization of auto-save intervals or if it provides an option for manual saves alongside auto-saving.

Recovery from Disruptions
Evaluation Task: Players should not lose significant progress due to unforeseen issues like crashes.
Evaluation Criteria: Test the game's recovery mechanism by simulating disruptions. If a crash occurs at a challenging game segment, does the player resume close to that point, or are they reverted to a much earlier stage?

Notification and Transparency
Evaluation Task: Players should be aware when the game is saving their progress.
Evaluation Criteria: Does the game display noticeable indicators, like icons or brief messages, during auto-save moments? This ensures players are informed about their progress being secured.

Redundancy in Saving
Evaluation Task: Incorporate multiple save slots or backup save files to prevent loss of progress due to corrupted save files.
Evaluation Criteria: Check if the game offers multiple save slots or creates backup save files periodically to prevent complete loss from a single corrupted file.

Player's Invested Time and Effort
Evaluation Task: The game's fail-safe mechanisms should demonstrate respect for the player's invested time and effort.
Evaluation Criteria: Gauge player feedback or conduct test sessions to determine if the fail-safes enhance their gaming experience and give them a sense of security.

By ensuring these evaluation tasks are met, developers can create not only a captivating game but also one that respects the player's time, providing a safe environment where the unpredictability of disruptions is mitigated. Proper fail-safe mechanisms signal a game's reliability and a developer's dedication to a holistic and gratifying player experience.

Evaluating the Prevent Pitfalls in Crucial Game Scenarios
In video games, specific junctures hold the power to shape a player's experience. High-stake decisions or game-changing events warrant precision. A mere slip-up during these phases can impact the entire game trajectory. To ensure players act with deliberation and to lessen the possibility of unintentional mistakes, game developers must incorporate specific protective measures.

Confirmation Steps
Evaluation Task: Assess whether the game incorporates verification prompts during crucial decision points.
Evaluation Criteria: During significant in-game actions (e.g., discarding a rare item or initiating a pivotal combat), does the game interface provide a momentary halt, prompting the player with a verification like "Are you certain about this action?"

Multisensory Feedback
Evaluation Task: Identify if the game utilizes visual, auditory, and tactile cues to accentuate the importance of a decision.
Evaluation Criteria: Does the game deploy bright visual indicators, unique sound alarms, or controller vibrations to signify high-stakes situations? These should effectively draw a player's focus to the criticality of their impending choice.

Engaging Challenges
Evaluation Task: Gauge if the game's challenges promote sustained attention and active engagement.
Evaluation Criteria: Are there tasks that push players to strategize thoughtfully? Does the game present storyline branches that carry long-term ramifications, ensuring players remain deeply engrossed and more resistant to distractions?

Graceful Failure and Recovery
Evaluation Task: Evaluate if the game allows players a way to rectify or recover from a mistake without disproportionate consequences.
Evaluation Criteria: If a player makes an inadvertent decision, does the game offer a means to undo or mitigate the outcome? Are there options to reattempt challenges or pathways to counteract the results of a mistaken choice?

Moreover, in the context of protection mechanics in a video game, the approach can be distilled into three overarching assumptions about game participants:

- Players frequently possess unstable and evolving preferences regarding their gameplay actions.
- Players might not always act logically during gameplay.

- Players often perceive themselves as more logical and informed than they truly are, leading to a desire for increased autonomy and reduced guidance.

Given these nuances, it's essential to gently guide player behavior while still respecting their autonomy and freedom of choice. Striking this delicate balance is crucial when evaluating this directive. Depending on the stakes of the game participation, implementing fail-safe mechanics might be of the utmost importance for nourishing a satisfying gaming experience. Nevertheless, the essence argues for aiming to find an equilibrium between providing a total freedom and hardwired guidance—a sort of a libertarian paternalism in the context of the game interface. Through mechanisms that guard players against unintentional mistakes during crucial moments, developers can furnish an environment where players can delve into challenges with both enthusiasm and assurance.

Evaluating the "Recognition" Rather Than "Recall" in the Interaction Interfaces

"Recognition" and "Recall" hold distinct meanings. While recognition refers to acknowledging something as familiar, recall entails actively retrieving specific details from memory. Within a gaming milieu:

- Recognition: Relates to how effortlessly players can spot and understand familiar elements.
- Recall: Challenges players to draw upon previous experiences and remember specifics.

An optimal design emphasizes recognition over recall, creating an environment that's both intuitive and player-centric. When engrossed in gameplay, players manage a multitude of cognitive tasks, from strategizing moves to delving into intricate storylines. Overburdening them with the need for memory recall can disrupt their flow and enjoyment. A recognition-centered approach, on the other hand, offers players clear, identifiable cues and symbols, simplifying their cognitive load. The evaluation factors for the design directive "Recognition Over Recall" in video game interfaces might be as follows:

Clarity of Icons and Symbols

- Are the game's icons and symbols easily distinguishable?
- Do they convey their intended meaning without ambiguity?

Consistency of Interaction Interface Elements

- Are similar actions represented consistently throughout the game?
- Are the cues, symbols, and icons used in a consistent manner in all scenarios?
- Are sounds used in a corresponding and coherent manner?

Intuitiveness of Interface Design

- Can players naturally predict the next step or action based on the current interface cues?
- Does the game's interaction interface direct the player's attention to the most important entity or the next logical undertaking?

Tooltip and Prompt Availability

- Are tooltips available for most, if not all, items or interface elements that might require them?
- Do these tooltips provide quick, clear information without overwhelming the player?

Context-Sensitive Guidance

- Are hints and prompts provided in scenarios where players might struggle or forget a previous instruction?
- Are these hints timely, relevant, and helpful without giving away too much?

Memory Load

- How often are players required to delve into their memory to progress or make decisions?
- Is the game designed in a way that minimizes the need for players to remember past events, keys, or actions?

Customization of Interface Elements

- Can players customize certain interface elements to better align with their recognition preferences?
- Is there modifiable settings that adjust how strong and how often prompts or hints appear in the interaction interface?

Testing and Community Opinion

- Have playtests been conducted to assess the effectiveness of the recognition-based elements?
- What feedback verdicts have the player base provided regarding the ease of recognition vs. the demand for recall?

Comparison to Industry Examples and Standards

- How does the game's implementation of the "Recognition Over Recall" principle compared to other popular games in its genre?
- Are there industry benchmarks or best practices that the game adheres to or deviates from?

Utilizing these evaluation criteria for the "Recognition Over Recall" offers game developers a structured framework to critically assess how well they have integrated this key design philosophy into their game's interface. By methodically examining each aspect, creators can gain deeper insights into areas that excel and those that might benefit from further refinement. Such a comprehensive evaluation does not just identify potential weak points; it also provides actionable feedback, empowering developers to make targeted improvements. This iterative process of evaluation and refinement ensures that the game's interface remains intuitive, minimizing the cognitive load on players. Ultimately, by emphasizing recognition over recall, game designers enhance the immersive quality of gameplay, leading to heightened player satisfaction and prolonged engagement.

However, it is important to remember that the above-mentioned aspects are a handful of examples, a game creator must be intuitive and realize what kind of barriers his/her game might impede on its participants depending on the game genre or context.

Evaluating the Feedback Upholding the Interplay

The core of any video game lies in its ability to communicate and engage with the player effectively. At its heart, every action, decision, or command within a game initiates a two-way dialogue between the player and the game interface. For game creators, it is crucial to ensure this conversation is both reassuring and informative, facilitating player agency and assurance.

Feedback Consistency

Begin by examining the consistency of feedback across various interactions. Every significant player action should be met with an appropriate response from the game, whether it is a simple jump, or a complex strategy move.

- Is feedback provided consistently across all significant interactions?
- Are there moments when player actions go unrecognized or unacknowledged by the game?

Feedback Modalities

- Visual Feedback: This is often the most immediate and recognizable form of feedback. Look for elements such as character animations, visual interface indications, or any visual cues that confirm player actions. For instance, does the enemy display any change when hit? Are there clear and distinct visual cues when a task is completed, or a level is achieved?
- Auditory Feedback: Sound can be a powerful tool in gaming, providing both ambiance and confirmation. Evaluate the quality, appropriateness, and timing of sound effects. Does the audio align with the player's actions, and does it enhance the overall emotional experience?
- Haptic Feedback: Especially relevant for console gaming, tactile feedback offers a tangible connection between action and response. Assess the sensitivity, timing,

and appropriateness of vibrations or other tactile responses. Does the feedback intensity match the gravity of the in-game action?

Feedback Timeliness and Loops
Ensure that the player feedback is almost instantaneous. Delays in the interface, even if minimal, can disorient players and break immersion.

- How quickly does the game respond to player actions?
- Are there noticeable lags that can hinder the player experience?
- Does the game provide immediate feedback when players make a choice, helping them to recognize the implications of their actions?
- Are there any mechanisms in place for players to easily revert or adjust their choices based on this feedback?

Interaction Interface Feedback Quality in Varied Scenarios
Use real-game scenarios to understand the effectiveness of feedback. For instance, in combat situations, assess if the combined visual, auditory, and haptic feedback contributes to a rich, immersive experience.

- For specific game scenarios (like combat or problem-solving), does the feedback enhance the player's immersion and understanding?
- Are there scenarios where feedback feels redundant or lacking?
- Does it amplify the urgency, thrill, and significance of player choices?

Player Reassurance
At its core, feedback serves to reassure players of their agency in the game world. Evaluate if the feedback mechanisms in place effectively convey to players that their actions have been recognized, processed, and have impacted the game world.

- Does the feedback accurately reflect the magnitude and consequence of the player's actions?
- Is the feedback scaled appropriately (e.g., more significant actions yield more noticeable feedback)?
- Do players feel a sense of agency, knowing their actions have tangible effects within the game world?
- Is there a balance between providing enough feedback without overwhelming or hand-holding the player?
- Can players adjust feedback settings (like turning off certain cues or adjusting haptic feedback intensity) to suit their preferences? Are there moments when feedback disrupts gameplay or breaks immersion?
- Are there instances where feedback could be streamlined or integrated more seamlessly?

Through a thorough analysis of the various components involved, game developers can effectively guarantee that their game not only effectively communicates with its players, but also actively listens and adapts to their actions, crafting an immersive and engaging experience that prioritizes player autonomy and confidence. By systematically evaluating these aspects, game developers can get a holistic understanding of how well they have integrated the principle of "Player Agency and Assurance" into their game design and where refinements might be beneficial.

Evaluating the Interface Responsiveness Foster Player Attentiveness
Responsiveness in a video game transcends mere feedback; it is a testament to how attuned the game is to a player's input. Essentially, it gauges the game's capability to process and manifest a player's action swiftly and precisely, resulting in fluid and organic gameplay. The hallmark of an optimally responsive game is its immediacy. When players press a button or make a choice, the game's reaction should be almost instantaneous, devoid of any perceptible lag. This immediacy fosters a game environment that feels lively and perpetually coordinated with the player's desires.

When assessing the Responsiveness in a video game, a useful lens is one that searches and identifies "Lapses." Lapses—disruptions in video game performance—in responsiveness can rupture the gaming experience. Whether it's an unresponsive jump, a character that seems out of sync with commands, or abilities that spring into action belatedly, such moments create friction, dampening the immersive experience and potentially heightening player aggravation. Conversely, a game that epitomizes peak responsiveness entrenches players further into its realm. Their in-game character or avatar mirrors their inputs in near-perfect harmony, making gameplay feel like a seamless dance of intent and execution. Here follows some other issues to assess and evaluate:

Immediate Reaction
Test the time lapse between a player's command and the game's reaction. It should feel nearly instantaneous. Calculate the time delay between a player's input and the game's response. The shorter this latency, the better the game's responsiveness.

Interruption Recovery
Evaluate how quickly the game regains its responsiveness after interruptions like pausing, accessing in-game menus, or when there's a sudden influx of on-screen action.

Fluidity
Observe if movements and actions flow naturally, without jitters or inconsistencies. Make sure to check the smoothness of characters' movements and animations following player commands. They should transition seamlessly without abrupt breaks.

Consistency of Game Response
Ensure that the game's responsiveness is uniform across various actions, levels, and scenarios. Assess if the game maintains consistent responsiveness across various actions, scenarios, or levels. There should not be certain areas or times where the game lags or feels slower.

Feedback Integration
While responsiveness deals with the immediacy of reactions, it should also be intertwined with appropriate feedback to signify the outcome of the player's action. The game should respond immediately to inputs with the associated feedback—mostly visual or auditory cues but preferably multimodal—should also be timely and not lag behind the action.

Responsiveness Across Different Devices, Platforms, and Settings
Evaluating the video game, it is important to consider its performance across different devices, platforms, and settings. This ensures that players have a consistent and responsive experience no matter what system they are using. It is also important to check if the game maintains its responsiveness when graphical settings are changed, as this can affect players with different capabilities. Cross-platform consistency is also important to examine, as a game may be responsive on one device but laggy on another, indicating optimization issues. Lastly, adaptability to settings should be checked to ensure the game remains responsive even when graphical settings are adjusted.

Player Special Settings Might Influence Responsiveness
Always gather insights from players. Investigate if players can adjust settings that might influence responsiveness, allowing them to tailor the experience to their preferences. Often, they can discern even subtle responsiveness issues that might escape a developer's eye. Gather player feedback specifically on the responsiveness of the game. Their firsthand experience will highlight areas of improvement.

Comparative Responsive Analysis
Compare and analyze the video game's responsiveness to other games in the same genre or category to determine its standing in the market. This benchmark will give an indication of where the game stands in terms of responsiveness when compared to other contemporary games.

These evaluation aspects can guide developers in identifying areas of strength and potential improvements, ensuring their game provides an optimal experience in terms of responsiveness. It is crucial for a game to respond quickly and accurately to player actions, as this helps players feel valued and immersed in the game world. Therefore, developers must carefully evaluate the responsiveness of their game during the evaluation phase to ensure that players feel respected and appreciated. By prioritizing responsiveness, developers can create a more engaging experience for players of varied circumstances. Feedback and Responsiveness are the unsung heroes of game design; this is true in interaction design as well as they are essential in providing a soft form of error prevention within the digital system. Both work behind the scenes, shaping the player's experience, building trust, and ensuring that the virtual worlds feel as alive and reactive as the real ones. By prioritizing these elements, game developers can craft games that are not just interactive but also engaging and facilitate attainable gaming experiences for a broader audience and become a powerful strategy for creating a more inclusive design culture.

6.4 Conclusion

The preceding chapter has elucidated how the four AGE design heuristics can offer an approach for evaluating the AGE level of the interaction interfaces in your video game. These heuristics enable game developers to accurately identify both strengths and areas for improvement in their projects, thereby enhancing the likelihood of delivering a universally engaging gaming experience. It is essential for developers to act promptly and transparently on these findings, not just as a matter of quality assurance, but also as a strategic means of community engagement and fan service—if these have been used for collecting insights for your AGE evaluation. In doing so, they can foster a sense of value and involvement among their players, thereby enriching the overall attainability of the intended game experience.

However, the utility of these evaluations is contingent on effective communication of the findings. Transforming complex data into comprehensible insights is vital. Employing visually intuitive tools—such as charts, graphs, and other graphical elements—serves to demystify intricate data sets, rendering them more accessible. This enhances the intelligibility of key themes and insights, facilitating better decision-making processes for both designers and stakeholders.

By emphasizing both the evaluative rigor through AGE design heuristics and the transparent communication of those evaluations, game developers can ensure that players from diverse backgrounds feel respected and valued. Ultimately, this dual focus equips developers to create more engaging, accessible, and successful video games for a wide array of players.

References

1. Aarseth, E. (2001). Computer game studies, year one. *Game Studies, 1*(1), 1–15.
2. Aarseth, E. J. (1997). *Cybertext: Perspectives on ergodic literature.* Johns Hopkins University Press.
3. Barone, E. (2016). Stardew Valley, Chuckelfish.
4. Bellotti, F., Berta, R., & Gloria, A. D. (2010). Designing effective serious games: Opportunities and challenges for research. *International Journal of Emerging Technologies in Learning (IJET), 5*(SI3), 22–35. https://doi.org/10.3991/ijet.v5s3.1500
5. CD Projekt. (2015). The Witcher 3: Wild Hunt. CD Projekt.
6. Cliffe, J. (2012), Counter-Strike—Global Offensive. Valve Corporation.
7. Deterding, S. (2018). Alibis for adult play. *Games and Culture, 13*(3), 260–279. https://doi.org/10.1177/1555412017721086
8. Engström, H. (2020). *Game development research.* University of Skövde.

9. Frasca, G. (2003). *Simulation versus narrative. The video game theory reader* (pp. 221–235).
10. FromSoftware. (2015). Bloodborne. Sony Computer Entertainment.
11. Fujibayashi, H. (2017). The Legend of Zelda: Breath of the Wild, Nintendo
12. Fullerton, T. (2019). Game design workshop: a playcentric approach to creating innovative games. 4th edition CRC press.
13. Gay, G., & Ralston, M. (2021). *Accessibility in serious game design* (Vol. 24). Scopus. https://doi.org/10.1017/s0958344012000183
14. Jooyaeian, E., & Khoshsaligheh, M. (2022). Translation solutions in professional video game localization in Iran. *Games and Culture, 17*(7–8), 1054–1074.
15. Krippendorff, K. (2005). *The semantic turn: A new foundation for design.* CRC Press.
16. Lazy Bear Games. (2018). Graveyard Keeper, tinyBuild.
17. LightSpeed & Quantum Studio. (2018). PUBG Mobile, Krafton, Tencent and VNG Games.
18. Mahatody, T., Sagar, M., & Kolski, C. (2010). State of the art on the cognitive walkthrough method, its variants and evolutions. *International Journal of Human-Computer Interaction, 26*(8), 741–785. https://doi.org/10.1080/10447311003781409
19. McGonigal, J. (2011). *Reality is broken: Why games make us better and how they can change the world.* Penguin.
20. Miyamoto, S., Yamauchi, H., & Tezuka, T. (1985). Super Mario Bros. Nintendo Entertainment System. Nintendo.
21. Miyazaki, H., Zin, N., Ishizaki, J., Kimijima, Y., Hirai, S., & Yoshida, H. (2011). Dark Soul I, From Software.
22. Miyazaki, H., Zin, N., Ishizaki, J., Kimijima, Y., Hirai, S., Yoshida, H. (2014). Dark Soul II, From Software.
23. Miyazaki, H., Zin, N., Ishizaki, J., Kimijima, Y., Hirai, S., Yoshida, H. (2016). Dark Soul III, From Software.
24. Mukhtar, Q. (2020). A multimodal approach to video games and the player experience. *Social Semiotics, 30*(5), 743–745. https://doi.org/10.1080/10350330.2019.1629524
25. Nealen, A., Saltsman, A., & Boxerman, E. (2011, June). Towards minimalist game design. In *Proceedings of the 6th International Conference on Foundations of Digital Games* (pp. 38–45).
26. Nintendo. (2017). Mario Kart 8 Deluxe. Nintendo.
27. Pathea Games. (2019). My Time in Portia, Team 17.
28. Persson, M. & Bergensten, J. (2009). Minecraft, Mojang.
29. Schatz, E., Cambier, R., Cambier, R. (2020). The last of us Part II, Naughty Dog.
30. Schell, J. (2019). *The art of game design: A book of lenses.* CRC Press.
31. Schonauer, C., Pintaric, T., Kaufmann, H., Kosterink, S. J., & Vollenbroek-Hutten, M. (2011). Chronic pain rehabilitation with a serious game using multimodal input. In *2011 International Conference on Virtual Rehabilitation* (Vol. 1, pp. 1–8). https://doi.org/10.1109/icvr.2011.5971855
32. Square Enix. (2016). Final Fantasy XV. Square Enix.
33. Super Evil Megacorp. (2014), Vainglory, Super Evil Megacorp & Rogue Games Inc.
34. Thorson, M. & Berry, N. (2018). Celeste, Maddy Makes Games.
35. Toh, W. (2019). *A multimodal approach to video games and the player experience.* https://doi.org/10.4324/9781351184779-2

Part III
Expanding the AGE Horizons Across Multiple Game Modalities

In the last part of this volume, we embark on a journey to further explore the frontiers of Attainable Game Experiences (AGE), with a keen focus on its applications across various game modalities currently having expansive growth and popularity. As the digital gaming landscape evolves, so does the need to ensure that these experiences are accessible and inclusive for a broader audience. Recognizing the growing ubiquity and diversity of digital gaming, the chapters within this part delve deeply into how Universal Design strategies can be harnessed to afford accessibility and inclusivity, irrespective of the modality and purpose of game participation.

Chapter 7 elucidates the principles behind "Universally Designed Game-Based Artifacts," offering insights into how game-like artifacts that harbor multipurpose for the participants can be crafted with a Universal Design approach that caters to the participants, regardless of their conditions or circumstances.

Chapter 8 moves into the immersive realm of "Universal Design in Extended Reality Games." Here, the complexities of designing for augmented and virtual reality experiences are examined, with discussions on contemporary best practices to ensure these emerging technologies remain inclusive and accessible.

Chapter 9 provides a deep dive into "Universal Design in Exergames," describing the undergoing fusion of physical activity and digital gaming. The chapter emphasizes AGE's unique challenges and opportunities within this game modality, focusing on creating exergames that are effective, engaging, and attainable for a broader audience.

Together, these three chapters underscore the versatility and adaptability of the AGE Universal Design philosophy, highlighting its potential to shape a more attainable game future for not just entertainment games but across a diverse range of game modalities.

Chapter 7
Attainable Game-Based-Artifacts—A Introspection of the Intersection of Fun and Function

Abstract In the last decade, the concepts "serious games" and "gamification"—ergo, game-based artifacts that harbor purposes that go beyond entertainment—have attracted increased public interest, acceptance, and adoption and have consequently undergone an exponential growth. Although with the growing prevalence and influence of these two game-based siblings in diverse areas such as sustainability, community engagement, corporate training, healthcare, governmental initiatives, and perhaps most consequential, formal education, it also becomes imperative to ensure that the "serious games" and "gamification" artifacts furnished experiences are attainable for its targeted audience. Simultaneously, these game-based concepts possess a multifaceted nature. Besides promoting an entertaining experience for the participants, they frequently encompass ideas that promote growth in participants' task performance, positively encourage sustainable behaviors, and stimulate the acquisition of new skills or the refinement of previously mastered competencies. Such utilitarian objectives differentiate game-based artifacts from the design space of traditional video games, as they must align with distinctive design directives and constraints postulated by their intended context. This chapter will comprehensively analyze the enablers and barriers that can impact your creation of game-based artifacts. Furthermore, it examines the appropriateness of serious games and gamification across varied scenarios and outlines strategies for crafting universally designed, inclusive games that cater to a broad audience. We aim to provide you with essential directions and insights to help you navigate these factors more easily and confidently. By doing so, you will be better equipped to produce top-quality game-based artifacts that are engaging and entertaining but also impactful, and effective.

Keywords Serious games · Gamification · Cognitive load · Accessibility · Inclusivity

A. Palmquist et al., *Universal Design in Video Games*, Human–Computer Interaction Series, https://doi.org/10.1007/978-3-031-30595-5_7

7.1 Within the Intersection of Function and Fun

Game-based artifacts serve as a potent medium, with data on the global player population highlighting the extensive influence and reach of digital gaming communities [70]. The burgeoning gamer population has warmly embraced the concept of utilizing video games and game-like artifacts [32], which has had an impact on a myriad of tasks and tools across a diverse range of contexts. Over the past couple of decades, technological innovations have increasingly incorporated design principles borrowed from entertainment gaming [38]. In the last decade, societal perceptions of activities traditionally categorized as either hedonic or utilitarian have undergone significant shifts. This change has blurred the boundaries between leisure and utility, allowing for a more nuanced understanding of the purposes behind various designs [40].

Game-based artifacts—such as serious games and gamification—have gained interest and momentum as these boundaries continue to blur. They currently stand as prolific areas with one foot in the entertainment game industry and the other in domains such as sustainability, community engagement, corporate training, healthcare, governmental initiatives, and formal education, to mention a few. With the rise in popularity and frequency of game-based artifacts, some of which may not be used by choice by the participating individual, it is critical that their conveyed game experiences are accessible to the intended participants.

However, before providing directives on how to achieve this, we must first and foremost distinguish what a game-based artifact and approach are. A game-based approach blends gaming elements with the aim of enhancing the participants'[1] engagement in a particular activity within the game-based artifact, or a related activity. These games are designed with objectives that go beyond mere entertainment. Traditional analogue games like chess and other board games have long served multi-functional roles, often acting as catalysts for personal growth, skill acquisition, or educational learning [23]. The design reasons and goals for a game-based approach might vary, although the idea is that the design goal will be more engaging for the target groups and, thus, easily achieved for the provider [16, 62].

Game-based approaches may include card games, board games, video games, or elements of game design. In this volume, we separate game-based approaches into two categories: serious games and Gamification. However, we are well aware of the myriad of categories, subcategories, and definitions used, sometimes interchangeably, in both the academic community and among practitioners in the industry (See further discussions in Engström [23]; Staller & Koerner [69]; Treiblmaier et al. [73]) (Figs. 7.1 and 7.2).

---

[1] In this chapter and Chap. 9 we diverge somewhat from the previously used terminology Player, as in serious game, gamification and exergame the participant does not necessary regard themselves as players when interacting with these technologies.

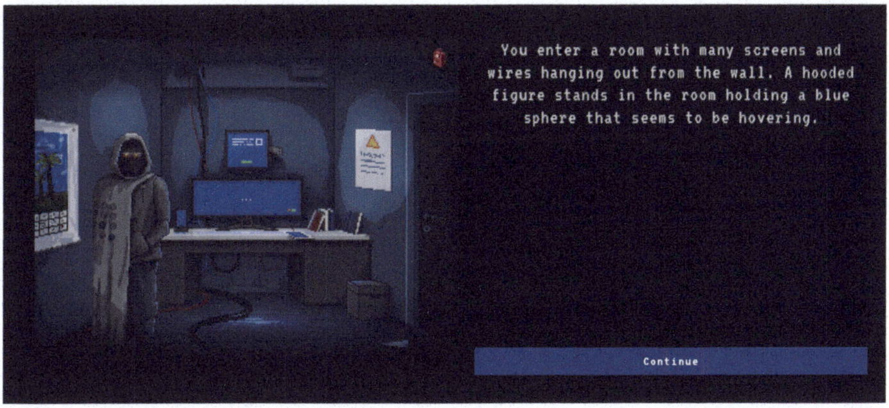

Fig. 7.1 The Chronicles of the blue sphere is a serious game designed for employer branding and talent acquisition using retro-pixel art and storytelling to attract software engineers interested in old-school RPGs. Copyright © [2021] by GWEN. This figure is reproduced herein with explicit permission from the copyright holder

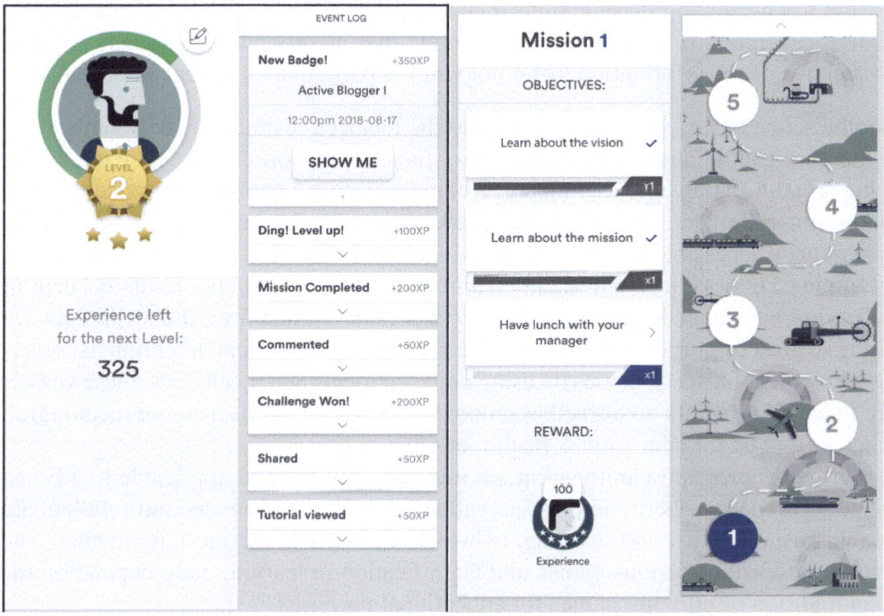

Fig. 7.2 Gamification designed for employer onboarding using game elements such as avatars, levels, points progression, and missions to facilitate newcomers to an international corporation. Figure from Palmquist [52] Permission: CC-BY-SA 4.0

What Are Serious Games?

Contrary to the name, serious games are not always focused on serious topics. Instead, they are games designed with a primary purpose that goes beyond entertainment. They find applications in various sectors, including healthcare, military training, education, and urban planning. The design of serious games involves a delicate balance of gameplay mechanics with non-entertainment goals to ensure that players remain engaged while committing to the additional alibi for play. Serious games deepen participants' insights into multifaceted human experiences. They create safe, controlled platforms for players to experiment with and navigate various aspects of social and interpersonal dynamics.

What Is Gamification?

Suppose serious games are complete games designed with a multipurpose that goes beyond entertainment. In that case, gamification involves taking game design elements—such as levels, badges, or avatars—and applying them to non-game contexts [20]. From community engagement for sustainability, health, and fitness to formal education and corporate training, gamification is used with the intention to engage and drive actions. Gamification design is often distinguished by its streamlined rules and gameplay frame that incorporate the already existing features of the information technology or the participant's virtual environments.

For the scope of this volume, delving into the nuanced distinctions between serious games and gamification is not our primary focus. Both approaches share the underlying principle that games—or elements of game design—can serve purposes beyond simple entertainment. Instead, our emphasis will be on strategies to make the gaming experiences accessible to a more diverse audience. Fundamentally, the underlying principle of both serious games and gamification is centered around the concept of delivering an elevated and engaging user experience. Therefore, the techniques for doing so must be purposefully designed to capture and hold users' attention. By leveraging on the mindset of games by using game elements and mechanics, these vessels are intended to create an attractive scope that the user regards as more meaningful, whether that be for educational, health, or other purposes.

Serious games and gamification are multidisciplinary and applicable to a broad range of domains where the most prevalent for both practitioners and scholars are health, sustainability, and learning, of which the latter is the most significant. The strong presence of serious games and Gamification in learning may depend on the long tradition of utilizing games for educational purposes [23].

Game-based learning currently stands as the most prominent field for these interactive artifacts, capturing the attention of both industry practitioners and academic scholars. This approach enjoys widespread adoption in formal educational settings, featuring a diverse array of specialized learning tools and platforms such as *Duolingo, Kahoot,* and *MinecraftEDU*, among others. These game-based learning platforms exemplify the rich variety of resources available for enhancing the educational experience.

Additionally, in the business landscape, organizations acknowledge and actively embrace serious games and Gamification as valuable tools for various corporate functions. Numerous international corporations have already integrated these gamified solutions into their workplace ecosystems [43]. These game-based technologies serve a myriad of purposes, ranging from expediting the familiarization process with newly acquired technologies [34] to streamlining employee onboarding procedures [54] and enhancing employer branding efforts [55]. The current discourse underscores the critical nature of Universal Design in serious games, scrutinizing potential challenges players may face in specific contexts. Furthermore, it explores the adaptability of serious games across diverse environments and presents strategies for the creation of universally accessible and inclusive serious games.

7.2 The Design Space of Game-Based Artifacts

In traditional game creation, the primary objective is often to captivate and entertain the player. In contrast, game-based approaches come with an added layer of "seriousness," which generally means they have educational, training, or other practical objectives beyond mere amusement. This added element of seriousness imposes specific requirements on both the development and gameplay, creating constraints that can have far-reaching consequences. For example, a serious game aimed at medical training must engage the player and provide accurate, valuable information and scenarios that mimic real world medical situations.

This dual demand for engagement and factual or practical accuracy creates a unique set of challenges for game designers, developers, and even players, who may have to balance the pursuit of in-game objectives with real-world learning outcomes.

While both regular and game-based artifacts aim to create engaging experiences, serious games and gamification have an added responsibility. They must also achieve specific, often complex, goals for a particular circumstance. This fundamental distinction influences every aspect of game-based development and gameplay.

The aim of accessibility in technology artifact design, as articulated by the World Wide Web Consortium in 2018, is to develop digital applications that are inclusive and accessible to as wide a range of users as possible. While games have been used for various purposes beyond mere entertainment since at least the 1970s [23], the field of serious games and gamification is experiencing not only robust growth in traditional areas and branching out into new domains, solidifying its influence and presence.

While entertainment is not the foremost priority in designing serious games and Gamification, it nonetheless plays a significant role. Despite their serious objectives, these games share a common lineage with their entertainment-focused counterparts in video gaming. Like an engaging video game, a well-crafted game-based artifact incorporates key design elements tailored to its specific context. These elements include purposeful decision-making opportunities and intriguing challenges. For instance, video games often revolve around engaging storylines. Striking a delicate balance between gameplay and skill acquisition in the game design potentiates participant engagement, making the learning experience compelling and immersive. Hopefully, the result is a learning experience that transforms instruction into an engrossing journey of discovery and personal development.

In contrast to conventional methods of information and communication, which often rely on the passive intake of information, serious games and gamification champion a more interactive and stimulating approach. They merge game-oriented design principles with intended user behaviors, aiming to produce a level of user engagement that surpasses traditional methods. Numerous theories and explanatory models have been developed to understand this phenomenon (for instance, see Krath et al. [39]). However, for the purposes of this text, the authors have chosen to focus on the psychological dimensions of hedonic and utilitarian aspects of technology to provide insights into these interactive platforms.

Van der Heijden [75] posits that the various attributes and characteristics of technologies convey either utilitarian or hedonic dimensions to users. Hedonic dimensions are designed with an emphasis on pleasure and enjoyment, typically related to leisure activities and home use. These systems aim for prolonged engagement and do not necessarily serve any external, practical goals. They are crafted to enrich the user's experience, providing intrinsic value through enjoyable interactions.

On the other hand, utilitarian dimensions are more task-oriented, focusing primarily on functionality and efficiency. These systems are often developed for business environments, where the ultimate objective is to enhance performance and streamline operations. In contrast to technology that embodies hedonic dimensions, where the perceived value is often related to enjoyment or pleasure, technology with utilitarian dimensions offers a more fruitful user-system interaction. In this context, the value lies in the system's instrumentality—its ability to facilitate tasks and enhance efficiency.

The distinction between hedonic and utilitarian has habitually been regarded as crucial because it informs the design, development, and evaluation of these artifacts. While hedonic artifacts strive for user engagement and satisfaction as measures of success, utilitarian artifacts aim for measurable improvements in task performance and operational efficiency. The distinction between hedonic and utilitarian dimensions also aids stakeholders in gaining a clearer understanding of the artifacts they are interacting with or deploying. As Köse et al. [40] point out, this differentiation helps clarify whether one is dealing with a "tool" designed for specific functions or a "toy" to provide enjoyment and entertainment. This nuanced understanding enables stakeholders to tailor their interaction or implementation strategies more effectively, ensuring that the technology is used in a manner most suitable for the particular needs and contexts at hand.

Adhering to Van der Heijdens' [75] concept of attributes and characteristics of technologies, it might be understood that entertainment games foremost act as a hedonic artifact created for leisure activities, while serious games and Gamification are often designed with foremost utilitarian purposes in mind.

Game-based technologies are inherently multidimensional, possessing both utilitarian and hedonic characteristics, as noted by Hamari and Koivisto [27]. The dominant design intent of technology determines whether it leans more toward a utilitarian or hedonic affinity. Utilitarian designs aim to bolster user performance and streamline task efficiency, while hedonic designs are engineered to enrich the user experience by making activities more enjoyable and engaging. The core goal of utilitarian design is to enhance productivity, while the central aim of hedonic design is to encourage prolonged usage [75]. Merging these utilitarian and hedonic design elements—particularly in the context of gamification—withholds an idea that the integration has the potential to yield a form of "prolonged productive use," wherein users are not only engaged over an extended period but are also more effective and efficient in accomplishing tasks. Crucially, the success of both serious games and Gamification is deeply rooted in the excellence of their design architecture. This is especially evident in how adeptly these designs incorporate multifaceted dimensions in terms of meaning and content [18, 21, 44, 49].

Designing serious games and gamification solutions that are better suited for individuals with specific conditions and circumstances adds a layer of complexity to the process. While many creators view this task as an added burden, the authors of this volume see it instead as an intellectual challenge. Moreover, they champion it as an essential element of "good design" (Fig. 7.3).

7.2.1 Gamification Design

When it comes to serious games and gamification, these multipurpose artifacts blend both hedonic and utilitarian design traits, necessitating a design and development approach that differs from creating "traditional" video games aimed solely at entertainment. A substantial body of literature exists on how to design and develop serious games and gamification, although a comprehensive discussion of this topic is beyond

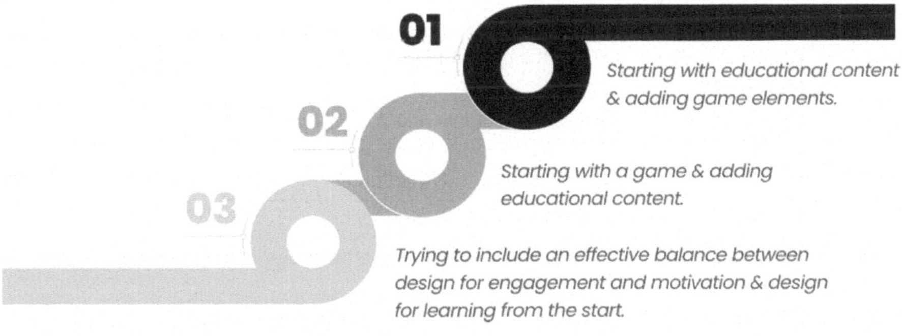

Fig. 7.3 Designing serious games and gamification solutions with attainable gameplay that still accomplish that artifact intent is a complex process

the scope of this volume. Nevertheless, offering some direction is pertinent, beginning with gamification. For an exhaustive list of frameworks related to gamification, one can refer to the systematic literature review by Mora et al. [49]. This review identified 40 unique design frameworks and sorted them into four primary domains: learning, health, business, and generic applications.

One prevalent design approach across these domains was User-Centered Design (UCD) [49]. UCD emphasizes understanding the user's needs, motivations, and behaviors at every stage of the design process, a construct that is embedded in Norman's [52] psychological/cognitive approach to design. This user-centric focus is essential for the success of any gamification project, as corroborated by further research, including a synthesis framework by Morschheuser et al. [51].

Recently, there has been a notable increase in the development of gamification frameworks that integrate multiple components to create a more comprehensive and inclusive design process [29, 51, 66]. These frameworks are designed to provide a more holistic approach to gamification, thereby enhancing the overall experience for users. Such frameworks aim to achieve the desired outcomes effectively and are gaining popularity among designers and developers alike. For instance, Morschheuser et al. [51] reviewed gamification design and development techniques and interviewed 25 practitioners to synthesize a comprehensive gamification design methodology. Based on the findings of their investigation, a seven-step process for gamification design was proposed (Table 7.1).

Regarding the skill set required for successful gamification design, experts in the field suggest that it necessitates a multidisciplinary approach. Knowledge of game design, behavioral science, and the specific context to be gamified are all essential [19, 38]. Furthermore, when the gamification is to be applied in a digital context, additional competencies in software development are required, including skills in software engineering, human–computer interaction (HCI), and information systems [51].

Table 7.1 Condensed overview of Morschheuser et al.'s [51] phases for engineering gamified software

Phases	Activity	Description
One	Project preparation	Establish a project plan
Two	User and context analysis	Analyze the context and Assess user needs and behaviors
Three	Ideation	Initiate ideation session(s)
Four	Design	Initiate ideation sessions
Five	Implementation	Decide, advise and manage the design of the implementation. Execute the gamification
Six	Evaluate success	Define if the objectives are met by the gamification artifact
Seven	Monitoring and management	Monitor the gamification artifact to better accommodate clients' needs (revise if needed)

The gamification design process has been considered "especially challenging" [28], as it compounds standard software development difficulties—such as prioritizing development tasks, time management, and limited team capacity—with unique risk factors, including skill deficits within the team, ambiguous project requirements, and insufficient standardizations [47].

In 2014, Landers introduced the Theory of Gamified Learning (ToGL), which posits that game elements should be carefully crafted based on various game attributes that significantly impact player behavior. According to Landers and his subsequent work with other researchers, these game attributes encompass diverse yet connected design dimensions (Table 7.2).

Applying attributes like the ones described above to specific game elements in the design is imperative for the implementation as it might lead to a myriad of processes that can affect participants' behavior and attitudes but not directly affect knowledge acquisition or skill development.

For example, in gamified learning environments, such as educational settings and training programs, participants do not directly acquire knowledge from the gamification artifacts themselves. Rather, the design of these gamified elements aims to

Table 7.2 Landers proposed game design attributes in ToGL

Game design attributes	Description
Action language	Refers to the mediums and interfaces that enable player-game interaction. An example would be integrating game console controllers into educational environments
Assessment	Pertains to methods used to evaluate achievements and track game progression. For instance, points can measure the quantity of correct answers in an educational exercise
Conflict/ challenge	Denotes the hurdles and challenges players face, such as teams vying for the most precise problem solution
Control	Highlights the player's ability to alter the game environment and the game's adaptive responses. For example, a student's choices could shape subsequent lessons
Environment	Represents the physical or digital spaces where players engage, from classroom settings to immersive 3D virtual worlds
Game fiction	Centers on the narrative and thematic components of the game. Traditional lessons might be reimagined as "adventures," weaving in storytelling elements like quests or mythical creatures
Human interaction	Examines the ways players interact, both in time and space
Immersion	Emphasizes the emotional and sensory depth players undergo, like replacing classroom boundaries with screens showing live imagery
Rules/goals	Involves presenting players with discernible objectives and milestones. This can be seen in detailed task guidelines or progress indicators showing task completion levels

modify the conditions surrounding the instructional content and context. The gamification design uses various game elements to influence participants' attitudes and behaviors toward both the content and the educational setting. The foremost goal is often to increase specific metrics, such as the amount of time spent engaging with the instructional material or participating actively in an environment. Landers et al. [42], gamification design consists of four fundamental constructs: Game Elements, Targeted Outcomes, Intermediary Individual Changes, and Personal and Situational Contexts (Fig. 7.4).

1. **Game Elements (Predictors)**: These encompass elements like storylines, points, and action languages, serving as initial triggers to spark specific outcomes. They can enhance user engagement, boost course completion rates, or promote energy-conserving behaviors.
2. **Targeted Outcomes (Criteria)**: These represent the ultimate objectives, whether it is heightened public engagement or a decrease in energy usage, which the game elements seek to realize.

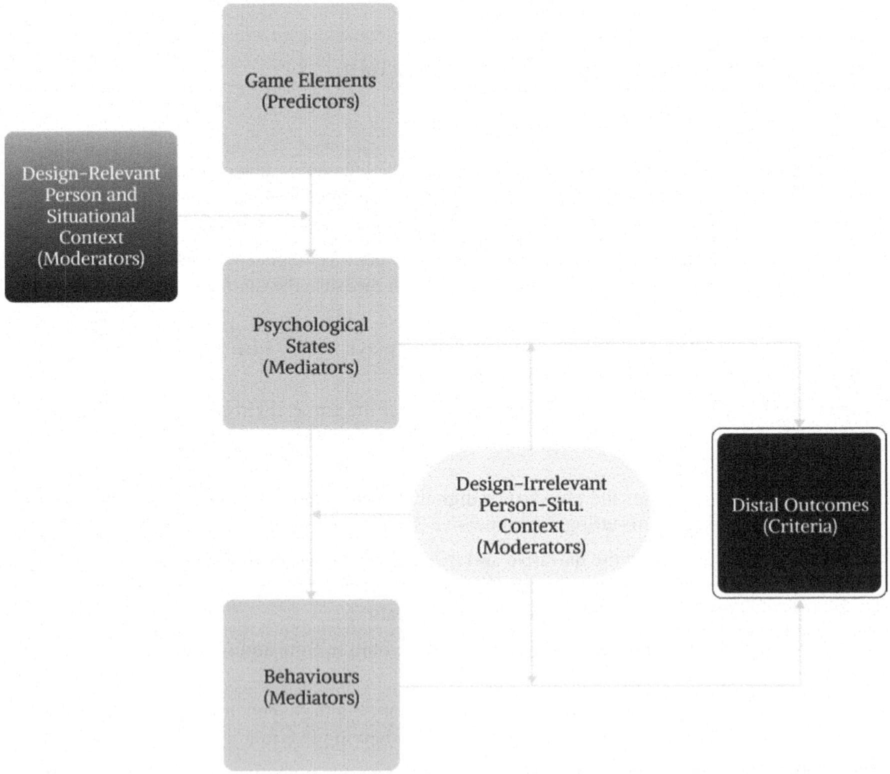

Fig. 7.4 A model illustrating the behavioral elements of gamification design (modified from Landers et al. [42])

3. **Intermediary Individual Changes (Mediators)**: These are the psychological and behavioral transformations in participants that connect game elements to the intended outcomes. As an example, a gamified academic program might focus on enhancing learning experiences, ultimately aiming to uplift graduation rates.
4. **Personal and Situational Contexts (Moderators)**: These are factors that can sway the impact of gamification techniques, taking into account participants' mental dispositions or the overarching environmental context.

Psychological and behavioral changes within individuals mediate the link between game elements and targeted outcomes. For example, a leaderboard may boost an employee's motivation to engage with training materials, enhancing their effort and leading to improved learning outcomes. Various moderating variables can influence this causal chain, including the context in which gamification occurs. The effectiveness of gamification can vary depending on individual participants and the broader situational factors.

The implementation context of the gamification artifact is crucial. Therefore, the gamification creators should outline the artifact after identifying the desired outcomes and relevant game elements to achieve them. Hence, it aligns with the specific context in which it will be used (See further Palmquist [57]).

Landers [41] suggests that a game element's influence is not confined to a single attribute; its impact depends on its design and the contextual factors affecting player behavior or attitudes. Thus, to create effective gamification, developers must carefully select game elements compatible with desired attributes. This requires a thorough understanding of the standards that must be met in order to ensure a successful outcome. By identifying the proper elements, developers can create engaging experiences that motivate users to achieve their goals and improve their performance. Gamification could be described as a frame that is implemented on a specific content in a system—a game frame. The game frame foremost aims to increase and/or decrease various user interactions with the system and its content, hopefully leading to a desirable usage of the artifact. It is important for the gamification designer to understand that gamification is very dependent on its structure and content (see further Reigeluth et al. [60]) regarding which outcome was desired for adding this "game frame."

Similarly, when gamification strategies are not properly balanced and overly emphasize either hedonic (pleasure-oriented) or utilitarian (functionality-oriented) elements, there is a potential risk that they may not effectively incentivize participation and engagement. In such cases, the implementation of gamification might not lead to sustained, productive usage or foster a sense of meaningful interaction with the platform or tool.

7.2.2 Serious Game Design

Regarding serious game design, in their comprehensive systematic review conducted by Ávila-Pesántez et al. [80], the researchers delved into the methodologies, frameworks, and models specifically applied to the design of serious games. Their analysis unearthed 11 distinct approaches commonly employed in this specialized area of game development. Furthermore, they identified an intricate process comprising 31 individual stages involved in crafting a serious game. These stages cover a wide range of elements, from initial concept development to the final stages of testing and deployment.

Notably, the study also shed light on the pedagogical underpinnings that influence serious game design. It discussed various learning strategies and educational theories that can be integrated into these games to make them more effective as teaching tools. Moreover, the research highlighted key factors that significantly impact the design process of serious games, possibly affecting their ultimate effectiveness and user engagement. Ávila-Pesántez et al. [80] serve as a valuable resource for anyone involved in the development or deployment of serious games. It offers a framework for understanding both the technical and educational dimensions, aiding in the creation of more effective and engaging serious games.

One of the most comprehensive approaches to the serious game is offered by Arnab and Clarke [4], which amalgamates frameworks and methodologies from four distinct application areas to construct a transdisciplinary hybrid model for game development. A key component of this hybrid model is the Mechanics Dynamics Aesthetics (MDA) framework, originally proposed by Hunicke et al. [31], which hails from the realm of game design. Another integral part of Arnab and Clarke's [4] hybrid models is the four-dimensional framework by De Freitas et al. [25], which is tailored for evaluating serious games and scrutinizing their design. Additionally, the hybrid model incorporates two other frameworks that span the development processes from pre-production through production to post-production.

Similarly, to the purpose of gamification, the fundamental objective of serious games is to disseminate important information, cultivate new skills, and induce behavioral change. Nevertheless, these game-based artifacts offer more conventional video game products in their approaches. They encapsulate a comprehensive game approach, intertwining the experiences with elements such as story, player journey, music, aesthetics, and interactivity. By doing so, they elevate content delivery to an immersive experience that has compromised several layers (Fig. 7.5).

Studies on game-based learning stress the significance of aligning game mechanics with instructional objectives to create effective *learning mechanics* in the serious game. This requires seamless integration of core tasks that players perform in the game with the learning goals [59]. The notion and approach are similar to Landers' [41] Game Elements Attributes in the ToGL model.

Serious games primarily aim to incorporate game design concepts in various domains. However, it is essential to note that serious games' foundational principles and objectives of serious games differ from those of traditional games. Therefore,

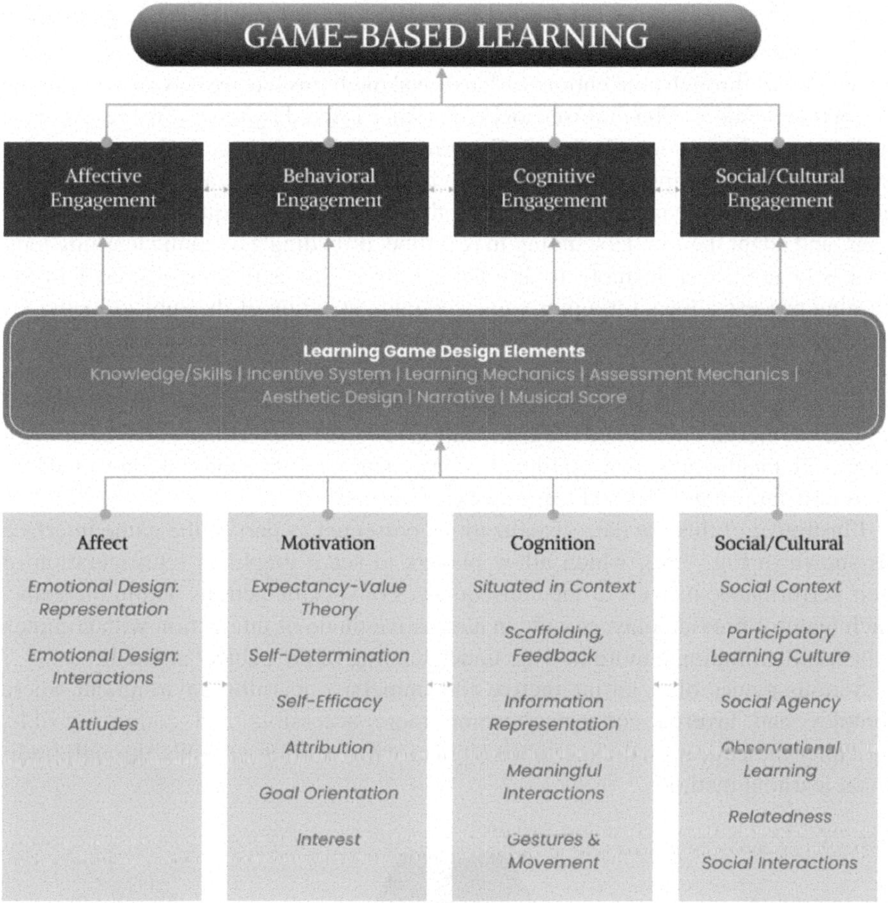

Fig. 7.5 An integrated framework for game-based learning design depicts various elements and mechanics useful for designing and elevating a serious game for instructional purposes (modified from Plass et al. [59])

direct transfers might not always be adequate and require adaptations [22]. This is because serious games aim to achieve educational, training, or therapeutic outcomes, while traditional games are designed for entertainment purposes. Therefore, the adaptation of game design concepts to suit the specific domain is crucial for the success and effectiveness of serious games, including the process of attributing the game mechanics in line with the context, making them learning/assessment mechanics. Nevertheless, although the creation process of regular games and serious games may differ, several of the game design directives in the AGE framework—especially from the Adjustable and Equitable Play heuristic—are also relevant for serious games. The design directives might include the possibility of adjustable interface components, modifiable input controllers, and alterable sound and graphical elements.

Through serious games, the interactive and immersive environment facilitates a deeper understanding of complex and nuanced concepts that may otherwise be difficult to convey through conventional educational mediums like textbooks, lectures, or instructional videos. The multisensory experience offered by serious games engages players on multiple cognitive levels, fostering retention and practical application of knowledge. For example, within a simulated game environment, a player can directly engage with theoretical principles, observe the immediate consequences of their decisions, and adapt their understanding in real time, providing a dynamic learning loop not easily replicated in more traditional settings. This active involvement in the learning process allows for a more nuanced understanding of the subject matter, as players can apply theoretical knowledge to simulated real-world challenges.

Moreover, the use of visual and auditory cues, as well as real-time feedback mechanisms within these games, contributes to enhanced comprehension and retention of complex subjects. The immediate gratification or corrective feedback offered through gaming elements motivates continued engagement with the material, thus enabling a more sustained and focused learning experience.

Illustrative of this are data visualizations presented as part of the game interface (as shown in Fig. 7.6.), which allow players to see a graphical representation of their performance metrics or the consequences of specific actions within the game. Such features provide players with an alternative mode of interaction with complex concepts, facilitating a more holistic understanding of the subject at hand.

Serious games offer an interactive and immersive learning environment where complex and layered concepts become more accessible and comprehensible, enriching the educational experience beyond what is often possible through traditional learning methods.

Fig. 7.6 Some of the claimed advantageous affordances that should compromise serious games

It is essential to address the challenges of developing game-based artifacts for their long-term viability and effectiveness. Developing serious games and gamification systems involves a substantial investment, often requiring a multidisciplinary team of experts ranging from game designers and developers to educational specialists and industry experts. Such a comprehensive approach is beneficial for the final product but can be resource-intensive, posing significant upfront costs.

Beyond initial development, the frequent updates necessary to maintain the relevance and effectiveness of these game-based solutions pose an additional financial burden. This is especially true in today's fast-paced technological environment, where software can quickly become outdated. The challenge extends beyond aesthetics or additional features; updates may be required to adapt to new research findings, compliance standards, or educational methodologies. Moreover, the constant need for updates could affect the affordability and, thereby, the accessibility of these tools, particularly for smaller organizations or disadvantaged communities.

The financial implications can be more nuanced when gamification is involved. Because gamification often integrates into existing systems—such as educational platforms or corporate training modules—any updates must also be compatible with those larger ecosystems. This adds another layer of complexity and potential cost.

To mitigate these challenges, developers of both serious games and gamification solutions can adopt a sustainable model that includes initial development and ongoing maintenance costs. Various funding strategies, such as public or private grants, partnerships, or subscription-based services, could be explored to make the projects financially viable in the long term.

Incorporating scalability and modularity in the design of both serious games and gamification platforms can also aid in reducing future costs. A modular framework would allow developers to update or adapt individual components without the necessity of revamping the entire system, thus providing a more cost-effective and agile approach to maintaining relevance. By planning for these financial challenges from the outset, both serious games and gamification initiatives can be designed to be more financially sustainable and broadly accessible.

7.3 Is the AGE Design Heuristics Right for All Game-Based Contexts?

Serious games and gamification find their application in diverse contexts, each necessitating the acquisition and mastery of particular skills performed in a specified routine. Therefore, your team must acknowledge these nuances during your serious games and Gamification design and development stages.

Consider the following scenario: A designer crafting serious games across various sectors might face challenges applying flexible design heuristics. The specific constraints dictated by these contexts require the participant to adhere to predetermined settings strictly. Failure to comply with these settings could make the participant ill-prepared for the real-life environments the Serious Game aims to reflect.

Take industries like the military, police, healthcare, fire services, maritime, and air-traffic control as examples. Each sector has unique protocols and practices that need to be adhered to, and straying from these can lead to serious real-world consequences.

For example, when developing a Serious Game for police officer training, it is crucial to design the game to familiarize participants with the adequate problem-solving procedures applicable to the specific law enforcement context. They must learn to adhere to specific tactical approaches and strategies, reflecting the real-world operational techniques of a police officer.

Similarly, in a healthcare-focused Serious Game, participants must follow specific medical procedures accurately, ensuring the game is not merely a hypothetical exercise but a practical reflection of the realities faced in healthcare settings. In a fire drill Serious Game scenario, the game must adhere to established fire safety protocols to develop crucial response skills for fire emergencies. In scenarios involving learning about corruption, serious games must integrate the corruption laws into gameplay to educate participants about the legal implications and potential repercussions of corrupt practices, helping to foster an understanding of ethical and legal conduct.

The serious games must accurately represent their respective real-world contexts to provide practical and applicable learning experiences. The serious games should not merely reflect the real-world environment but must also enforce the regulations and procedures that govern these sectors. Thus, serious games' design and development process must consider these unique characteristics and constraints to ensure participants acquire the intended skills and knowledge effectively.

It is crucial to remember that a serious game is not an exact replication of reality but rather a reflection of it. This distinction is fundamental as it underscores the game's purpose: providing a cost-effective learning and skill development platform. This reflection of reality is intentionally designed to be more accessible than the scenarios it mirrors or a simulation of it. It allows learners to experience and navigate challenging situations or complex processes within a consequence-free environment, which might be impossible, hazardous, or prohibitively expensive to replicate in the real world.

However, this simplified reflection also carries limitations. Only some aspects of reality can be fully encapsulated within the Serious Game context. Certain topics or situations need to be more complex to be accurately represented within the game framework. Ignoring this could lead to oversimplifications or misinterpretations, potentially detracting from the intended learning outcomes.

Therefore, while serious games offer an engaging and immersive learning environment, it is important to recognize their limitations and consider the subject matter and learning objectives when designing them. Doing so will help ensure they are effective, enjoyable, ethically sound, and contextually accurate.

Current understanding and recognition of the needs of staff members with disorders must be improved. This results in many of these individuals' facing disadvantages in the workplace [77]. Factors such as physical accessibility, provision of assistive technology, and discrimination or unconscious bias can present significant barriers. More comprehensive education and policy implementation are required for employers and colleagues to support and accommodate staff members with disorders. Simultaneously, there is a pressing concern regarding including and integrating students with disorders within mainstream education. Despite strides in inclusive education policies and practices, challenges persist. These include a lack of appropriate instructional modifications, insufficient teacher training, and inadequate peer support.

Furthermore, the question of resource availability is of paramount importance. Providing an inclusive educational environment is often resource-intensive, requiring specialized equipment, software, or personal aids. Additionally, teachers and support staff may require professional development and training to support learners with disorders effectively. Inclusive education is not merely a matter of physical integration but also requires an environment that promotes social and academic progress. Without sufficient resources, full and effective inclusion of disabled students in mainstream education will remain elusive.

The workforce and the educational system need to adopt a more holistic approach to disorders, focusing on both access and integration. Further, resource allocation must be prioritized to ensure that inclusion and integration are more than aspirational objectives.

7.4 AGE Directives for Game-Based Artifacts

As discussed above, the design process for gamification and serious games presents a complex, multi-layered challenge. These interactive platforms must delicately balance two objectives: engaging participants with an enjoyable, exciting experience while also serving as tools for learning or other specific purposes. To achieve this nuanced harmony, designers need to draw upon principles from various fields in conjunction with gameplay mechanics, thereby crafting a truly immersive and engaging environment. Given that Gamification and serious games can appear in a broad array of domains, serving functions beyond mere entertainment, this balance becomes all the more critical to achieve. Crafted to provide user engagement, gamification and serious games must cater not only to seasoned gamers and the casual players but also to those entirely new to the concept of games having multipurpose or the gaming culture.

In serious games and gamification, the challenge of crafting artifacts with better attainable experiences gains an additional layer of complexity. While designing games suitable for individuals with various disorders might initially seem daunting, reframing this as an essential aspect of responsible game design rather than an "extra" burden is important. The AGE directions and heuristics are especially critical when dealing with serious games and gamification, which aim not just to entertain but also to impart valuable knowledge or skills. This emphasizes ensuring that all facets of the game-based product—from gameplay mechanics and educational content to tutorials and user interfaces—are attainable.

For visually impaired participants, including those who are blind or nearsighted, designers can incorporate features like text-to-speech for game instructions or utilize haptic feedback as a substitute for visual cues. Audio descriptions could be employed to communicate crucial visual information.

For those with auditory impairments, visual or tactile elements can replace critical auditory cues. For example, subtitles or visual signals could accompany significant audio cues in a language-learning game, ensuring the information is accessible.

Individuals with speech disorders, such as apraxia, dysarthria, or stuttering—also require special consideration, especially in games where communication is vital to achieving objectives. In such cases, alternative modes of communication like text chats or symbolic gestures can be integrated to ensure inclusive participation.

Designers and developers of serious games and gamification can create a more inclusive environment by thoughtfully incorporating audio, visual, and tactile elements that cater to diverse sensory needs. This approach can help to ensure that all participants are able to engage with the content and derive maximum benefit from the experience (Fig. 7.7).

Moreover, when designing and developing game-based activities catering to individuals with cognitive and learning conditions, it is important to consider their unique needs and abilities. To best afford an attainable experience, the game-based artifact should incorporate customizable difficulty levels that can be adjusted to accommodate different learning speeds or provide step-by-step tutorials and optional hints

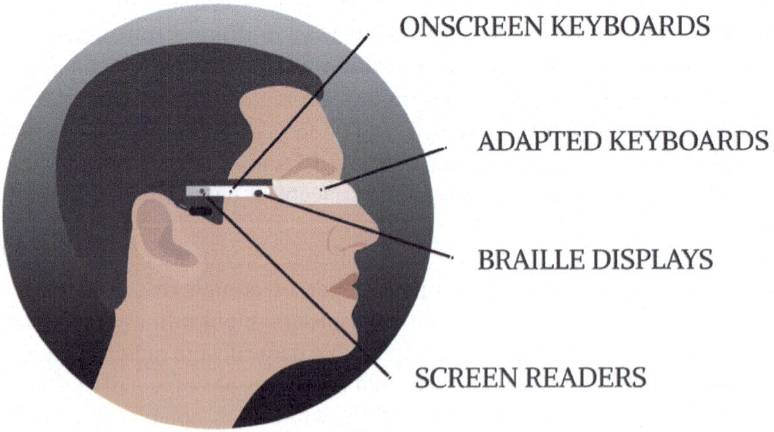

Fig. 7.7 By harnessing contemporary assistive technologies, game creators can broaden the attainability of game-based experiences

to aid those who struggle with attention, memory, language processing, reading, or reasoning. By providing these features, participants with cognitive and learning disorders can engage in a meaningful way and experience success in the activity.

Ensuring attainable gameplay experiences in serious games and gamification goes well beyond the mere mechanics of accessibility and inclusion; it also encompasses the richness of human diversity in all its forms. To truly resonate with a broad spectrum of players, the content within such games should be a tapestry of varied abilities, races, genders, and cultures. The goal is not just to create game-based artifacts that are playable by everyone but to build experiences that are deeply meaningful and relatable to each individual. By incorporating diverse characters, storylines, and scenarios, designers can offer players more than just a game; they can offer a mirror of the world in which we live. This reflection can be a powerful tool for empathy and understanding, allowing players to walk in the shoes of individuals who are different from them in significant ways. A diverse representation can facilitate a sense of belonging among players who might not often see themselves represented in digital media. This can be empowering and validating, enhancing the game's overall impact not just as a tool for learning or skill development but also as a catalyst for social change. A comprehensive approach to diversity can also extend to the challenges and objectives within the game. The tasks players must complete or the skills they must acquire could be designed to reflect a variety of cultural norms or values, making the experience more inclusive and educational.

Attainable gameplay in the context of serious games and gamification is a multidimensional concept. It is not enough to make a game accessible; it should also be inclusive in its narrative and objectives, offering a genuinely enriching experience that speaks to the diverse realities of its players. This level of detail enriches the educational and empathetic potential of serious games, making them more engaging to play and more impactful as tools for learning and growth.

The utilization of AGE heuristics is not merely an ethical choice but a critical one, particularly in serious games and gamification. Through thoughtful design that incorporates a variety of needs and preferences, serious games can become a powerful tool for inclusive education and skill development. The goal is to create experiences that are not only attainable but also deeply enriching, fulfilling the dual purpose of the game-based artifact to influence and engage. For the successful design of a universal game-based artifact, there are compelling reasons to involve various communities with disorders in the game's design process. These reasons extend beyond merely ensuring the game's usability and usefulness; they also encompass a range of broader social and individual benefits. By actively involving these communities, game developers can foster greater inclusivity, cultivate empathy, and challenge societal stereotypes. Additionally, developers should thoughtfully incorporate assistive technologies. These may encompass software features like screen readers or hardware devices such as adaptive controllers. Integrating such technologies can heighten the game's attainability, paving the way for an inclusive gaming experience. This proactive approach ensures that all participants can enjoy the game, regardless of their abilities or backgrounds.

7.5 Design Constraints for Game-Based Artifacts

When considering the game creation team organization, serious game and gamification development diverges from the conventions of traditional video game development. It necessitates a balance between embracing the artistic and aesthetic nuances of game creation and addressing organizational challenges [23, 22].

It is essential to underscore the significant differences between entertainment games and games with ambitions beyond amusement. Creating a successful video game for entertainment is a challenging feat, yet creating a satisfying gaming experience that should also have a fruitful impact on other dimensions and functions, such as the user's mindset and habits, is even tougher.

The body of knowledge concerning this type of game creation is fairly unanimous in stating that development must be carried out with an explicit and meticulously systematized strategy [58]. This should be done in collaboration with individuals knowledgeable in the subjects being conveyed, stakeholder groups having an interest within the implementation context of the game-based artifact, and at times—especially when dealing with game-based solutions for learning and training—people with experiences from the learning sciences.

The International Game Developers Association's Accessibility Special Interest Group IGDA GASIG [33] offers a comprehensive list of guidelines aimed at making games more accessible to a broader audience. While originally designed for entertainment games, many of these principles can be seamlessly adapted for game-based artifacts and several of them are more implicitly described in Chaps. 3–5. However, it is essential to note that these guidelines are not one-size-fits-all. Game designers and developers should interpret and implement these features based on the unique demands and objectives of the specific serious game or gamification approach they plan to implement. By doing so, they can create a more inclusive and accessible learning environment.

Moreover, in their study, Gay and Ralstone [26] argue that the discourse on serious games in formal education often overlooks the necessity of accommodating a diverse range of learners. While the term "diverse" primarily refers to learners with disabilities in this context, it also encompasses students for whom English is a second language, those using outdated technology, and individuals with limited internet access, among other scenarios.

These variables significantly impact how effectively a learner can engage with educational material. Beyond the basics of perceptual accessibility—ensuring that content can be seen, heard, or even touched—cognitive aspects also warrant attention for inclusivity. According to the Learning Disabilities, Access and Cognitive (LDAC) study (2020), elements like font and text spacing, the complexity of the visual environment (e.g., overly cluttered content), and potential distractions such as moving or flashing elements can all hinder a learner's capacity to absorb and understand the material.

Adaptability is vital to make game-based experiences attainable in the formal educational context. For example, students who have reading difficulties should be able to employ assistive technologies like Text-to-Speech (TTS) applications to convert text into audible content. When text is embedded in images or presented in multimedia formats that cannot be parsed by TTS technology, it erects a significant barrier for learners who are dependent on these tools. However, such challenges are often straightforward to overcome, merely requiring that text be presented in a format that is compatible with assistive technologies, as opposed to being locked in graphical representations.

Additionally, for students facing attention-related challenges like ADHD, certain design elements in game-based learning—such as particle effects, often referred to as "juiciness"—can serve as distractions rather than enhancements, thereby hindering learning and development. One prevalent concern is cluttered interface design, which can make it challenging for learners to locate crucial elements. Similarly, interfaces that divert attention away from important content can impair comprehension. Dynamic content, such as flashing advertising banners, can exacerbate this issue by drawing a student's focus away from the educational material, further affecting their ability to understand the content, as noted by the World Wide Web Consortium (W3C) in 2017.

Gamification and serious game implementation have several other factors directing their design space; we are going to address four of them in the upcoming chapters, but we feel a need to stress that there are several more to take into consideration depending on the setting and culture of the implementation.

7.5.1 Game-Based Artifacts and the Issue of Increased Cognitive Load

As stated previously, striking the right balance between entertainment and performance is crucial in creating game-based artifacts; this is particularly important when considering cognitive load. Cognitive load refers to the mental effort required to process information and perform tasks. While game elements such as rich visuals, interactive features, and dynamic feedback can enhance engagement, they can also impose an additional cognitive burden on the audience. A challenge that arises in association with the distractions that game-based artifacts might cause is the potential of increased cognitive load that they can place on the individuals using them. Cognitive load refers to the amount of mental effort and resources required to understand, navigate, and interact with the technology. As game-based artifacts have multipurpose cognitive load is crucial to concern as it might impede the purpose that goes beyond amusement.

In an academic study by Njå (in review), the performance of language-learning students in serious games was found to vary significantly. This variation was attributed to distinct elements in game design, particularly the level of "juiciness," which refers to the aesthetic richness and dynamic elements present in a game. In

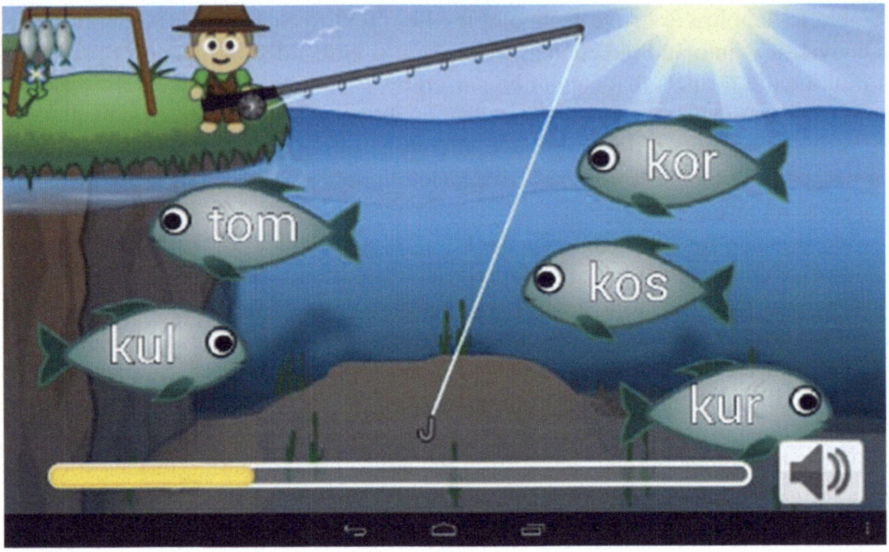

Fig. 7.8 One of the serious game modes comprising numerous elements providing the participant's stimuli that resonated imposed a high cognitive load on the participants. Figure from Njå et al. (in review). Permission: CC-BY-SA 4.0

the games being studied, items—in this case, words—were organized into two asynchronously moving clusters. Participants were tasked with forming words by tracking and combining these moving textual elements on the graphical interface. In game modes with higher "juiciness," both visual and auditory feedback were enhanced. These modes also introduced additional moving items and divided the interactive elements into two vertical zones on the left and right sides of the user interface (Fig. 7.8).

Participants playing in the "juicer" game models demonstrated longer response times, lagging by approximately one second compared to their performance in less juicy modes. They also exhibited lower accuracy rates in combining items to form words, as well as a reduced success rate in correct word formation overall. Njå and colleagues reasoned that the increased number of interactive items and amplified feedback stimuli contributed to a higher cognitive load for the participants. As a result, game modes with enriched feedback and more complex mechanics required more cognitive resources, which in turn likely led to the observed disparities in participant performance.

The theory of cognitive load plays a crucial role in various facets of AGE interaction interface design, particularly for game-based products with multifaceted purposes that transcend mere human pleasure-seeking. Consequently, this chapter will provide a detailed exploration and discourse on cognitive load theory. Understanding how to optimize cognitive load is essential for ensuring that game-based products are not only captivating but also pedagogically effective, making their intended full experiences attainable. The concept of cognitive load has longstanding roots in psychology, dating back to the 1950s. It underscores the idea that working memory has finite capacity—a notion first popularized by George Miller [48] in his seminal article, "The Magical Number Seven, Plus or Minus Two." Miller's work laid the foundation for our understanding of how limitations in working memory can impact learning and task performance. Miller argued that people could only hold about seven items in their working memory at once, although this number has been revised downward to around five [78]. This limitation is critical from a learning perspective, as overloading working memory can impair learning and hinder acquiring new knowledge and skills [37].

The concept of the cognitive load has proven incredibly useful in understanding how design choices impact performance, particularly in human–computer interaction (HCI) [12, 53]. The theory draws upon knowledge about learning that has been proven effective in the HCI field [50]. It provides insights into how various design decisions, such as the user interface or auditory elements, affect the users' mental process [71].

Cognitive load theory concerns how cognitive resources are directed and utilized during learning and problem-solving. Cognitive load refers to the total effort required for working memory. Given that working memory is limited, instructional designers must strive to reduce unnecessary cognitive load whenever possible. The central tenet of cognitive load theory identifies three significant sources of cognitive load. The first, intrinsic cognitive load, is caused by the inherent complexity and difficulty of the task. The second, external cognitive load, is caused by the task's presentation features, such as distractions or unnecessary information [12]. Finally, germane cognitive load is the effort required to learn and process information in a way that can be committed to long-term memory [71].

Drawing from the cognitive perspective and the principle of cognitive load, designing interaction interfaces of game-based artifacts that ensure adequate student comprehension without overwhelming them is crucial. Several didactic methodologies have been proposed to mitigate high cognitive load and bolster student growth within game-based learning contexts. For instance, Rosenshine [61] underscores the merits of "direct instruction" within game-based learning interfaces—this indicates that interaction interfaces should offer:

- Lucid explanations of primary concepts.
- Demonstrations of the intended behaviors or skills.
- Scenarios for both guided and autonomous practice.

Likewise, Coe et al. [14] emphasize the interface design's role in diminishing extraneous cognitive load. Game-based learning designs should:

- Minimize visual and auditory distractions.
- Convey critical information in a coherent and streamlined manner.

The cognitive perspective offers profound insights into human learning and information processing, highlighting working memory's constraints and the significance of adeptly managing cognitive load. When the interaction interfaces of game-based learning products are built upon cognitive science tenets, they can more effectively navigate these constraints, leading students to more fruitful learning outcomes.

The amount and complexity of information students are expected to learn can be overwhelming, leading to cognitive overload and decreased learning outcomes. Being aware of the limitations of cognition is crucial, as an excessive workload on working memory effectively renders learning impossible [37]. Recently, there has been an increasing discussion about the importance of considering students' cognitive load during the design and implementation of higher education courses [14].

Conceivably the most significant criticism of cognitive load theory in the learning sciences is the lack of a reliable and valid measurement method to detect, estimate, and assess it. Therefore, without an agreed-upon measurement method for determining cognitive load, the approach faces challenges in being recognized as reliable. Standardizing a comprehensive measurement method for assessing cognitive load has long been debated but has yet to be agreed upon. Researchers in the learning sciences often rely on subjective ratings, physiological measurements, or both to assess cognitive load.

Subjective ratings involve asking participants to rate their perceived level of mental effort or workload during a task using self-report measures such as the NASA Task Load Index (NASA-TLX) or the Subjective Mental Effort Questionnaire (SMEQ). However, subjective ratings are inherently limited since they depend on participants' ability to accurately report their mental effort, which may be influenced by attitude, motivation, bias, and personal stake. These factors can influence the accuracy of self-reported cognitive load, making it difficult to draw reliable conclusions from subjective ratings alone.

Physiological measurements are another approach to assessing cognitive load. These measurements include heart rate variability, electroencephalography (EEG), or pupillometry. Heart rate variability is the variation in time between successive heartbeats and is a beneficial physiological indicator of cognitive load. Electroencephalography (EEG) measures electrical activity in the brain and can be used to detect changes in brain waves associated with cognitive load. Pupillometry involves measuring changes in pupil size and is used to assess cognitive load based on changes in pupillary dilation, an indicator of mental effort. While physiological measurements offer a more objective approach to measuring cognitive load than the user's subjective ratings, they often require specialized equipment, which may not be practical or feasible in all contexts, such as real-world situations like the classroom. Additionally, these methods have difficulty differentiating between different types of cognitive load, for instance, intrinsic versus extraneous load.

To address the criticism that there is no standardized measurement method for cognitive load, researchers have proposed using multiple methods to obtain a more comprehensive understanding of cognitive load [53]. Others have suggested that researchers should focus on specific aspects of cognitive load, such as working memory load, to understand better how different mental efforts affect learning and problem-solving [71].

In HCI and UX, the concept of cognitive load is often used concerning evaluating the usability principles in the graphical interaction interface [24, 30]. In these strands, cognitive load is an often used theoretical lens for analyzing or interpreting the user's mental effort and/or the cognitive resources required to begin and complete a task in the user interface—not to analyze various strains on the individual's memory when acquiring a skill or comprehending a subject. Consequently, HCI has several more procedures that can be used to measure cognitive load beyond the approaches of subjective ratings and physiological measures, such as performance and observational measurement, as well as dual-task paradigms.

Performance measures are a commonly used method for evaluating cognitive load in HCI. These measures assess how well users perform a task and can be used to infer the level of cognitive load required to complete that task. The idea is that more mentally demanding tasks will take longer to complete, involve more errors, or exhibit more hesitation. The performance approach to cognitive load employs several agreed-upon variables. A generally employed performance measure is user response time, which refers to the time it takes a user to react to a stimulus delivered by the technology. The response time measurement variable is used in HCI research to infer the level of cognitive load required to interpret, commence, and complete a task [8, 53]. Other performance measures used to assess cognitive load in various human–computer contexts are "user error rate," "user hesitation," and "user memory facilitation in the technology configuration" [15, 64]. See Fig. 7.9.

These measures help evaluate the effectiveness and usability of technology interfaces and help designers identify areas where improvements can be made to reduce cognitive load, reduce the level of stimuli, enhance interaction interface usability by redesigning its intended trajectories, or increase the feedback cues to the players.

In designing interaction interfaces intending to increase the audience's attainability of game-based artifacts, obtaining an undemanding cognitive load assessment is key. By amalgamating various metrics—ranging from performance measures to subjective feedback and physiological markers—researchers can gain a holistic view of cognitive load in human–computer interaction (HCI). For instance, Bosch et al. [8] incorporated response time indices as a tool to gauge cognitive load within a game-based tutoring interface. Meanwhile, Cowley et al. [15] provided an overview of the prevailing methodologies used to measure cognitive load in multimedia learning interfaces. Such insights are crucial for fine-tuning the interaction design of game-based learning products to ensure optimal user experience. Seyderhelm et al. [65] evaluated cognitive load through Game-Task Difficulty. They employed three distinct metrics to measure cognitive load: time, accuracy, and accuracy of a secondary task. These results were subsequently consolidated into a comprehensive combined score.

Moreover, designing interaction interfaces for serious games or gamification for learning, it is even more vital to minimize the sources of cognitive load that are not essential to the learning process [53]. This may involve reducing the number of distractors in the game or presenting information clearly and concisely. Research has suggested that three to five options can be preferable to avoid overwhelming players with too much information [50]. Cowley et al. [15] argue that playing video games is not a simple task but rather a complex one that involves multiple cognitive processes simultaneously. They suggest that gaming experiences impose cognitive load on players in several ways. For example, players must make strategic decisions, react to unexpected events, and coordinate their actions in sequences. These activities require players to use their attentional and working memory resources,

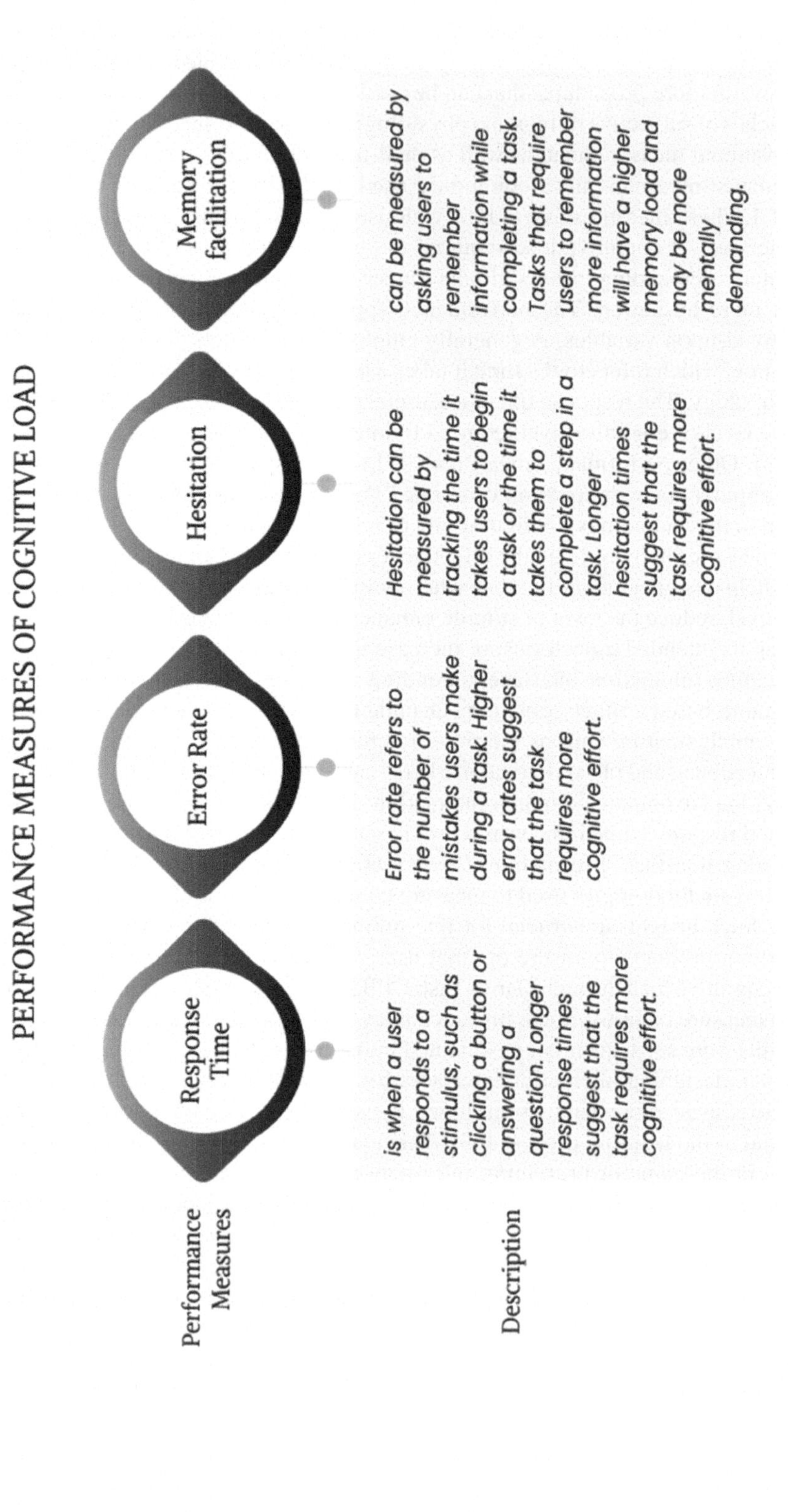

Fig. 7.9 Approaches to assessment cognitive load

leading to an increased cognitive load. Furthermore, Cowley et al. [15] suggest that the complexity of video games is wider than the game- mechanics and tasks that players are presented with. Instead, it also includes other aspects of gaming, such as social and emotional, like adapting to the social norms and expectations of the game's circumstances and handling emotions like frustration and enjoyment to hold affinities with other participants. These aspects impose a cognitive load on participants.

Additionally, in the context of multimodal technologies, it has been argued that the interaction interface providing clear feedback is essential for reducing cognitive load and ensuring users understand their actions' outcomes [46]. According to Mayer's [46] cognitive perspective on multimodal technology, user engagement with them can be broken down into a three-step process:

- **Step 1**: Users filter and select the information displayed on the game interaction interface.
- **Step 2**: The selected information is then structured into visual and verbal models within their working memory.
- **Step 3**: These models are then assimilated with pre-existing knowledge and with one another.

Adhering to this three-step process when devising an interaction interface, the designer might facilitate the user's learning trajectory and learning experience by focusing their attention on what actually matters in the game-based learning environment. Participation in a game-based learning environment should not concern understanding how to interact with the game technology—it is only the form that shall expedite personal growth. Interaction interfaces enabling users to quickly develop a familiarity and understanding of the features and frames of the multimodal learning technology might assist them in commencing their skill development more efficiently.

Understanding the basic concepts of cognitive load is a valuable tool for an AGE designer seeking to create a more attainable serious game and/or gamification tool. By minimizing unnecessary "white noise" within the interaction interfaces and providing straightforward user feedback, designers can decrease the cognitive load, assisting players in retaining the information of importance more effectively.

AGE designers aiming to apply the cognitive perspective to their video game interfaces should focus on identifying and evaluating the game elements contributing to the increasing cognitive load, which obstructs the processing of instructional content [59]. The focus could include determining the best practice to represent the content and designing learning mechanics that engage the learner to facilitate the intended cognitive outcomes [59].

Game creators must also consider the cognitive load experienced by the participants during gameplay, which is the cognitive demand of processing the meaning of various game elements [36]. While not directly in the context of game-based artifacts, yet, Mayer [46] recommends that creators of multimodal technology should aim to reduce unnecessary processing (extraneous), manage necessary processing (essential), and encourage investment of mental effort by the learner (generative processing). By doing so, the creators can effectively reduce the imposed cognitive load by the technology, facilitate skill development, and improve the learning experience.

It is clear that the allure of the cognitive load theory as a design principle for your video game's AGE design is compelling. However, we urge prudence in its application to your interface design. Research using the cognitive load theory in gaming often faces criticism for its settings, as many studies are conducted in experimental labs rather than real-world contexts [72]. Another point of contention is the comparison of games to other digital media delivering similar content [1]. Additionally, studies examining the cognitive load in gaming tend to focus on small sample sizes and short gameplay intervals [45, 59]. Appel et al. [2] highlight that the primary methodology to measure cognitive load in serious games revolves around behavioral and performance metrics.

On a positive note, in the HCI field, many researchers complement their studies with physiological indicators of cognitive load. Techniques include functional near-infrared spectroscopy (fNIRS), cardiac assessments, galvanic skin responses, and eye-tracking [2].

As previous research has deemed it essential to identify the game design elements that affect users' cognitive load [2, 46, 59], we propose design metrics for predicting cognitive load in the context of serious games and gamification artifacts. Specifically, it is important to examine the relationship between participants' reactions to elements utilized in the design.

7.5.2 *Various Stakeholders Having Conflicting Interest in the Game-Based Artifact*

To harness the potential of these game-based tools, it is paramount to champion making them not only attainable but also understandable for stakeholders other than the intended audience, such as teachers, managers, and procurement officers. Incorporating game-based tools, organizational culture, and norms into professional settings can be a challenging task due to the resistance of stakeholders. Palmquist [54] found that participants who were inexperienced with games showed increased hesitancy in adopting game-based technology for workplace learning. The intended participants and other corporate stakeholders interested in the game-based implementation often struggled to balance gamification's practical and pleasure-driven aspects. Users tended to resist overly playful elements and aesthetics, viewing them as hindrances to their learning journey.

Moreover, the organizational managers showed increased negativity toward the playful graphical aspects and gameful language, indicating these aspects to be too juvenile for the corporate context [17, 57]. A conceptual paper by Dale [17] recommends a more sophisticated approach to presenting and unpacking the game-based artifacts in more traditional workplace settings. Both Palmquist [57] and Dale's [17] conclusions imply that strategic implementation requires a deeper understanding of the corporate culture of gamification techniques to engage stakeholders and achieve desired outcomes effectively. Thus, in the format of the AGE Adjustable & Equitable Play tailoring the game-based artifact so they fit the specific circumstances and demographics, developers can increase the likelihood of making their game better attainable for the intended audience, achieving the desired outcomes, whether they are educational goals, skills development, or simply increase the user engagement and activity in the context. This level of customization is not just an added feature but a necessity for ensuring that the gaming experience is both meaningful and impactful for its intended audience.

In most settings, participants engaging in game-based scenarios generally are not doing so solely for the amusement of gaming; they have utilitarian objectives in mind. Likewise, the stakeholders who commission these game-based tools often expect them to serve a more utilitarian function, improving or replacing traditional processes.

However, the utilitarian focus should not overshadow the importance of making these game-based experiences attainable. Regardless of participants' conditions, abilities, technological expertise, or previous exposure to games and gaming, these resources should be designed to allow for comprehensive participation for everyone within the intended audience. Making such a commitment as a game creator goes beyond mere tokenism; it forms a cornerstone of the core design philosophy that shapes your game-based artifacts and, consequently, your brand's reputation. By adhering to the AGE Heuristics and incorporating design directives of the framework, your serious games and gamification products increase their potential user base and enhance the quality of the gameplay experience. In doing so, these artifacts can successfully fulfill their utilitarian objectives while excelling within the design space created for them.

7.5.3 *Technology Constraints in Game-Based Artifacts*

As described in Chap. 2, the available technology influences the design of the interaction interface based on its viability in the given context. The overarching design constraint, "Technological Constraints/Capabilities," takes on heightened significance when applied to game-based artifacts. It has been empirically shown that an organization's digital readiness—defined as the level of digital maturity an organization maintains for the successful implementation of digital tools, often highlights discrepancies between the organization's stated and actual preparedness for adopting digital artifacts (see further Carvalho et al. [11]; Chanias & Hess [13])—is a critical factor in the success of game-based implementations within that organization [35, 34, 57]. This preparedness not only enhances the efficacy of the game-based interventions but also contributes to more enriching and achievable experiences for the participants involved.

Studies have pinpointed technological limitations as a major hurdle in effectively deploying game-based initiatives. Specifically, research has indicated that the existing technological equipment and infrastructure within many organizations are often too antiquated to support seamless game-based implementations [35, 34, 43, 57]. The compatibility between the game-based technology and the organization's existing digital ecosystem is, therefore, a critical consideration [34]. Using outdated systems can not only hamper the user experience but may also compromise the data integrity and security associated with these implementations.

Moreover, Jedel and Palmquist [34] argue that disparities in technological access across different organizational groups can also impact the rollout and adoption of game-based initiatives. This underscores the importance of conducting a comprehensive assessment of the organization's digital landscape, factoring in variances in technological access among various departments, teams, or even individual employees. Such an assessment will enable organizations to develop a more tailored approach, thus expediting the endorsement and acceptance of these game-based interventions.

The "readiness" of an organization's digital infrastructure—as well as the accessibility of this infrastructure to employees—is paramount for the successful implementation of game-based strategies. Organizations should prioritize investing in up-to-date technological systems and ensuring equitable access to these resources as a foundational step in leveraging the full benefits of game-based learning or gamification.

This highlighting the critical role of digital readiness and technological compatibility in the successful implementation of game-based interventions aligns with the conclusions of prior empirical research. For instance, a study by Smy et al. [67] on game-based implementations reinforced the importance of a strong technological fit within organizational settings. Similarly, research conducted by Vanduhe et al. [76] on the intention to incorporate game-based solutions into Learning Management System (LMS) courses also emphasized that technological compatibility is a key determinant of success. Collectively, these studies point to a consistent theme: the successful incorporation of game-based technologies into an organization requires careful consideration of how well these innovations mesh with the existing technological environment. This underlines the importance of conducting comprehensive digital readiness assessments before undertaking such initiatives, as doing so can pave the way for more effective and sustainable implementations.

7.5.4 The Audience Demographics

In addition to being multifaceted, games that are outlined to offer an experience that is both engaging and productive within a given context must also be meticulously customized to suit the specific circumstances and demographics of the target audience. This means the design considerations extend beyond simply making the game enjoyable or educationally sound. Developers must delve into the nuances of the setting in which the game will be deployed, the age group it targets, the cultural background of the players, and any other relevant factors that could influence user engagement and the game's efficacy. For instance, a game aimed at educating elderly individuals about technology will likely require a different interface, pacing, and instructional guidance compared to a game designed for tech-savvy teenagers. Similarly, a game used for corporate training may need to incorporate industry-specific jargon and scenarios to make it contextually relevant and effective.

Within the intersection of Heuristics for Logical Play as well as Adjustable and Equitable Play, it becomes clear that the game creators must take their audience demographics into consideration, ensuring that the game-based artifact appears logical for them as well as being able to adjust to make it attainable. Audience demographics play a significant role in game-based learning, particularly when considering age. In order to create a fair and attainable game-based experience for the intended participants, it is vital to consider the specific needs and preferences of different age groups. By doing so, game developers can ensure that their games are accessible and engaging for everyone, regardless of age.

At the same time, the topic of age is deceptive in relation to games, and there is much bias surrounding it. Contrary to the prevalent notion that younger stakeholders are naturally more inclined to adopt game-based products due to their assumed familiarity with gaming, a body of research suggests that age may not be as pivotal a factor as once thought. Various studies have interrogated this assumption, casting doubt on the idea that age alone significantly influences the acceptance and integration of game-based artifacts in different settings [3, 7, 43].

Consequently, to effectively address the demographic challenges that may arise in making your game-based artifact more accessible and appealing, we strongly recommend adopting a participatory design approach. This method, which is thoroughly detailed in Chap. 3 of this book, engages potential users—across varying age groups and backgrounds—in the design process. By involving stakeholders early on and throughout the project's lifecycle, you can gather invaluable insights into their needs, preferences, and limitations. This participatory strategy not only allows for the tailoring of the game elements to the specific audience but also potentially increases user acceptance and engagement, regardless of age or prior gaming experience.

7.5.5 Game Literacy—An Important Consideration Applying Game-Based Experiences

Crafted to provide user engagement, Gamification and serious games must cater not only to seasoned gamers and the casual players but also to those entirely new to the concept of games having multipurpose or the gaming culture. Video games often act as an intercultural medium, providing a platform where a diverse group of players can engage, collaborate, and interact, creating a rich tapestry of shared experiences and interactions [10]. Different user groups appear to harbor varying perceptions regarding the merits and rationale of serious games and gamification. These perceptions are often shaped by their understanding—or lack thereof—of entertainment games and game-based learning, commonly referred to as "game literacy." The importance of game literacy is being increasingly recognized as a critical skill for the future. This is due to the already significant and continually growing interest in gaming among diverse demographics [79]. Game literacy is broadly understood as the comprehension of the essential nature of games, including their design elements and mechanics [63, 79]. Research suggests that individuals with a high level of game literacy are generally more open to and interested in engaging with game-based artifacts [5, 9, 34, 68]. This elevated interest likely stems from their nuanced understanding of how such systems operate, which in turn enhances their willingness to explore and adopt game-based solutions.

Research has indicated that various stakeholders—including procurement officers [56], adult learners [35], and managers [34]—have shown a lack of game literacy, particularly in the context of gamified workplace learning. This gap in understanding may influence the perceptions of game-based artifacts. Specifically, their views are often shaped by their direct interactions with the gamified design artifacts within a corporate learning environment. Conversely, another study found that when the stakeholder groups had high levels of game literacy, the focus of the discussion shifted toward personal preferences regarding the gamified training technology [55].

Drawing from the above body of knowledge indicates that introducing game-based artifacts into an organizational setting is not a simple "drop-and-go" operation, especially in environments with a prevailing skepticism or low levels of game literacy. In such cases, designers and developers have a crucial role to play in educating clients about the fundamentals of game design. This educational process not only fosters a more informed and nuanced understanding of how these game-based systems work but also helps to mitigate resistance or skepticism toward their implementation. By empowering clients with a foundational understanding of game design principles, designers and developers can facilitate a smoother, more effective integration of game-based solutions into the organization, thereby optimizing their utility and impact. The role of game literacy as a cornerstone in interpretation is further corroborated by game-based learning and its adoption in formal education [68].

Especially in the corporate environments, the intended participants' game literacy wields considerable influence over the interpretation and comprehension of game-based products. Individuals' advanced game literacy tends to engage in more in-depth discussion and debate regarding the artifacts' design nuances [57]. However, those lacking in this literacy might harbor misconceptions or reservations [3, 6]. It is pivotal to understand that possessing game literacy does not automatically translate to acceptance, but it does equip the participants with the tools to contextualize instructional gamification more effectively.

Incorporating game literacy as a guiding directive within the AGE framework and its heuristics aims to ensure that intended participants have a clear understanding of both the purpose and function of game-based artifacts, as well as the underlying game elements and mechanics. This heightened awareness can enhance engagement, optimize user experience, and ultimately contribute to the successful deployment of the game-based solution.

7.5.6 Game-Based Artifacts Contextualized via the AGE Framework

Applying the above discussion to the context of AGE it is obvious that that serious games and gamification initiatives have to operate under certain conditions that may not be present in traditional entertainment games. These conditions shape the design space process and often necessitate different approaches to ensure the intended purposes is achieved and that certain outcomes are fulfilled. From the four categories deliberated earlier we encapsulate that these challenges and considerations affecting three of the AGE heuristics: Logical Play, Adjustable and Equitable Play, and to some extent Fair and Flexible Play (Fig. 7.9). Although it should be noted that this painted with exceptionally broad strokes and might vary depending on the context of the implementation (Fig. 7.10).

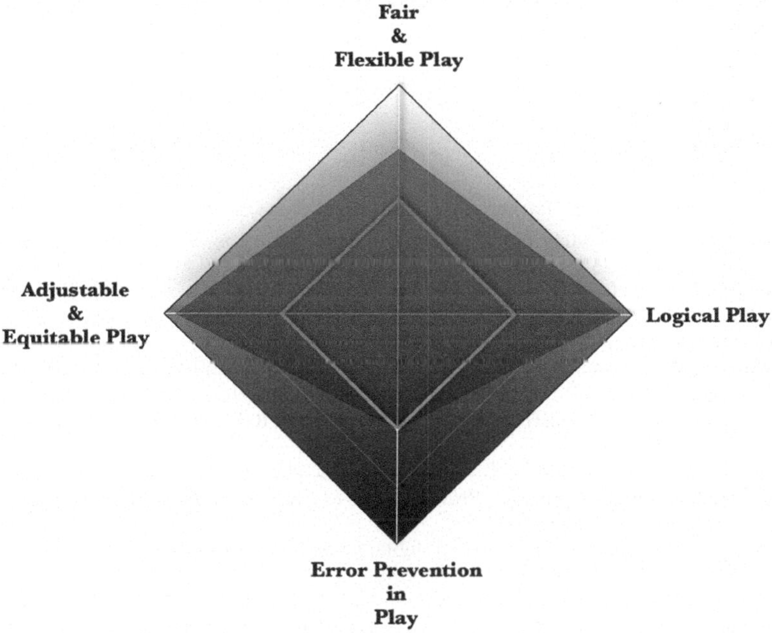

Fig. 7.10 Shadowed areas in the AGE matrix highlighting the heuristics concerned when employed within the design space of game-based artifacts

7.6 Conclusion

The future landscape of serious games and gamification is poised for substantial growth and transformation in the forthcoming years. This evolution is driven by groundbreaking innovations in technology, design methodologies, and diverse applications spanning various sectors as these game-based strategies gain traction and prominence, their potential as formidable learning instruments becomes more pronounced.

Looking forward, serious games and gamification find utility in diverse fields such as healthcare, military training, corporate training, and driving social change. Technological advancements, notably in virtual reality (VR), augmented reality (AR), and artificial intelligence (AI), are supercharging the experience and effectiveness of serious games. Contemporary games often harness adaptive learning algorithms, personalizing the user experience based on performance, learning pace, and individual preferences. This adaptability enhances their standing as potent educational instruments.

References

1. Adams, D. M., Mayer, R. E., MacNamara, A., Koenig, A., & Wainess, R. (2012). Narrative games for learning: Testing the discovery and narrative hypotheses. *Journal of educational psychology, 104*(1), 235.
2. Appel, T., Gerjets, P., Hoffman, S., Moeller, K., Ninaus, M., Scharinger, C., Sevcenko, N., Wortha, F., & Kasneci, E. (2021). Cross-task and cross-participant classification of cognitive load in an emergency simulation game. *IEEE Transactions on Affective Computing.*
3. Armstrong, M. B., Landers, R. N., & Collmus, A. B. (2016). Gamifying recruitment, selection, training, and performance management. In H. Gangadharbatla & D.Z. Davis (Eds.), *Emerging research and Trends in gamification* (Vol. I, pp. 140–165). IGI Global. https://doi.org/10.4018/978-1-4666-8651-9.ch007
4. Arnab, S., & Clarke, S. (2017). Towards a trans-disciplinary methodology for a game-based intervention development process. *British Journal of Educational Technology, 48*(2), 279–312. https://doi.org/10.1111/bjet.12377
5. Bacalja, A. (2022). A critical review of digital game literacies in the English classroom. *L1-Educational Studies in Language and Literature*, 1–28.
6. Baxter, R. J., Holderness, D. K., & Wood, D. A. (2017). The effects of gamification on corporate compliance training: A partial replication and field study of true office anti-corruption training programs. *Journal of Forensic Accounting Research, 2*(1), A20–A30. https://doi.org/10.2308/jfar-51725
7. Bittner, J. V., & Shipper, J. (2014). Motivational effects and age differences of gamification in product advertising. *Journal of Consumer Marketing, 31*(5), 391–400. https://doi.org/10.1108/jcm-04-2014-0945
8. Bosch, N., D'Mello, S. K., Baker, R. S., Ocumpaugh, J., Shute, V., Ventura, M., Wang, L., & Zhao, W. (2016). Detecting student emotions in computer-enabled classrooms. *International Joint Conference on Artificial Intelligence, 16*, 4125–4129
9. Brooks, A. L., Brooks, E., & Sylla, C. (Eds.). (2019, October 24–26). *Interactivity, game creation, design, learning, and innovation.* 7th EAI International Conference, ArtsIT 2018, and 3rd EAI International Conference, DLI 2018, ICTCC 2018, Braga, Portugal, Proceedings, Vol. 265. Springer.

10. Cairns, P., Power, C., Barlet, M., & Haynes, G. (2019). Future design of accessibility in games: A design vocabulary. *International Journal of Human-Computer Studies*, 131, 64–71.
11. Carvalho, J. V., Pereira, R. H., & Rocha, A. (2018). Maturity models of education information systems and technologies: A systematic literature review. *Iberian Conference on Information Systems and Technologies*, June, 1–7. https://doi.org/10.23919/CISTI.2018.8399339
12. Chandler, P., & Sweller, J. (1991). Cognitive load theory and the format of instruction. *Cognition and Instruction, 8*(4), 293–332.
13. Chanias, S., & Hess, T. (2016). How digital are we? Maturity models for the assessment of a company's status in the digital transformation. ePub Uni München. https://epub.ub.uni-muenchen.de/57622/
14. Coe, R., Rauch, C. J., Kime, S., & Singleton, D. (2020). *Great teaching toolkit: Evidence review.*
15. Cowley, B., Ravaja, N., & Heikura, T. (2013). Cardiovascular physiology predicts learning effects in a serious game activity. *Computers & Education, 60*(1), 299–309. ISSN 0361315. https://doi.org/10.1016/j.compedu.2012.07.014
16. Csikszentmihalyi, M. (2000). *Beyond boredom and anxiety*. Jossey-Bass.
17. Dale, S. (2014). Gamification. *Business Information Review, 31*(2), 82–90. https://doi.org/10.1177/0266382114538350
18. Dao, T. T., Tannous, H., Pouletaut, P., Gamet, D., Istrate, D., & Tho, M. C. H. B. (2016). Interactive and connected rehabilitation systems for e-Health. *IRBM, 37*(5–6), 289–296.
19. Deterding, S. (2015). The lens of intrinsic skill atoms: A method for gameful design. *Human-Computer Interaction, 30*(3–4), 294–335. https://doi.org/10.1080/07370024.2014.993471
20. Deterding, S., Dixon, D., Khaled, R., & Nacke, L. (2011, September). *From game design elements to gamefulness: Defining "gamification"*. Proceedings of the 15th international academic MindTrek conference: Envisioning future media environments, pp. 9–15.
21. Ding, Q., Stevenson, I. H., Wang, N., Li, W., Sun, Y., Wang, Q., Kording, K., & Wei, K. (2013). Motion games improve balance control in stroke survivors: A preliminary study based on the principle of constraint-induced movement therapy. *Displays, 34*(2), 125–131.
22. Engström, H., & Backlund, P. (2022). Serious games design knowledge: Experiences from a decade (+) of serious games development. *EAI Endorsed Transactions on Serious Games, 6*(1), 1–13.
23. Engström, H. (2020). *Game development research*. University of Skövde.
24. Feinberg, S., & Murphy, M. (2000). *Applying cognitive load theory to the design of web-based instruction*. 18th Annual Conference on Computer Documentation. IPCC SIGDOC 2000. Technology and Teamwork. Proceedings. IEEE Professional Communication Society International Professional Communication Conference an, pp. 353–360. IEEE.
25. De Freitas, S., Rebolledo-Mendez, G., Liarokapis, F., Magoulas, G., & Poulovassilis, A. (2010). Learning as immersive experiences: Using the four-dimensional framework for designing and evaluating immersive learning experiences in a virtual world. *British Journal of Educational Technology, 41*(1), 69–85.
26. Gay, G., & Ralston, M. (2021). Accessibility in serious game design (Vol. 24).
27. Hamari, J., & Koivisto, J. (2015). Why do people use gamification ser- vices? *International Journal of Information Management, 35*(4), 419–431. https://doi.org/10.1016/j.ijinfomgt.2015.04.006
28. Hassan, L., Morschheuser, B., Alexan, N., & Hamari, J. (2018). First-hand experience of why gamification projects fail and what could be done about it. *CEUR Workshop Proceedings, 2186*, 141–150.
29. Helmefalk, M. (2019). An interdisciplinary perspective on gamification: Mechanics, psychological mediators and outcomes. *International Journal of Serious Games, 6*(1), 3–26. https://doi.org/10.17083/ijsg.v6i1.262
30. Hollender, N., Hofmann, C., Deneke, M., & Schmitz, B. (2010). Integrating cognitive load theory and concepts of human–computer interaction. *Computers in Human Behavior, 26*(6), 1278–1288.

31. Hunicke, R., Leblanc, M., & Zubek, R. (2004). *MDA: A formal approach to game design and game research.* AAAI Workshop-Technical Report, WS-04-04, 1–5.
32. Huotari, K., & Hamari, J. (2017). A definition for gamification: Anchoring gamification in the service marketing literature. *Electronic Markets, 27*(1). https://doi.org/10.1007/s12525-015-0212-z
33. IGDA GASIG (2020). IGDA Game Accessibility SIG. Available at: https://igda-gasig.org/ (Accessed Febuary 14, 2024).
34. Jedel, I., Palmquist, A., & Gillberg, D. (2021). A practical view of gamifying information systems for the future. *International Journal of Gaming and Computer-Mediated Simulations (IJGCMS), 13*(4), 1–13.
35. Jedel, I., & Palmquist, A. (2021, April 28–30). Factors related to the use and perception of a gamified application for employee onboarding. In *Human Interaction, Emerging Technologies and Future Applications IV: Proceedings of the 4th International Conference on Human Interaction and Emerging Technologies: Future Applications (IHIET–AI 2021)* (pp. 653–661). Springer International Publishing.
36. Kalyuga, S., & Plass, J. L. (2009). Evaluating and managing cognitive load in games. In *Handbook of research on effective electronic gaming in education* (pp. 719–737). IGI Global.
37. Kirschner, P., & Hendrick, C. (2020). *How learning happens: Seminal works in educational psychology and what they mean in practice.* Routledge.
38. Koivisto, J., & Hamari, J. (2019). The rise of motivational information systems: A review of gamification research. *International Journal of Information Management, 45*, 191–210. https://doi.org/10.1016/j.ijinfomgt.2018.10.013
39. Krath, J., Schürmann, L., & von Korflesch, F. (2021). Revealing the theoretical basis of gamification: A systematic review and analysis of theory in research on gamification, serious games and game-based learning. *Computers in Human Behavior, 125*. https://doi.org/10.1016/j.chb.2021.106963
40. Köse, D. B., Morschheuser, B., & Hamari, J. (2019). Is it a tool or a toy? How user's conception of a system's purpose affects their experience and use. *International Journal of Information Management, 49*, 461–474. https://doi.org/10.1016/j.ijinfomgt.2019.07.016
41. Landers, R. N. (2014). Developing a theory of gamified learning. *Simulation & Gaming, 45*(6), 752–768. https://doi.org/10.1177/1046878114563660
42. Landers, R. N., & Landers, A. K. (2014). An empirical test of the theory of gamified learning: The effect of leaderboards on time-on-task and academic performance. *Simulation & Gaming, 45*(6), 769–785.
43. Larson, K. (2020). Serious games and gamification in the corporate training environment: A literature review. *TechTrends, 64*(2), 319–328. https://doi.org/10.1007/s11528-019-00446-7
44. Liu, D., Santhanam, R., & Webster, J. (2017). Toward meaningful engagement: A framework for design and research of gamified information systems 1. *MIS Quarterly, 41*(4), 1011–1034. https://doi.org/10.25300/misq/2017/41.4.01
45. Mayer, R. E., & Johnson, C. I. (2010). Adding instructional features that promote learning in a game-like environment. *Journal of Educational Computing Research, 42*(3), 241–265.
46. Mayer, R. E. (2014). Cognitive theory of multimedia learning. In R. E. Mayer (Ed.), *The Cambridge handbook of multimedia learning* (pp. 43–71). Cambridge University Press. https://doi.org/10.1017/CBO9781139547369.005
47. Menezes, J., Gusmão, C., & Moura, H. (2019). Risk factors in software development projects: A systematic literature review. *Software Quality Journal, 27*(3), 1149–1174. https://doi.org/10.1007/s11219-018-9427-5
48. Miller, G. A. (1956). The magical number seven, plus or minus two: Some limits on our capacity for processing information. *Psychological review, 63*(2), 81.
49. Mora, A., Riera, D., González, C., & Arnedo-Moreno, J. (2017). Gamification: A systematic review of design frameworks. *Journal of Computing in Higher Education, 29*(3), 516–548. https://doi.org/10.1007/s12528-017-9150-4
50. Moreno, R., & Mayer, R. (2007). Interactive multimodal learning environments: Special issue on interactive learning environments: Contemporary issues and trends. *Educational psychology review, 19*, 309–326.

51. Morschheuser, B., Hassan, L., Werder, K., & Hamari, J. (2018). How to design gamification? A method for engineering gamified software. *Information and Software Technology, 95*, 219–237. https://doi.org/10.1016/j.infsof.2017.10.015
52. Norman, D (1988). *The psychology of everyday things*. Basic Books.
53. Paas, F., Renkl, A., & Sweller, J. (2003). Cognitive load theory and instructional design: Recent developments. *Educational psychologist, 38*(1), 1–4.
54. Palmquist, A. (2023). Design elements of conflict: A design study of a gamified smartphone application for employee onboarding. *Technology, Knowledge, Learning, 28*, 1133–1173. https://doi.org/10.1007/s10758-023-09657-7
55. Palmquist, A. (2023). Stakeholders' design preferences for instructional gamification. *Behaviour & Information Technology*. https://doi.org/10.1080/0144929X.2023.2255905
56. Palmquist, A. (2021). *Lost in translation: A study of (mis)conceptions, (mis)communication and concerns when implementing gamification in corporate (re)training*. Proceedings of the 54th Hawaii International Conference on System Sciences. https://doi.org/10.24251/hicss.2021.166
57. Palmquist, A. (2023). *Plug & play? Stakeholders' co-meaning making of gamification implementations in workplace learning environments*. Dissertation University of Gothenburg Department of Applied Information Technology
58. Pendleton, A., & Okolica, J. (2019, November 27–29). *Creating serious games with the game design matrix*. In Proceedings of the International Conference on Games and Learning Alliance, Athens, Greece, pp. 530–539. Springer: Cham, Switzerland.
59. Plass, J. L., Homer, B. D., & Kinzer, C. K. (2015). Foundations of game-based learning. *Educational Psychologist, 50*(4), 258–283. https://doi.org/10.1080/00461520.2015.1122533
60. Reigeluth, C. M., Beatty, B. J., & Myers, R. D. (2016). *Instructional-design theories and models* (Vol. IV). Routledge. https://doi.org/10.4324/9781315795478
61. Rosenshine, B. (2012). Principles of instruction: Research-based strategies that all teachers should know. *American educator, 36*(1), 12.
62. Ryan, R. M., Rigby, C. S., & Przybylski, A. (2006). The motivational pull of video games: A self-determination theory approach. *Motivation and Emotion, 30*(4), 344–360.
63. Salen, K. (2007). Gaming literacies: A game design study in action. *Journal of Educational Multimedia and Hypermedia, 16*(3), 301–322.
64. Salvucci, D. D., & Taatgen, N. A. (2010). *The multitasking mind*. Oxford University Press.
65. Seyderhelm, A. J., & Blackmore, K. L. (2023). How hard is it really? Assessing game-task difficulty through real-time measures of performance and cognitive load. *Simulation & Gaming, 54*(3), 294–321.
66. Shahri, A., Hosseini, M., Phalp, K., Taylor, J., & Ali, R. (2019). How to engineer gamification: The consensus, the best practice and the grey areas. *Journal of Organizational and End User Computing, 31*(1), 39–60. https://doi.org/10.4018/JOEUC.2019010103
67. Smy, P. J., Donald, I., Scott-Brown, K., & Falconer, R. E. (2020). Digital training in the aeronautical industry: Measuring the usability of two mobile applications. *Frontiers in Computer Science, 2*, 22. https://doi.org/10.3389/fcomp.2020.00022
68. Squire, K. (2006). From content to context: Videogames as designed experience. *Educational Researcher, 35*(8), 19–29.
69. Staller, M. S., & Koerner, S. (2021). Beyond classical definition: The non-definition of gamification. *SN Computer Science, 2*(2), 88. https://doi.org/10.1007/s42979-021-00472-4
70. Steinkuehler, C. (2006, November 23). *Massively multiparticipant online games-based learning, M3-interdisciplinary aspects on digital media & education, workshop*. Wein, Austria.
71. Sweller, J., Ayres, P., Kalyuga, S., Sweller, J., Ayres, P., & Kalyuga, S. (2011). Measuring cognitive load. *Cognitive Load Theory*, 71–85.
72. Tobias, S., Fletcher, J. D., & Wind, A. P. (2014). Game-based learning. In *Handbook of research on educational communications and technology* (pp. 485–503).
73. Treiblmaier, H., Putz, L.-M., & Lowry, P. B. (2018). Research commentary: Setting a definition, context, and theory-based research agenda for the gamification of non-gaming applications. *AIS Transactions on Human-Computer Interaction*, 129–163. https://doi.org/10.17705/1thci.00107

74. Van der Heijden, B., Burgers, M. J., Kaan, M., Lamberts, B. F., Migchelbrink, K., Van den Ouweland, R. C. P. M., & Meijer, T. (2020). Gamification in Dutch businesses: An explorative case study. *SAGE Open, 10*(4).
75. Van der Heijden. (2004). User acceptance of hedonic information systems. *MIS Quarterly, 28*(4), 695. https://doi.org/10.2307/25148660
76. Vanduhe, V. Z., Nat, M., & Hasan, H. F. (2020). Continuance intentions to use gamification for training in higher education: Integrating the technology acceptance model (TAM), social motivation, and task technology fit (TTF). *IEEE Access, 8*, 21473–21484. https://doi.org/10.1109/ACCESS.2020.2966179
77. Waterfield, B., Beagan, B. B., & Weinberg, M. (2018). Disabled academics: A case study in Canadian universities. *Disordery & Society, 33*(3), 327–348.
78. Weinstein, Y., Sumeracki, M., & Caviglioli, O. (2018). *Understanding how we learn: A visual guide*. Routledge.
79. Zimmerman, E. (2008). Gaming literacy: Game design as a model for literacy in the twenty-first century. In *The video game theory reader* (Vol. 2, pp. 45–54). Routledge.
80. Ávila-Pesántez, D., Rivera, L. A., & Alban, M. S. (2017). Approaches for serious game design: A systematic literature review. *Computers in Education Journal, 8*(3).

Chapter 8
Universal Design in Extended Realities

Abstract The domain of extended reality (XR) has undergone considerable advancements and has brought forth an assortment of gaming experiences that cater to both hedonic and utilitarian contexts. In this chapter, we delve into the various aspects of XR technologies and explore their potential for making their highly immersive gaming experiences more accessible to audiences across diverse levels. We examine the technological innovations that have broadened the scope of XR and discuss its growing influence in the gaming industry. Moreover, we explore the remarkable impact of virtual reality (VR) on gaming, analyzing its potential for engaging players while highlighting the challenges it poses. Lastly, we outline the design directives and constraints for XR game applications that can be used by individuals with different conditions or those seeking to engage in such games. Finally, we emphasize the essentiality of accessibility and inclusivity in the development and deployment of XR game technologies, particularly in the gaming sector. Through this comprehensive overview, we aim to shed light on the multifaceted roles and transformative potential of XR in contemporary society.

Keywords Extended reality · Virtual reality · Augmented reality · Design directives · Cybersickness · Video game

8.1 A Brave New Reality for Game Creators

Extended Reality (XR) serves as a comprehensive term that encompasses Virtual Reality (VR), Augmented Reality (AR), and Mixed Reality (MR) while also leaving room for future developments and technologies in this rapidly evolving field. XR is not confined solely to these three realms. Instead, it represents any current or upcoming human–computer interaction that utilizes graphic technology combined with wearable devices. Moreover, arguments exist that XR should not stand for "Extended Reality." Instead, the "X" should serve as a placeholder for all emerging reality formats, as described by Rauschnabel et al. [27].

A. Palmquist et al., *Universal Design in Video Games*, Human–Computer Interaction Series, https://doi.org/10.1007/978-3-031-30595-5_8

At its core, XR aims to bridge the gap between the virtual and physical worlds, creating immersive experiences that can be seamlessly integrated into our everyday lives [27]. This technology has a broad reach, influencing various domains, from psychology to aviation simulations, demonstrating the enormous potential for inclusivity and development [27].

One industry that XR is currently transforming is gaming. By superimposing digital information onto the real world (AR), fully immersing participants in a synthetic environment (VR), or blending elements of both (MR), XR gaming takes participant engagement and interactive entertainment to unprecedented heights. These technologies allow gamers not just to observe but to interact with and influence the game environment, offering an unprecedented level of realism and immersion. XR gaming goes beyond visual engagement; it offers a multisensory gaming experience. Participants can touch, manipulate, and navigate digital objects and environments in ways that traditional gaming platforms cannot offer. This fusion of real and virtual worlds results in more immersive, engaging, and realistic gaming experiences, pushing the boundaries of gameplay and storytelling.

The advent of wearable devices, such as Head-Mounted Displays (HMDs), haptic feedback gloves, and motion-tracking sensors, has significantly enriched the gaming experience. These devices enhance the connection between the participant and the game, allowing for more intuitive and realistic interactions. In VR gaming, for instance, participants can navigate a digital world, handle virtual objects, and execute actions as they would in the real world. Similarly, AR games enable participants to interact with digital elements superimposed onto their physical surroundings, creating a unique blend of real and virtual gameplay.

XR gaming is not just about entertainment; it also opens new avenues for learning, social interaction, and therapeutic interventions. For instance, educational games can utilize XR to create engaging and interactive learning experiences, while multi-participant games can foster social connections among participants worldwide.

The potential for Universal Design in XR gaming is substantial. Given its ability to simulate various experiences—from replicating the adrenaline rush of skydiving to allowing participants to explore historical events firsthand—XR offers a level of accessibility previously unimaginable. This technology enables a broad range of gamers, irrespective of their physical abilities or geographical locations, to participate in shared gaming experiences.

However, along with its immense potential, XR gaming also presents particular challenges, such as cost, hardware requirements, and player comfort. As technology continues to evolve, developers are working to overcome these obstacles and make XR gaming more accessible and enjoyable for everyone. The impact of XR on the gaming industry is transformative, offering novel and exciting ways for participants to engage with digital content.

8.2 Virtual Reality

As it currently stands, Virtual Reality (VR) is the most prevalent form of extended reality. VR is typically described as an immersive, computer-generated experience that unfolds within a simulated environment, wherein the user is entirely immersed within an artificially constructed realm. Distinguishingly, in the context of VR, there is no direct interaction between the real world and this simulated reality; the user does not simultaneously engage with both the real and the artificial environments [4].

Various forms of VR exist, each providing different degrees of immersion and user engagement within the virtual world. The extent of the user's immersive experience can range from fully enveloping to somewhat detached, based on the type of VR in use. At the full immersion spectrum are Head-Mounted Displays (HMDs) which offer users a highly immersive experience by clearly delineating the physical world and the virtual environment. These systems provide a comprehensive sensory experience, immersing the user fully in a digitally generated world. VR allows for a significant degree of user engagement within the simulated environment [16].

Beyond the World of Entertainment

Advancements in VR technology have also led to the development of video mapping and 360-degree films. Video mapping transforms ordinary objects or rooms into dynamic 3D displays, allowing users to interact with their environment in novel and immersive ways. Similarly, 360-degree films place the user within a wholly digital environment, which can be either a live-action setting or a computer-generated world. This format offers a unique blend of traditional filmmaking and VR technology, enabling a level of immersion not possible with conventional video. In particular, the humanitarian sector has found significant use for VR 360 films due to their comparative affordability and efficiency in production. These films offer a powerful tool for storytelling and advocacy, transporting viewers into the heart of humanitarian crises and fostering a deeper level of empathy and understanding than traditional media formats.

VR Gaming—A Fast Developing Domain

VR gaming represents a significant and rapidly expanding Reality (VR) gaming has emerged as a groundbreaking and swiftly evolving facet of VR technology, fundamentally altering the landscape of video gaming as we know it [19]. Going beyond the two-dimensional plane of traditional video games, VR gaming engrosses players in a meticulously crafted, three-dimensional virtual environment that they can actively traverse and manipulate [28]. This transformative shift in gaming paradigms is fueled by refined and relatively cheap hardware such as Head-Mounted Displays (HMDs), also known as the VR helmet. The VR helmet technologies often come equipped with hand-held controllers with motion-tracking systems (Fig. 8.1).

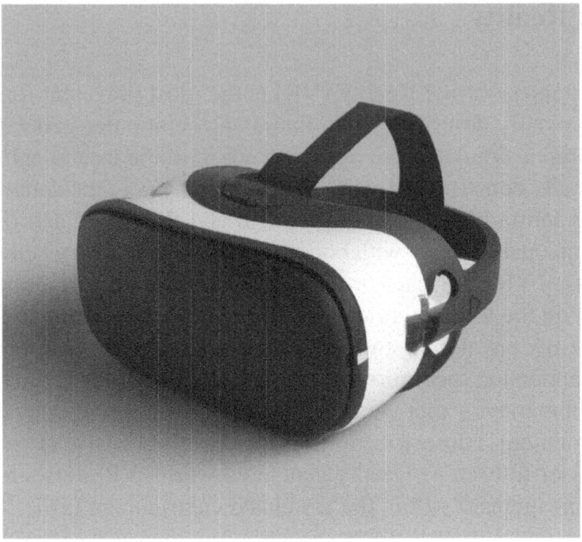

Fig. 8.1 A wireless VR helmet common in gaming

Notable examples of this type of equipment rigged for gaming include but are not limited to, kits Oculus Rift, PlayStation VR, and HTC Vive. These elements synergistically offer a holistic gaming experience that closely mimics real-world interactions. Gamers can navigate virtual landscapes, manipulate digital objects, and execute complex actions, all in a manner that mirrors their natural, real-world movements.

Further adding a tactile dimension to this immersive milieu are advancements in haptic technology. VR gaming systems often incorporate haptic feedback mechanisms that provide players with physical sensations, such as vibrations or resistance, corresponding to their in-game activities. This multisensory engagement significantly amplifies the player's sense of presence and immersion in the digital realm. In stark contrast to more traditional video aiming, which restricts players to the one-dimensional viewing space of a computer or television screen, VR gaming transcends these limitations by virtually inserting the participant into the gaming environment [2]. This is achieved by transforming the player's entire field of vision into an interactive digital canvas, escalating engagement to unparalleled heights. This offers a level of immersion that makes the boundary between the digital and the physical worlds increasingly porous, allowing for a more enriched and engaging interactive experience. VR gaming represents a monumental leap in the evolution of video gaming, offering a multisensory, interactive experience that traditional gaming platforms simply cannot match. Enabled by technological advancements in HMDs, motion tracking, and haptic feedback, VR gaming offers an extraordinarily immersive environment that captures not just the vision but the full sensorial attention of the player, further blurring the lines between the virtual and the real. It is becoming increasingly apparent that the potential of VR is vast and varied as it has significantly impacted the gaming industry. In recent years, we have seen the emergence of a wide range of VR games, from action and adventure titles to sports, racing, and even educational games. As technology continues to evolve, we can expect to see even more exciting and immersive gaming experiences in the future. VR's possibilities are exciting, and how this technology will continue to shape the gaming landscape in the future.

Potential Challenges for VR Gaming

Alongside the advancements of VR gaming, it also presents certain challenges, including cost, hardware requirements, and physical discomfort or motion sickness experienced by some participants [20]. As technology continues to evolve, developers are constantly seeking solutions to these issues, striving to make VR gaming more accessible and enjoyable for all.

VR technology has emerged as a transformative tool for individuals with physical conditions. By crafting immersive environments that mimic real-life scenarios, VR allows these individuals to transcend the constraints of their physical conditions, enabling them to broaden their horizons, acquire new skills, and shape their attitudes.

Through the medium of VR, people with physical disorders can immerse themselves in various activities, an approach that has been shown to improve motor skills, balance, and coordination in rehabilitation. This immersive technology offers a safe and controlled setting that minimizes potential harm or discomfort. According to Rueda [30], firsthand experiences facilitated by VR can lead to a deepened understanding and empathy, prompting societal change toward a more inclusive and compassionate society.

VR game creation stands out among the extended reality family due to it having gained significant traction in the indie gaming community [19]. It has reached a high level of technological sophistication and is poised for widespread commercialization. At this critical juncture lies a unique opportunity to embed principles of accessibility and inclusivity into the very foundation of VR game design and development. Establishing cross-industry standards and guidelines in this arena could set a benchmark for high-quality, accessible gameplay experiences. Such innovations have the potential to exponentially expand the medium's impact and reach.

8.3 Augmented Reality—Bridging the Digital and Physical Worlds

Augmented Reality (AR) serves as a fascinating intersection between the digital and physical realms. Unlike Virtual Reality, which immerses users in a completely virtual environment, AR allows simultaneous interaction with real-world and computer-generated elements. It accomplishes this by superimposing digital information—text, images, or 3D models—onto the user's real-world view through devices such as smartphones, tablets, or AR glasses Santos et al. [32].

In the Sphere of Digital Gaming
Regarding the gaming industry, AR offers an innovative approach by intertwining digital gameplay elements with real-world settings and components. For example, the hugely popular mobile game Pokémon GO is a textbook illustration of AR's capabilities. In this game, players traverse real-world locations to capture virtual Pokémon that appears on their mobile screens, overlaid onto their actual surroundings. This successful integration shows how AR can enhance player engagement, not by replacing Reality but by enriching it with a seamless blend of digital elements.

Enhancing Reality, One Layer at a Time
AR's unique selling point lies in its ability to augment our perception of Reality rather than replace it. It adds a new dimension to our experiences by introducing digital layers that interact with our physical environment. These layers can range from simple informational tags to complex, interactive 3D models, serving various functions from entertainment to education. By weaving together, the tangible and the virtual, AR offers a rich tapestry of experiences that can profoundly enrich our interactions with the world around us. Whether it is a history lesson coming to life through interactive AR timelines or a shopping experience enhanced by virtual try-ons, AR has the potential to revolutionize the way we engage with our surroundings. Augmented Reality serves as a transformative technology that enriches our Reality, opening up a realm of possibilities for enhanced interaction, immersion, and engagement. Its seamless fusion of digital and real-world elements holds the promise of shaping a multitude of industries, from gaming to education and retail, offering an exciting future brimming with untapped potential.

8.4 Mixed Reality—A Convergence of the Real and Virtual Worlds

Mixed Reality (MR) represents the next frontier in the evolution of human–computer interaction, taking the best of both Augmented Reality (AR) and Virtual Reality (VR) to create a unique experience. It fuses real-world and digital elements in a way that allows them to coexist and interact in real time. MR layers virtual information onto our actual environment, firmly anchoring digital graphics so they can interact meaningfully with real-world structures and objects Kang, [17].

Interaction Between the Real and Virtual Worlds
One of the notable features of MR technology is its capability to enable complex interactions between the real and virtual worlds. By utilizing refined sensing and imaging technologies, MR empowers individuals to actively engage with and manipulate physical objects and virtual elements that are present in their immediate surroundings. This unique ability to seamlessly blend the physical and digital worlds sets MR apart from its sibling VR, making it an innovative and exciting technology for video game creators. Imagine wearing a headset that allows you to interact with holograms in your real-world space using your hands or specialized controllers. This way, you can experience high game immersion without losing touch with your surroundings; you do not need to remove your headset to switch between the two realities.

A New Realm for Gaming and Beyond
In the context of gaming, MR offers a revolutionary experience that blurs the boundaries between reality and digital fantasy [23]. Picture a game where you could build a virtual fortress in your living room and then physically walk around it, viewing it from all angles and even interacting with its elements as though it were a physical structure. Alternatively, consider a scenario where game characters could "exit" your screen and roam your environment, responding to real-world objects and obstacles. The game evolves as you do, reflecting both your virtual actions and real-world choices, resulting in an unparalleled gaming experience that has the potential to redefine how players interact with digital worlds.

Expanding Boundaries
MR does not stop at gaming; its applications are boundless. From medical training simulators that allow doctors to practice surgeries in a controlled yet realistic environment to collaborative workplace solutions that blend physical and digital workspaces, MR is effectively erasing the lines that separate our digital and physical lives. Educational platforms can also benefit from MR, providing students with immersive, hands-on learning experiences that are otherwise difficult to replicate. Mixed Reality technology is more than just a new medium; it is a groundbreaking technology that can redefine our interactions with the real and virtual worlds. It stretches the boundaries of what is possible, enabling a rich, interactive experience that interests a wide array of industries, not only the game industry, with its entertainment games and game-based artifacts, but also education, healthcare, automotive, and beyond.

8.5 XR Game Design Approaches

While numerous human–computer interaction methodologies can be applied to developing XR systems, many researchers contend that achieving excellence requires addressing distinct design and implementation nuances unique to XR [31]. There is currently no comprehensive or dominant design approach in the domain of XR games; however, among the three strands that compose the XR technology design space. User-centered Design (UCD) and User Experience (UX) have a strong presence, being both fundamental aspects of design philosophy and evaluative methodology. There are, of course, other design procedures for XR games. However, as UCD and UX are both applicable and meaningful design lenses in the AGE interaction interface framework, they will be described more in-depth.

Game creators seeking to make their XR gameplay more attainable should begin by outlining the desired player activities and the XR game responses to the players' behavioral interaction. Before commencing the design investigation for the XR interaction interfaces, it is vital to determine which of the immersive environments is most fitting as VR, AR, and MR game systems offer different experiences as well as mandating quite distinct game creator skills. When this is accomplished, it follows two design sections: the first focuses on the XR game basics, and the second on the XR game specifics. The sections are recommended to be conducted simultaneously and iteratively in tandem with the design investigation for continuously informing the creation process (see further Chap. 3).

The first section follows the suggested approach by de Clerk et al. [43] for designing interaction interfaces specific to XR. de Clerk et al. [43] argue that a meticulous analysis of the intended context is paramount as a point of departure. Within the XR game design space, this involves delving into an understanding of the target audiences, deciphering their objectives within the XR game, and discerning the tasks they are projected to undertake within the XR in-game environment. For XR games, it also necessitates a contemplation of their potential "own" environments wherein they are anticipated to participate and immerse themselves in the gameplay. The first section is fundamental for understanding how to make your XR game experiences more straightforward for a diverse audience, as it creates a tentative roadmap for what you and your team need to address. After the first section, the creation process becomes more specific and detailed.

In the second section, the design process can focus on specific XR game design patterns and directions to ensure genuine and immersive interactions. The process could involve attentively crafting spatial and behavioral dynamics, fostering naturalistic conversations, understanding multidimensional spaces, and providing navigation cues and spatial audio cues. The second section is not as fundamental as the first, occurring as an accompaniment with the overarching goal of leveraging the XR game's multidimensional capabilities to create a player-centric, attainable experience that minimizes discomfort or cybersickness.

These two design sections can be used as an initial design strategy for your interaction interface in the XR game environment. Assure that you aim to align your design with the outcome of the design investigation, ensuring it corresponds to players' expectations and thus enriches their overall gameplay experience to become fully absorbed in the XR environment.

Regarding XR evaluation, the ambition is to transcend the confines of "traditional" task-centric usability assessments to embrace a comprehensive range of metrics. Following the recommendation of Scapin et al. [33], the selection of the metrics should encapsulate dynamic, context-sensitive, and subjective elements of an individual's experience during interaction with the technology—in our case, the XR game. Multifaceted evaluation methodologies are indispensable for the progressive development of XR gaming technologies. However, there is currently a lack of specific evaluation tools dedicated to XR technology [5, 7].

Given the unique capabilities of XR game evaluations concerning multidimensional object interaction, locomotion, multimodal system output, incorporating visual, auditory, and haptic feedback, and collaborative XR game experiences in shared spaces would be exciting and yield meaningful assessments of XR games. Currently, however, no authorized and standardized methods exist [31].

The existing XR evaluation methods are multifactor usability methods divided into qualitative and quantitative approaches predicated on the user—in the context of the book, the player—involvement. The approaches originate from two standard usability evaluation methodologies: inspection methods—focusing on the XR game *artefact*—and player testing—focusing on the XR game *player*—a simplified conception of them is presented in Table 8.1.

To align with your XR game's goals, scope, and audience, you and your team should develop the appropriate protocols and benchmarks for the test sessions. If you are intrigued by the approaches in Table 8.1 but are unsure of how to begin, here is a basic outline for an assessment flow to measure the attainability of your XR artifact's gameplay and experiences. Naturally, this is within the context of the AGE heuristics, starting with:

(1) an XR game task analysis, followed by (2) an expert-led XR game inspection, then a (3) qualitative player testing for understanding the audience perspectives and thoughts on the XR games furnished experiences, interaction possibilities, and perceived affordances, and concludes with a (4) quantitative assessment to

Table 8.1 Common assessment approaches for XR environments

Evaluation form	Inspection methods: do not require players	Player testing: requires players
Qualitative	Heuristic evaluation Cognitive walkthrough	Focus groups discussion Interviews Observation Questionnaires Think-aloud approaches
Quantitative	Performance models • GOMS • KLM	Formative evaluations Summative evaluations

gauge attainability of the XR game experiences, what it requires regarding player performance, understanding, and condition.

While earlier chapters in the volume delved into optimizing video game systems through their interaction interfaces with a focus on screens, smartphones, mouses and keyboards, D-pad controllers, and eye-tracking, XR games introduce various interaction techniques, which are somewhat different from most video games, yet share some similarities with Exergames (Chap. 9).

Gesture recognition stands out as a cornerstone of interaction in XR environments, perhaps mainly in VR games. The gestures involve tracking and interpreting human movement and positioning to identify specific, meaningful gestures [37]. These gestures can be employed to select and manipulate objects, guide navigation, modify the environment, and execute contextually relevant commands. Thus, as an XR video game that operates within a multidimensional space, it is paramount to furnish players with interface compositions that are not only immersive but also integrate well with their circumstances for participation, making the XR experience attainable. The integration must guarantee that the digital and physical worlds coalesce smoothly, not only to provide players with a holistic and attractive gameplay experience but also to make the XR game participation secure and harmless. Designing with the game audience's personal space in mind must be prioritized so the XR game accommodates player interactions. If players find themselves in a space restricting movement or in-game actions, the interaction interface should proactively detect such limitations. The interface should then guide the player to relocate to a more suitable area before initiating or continuing with the gameplay—a feature in many VR games but far from all. Leveraging real-world environmental cues to inform players about spatial requirements enhances safety, making the interaction interface appear meaningful. See Fig. 8.2.

8.6 AGE Heuristics Design Directives for XR Games

XR offers promising new opportunities for improving accessibility, inclusivity, and customization in the gaming industry, benefiting a diverse array of players. With the capacity to create highly immersive, digitally enhanced environments, XR can be specifically tailored to meet individual requirements, radically altering the landscape of player-game interactions and overall game experiences.

One of the significant advantages of XR is its ability to cater to players with sensory impairments. For instance, it can accommodate visual impairments by adjusting game elements like color contrast and font size. For those with auditory impairments, XR environments can incorporate spatial audio cues, providing an additional sensory dimension to improve the gaming experience.

Furthermore, XR technology is equipped with an extensive array of motion controls. These can be adapted to align with the physical capabilities and comfort levels of individual players, thereby fostering a more personalized and inclusive gaming experience. The ability to adapt game controls to player's specific physical

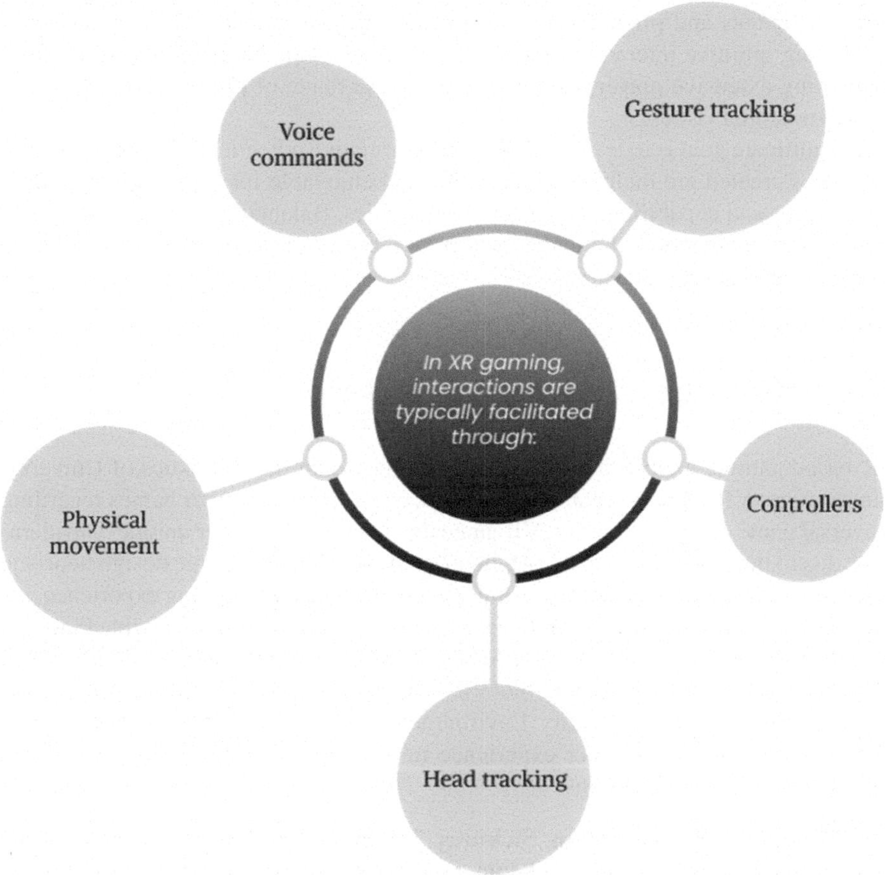

Fig. 8.2 Common interaction interfaces in XR games

capacities helps to create an environment where anyone can participate and enjoy the game, irrespective of their physical abilities.

Nevertheless, along with its significant advancements, XR introduces its own set of challenges to game accessibility. The complexity and novelty of XR technology can be daunting to some players, making the technology difficult to navigate and potentially discouraging participation.

Another critical issue is the risk of XR exacerbating existing accessibility problems found in traditional gaming or introducing entirely new ones. For example, XR environments often include fast-paced motion or intense visual effects. These elements, while immersive and thrilling for some, may pose difficulties for players prone to motion sickness or sensory overload. This could unintentionally create an environment that's stressful or even unplayable for these individuals.

Therefore, while XR technology has impacted the gaming industry, its potential issues should not be overlooked. Game designers and developers must understand these challenges and proactively work toward mitigating them. This would entail developing intuitive interaction interfaces, creating adaptable gaming settings, and conducting extensive player testing with a diverse range of players to identify and resolve potential issues.

The ultimate goal is to leverage XR's transformative potential while ensuring that the games created are inclusive, accessible, and enjoyable for everyone, regardless of their physical capabilities or sensory sensitivities. Balancing XR's unique opportunities with its inherent challenges will pave the way for an exciting and inclusive future for the gaming industry.

8.6.1 AGE Design Directives for VR Games

VR-based gaming experiences offer potential regarding the Heuristics of Universal game design. VR shares similar challenges as consoles or computer games regarding universal game design. However, VR game development has other unique considerations due to the platform format [14]. In order to apply the five-game design heuristic proposed in this volume to achieve a universally designed VR gaming experience, we suggest adding the following directives, which have a basis in the Accessible Platform Architectures Working Groups "XR Accessibility User Requirements" (W3C, [39]), MetaQuest's "Designing Accessible VR" [6], University of Melbourne overview "Accessibility of Virtual Reality Environments" Normand, [25], and the authors joint teaching and practitioner experience in designing and developing VR-based games and similar applications.

1. **Mitigate VR Simulation Sickness Triggers**: VR can sometimes induce discomfort, nausea, and a phenomenon known as "cybersickness." To mitigate these effects, developers must create mechanisms to modulate elements that often trigger such symptoms. One such approach could be a "comfort mode," encompassing features like teleportation as an alternative to smooth locomotion or snap turning instead of smooth turning. Dynamic field-of-view adjustments can also help make the VR experience more comfortable, reducing cybersickness. Furthermore, developers must incorporate these features in a manner that is easily accessible, even in the middle of gameplay, enabling participants to control their experience effectively.
2. **Promote Accessibility for Varied Body Types in VR**: Given the wide range of physical abilities and ranges of motion among participants, developers need to ensure that VR gaming experiences accommodate this diversity. The directive means making input methods adaptable and flexible. Players should be able to adjust the VR environment's height according to their physical stature. Additionally, essential objects or interaction points should not be positioned in areas that are hard to reach. Striving for an environment that adapts to the participant rather than vice versa ensures a more inclusive gaming experience.

3. **Minimize Reliance on Motion Tracking and Head/Body Rotation**: While motion tracking and head or body rotation enhance immersion in VR, they can potentially alienate participants with limited mobility. Developers should, therefore, create alternative mechanisms for these participants. One possibility is to allow the use of controllers for movement. Additionally, offering seating options can ensure that the game remains inclusive and accessible to all participants. Inclusivity entails ensuring that everyone can enjoy the game to the fullest, regardless of physical capabilities.
4. **Field-of-View Adjustments**: A participant's comfort level can vary widely when it comes to the field of view. Some participants may prefer a wide field of view for enhanced immersion, while others may find that it contributes to motion sickness. Developers can cater to this diversity by allowing adjustments to the field of view. This flexibility allows participants to customize their visual experience, potentially increasing their overall play time by reducing discomfort. Providing a range of options for field-of-view adjustments can make the VR experience more enjoyable and inclusive.
5. **Maintain Essential Information Within the Participant's Line-of-Sight**: Participants must access vital information quickly and efficiently in VR. This requirement can be addressed by ensuring that HUD elements and other critical information are placed within the central field of view. Alternatively, developers could also employ auditory cues and other indicators to draw the participant's attention to essential off-screen events. By doing so, developers can prevent participants from missing crucial game information, thus improving their overall gaming experience.
6. **Facilitate Player Calibration and Ensure Device Independence**: One of the essential facets of player comfort and control in VR is the flexibility to recalibrate the game according to the participant's current position, focus, and orientation. In VR, aligning physical and virtual spaces is critical for an optimal gaming experience. This necessitates a calibration mechanism that is straightforward, intuitive, and accessible during gameplay, potentially as simple as a button press to reset the view or a more detailed calibration process to establish the play area, the participant's height, and tracking accuracy. Device independence underscores the need for these calibration features to function seamlessly across various VR headsets. This demands a comprehensive approach from developers while creating calibration procedures, considering different devices' unique capabilities and constraints. Adjustable zoom levels or focus are crucial for gamers with diverse visual capabilities. For instance, the game could offer features that allow players to magnify specific game sections or adjust the visual field's clarity to cater to conditions like nearsightedness or farsightedness. Ultimately, empowering players with the control to personalize their gaming experience to their comfort, preferences, and physical conditions is a key component of inclusivity in VR gaming.
7. **Support Multiple Locomotion Styles in VR Games**: Given the diverse range of participant preferences and physical abilities, VR games should support a variety of locomotion styles to cater to as many participants as possible.

Some participants may prefer traditional "stick" locomotion, where movement is controlled with the thumbstick on a controller. In contrast, others may find this causes motion sickness and prefer "teleportation" style locomotion, where the participant selects a point in the environment and is instantly transported there. Another option is "physical" locomotion, where the participant's real-world movements are translated into the game, but this may be tiring or impractical for some participants. By providing a range of options, developers can ensure that their game is accessible and enjoyable for all participants, regardless of their physical abilities or comfort levels.

8. **Provide an Option to Select a Dominant Hand**: VR games need to acknowledge and accommodate the fact that not all participants have the same dominant hand. For a truly inclusive gaming experience, participants should be given the option to select their dominant hand at the start of the game. This choice would influence controls, the handedness of in-game avatars, and other interactions within the game. By providing this option, developers ensure left-handed participants have the same smooth and intuitive experience as right-handed participants. Accomplishing this also helps in cases where a participant might have a disability or injury that affects one hand, as they can choose to use their other hand for primary interactions.
9. **Incorporate Adjustable Comfort Settings**: Besides the well-documented phenomenon of simulation sickness, other aspects of the VR experience can contribute to participant discomfort. These include the intensity of movement, speed, degree of visual effects, or the realism level of certain simulations. Developers can address this by implementing a variety of adjustable comfort settings within their VR games. By allowing participants to modify these settings, developers can mitigate potential discomfort and broaden the appeal of their games, making them more inclusive and accessible for individuals with different comfort thresholds.
10. **Enable Haptic Feedback Customization**: While haptic feedback can enhance immersion in VR games, its intensity can be off-putting or uncomfortable for some participants. By offering the ability to customize or disable haptic feedback, developers can cater to a broader audience. Participants who prefer a more tactile experience can opt for more intense feedback, while others who might find such feedback overwhelming can choose to reduce it or turn it off altogether.
11. **Assure Visual Clarity**: VR displays, due to their proximity to the player's eyes, necessitate clear, sharp visuals for an optimal experience. Developers should thus provide participants with options to adjust the VR display's clarity or sharpness. Visual clarity is particularly important for players who cannot wear their corrective lenses while using the VR headset, allowing them to enjoy the VR experience without visual strain.
12. **Ensure Compatibility with Assistive Technologies**: In the spirit of inclusivity, it is crucial that VR games be designed to work seamlessly with existing assistive technologies. For example, supporting text-to-speech technology can make a VR game significantly more accessible to visually impaired participants.

Accomplishing this not only extends the game's reach to a broader audience but also ensures that every participant has the means to engage fully with the gaming experience.

13. **Implement Regular Break Reminders**: Extended periods of immersion in VR can lead to both physical and mental fatigue. Developers can incorporate periodic break reminders into their VR games to address this. These reminders can encourage participants to take short breaks, manage their game time effectively, and maintain a healthy balance between their VR and real-world experiences. Ultimately, prioritizing participant well-being contributes to a more positive gaming experience and ensures the sustainability of participant engagement over time.
14. **Creating a Safe Virtual Environment**: A key aspect of player comfort and enjoyment in VR is the sense of safety. It involves both the game content and the physical environment in which the game is played. Ensuring that game content is suitable and non-threatening means avoiding unexpected, alarming events or visuals that may cause distress. This also extends to in-game characters and AI that should behave in ways that do not threaten or discomfort the participant. As VR involves movement within a physical space, safety also means preventing real-world accidents. This requires clearly defined in-game boundaries corresponding to the participant's real-world play area. To further enhance safety, developers can incorporate in-game alerts that activate when participants approach the edge of their play area or are about to encounter real-world obstacles. This can be achieved using advanced object and environment detection technologies or simpler mechanisms like player-defined play areas. The ability to quickly pause or exit the game is also an important safety feature.
15. **Implementing Easy-to-Read UI Elements**: The interaction interfaces play a critical role in VR games as they are providing crucial communication to the players facilitating interaction with the real world and the game world. However, due to the immersive nature of VR and the variety of display technologies used, UI elements such as text, icons, and indicators need to be designed with exceptional clarity. This means they should be large enough to read comfortably, with high contrast against their backgrounds, and appear at a comfortable distance for the player's eyes. To ensure accessibility for all players, developers should provide options to customize the UI. Participants should be able to adjust these elements' size and appearance distance according to their preference or need. Additionally, contrasting colors and simple backgrounds can make important information stand out more clearly and be easier to process. To further enhance accessibility, developers could consider offering a variety of UI themes or color schemes, including options suitable for participants with different color vision deficiencies.

The strategies and outlined above will enable you and your team to foster inclusivity, delivering a VR gaming experience that feels deeply personalized and meticulously crafted for your audience. By adhering to these guidelines, you can design a gaming environment that is both immersive and representative, resonating with a broad spectrum of players. Your audience will appreciate the relevance of the design, seeing themselves reflected in it, as the inclusive features will enable them to fully engage with the VR gaming experience, seeing their own desires mirrored within the game. However, remember that these are merely guidelines. The most effective method for ensuring accessibility lies in involving participants with diverse needs in your testing process as early as possible. This proactive involvement enables you to identify and address any potential accessibility challenges head-on.

8.6.2 AGE Design Directives for Mixed Reality Games

Mixed Reality (MR) games present a distinct set of opportunities and challenges for designers and developers striving to design inclusive and accessible experiences. Many of the principles discussed for VR gaming remain applicable to MR, but there are additional considerations unique to this specific context. Our knowledge base draws from several sources, including Microsoft's "Designing for Mixed Reality" (2020), Qualcomm's "Best Practices Guide for Mixed Reality" (2021), Stanney et al. [35] and our hands-on teaching and practitioner experience in the design and development of MR-based games and similar applications.

1. **Implement Environment Scanning**: MR games often require participants to move and interact within their physical environment. For this reason, MR games should implement comprehensive environment scanning tools to avoid real-world obstacles and create safer virtual environments. Safety alerts could be triggered when the participant is nearing a real-world obstacle.
2. **Support Indoor and Outdoor Participation**: Different MR experiences may be better suited for indoor or outdoor environments. Whenever possible, design your game to support both, or to work well within the constraints of different types of spaces.
3. **Ensure Privacy**: MR games can sometimes involve capturing images or videos of the participant's real-world environment. It is essential to ensure privacy by informing participants about this data collection, explaining how this data will be used and stored, and obtaining the necessary permissions.
4. **Consider Lighting Conditions**: MR experiences can be influenced by real-world lighting conditions. For a consistent and accessible experience, developers need to ensure that the game visuals are clear and visible under various lighting conditions.
5. **Optimize for Different Devices**: MR games can be experienced on various platforms, from smartphones to sophisticated headsets. Each of these devices has different capabilities and constraints, and the game needs to be optimized to work well on all of them to ensure broad accessibility.
6. **Implement Intuitive Controls**: In MR, participants interact with the game using natural movements and gestures in the real world. These controls should be as

intuitive as possible, and the game should provide clear feedback on the participant's actions. Additionally, consider offering alternatives for participants who may have limited mobility or other physical constraints.

7. **Context-Aware Design**: MR games do not control the environment in which they are played. This means that developers need to design flexible experiences that can adapt to a wide variety of contexts. This includes considerations such as different room sizes, outdoor and indoor environments, and the presence of other people in the space.

Remember, these are just directives. As always, we recommend that the most effective way to ensure accessibility is to involve participants with diverse needs in your testing process as early as possible. That way, you can uncover any potential accessibility issues and address them directly.

8.6.3 AGE Design Directives for Augmented Reality Game

AR games present unique opportunities and challenges for game designers and developers who aim to craft inclusive, accessible, and tailored experiences. While many of the principles we suggested for VR and MR gaming remain relevant, AR brings forth a distinct set of considerations, particularly involving mobile devices. Therefore, we propose the following guidelines to aid in the creation of AR games that embrace both accessibility and inclusivity:

Robust Environment Recognition
To accomplish engaging and interactive augmented reality experiences, your game must understand the player's real-world surroundings in-depth. This requires sophisticated environment recognition technologies to identify surfaces (through plane detection) and objects (using object recognition) and understand the spatial depth to place virtual elements accurately. By ensuring your game can interact seamlessly with various environments, you reduce the risk of breaking immersion due to technological limitations.

Adjust for Lighting Conditions
Given that AR involves layering virtual elements over the real world, lighting conditions can drastically affect the visibility and realism of your game. Designing your AR elements to adjust according to real-world lighting conditions is crucial. This might involve brightening virtual elements in low light, reducing glare in bright light, or using real-time shadows to create a sense of depth and realism. Players can tailor their AR experience to their specific needs or preferences by providing manual settings.

Ensure Clear Visuals and Readability

Text and other visual interface elements overlay the real-world view in AR. These elements should be clear and easy to read against a variety of backdrops and in different lighting conditions. High-contrast colors can help elements stand out, while drop shadows can provide further distinction against busy backgrounds. Additionally, allowing players to adjust text size, brightness, or contrast can ensure a more accessible and personalized experience.

Provide Intuitive Interaction Methods

Interaction methods should be natural and intuitive to create a seamless gaming experience. This could involve physical movements, like pointing or tilting the device, or screen-based interactions, like swiping or tapping. For inclusivity, always offer alternative methods of interaction, considering players with varying physical abilities or preferences. For instance, options for touchless controls or voice commands can offer a more accessible experience for some players.

Respect Player Privacy

Since AR games often involve capturing real-world images or data, privacy becomes a paramount concern. Inform players why you need certain permissions and how the data will be used and stored. Wherever possible, minimize data collection to only what is necessary for the game. By building trust with your players, you foster a respectful gaming environment.

Optimize for Different Devices and Performance Levels

AR games can be played on various devices, each with its capabilities and limitations. Ensure your game is optimized to run smoothly across different devices, considering factors like display resolution, processing power, and battery life. By offering settings that allow players to balance visual quality with performance, you can cater to a wider range of devices and player preferences.

Allow for Flexible Gameplay

Given the nature of AR, players will interact with your game in a wide variety of environments. Your game should adapt to different conditions, whether played in a small room, noisy outdoor park, or a quiet office. This might involve allowing for gameplay that can be enjoyed in short bursts or over extended periods or offering options for sound notifications, subtitles, or vibration alerts to cater to different environments and player needs.

Consider Spatial Audio

Audio cues are essential in crafting an immersive AR experience and providing accessibility. Spatial audio, which gives the illusion of sound originating from a specific point in space, can be a powerful tool for guiding player attention and interaction within the game. However, it is essential to consider the potential for sensory overload or discomfort and provide the means to adjust or disable spatial audio. This way, you cater to a broader range of auditory sensitivities and preferences.

Allow for Pause and Save Functionality
Real-world interruptions can often be unpredictable. It is crucial to allow players to pause their AR experience at any point and resume where they left off. Incorporate a robust save system that enables players to retain their progress, even if they suddenly need to exit the game. This flexibility can drastically enhance the player's experience, especially during more prolonged or physically demanding sessions.

Implement Multimodal Feedback
Providing feedback through multiple visual, auditory, and haptic channels can significantly enhance immersion and accessibility in AR games. For instance, haptic feedback, which involves vibrations or tactile responses from the device, can provide a sense of touch that matches the visual and audio input, enriching the overall sensory experience. It also serves as a valuable accessibility tool, offering alternative cues for players with visual or auditory impairments.

Provide Detailed Interface Instructions
AR can often present a novel interaction paradigm for many players. Therefore, comprehensive instructions and tutorials are essential to familiarize players with the AR interface, interactions, and game rules. These instructions should be clear, concise, and easily accessible at any point during the game. Visual aids, such as diagrams or animations, can be beneficial in conveying more complex mechanics or interactions.

Consider Power Consumption
Given the computationally intensive nature of AR, power consumption can be a significant concern. Optimize your game's performance to be as power-efficient as possible, minimizing unnecessary processor or GPU load. This could involve simplifying graphical assets, optimizing code, or implementing smart power management systems that scale performance based on device capability or battery level. Also, notifying players about their device's low battery level can prevent unexpected game interruptions, ensuring a more consistent and enjoyable experience.

Adhering to these design directives, you will be well on your way to creating an AR game experience that is immersive, accessible, and considerate of a wider range of player needs and preferences. Certainly, the integration of digital and physical worlds in AR gaming surfaces complexities in the realm of property rights and has already sparked several legal disputes. These disputes are tied to varied representations of physical spaces within AR games, potential harm to public property, and trespassing or disturbances linked to in-game activities on private property. Thus, the development of AR games undeniably introduces new ethical challenges in areas such as intellectual property, privacy, and safety, calling for more comprehensive and universally applicable solutions. As AR games become more prevalent, a growing volume of data will be collected on players and their environments. This raises substantial privacy issues regarding data ownership, secure storage, and appropriate access Enyedy et al. [8]. Another concern is whether individuals can opt out of being recorded or having their surroundings scanned during AR gameplay. Copyright issues are also entering the fray. The immersive nature of AR games hinges on the ability to contextualize information through overlaying text, images, and game artifacts onto the real world. This has the potential to infringe upon the copyright owner's exclusive rights to reproduction and alteration.

In the game development sphere, the fusion of physical and digital spaces in AR gaming opens innovative avenues for monetization and player engagement. For instance, a game developer could partner with businesses to offer augmented experiences at specific locations, integrating curated content into physical spaces. However, the line between enhancing player experience and overstepping boundaries can be thin. Iconic landmarks or logos might be used as augmented markers within the game and altered to suit the game's narrative. This might lead to third parties using existing physical advertisements for their own gains, undermining original ad placements. At its worst, it could risk turning cultural landmarks into digital billboards cluttered with in-game elements Santos et al. [32]. These challenges underscore the importance of ethical and respectful game design when it comes to integrating AR technologies.

8.7 AGE Heuristics Design Constraints for XR Gaming

The cornerstone of developing a compelling XR game rests within the defined boundaries and established criteria of certain key design drivers. Two primary drivers significantly shaping the XR game design space are Technological Constraints/Capabilities and the Goal and Purpose of the Game. These drivers concurrently limit and enable the implementation of our universal game design heuristics.

Firstly, the heuristic, Fair and Flexible Play, which in the XR gaming context expands its focus by addressing the diverse body types, locomotion styles, and sensory preferences of the participants. Secondly, the heuristic Adjustable and Equitable Play, which in the XR gaming environment extends its scope to ensure that physical factors such as the effort, proportions, and spaces for participation can be customized. By considering and aligning these design drivers and heuristics, the game design has the possibility to promote a more inclusive, adaptable, and immersive XR gaming experience.

8.7.1 The Fair and Flexible Play Heuristic in XR Game Creations

The Fair and Flexible Play heuristic for the Universal Gaming Experience carries significant implications within the XR gaming context. The fundamental principle here is to provide multiple means of representation, thereby stressing the importance of flexible methods for presenting and conveying information.

In the XR gaming context, Fair and Flexible Play goes beyond the standard ergonomic features—such as visual cues, auditory signals, and tactile feedback—striving to make the game content widely accessible to a diverse range of game participants. It aims to level the playing field for the player, ensuring that XR games are enjoyable, irrespective of the participant's physical abilities, spaces, and circumstances.

The design drivers in the context of XR gaming stipulate the creation and incorporation of various input procedures to consider and cater to the various body types, locomotion styles, and sensory preferences so granular that even the participants' handedness is considered. The design driver, "Technological Constraints/Capabilities," is critical regarding Fair and Flexible Play; it assists you in ensuring that your XR game provides a comparable experience for a wide variety of participants enabling them to engage and execute the game tasks in a way that suits their conditions without undermining the quality of the game content. Still, even though XR Games have capabilities for a vaster inclusion than some Computer and Console games, they also come with constraints that must be recognized and adhered to in the game design and development process.

Besides its standard outlook, the heuristic of Fair and Flexible Play in XR gaming seeks to create an inclusive gaming environment where every participant, regardless of their physical, cognitive, or sensory abilities, can engage and thrive, challenging the game developers to implement creative and innovative interventions and solution specified by the determined XR game project's existing technological constraints and capabilities. By experimenting with relatively novel functionalities that XR harboring, affording, and fostering unique forms of interactions are achievable, which aren't readily achievable in the physical world, participants can delve into and push the boundaries of possibility.

8.7.2 Adjustable and Equitable Play Heuristic in XR Game Creations

The Fair and Flexible Play heuristic in XR encompasses the design elements of the XR gaming experience that directly infiltrate the player's realm. This heuristic inspires your development team to create diverse engagement methods, cultivating an environment brimming with options that pique interest, fuel persistence, and drive excitement around the gaming adventure. It transcends simple alternative control schemes or difficulty levels in XR gaming, focusing more on how players interact with and explore the XR game. It includes offering varying approaches to engaging with the game world, empowering players to select their preferred controls, and accommodating different play styles—casual or intense.

The essence of this heuristic is to allow players to exert their influence within the XR gameplay, augmenting their individual level of immersion and emotional investment. Through the thoughtful application of Adjustable and Equitable Play, designers can foster a more profound connection between players and the virtual environment, facilitating an experience that truly resonates with them.

Adjustable and Equitable Play advocates for a versatile gaming experience that caters to a wide array of players' needs, regardless of body size, posture, mobility, or available space. It accommodates the potential use of assistive devices or personal assistance, ensuring a universally equitable gaming experience. Its inclusive nature extends to guaranteeing that the XR game can be adjusted to provide ample space for participation and can adapt interactions based on the individual's specific circumstances.

This heuristic serves as a guide to providing players with a plethora of options to engage with the game according to their physical condition, cognitive capabilities, and available space for participation and interaction. Nevertheless, it is crucial to recognize that the actualization of the Adjustable and Equitable Play heuristic can be influenced by unique Design Drivers intrinsic to each XR platform.

Consider an AR game that takes cues from Pokemon Go within a pirate treasure hunt context. This Pirate Treasure Hunt game relies heavily on smartphone devices for input control, using features like the device's camera and GPS technology with a dual purpose: to stimulate physical activity among players and support local businesses by directing foot traffic toward them. The game design skillfully intertwines physical engagement and community enhancement, yielding captivating gameplay. However, the two objectives of the game—promoting physical activity and boosting local businesses—showcase the intricate interplay between the Adjustable and Equitable Play heuristic and the specific Design Drivers of the AR game. In such a setting, indiscriminate application of the Adjustable and Equitable Play heuristic could lead to players hoarding treasures, overpowering their competitors, and dominating the leaderboard. This scenario could disrupt the equilibrium and camaraderie within the gaming community.

In this regard, the thoughtful implementation of this heuristic is vital, making necessary adjustments based on the gameplay mechanics in the Treasure Hunt game, particularly those related to GPS, camera, and smartphone usage. Striking an ideal balance is essential in maintaining an engaging, competitive, and enjoyable gaming atmosphere. Therefore, the prudent application of Adjustable and Equitable Play, adjusted according to gameplay mechanics associated with diverse features, is paramount (Fig. 8.3).

Examining the development process of an XR game using the AGE heuristics matrix, emphasis should be placed on the "Adjustable and Equitable Play" and "Fair and Flexible Play" heuristics. However, the other two heuristics in the framework should not be overlooked, as they also play a critical role in making the gameplay

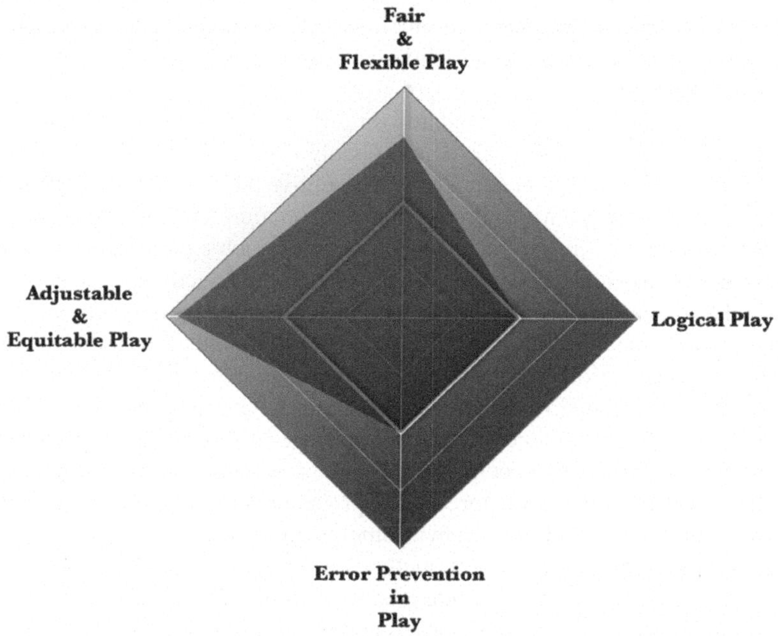

Fig. 8.3 The AGE heuristics matrix applied to XR games highlights the prominence of "Adjustable and Equitable Play" and "Fair and Flexible Play," while maintaining the importance of the other two core heuristics

more attainable (Fig. 8.2). Despite that, there are additional factors that govern the design space of XR games, which we need to address.

8.7.3 The Cognitive Burden in XR Gaming

The domain of XR gaming, still relatively nascent, hosts a broad audience unfamiliar with its unique experiences. As the field currently lacks a robust set of standards or agreed-upon best practices, in some cases, it becomes paramount to ensure the initial experiences are neither overly intense nor cognitively taxing. An excessive sensory or cognitive stimulus during an introductory XR gaming experience could lead to cognitive (over)load (see further Chap. 7).

Providing a suggestion of best practice for an indie game studio, without access to a usability testing lab, how to best measure cognitive load in XR environments is challenging for several reasons; Mainly due to the level of cognitive burden caused by the XR technologies can vary widely (1) across the three modalities (AR, MR, and VR), (2) within the three modalities depending on, e.g., in-game tasks, goal, locomotion, and level of provided stimuli, and (3) individual players' familiarity with the three modalities' different experiences and skill levels, complicating the accurate assessment of cognitive demands. Aiming to deliver attainable game experiences in your XR game, considerate these modalities variating impact on the level of cognitive burden is fundamental.

Moreover, the lack of design standards for XR environments offers unique challenges. For instance, you and your team probably need to decide your benchmarks for what is a decent outcome of a playtest on cognitive burden. Habitually, XR experiences are often more intense and potentially more complex than other interaction interfaces, making deciding if your artifacts provide such a penetrating and overly uncanny digital experience burdening cognition a multifaceted challenge.

It is highly recommended to take the feedback provided by the participants seriously and give it due consideration. Additionally, being attentive and observant of their behavior and reactions during the process is essential. Adaptability to their needs and preferences can result in a more positive and productive outcome of your XR test. Enclosing thoroughly examined the factors mentioned above and carefully weighing them against your project's specific requirements, we suggest, with support from Stanney et al. [35], the following three set of procedures for appraising the cognitive burden projected in your XR game environment (Fig. 8.4).

Experts suggest integrating various methods to obtain a thorough and precise evaluation of cognitive load within extended reality settings. This approach is necessary as each method has its own set of strengths and weaknesses. By combining different techniques, we can better understand the cognitive demands imposed on players in extended reality environments. This will enable us to develop practical solutions that optimize player experiences while minimizing cognitive overload.

Still, as excessive sensory or cognitive stimuli during an initial XR gaming experience can negatively affect the player's perception and impede the adoption of your XR game, your game should make allowances for those unacquainted with the XR concept is crucial. These players should be allowed to familiarize themselves with XR's unique physical and sensory navigation. For instance, first-time participants ought to be provided with a safe environment where they can learn to navigate the virtual environment of the XR game and comprehend how to safely maneuver and avoid obstacles within this virtual setting before progressing into the more immersive aspects of XR gaming. Providing an optional initial acclimatization phase will likely bolster player comfort, acceptance, and overall enjoyment of your XR game. Creating safe spaces in XR gaming involves providing an acclimatization trajectory for players to familiarize themselves with the unfamiliar environment. This strategy ensures player comfort, understanding, and safety, enabling players to gain confidence in their virtual interactions.

Onboarding
Begin with an intuitive onboarding process that introduces the XR interface and controls to the players. This process should educate them about game mechanics, navigation, and interaction within the XR environment.

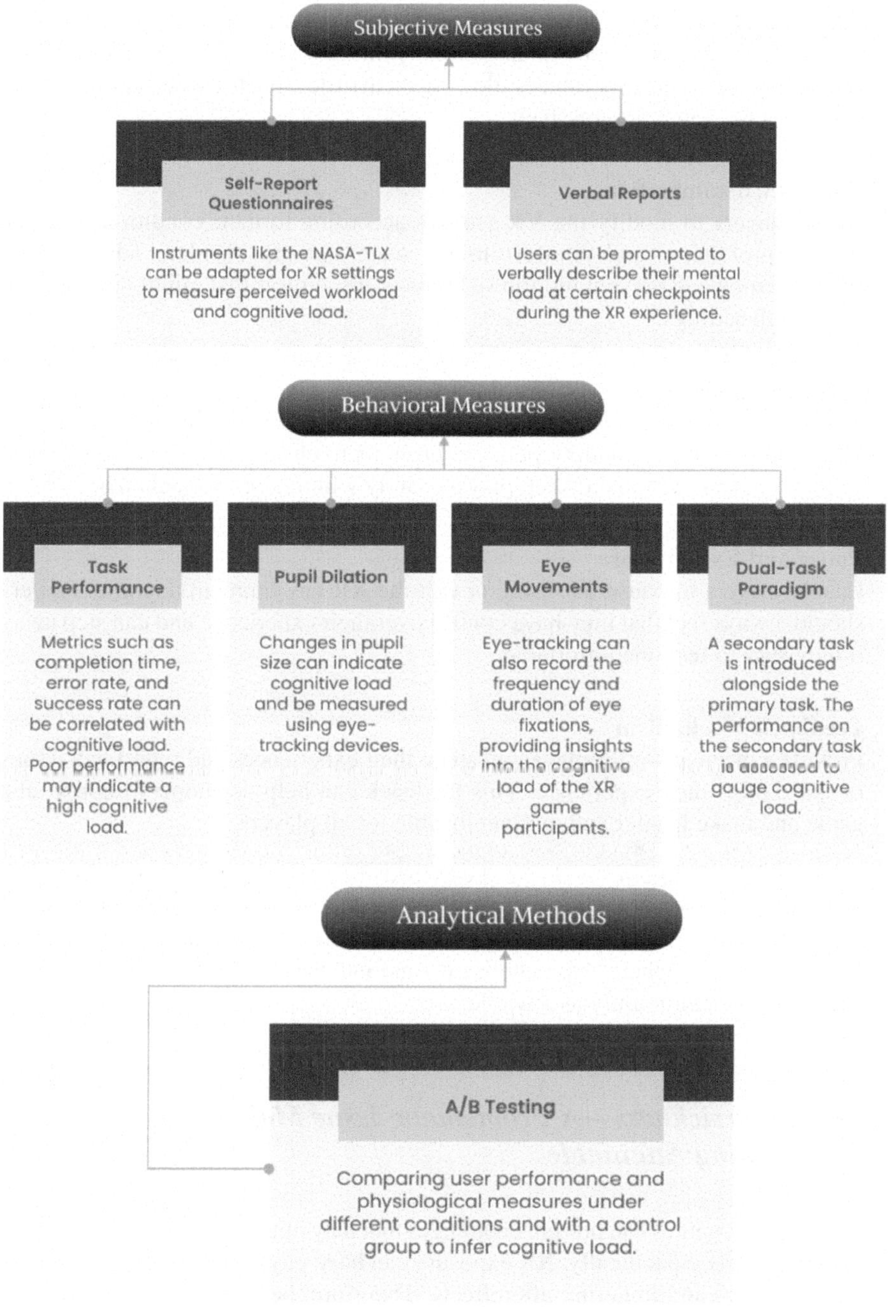

Fig. 8.4 Three set of procedures for appraising the cognitive load in XR games

Gradually Increased Complexity
Start with simple, linear tasks that gradually increase in complexity. This method eases players into the experience, allowing them to develop their skills and comfort level with the game progressively.

Control Customization
Allow players to modify the VR settings according to their condition, circumstances preference and comfort might seem like an obsolete advice. This customization can prevent motion sickness or discomfort that might occur due to the default settings.

Safety Reminders
Regularly remind players about their physical surroundings to prevent accidents. This could involve providing periodic prompts to check their physical space or using boundary systems to keep players safely within a predefined area.

Pause and Exit Options
Enable players to pause the game or exit the XR environment anytime. Players should always feel that they have control over their experience and can step away if they start to feel uncomfortable.

Feedback Mechanism
Provide a mechanism for players to share their experiences and report any issues or discomfort they experience. This feedback can help developers improve the game and make it safer and more enjoyable for all players.

By adopting and adhering to these prescribed measures, you have the ability to establish an environment that is not only more secure but also more welcoming to all players who engage with XR gaming platforms. This demonstrates a commitment to fostering an atmosphere that is both safe and inclusive and reflects positively on the values of the community as a whole.

8.7.4 Cybersickness—A Problematic Issue Making XR Gaming Attainable

Exposure to XR games can present challenges that may hinder participation and raise liability concerns. Specifically, XR exposure can have physiological effects, mainly causing sickness and lingering aftereffects. Therefore, being aware of these issues when developing games using XR technologies is crucial.

Exposure to XR can result in symptoms resembling motion sickness and other negative side effects such as balance disruptions, visual strain, and altered hand–eye coordination [34]. This type of discomfort stemming from XR systems is often termed as "cybersickness" [21]. Typical symptoms encompass dizziness, fatigue, headaches, nausea, visual tiredness, and a general sense of unease [31]. Notably, these effects tend to be more severe in VR compared to AR/MR.

In VR, studies have shown that over 80% of users experience some form of discomfort, with around 12% stopping their VR sessions early due to these negative effects [34]. The likelihood and severity of these issues tend to rise with extended VR usage [31].

In contrast, AR/MR users often face milder symptoms than VR users [38]. This may be attributed to the real-world elements in AR/MR serving as stable reference points, reducing the discrepancies between virtual movement and actual physical sensations. However, AR displays still introduce visual strain due to the conflict between vergence and accommodation. While the overall strain on the visual system is evident, AR users generally experience discomfort rather than disorientation and rarely experience severe symptoms like nausea [15]. Individuals typically undergo a physiological adjustment to mitigate negative effects during XR experiences. This adjustment is a natural response to inconsistencies within the XR environment, triggered by the adaptability of the human nervous system [41].

Thus, XR game interfaces aiming for an optimal gaming experience should prioritize player comfort, mitigate risks, and alert players about possible aftereffects. Various design strategies can be employed to alleviate cybersickness, including (Table 8.2).

Incorporating these cybersickness prevention methods improves the XR experience and diminishes the chance of negative side effects. For instance, Batman Arkham VR (Kohler, [18]) employs these tactics. It combines a brief 400 ms of movement with peripheral blur during transitions, followed by a visual "blink" and a gradual return, preserving immersion while offering multiple protective layers against cybersickness.

8.7.5 Achieving Attainable Gameplay in XR Game Technology

Harnessing XR technology effectively necessitates that both hardware and software are not only accessible but are also compatible with and supportive of assistive technologies utilized by individuals with certain conditions or special circumstances for participating. As delineated by Padrao et al. [26] and Ross et al. [29], the current XR landscape is marked by several significant challenges:

Physical Constraints
Presently, XR technologies typically demand precise tracking and an exact mirroring of body movements. This high-fidelity motion capture focus can pose substantial barriers for individuals with physical limitations, curtailing their ability to fully engage with XR experiences.

Table 8.2 Design driver for minimizing player cybersickness and harm in XR games

XR design driver	Description
Multisensory feedback techniques	Offering multisensory feedback to diminish sensory mismatches
Visual-vestibular synchronization	Introducing synchronized physical movement with visual movement, like using a motion base, to mitigate visual-vestibular discrepancies [3]
	Encouraging users to adjust their head/body in line with the virtual motion they are experiencing, decreasing visual-vestibular conflicts [40]
Modifiable viewpoint and motion settings	Allowing players active viewpoint management through swift head-tracking [34]
Provide reference frames	Presenting reference frames, like a consistent visual backdrop aligned with users' physical senses, to help users assess virtual movement [34]
Provide 3D audio feedback and cues	Incorporating 3D audio environments and directional signals that inform users of their position relative to other sites [11]
Multisensory cues	Enabling P-Layers to foresee motion using multisensory cues across the interaction interfaces
Allow teleportation and movement techniques	Applying a layered teleportation design that fuses techniques like peripheral blur, dynamic field of view adjustment, blink transition, and quick movement [22]
	Blink teleportation, which minimizes visible motion, has been shown to counteract cybersickness effectively. However, it momentarily removes users from the XR environment, potentially lessening immersion [24]
	Swift, brief movements in XR maintain immersion and considerably reduce motion sickness [13]
Visual techniques for cybersickness reduction	Peripheral blur limits the player's perception, lowering cybersickness caused by visual-vestibular mismatch [10]
	Visual cues that sync with users' sense of balance, like a consistent horizon or a fixed vehicle dashboard, can be beneficial

Visual Impairments

XR platforms predominantly rely on visual cues, which create obstacles for individuals with visual impairments, hindering their ability to wholly engage with the virtual environment. This heavy reliance on visual stimuli inadvertently leaves out a substantial segment of potential players. Nonetheless, the continuous endeavors of researchers and developers are making strides toward resolving these issues, and promising solutions have started to take shape.

Spatial Audio Cues

To facilitate navigation and interaction within virtual environments, spatial audio cues can be deployed as an efficient tool. This strategy allows players to comprehend their surroundings using auditory cues. Initiatives like Google's Daydream

Labs are leading significant experiments in this domain, investigating ways to harness audio for improved accessibility in XR.

The ongoing advancements and research in these areas could unlock a more comprehensive array of opportunities, reinforcing the commitment to make the thrilling domain of XR accessible to all, regardless of their physical or sensory capabilities.

8.8 Conclusion

XR games are rapidly gaining traction in game development. As a result, there is a growing need to tailor these immersive gaming experiences to make them more accessible to a broader audience. While there is a recognition of the importance of designing XR games with accessibility in mind to cater to a broad spectrum of players, the relatively new nature of XR means there is not yet a universally agreed-upon approach for doing this proper. Hence, in this chapter, we have explored insights from neighboring fields.

A well-rooted perspective in HCI, interaction design, as well as UCD and design ethnography, emphasizes iterative strategies in technology development. Primarily in these domains, iterative strategies aim to enhance the usability of the artifact. Within such a technological development cycle, artifacts are regularly evaluated with their target audience. This process drives continuous improvements to the artifact until the desired optimization level is reached, ensuring they are best suited for their intended purpose and usage (Gonzalez-Franco et al. [12]; Zhao et al. [42]).

In the context of the AGE heuristics, ideas stemming from more utilitarian technology development, such as accomplishing more regular inspections of XR gameplay attainability, are crucial. With the aim of enhancing attainability by modifying components in the interaction interface after each review. Such ideas could stand as an essential aspect not only of XR games but also of overall game creation processes that strive to increase their game experiences' attainability.

In making XR gaming more attainable for a broader audience, we argue that an iterative design approach may be even more beneficial than in other areas of game creation. Especially because the collective knowledge of extensive XR game creation is relatively less developed than other digital gaming modalities. Creating a universally attainable gaming experience requires an in-depth understanding of the participants and the game's context, the conditions for participation, and the physical environment where gaming takes place. XR game designers must deeply contemplate the interaction dynamics between the envisioned XR game and its players. An iterative approach to XR game development aids in pinpointing and addressing potential challenges, refining the gaming experience to be as immersive, accessible, and inclusive as possible. By achieving this, XR gaming can genuinely realize its potential as arguably the most immersive game modality available today, offering unique experiences that cater to players with permanent and situational barriers to participation (see Falconer et al. [9]; Heilemann et al. [14]).

References

1. Bellini, H. (2018, May 21). *Episode 93: Beyond VR & AR: Extended reality to transform our lives as consumers* (J. Siewert, Interviewer). Goldman Sachs Exchanges Podcast.
2. Bodzin, A., Junior, R. A., Hammond, T., & Anastasio, D. (2021). Investigating engagement and flow with a placed-based immersive virtual reality game. *Journal of Science Education and Technology, 30*, 347–360.
3. Bos, J. E. (2015). Less sickness with more motion and/or mental distraction. *Journal of Vestibular Research, 25*, 23–33.
4. Bradley, C. F. (2003). *Virtual worlds, real rules.* New York Law School Review.
5. Cavalcanti, V. C., de Santana, M. I., Da Gama, A. E. F., et al. (2018). Usability assessments for augmented reality motor rehabilitation solutions: A systematic review. *International Journal of Computer Games Technology, 23*, 1–18. https://doi.org/10.1155/2018/5387896
6. Designing Accessible VR | Oculus Developers Meta Quest. (2023). https://developer.oculus.com/resources/design-accessible-vr/. Accessed: September 12.
7. Dey, A., Billinghurst, M., Lindeman, R. W., & Swan, J. E. (2018). A systematic review of 10 years of augmented reality usability studies: 2005 to 2014. *Frontiers in Robotics & AI, 5*(37). https://doi.org/10.3389/frobt.2018.00037
8. Enyedy, N., Danish, J. A., & DeLiema, D. (2015). Constructing liminal blends in a collaborative augmented-reality learning environment. International Journal of Computer-Supported Collaborative Learning, 10, 7-34
9. Falconer, C.J., Slater, M., Rovira, A., King, J.A., Gilbert, P., Antley, A., and Brewin, C.R. Embodying Compassion: A Virtual Reality Paradigm for Overcoming Excessive Self-Criticism. PLoS One, 2014, 9(11), November 12, 2014.
10. Fernandes, A. S., & Feiner, S. K. (2016). *Combating VR sickness through subtle dynamic field-of-view modification.* IEEE Symposium on 3D User Interfaces, pp. 201–210. https://ieeexplore.ieee.org/document/7460053
11. Gartenberg, C. (2018). Microsoft's new Soundscape iOS app is designed to help the visually impaired navigate cities: 3D audio cues help mark waypoints, intersections, and points of interest. *The Verge.* https://www.theverge.com/circuitbreaker/2018/3/1/17067122/microsoft-soundscape-ios-app-3d-audio-visually-impaired-blind-navigation
12. Gonzalez-Franco, M., Bellido, A. I., Blom, K. J., Slater, M., & Rodriguez-Fornells, A. (2016). The neurological traces of look-alike avatars. Frontiers in human neuroscience, 10, 392.
13. Habgood, M. P., Moore, D., Wilson, D., & Alapont, S. (2018). Rapid, continuous movement between nodes as an accessible virtual reality locomotion technique. In *2018 IEEE virtual reality (VR)* (pp. 1–9). Reutlingen, Germany. http://shura.shu.ac.uk/18594/
14. Heilemann, F., Zimmermann, G., & Münster, P. (2021). Accessibility guidelines for VR Games—A comparison and synthesis of a comprehensive set. *Frontiers Virtual Reality, 2*, 697504.
15. Hughes, C. L., Bailey, P. S., Ruiz, E., Fidopiastis, C. M., Taranta, N. R., & Stanney, K. M. (2020). The psychometrics of cybersickness in augmented reality. *Frontiers in Virtual Reality: Virtual Reality & Human Behavior, 1*, 602954. https://doi.org/10.3389/frvir.2020.602954
16. Jaron Lanier, V. M. (2017). *The RealityMashers: Augmented reality wide field-of-view optical see-through head mounted displays.* Massachusetts Institute for Technology (MIT).
17. Kang, A. R., Blackburn, J., Kwak, H., & Kim, H. K. (2017, April). I would not plant apple trees if the world will be wiped: Analyzing hundreds of millions of behavioral records of players during an MMORPG beta test. In Proceedings of the 26th International Conference on World Wide Web Companion (pp. 435-444).
18. Kohler, C. (2016). Batman: Arkham VR is smart, scary, and (very) short. Wired. https://www.wired.com/2016/10/arkham-vr-review/ (Accessed February 20, 2024).
19. Korkut, E. H., & Surer, E. (2023). Visualization in virtual reality: A systematic review. *Virtual Reality*, 1–34.

20. Madary, M., Metzinger, T.K.: Real virtuality: A code of ethical conduct. Recommendations for good scientific practice and the consumers of VR-technology. Frontiers Robotics AI. 3, (2016). https://doi.org/10.3389/FROBT.2016.00003
21. McCauley, M. E., & Sharkey, T. J. (1992). Cybersickness: Perception of self-motion in virtual environments. *Presence: Teleoperators and Virtual Environments, 1*(3), 311–318.
22. Milik, S. (2018, July 17). VR locomotion: Teleblur is the new sheriff in town. *Big Immersive.* http://blog.bigimmersive.com/vr-locomotion-teleblur-is-the-new-sheriff-in-town/. Accessed: 29 September 2023.
23. Moussaid, M. K. (2016). *Crowd behavior during high-stress evacuations in an immersive virtual environment.* Max Planck Institute for Human Development, Disney Research Zurich, ETH Zurich, Rutgers University. Berlin: Journal of the Royal Society Interface.
24. Neimark, D. (2019). XR design: Patterns for interactions. *UX Matters: Evolution of XD Design Principles.* https://www.uxmatters.com/mt/archives/2019/01/xr-design-patterns-for-interactions.php
25. Normand, A. (2019). Accessibility of Virtual Reality Environments. https://www.unimelb.edu.au/accessibility/virtual-reality(Accessed February 19, 2024).
26. Padrao, G., Gonzalez-Franco, M., Sanchez-Vives, M. V., Slater, M., & Rodriguez-Fornells, A. (2016). Violating body movement semantics: Neural signatures of self-generated and external-generated errors. Neuroimage, 124, 147-156.
27. Rauschnabel, P. A., Felix, R., Hinsch, C., Shahab, H., & Alt, F. (2022). What is XR? Towards a framework for augmented and virtual reality. *Computers in Human Behavior, 133*, 107289.
28. Roeth, J. T. (2018). *The same game in 2D, 3D, or HMD virtual reality—How does technology impact game evaluation and brand placement.* Alpen-Adria-Universitat Austria.
29. Ross, A.S., Cutrell, E., Fiannaca, A., Kneisel, M., & Morris, M. R. (2019) *Use cases and impact of audio-based virtual exploration.* CHI 2019 Workshop on Hacking Blind Navigation.
30. Rueda, J. (2023). Doing Good with Virtual Reality: The Ethics of Using Virtual Simulations for Improving Human Morality. In Kissel, A. & Ramirez., E. J., Exploring Extended Realities: Metaphysical, Psychological, and Ethical Challenges (pp. 188-212). NY: Routledge. https://doi.org/10.4324/9781003359494
31. Salvendy, G., & Karwowski, W. (2021). *Handbook of human factors and ergonomics* (5th ed.). Wiley.
32. Santos, M. E. C., Chen, A., Taketomi, T., et al. (2014). Augmented reality learning experiences: survey of prototype design and evaluation. IEEE Transactions on Learning Technologies, 7(1), 38–56. https://doi.org/10.1109/TLT.2013.37
33. Scapin, D. L., Senach, B., Trousse, B., et al. (2012). User experience: Buzzword or new paradigm? ACHI 2012: The Fifth International Conference on Advances in Computer-Human Interaction (pp. 336–341). Valencia, Spain. https://hal.inria.fr/hal-00769619
34. Stanney, K., Fidopiastis, C., & Foster, L. (2020). Virtual reality is sexist: But it does not have to be. *Frontiers in Robotics & AI-Virtual Environments, 7*(4). https://doi.org/10.3389/frobt.2020.00004
35. Stanney, K., Nye, H., Haddad, S., Hale, K., Padron, C., & Cohn, J. (2021). Extended reality (XR) environments. In *Handbook of human factors and ergonomics* (pp. 782–815).
36. Steuer, J., Biocca, F., & Levy, M. R. (1995). Defining virtual reality: Dimensions determining telepresence. *Communication in the Age of Virtual Reality, 33*, 37–39.
37. Turk, M. (2014). Gesture recognition. In K. Ikeuchi (Ed.), *Computer vision: A reference guide* (pp. 346–349). Springer-Verlag.
38. Vovk, A., Wild, F., Guest, W., & Kuula, T. (2018). *Simulator sickness in augmented reality training using the Microsoft HoloLens.* In Proceedings of the 2018 CHI Conference on Human Factors in Computing Systems, Paper 209, pp. 1–9. Montreal, Canada. https://doi.org/10.1145/3173574.3173783
39. W3C (2020). XR Accessibility User Requirements. https://www.w3.org/TR/xaur/(Accessed February 20, 2024).
40. Wada, Y., Nishiike, S., Kitahara, T., et al. (2016). Effects of repeated snowboard exercise in virtual reality with time lags of the visual scene behind body rotation on head stability

and subjective slalom run performance in healthy young subjects. *Acta Oto-Laryngologica, 136*(11), 1121–1124. https://doi.org/10.1080/00016489.2016.1193890
41. Welch, R. B. (1978). *Perceptual modification: Adapting to altered sensory environments.* Academic Press.
42. Zhao, Y., Bennett, C., Benko, H., Cutrell, E., Holz, C., Morris, M.R., & Sinclair, M. (2018). *Enabling people with visual impairments to navigate virtual reality with a haptic and auditory cane simulation.* Proceedings of CHI 2018.
43. de Clerk, M., Dangelmaier, M., Schmierer, G., & Spath, D. (2019, 21 March). User-centered design of interaction techniques for VR-based auto-motive design reviews. *Frontiers in Robotics and AI, 6*(3). https://doi.org/10.3389/frobt.2019.00013

Chapter 9
Universal Design in Exergames

Abstract Exergames offers an exciting avenue for game developers both in terms of heightening the player experience and promoting health-related outcomes. Common to all exergames is the use of movements during gameplay. Previous research has shown that by incorporating movements into gameplay can facilitate the additional enjoyment, immersion, and game challenge of exergames. Balancing the inclusion of movements with the already complex terrain of the game design introduces new challenges that exergame designers need to be aware of, especially in striving for a universally attainable game experience. Consequently, design constraints and attainable game design heuristics need to be understood in light of the exergames' movement-based nature. This chapter introduces the concept of exergames, what they are, how they vary from one another, and the complicated dynamics that can arise in combining enjoyment with utilitarian purposes behind movements. Thereafter exergames are discussed in relation to the Universal Design perspective and the AGE framework presented in Chap. 2. The purpose of the chapter is to provide you with insights about the unique nature of exergames compared to non-movement-based games and what it can imply in striving toward attainable exergame experiences.

Keywords Exergame · Movement-based game · Exertion game · Design heuristics · Accessibility

9.1 Introduction

In the past decade, the world has witnessed the rise of "exergames," a fusion of "exercise" and "games" that amalgamates physical activity with the engaging medium of video games [16]. Exergames are also referred to as exertion games, full-body interactive games, active video games, and movement-based games, highlighting their intent to promote exertion, physical activity, and specific movements. Several factors have contributed to the growing interest in exergaming. Among these are the recent technological advancements allowing individuals to play these games at home or while doing other arbitrary tasks. Well-known instances include "Just Dance" [47], "Wii

A. Palmquist et al., *Universal Design in Video Games*, Human–Computer Interaction Series, https://doi.org/10.1007/978-3-031-30595-5_9

Fit" [32], and "Pokémon Go" [31]. These games leverage advanced technology that monitors body movement to foster an environment conducive to physical activity. By necessitating player movement as an integral part of gameplay, exergames provide an enjoyable and interactive alternative to traditional exercise.

The appeal of exergames is not confined to a specific user group; instead, it transcends traditional demographics and interests, reaching a vast array of individuals in various contexts [1, 43]. The universal appeal is demonstrated in its enterprise's varied target age groups, encompassing young children to the elderly [46]. Not only are exergames engaging and motivational for both the proficient and novice gamer, but they also possess the potential to increase physical activity duration and intensity, thereby improving perceptual motor skills, strength, balance, and motivation [34]. As a business model, exergaming has been regarded as prosperous [5], which has made it possible to carve out a place for itself in various contexts, becoming a novel game category under the expansive video game umbrella.

The design of exergames introduces new challenges in designing an attainable game experience. Accessibility and inclusivity cannot solely be regarded from the game interface or physical game controllers but also need to encompass the movement that drives the gameplay. This chapter focuses on the movement-based nature of exergames and their implication on the Universal Design of exergaming. While the chapter does not address the design methodology of exergames specifically, it is essential to note the inclusion of different stakeholders is necessary to achieve an attainable game experience. Primarily, the experience of players representing the target user group needs to be considered in relation to the game experience and in relation to the effect on health-related outcomes. Measuring health-related outcomes can take time; however, initial measures such as the user's heart rate after playing, experience of the movements utilized, physical exertion, and muscular strain can be included in early user testing. Other exergames stakeholders—parents, hospital personnel, trainers, caregivers, etc.—have been displayed to be tense about adopting exergames into their repertoire [14]. Particularly among parents about the potential feebleness of exergaming when it comes to its benefit to their own children [27]. For successful exergame implementation, it is therefore crucial to include the main stakeholders in the initial design phases. To gain trust, the main stakeholder can also be informed about progress achieved during exergame play. Implementing a comprehensive dashboard for monitoring participant data could be highly beneficial. Such a feature would provide relevant information to the exergame stakeholders, including players' performance metrics, progress reports, and engagement levels. By offering real-time data analysis and personalized feedback, such dashboards would enhance the user experience, encourage player motivation, and ultimately contribute to the overall success and effectiveness of exergaming.

9.2 The Purpose Behind Exergaming

As with other game-based artifacts (see Chap. 6), the purpose behind exergames is in most cases, dual. On the one hand, exergame designers often target specific utilitarian purposes associated with the benefits of movements. These utilitarian purposes can include a vast spectrum of health-related benefits, from target intervention in healthcare practices to more general physical activity-promoting initiatives.

On the other hand, exergame designers want to elicit the enjoyable, hedonic nature of video game play. The enjoyment associated with movement (Bianchi-Bertthouze et al. [4]) has led researchers to explore exergames as a medium of gameplay that can generate positive gaming experiences that extend those of non-movement-based games.

Game creators who want to develop successful universally designed exergames within and outside healthcare practices first need to understand the utilitarian and hedonic dimensions as well as their interrelatedness.

9.2.1 The Utilitarian Dimension of Exergames

Exergames have been developed for a myriad of different purposes. By utilizing movements, exergame designers can target specific outcomes they want to attain, for example, the health-related benefits associated with exercise or the rehabilitation and treatment associated with doing specific movements. The growing popularity of the exergame industry has spurred the scholar's various investigations of the assertions regarding its usefulness. In academic research, the exergaming domain is diverse, mirroring a plethora of research disciplines, and finds application in various fields. Exergame design and research have been conducted for specific health-related purposes such as rehabilitation [50], fall prevention [8], treatment [2], increased motor control [48], and improved mental health [21]. Other exergames have been designed and researched in terms of the general increase of physical activity by utilizing exergames as a form of exercise [23] and as a means to decrease sedentary behavior [3]. In research, exergames have predominantly been designed and evaluated for the elderly and younger age groups [1]. Exergames have for example been shown to motivate children to exercise more and serve as a functional tool for rehabilitation for the elderly in healthcare settings [38].

While evidence indicates that exergaming can foster health improvement via increased physical activity, the potential of exergames needs to be investigated more to grasp and understand best practices fully. However, the appeal of exergaming seems to lie in their potential to engage individuals in physical activity that normally would not have bothered them. Even being a relatively immature research field, studies have displayed a number of challenges with exergames in terms of promoting health-related benefits. For instance, sustaining long-term engagement in exergaming presents a challenge [3, 45], being something of a novelty effect—which it shares with other game-based practices [17].

9.2.2 The Hedonic Dimension of Exergames

The inclusion of movements in exergames does not only imply that health-related outcomes can be targeted but also that enjoyable, hedonic, psychological experiences can be elicited. Promoting an enjoyable experience in exergames is crucial as it motivates people to keep playing, thus engaging in the movements that can promote health-related benefits. Researchers have explored the unique dimensions of exergame play that distinguish exergames from non-movement-based games in terms of positive psychological experience.

One suggested distinction between exergames and non-motion based games is that exergames can contribute to positive game experiences due to the enjoyment associated with moving one's body. Several studies have shown positive correlations between physical exertion and enjoyment in exergames [27]. At the same time, including too high levels of exertion has been found to be problematic, as overexertion can cause a negative experience. For exergames to generate sufficient levels of exertion for enjoyment while not resulting in overexertion, previous studies have suggested several recommendations. The include activating several parts of the body during exergame play, thus distributing fatigue more equally and not overextending a certain body part, as well as balancing the level of exertion in accordance with the length of gameplay [18, 22, 40]. Shorter gameplay durations, such as those introduced in short-form casual exergames, can generate higher degrees of exertion, while longer format exergames, intended to be played over longer periods of time, should mindfully introduce different levels of exertion over time.

Another distinction between exergames and non-motion based games is that exergames can provide a more immersive experience due to the natural mapping of movements. Natural mapping refers to the extent to which the players perceive that the game controls are mapped to the changes in the game in a manner that is logical and aligned with expectations [42]. Previous research has shown that higher natural mapping of movement in relation to a game can promote higher enjoyment and immersion [29]. Hitting a ball in a game for example, through swinging one's arm, can result in higher nature mapping, producing a more immersive and enjoyable experience, compared to pressing a button to hit the ball in the game, which holds no logical connection to the experience of hitting a ball in real life.

Finally, exergames can contribute to enjoyment due to the additional challenge introduced through exertion. As proposed in the dual flow model of exergames, adapting challenges in accordance with skill should not only be considered from a gameplay perspective but should also encompass balancing the physical intensity of the game with the player's fitness levels [41]. Introducing exertion strategically into the game by adapting the players' current physical capability to the one required to play the game can thus be a way to create higher game challenge and enjoyment in exergames [22].

9.2.3 Balancing the Benefits of Movement with the Enjoyment of Games

According to Roure et al. [36], exergames can effectively induce a high level of situational interest[1] in exercise by adding an appealing framing of exercise activities to individuals' opinions. However, even though exergames stimulate a high level of situational interest, their introduction does not guarantee a sustained increase in physical activity [36]. Furthermore, even if individuals do increase their physical activity through exergaming, they might not achieve the activity levels necessary to ensure positive health effects compared to traditional physical activities [6]. Therefore, it has been proposed that developing exergames intended to promote health-related physical activity necessitates a more holistic, design-based approach [6, 36].

The holistic, design-based approach of exergames needs to consider the balance between eliciting the health-related outcomes intended (from the utilitarian perspective) with the psychological outcomes related to the experience of the game (from the hedonic perspective). Like traditional exercise varies in quantitative and qualitative attributes [35], so do exergames. According to Pesce [35], quantitative factors like duration and intensity fall under a "medical" perspective. On the other hand, qualitative aspects like the type or mode of exercise pertain to non-physical dimensions of exercise tasks, such as cognitive or coordinative demands. In exergaming, the interaction of these factors might be crucial to reap benefits in physical, cognitive, and psychosocial target variables. The duration and intensity of the physical movements, together with the exercise task, can influence the physical benefits along with the psychological experience of the exergame. Too high duration and intensity can, for example, lead to a negative experience by players due to extended fatigue [27]. From the utilitarian perspective, however, not producing sufficient levels of exertion can result in not gaining the intended physical benefit that was intended with the game. The cognitive and coordinative demands of the exergame can in turn influence the psychological experience of the game, as too high cognitive demands can negatively impact the player experience [22]. Simultaneously, the cognitive and coordinative demands can influence the physical benefit as too high complexity in movements can result in players not being able to perform the movements correctly or with sufficient levels of intensity.

Exergames, due to their multidisciplinary nature, currently lack a universally agreed-upon theoretical framework. Consequently, there exist various design proposals for these games [44]. The process of designing and developing exergames

[1] Situational interest is a multidimensional concept from motivational psychology that comprises five aspects: novelty, challenge, demand for attention, intention to explore, and immediate enjoyment.

necessitates careful adaptations to numerous game design elements, including game mechanics, interfaces, and gameplay, to suit the particular needs and opportunities presented by the exergaming space. The movement-based nature of exergames also implies that the game elements need to be adapted and modified in accordance with the physical demand introduced in the game. These modifications are integral to the successful completion of in-game tasks and can significantly enhance both the efficacy and appeal of exergaming [49]. Examples of such adjustments might encompass altering the user interface for increased intuitiveness, ensuring the interface is secure for player safety, regulating the game's pace to match the player's physical capacity, and modulating the difficulty of the tasks within the game to align with the player's skill level.

More research is needed to understand the complex relationship between the hedonic and utilitarian dimensions of exergames. Current exergame guidelines focus on the hedonic dimension of exergames, often neglecting the utilitarian dimension and the interrelation between the hedonic and utilitarian dimensions [44]. From a practical perspective, those who intend to design exergames should pay careful consideration to the reason for playing the game along with the intended experience of the game and how these aspects interplay. For example, some types of exergames are developed solely for entertainment purposes, putting more emphasis on how movements can positively influence the in-game experience. Other types of exergames were developed to increase physical activity, putting more emphasis on how exertion can be generated by incorporating a specific game design that is enjoyable enough to keep stimulating players. In both cases, it is, however, important to have an awareness of how the physical movements affect the psychological experience and vice versa. This dynamic interplay should always be a focal point of exergame design (Fig. 9.1). The physical movements utilized in gameplay can contribute to the player experiencing the gameplay as more or less enjoyable. The same holds true from the opposite perspective. The psychological game experience affects how and to what extent movements are used during gameplay.

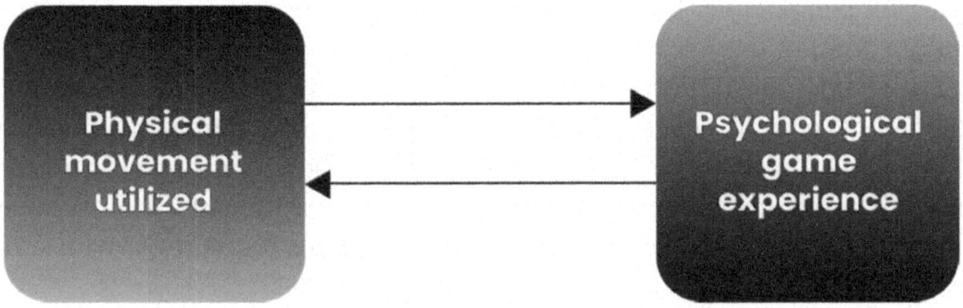

Fig. 9.1 The interplay between physical activities and gameplay experiences is foundational in a exergame composition

9.2.4 The Attainable Exergame Experience

Based on the definition of universally designed games introduced in Chap. 1, a Universal Design approach toward exergaming should involve striving toward an attainable game experience for people with all abilities. In exergames, compared to non-motion-based games, the attainable game experience needs to include a consideration of movements. As has previously been discussed throughout the chapters of this book, offering flexibility in terms of game controllers can enable more attainable game experiences. Game controllers are the way in which players influence a game [24]. The core mechanism that distinguishes exergames from non-movement-based games is the utilization of movement-based controllers [25]. In Chap. 3, input controllers are discussed from a Universal Design perspective in relation to non-movement-based games. For exergames, the movement-based controllers, i.e., the movements utilized to control the game can take on different forms. One distinction is between exergames that utilize tangible controllers compared to exergames that do not use tangible controllers but instead only rely on the bodily movements performed by players. Based on the notion of naturally mapped controllers, Skalski et al. [42] define the following three types of controllers used in exergames, from less to more naturally mapped:

- Kinesic naturally mapped controllers: using bodily movements that correspond to the actions in the game without the use of tangible controllers. Microsoft Kinect for Xbox 360 [30] utilizes such mapping by identifying the movements of the player without requiring a physical game controller to be held while interacting with the game.
- Incomplete tangible natural mapped controllers: using controllers that simulate but differ from the object in the game. Nintendo Wii [33] utilizes such mapping by including a physical game controller that represents different objects in different games.
- Realistic, tangible naturally mapped controllers: using realistic and tangible controllers. Guitar Hero [20] utilizes such mapping by utilizing a physical game controller that represents a guitar, directly corresponding to the game.

The type of naturally mapped controller used in an exergame affects the game's accessibility and attainability. For exergames that include kinesic controllers, game attainability depends primarily on a person who is able to perform the intended movements in an accurate and timely way. For exergames that include incomplete or realistic tangible controllers, the game attainability will depend both on whether a person is able to perform the intended movement and if the person is able to operate the tangible controller. People with limited motor functions might, for example, have a difficult time gripping tangible controllers for the gameplay duration. Kinesic controllers, incomplete tangible controllers, and realistic, tangible controllers can also introduce higher or lower ambiguity of movements, that is, the precision required in movements for the in-game action to occur.

The choice and design of game controllers in exergames affect the attainability, game experience, and efficiency of the game. The consideration of which type of mapping is utilized in game controllers, as well as the movements required and their precision, needs to be balanced in accordance with the purpose of the game. An exergame developed for entertainment purposes might emphasize the natural mapping of game controllers and put less emphasis on movement precision, whereas exergames used for rehabilitation purposes might emphasize natural mapping less and put more emphasis on movement precision. For an exergame experience to be attainable for people in the targeted user group, designers need to be cautious about how the choice of game controllers affects the accessibility and game experience. For example, introducing movements that activate several parts of the body to distribute fatigue more equally could positively impact the game experience but also lead to excluding players who are not able to use certain body parts.

9.3 Universal Exergame Design Through the AGE Framework

To guide the application of Universal Design in the context of exergaming, the AGE (attainable game experience) framework presented in Chap. 2 can provide an understanding of some of the aspects that should be considered. As exergames differ to a large extent depending on their purpose, the application of heuristics also needs to be understood from the specific design space for your game. The current section provides an overview of how the heuristics and design constraints can be viewed in light of exergame design. Notably, the application of the AGE heuristics in the upcoming discussion focuses on the movement-based nature of exergames. Following our discussion on the AGE design heuristics and design constraints in relation to exergames, we detail a specific case (Exergames for Stroke rehabilitation) that can offer guidance on how the AGE framework can be applied to exergame design.

9.3.1 AGE Design Heuristics for Exergaming

The design heuristics for an attainable game experience presented in Chap. 2 can provide a valuable perspective in navigating the complex terrain of designing an attainable exergame experience that considers hedonic and utilitarian perspectives to varying extents. The vast purposes that can underlie exergame design imply that the heuristics need to be applied to the specific type of exergame that is designed to varying extents. In other words, the design heuristics need to be understood in relation to the design constraints.

Fair and Flexible Play heuristic puts forth that gameplay should be perceived as fair, allowing participants from a broad audience with differing conditions and abilities to take part in the game, and Flexible, providing interfaces with adjustable settings and alternative controller inputs. To make exergaming fair, special emphasis should be made regarding people's motor and mobility conditions, understanding that not all people can or are comfortable with moving in similar manners. A potential pitfall that game designers face in the development of exergames is only testing the movement-based interactions on themselves, thus neglecting an understanding of the movement-related abilities and preferences of the target user group. Including Fair and Flexible play in the context of exergames involves alternative ways of interacting with the game through movements through careful consideration of the conditions and characteristics of the user group. For example, while some players are able to interact with the game standing up, this might not hold true for all players. Including options for playing exergames standing or seated could, therefore, provide more attainable gameplay through adhering to the heuristic of Fair and Flexible gameplay. Exergames can also offer various different movements that can be used to interact with the game, adhering to player preferences.

Adjustable and Equitable Play heuristic underscores that games should provide features that tailor and personalize the gameplay experience. In exergames, a crucial aspect of Adjustable and Equitable Play concerns that players should have an equitable chance to enjoy and compete in games. Introducing alternative ways to interact with a game through being able to adapt the movements utilized to interact with the game (in order to create a Fair and Flexible game) risks negatively impacting the player experience in the exergame. For instance, if the alternative player mode utilizes more complex movement and thus becomes more difficult compared to the traditional player mode, some players will get an unfair advantage compared to others, resulting in non-equitable play. Furthermore, from the utilitarian dimension, it is of essence to be mindful of which health-related consequences the alternative ways of interacting with the game have. For example, if an exergame is designed to promote exertion, all different modes of interacting with the game need to be considered in the evaluation of the exertion generated through game play.

Logical Play heuristic refers to creating comprehensible, intuitive, and logical games that appear meaningful to the players. While the Logical Play heuristic is important to consider in crafting an attainable game experience in all games, it can be considered even more important in the context of exergames. Due to the dual focus and the screen and the body, the cognitive complexity of exergames compared to non-motion based games becomes higher [22]. Playing exergames requires attention, not only in terms of following and interacting with the video game displayed on a screen but also to the body. Exergames also require that the players familiarize themselves not only with the game itself but also with the movements. Guidance and reassurance should, therefore, be provided to the players as they embark on their gaming journey. The Logical Play heuristic becomes even more crucial in exergames utilizing more complex movements for interaction.

Error Prevention in Play heuristic refers to preventing players from committing easily avoidable mistakes. Players who make mistakes in terms of not performing movements correctly can experience frustration due to the game not reacting as expected. Mistakes can also result in injury. Preventing errors from occurring during exergame play thus becomes crucial. One aspect to consider is to provide clear feedback to players regarding their movements and indicate how players need to adjust their movements in order for the game to respond. More importantly, exergame designers need to prevent injuries that can occur both from the surrounding environment and the improper or overuse of movements. Strategies to reduce injury-related errors could include making players aware of their surroundings during exergame play, providing information about the risks of performing movements incorrectly and nudging or forcing players to take breaks during longer durations of gameplay.

9.3.2 AGE Design Constraints for Exergaming

An important first step for applying a Universal Design lens to your video game is clarifying the design constraints. In exergames, this is essential. Not only do the goal and purpose of exergames vary to a significant extent, but including a broader audience, while beneficial for long-term gains, can imply large investments in technological capabilities. The specific purpose and goal and technological constraints of the exergame put more or less emphasis on the AGE heuristics. For example, a game designed with the intention to promote short breaks should emphasize the logical play heuristic more, as people will have less time to invest in the game experience, whereas a game designed with the intention of longer format hedonic experiences might put more emphasis on the Fair and Flexible play heuristic, allowing players to interact with the game according to their own preferences. In Chap. 2, the following three main design constraints are presented, which help to define the design space of your exergame:

The Goal and Purpose of the Game
Defining the purpose of the exergame is crucial as it provides an understanding of the target group of the game and limits the design space in terms of the duration of the game and the movements utilized. A first step in understanding the goal and purpose of an exergame is to define the balance between the utilitarian and hedonic goals of the game. Utilitarian objectives can be more (such as increased motor control for the elderly) or less (such as promoting physical activity) specific. Exergames can also neglect utilitarian objectives and instead focus on

creating enjoyable experiences through the enjoyment of movement, immersive possibilities of natural mapping, and the additional challenge introduced by exertion.

The Game Technological Constraints/Capabilities
The availability or possible investment in technological resources should also be carefully considered. In exergames, different devices utilized imply different technological investments. In console kinetically mapped exergames, for example, motion detection devices are required with varying levels of precision depending on the purpose of the exergame.

Requirements of the Game Genre
The over-encompassing exergame genre requires notable consideration of the Error Prevention in Play heuristic, specifically concerning the avoidance of injuries. Exergames developed for medical interventions also need to adhere to specific regulation standards and practices, often designed in collaboration with healthcare professionals.

9.3.3 The AGE Framework Applied to Exergames for Stroke Rehabilitation

In the present therapeutic landscape, exergames are swiftly becoming a noteworthy adjunct to established rehabilitation techniques, particularly in contemporary stroke rehabilitation practices [10]. These exergames serve to merge physical exertion with cognitive challenges, creating an engaging medium that supports stroke survivors on their path to recovery. Exergames have demonstrated the potential to facilitate enhanced motor function, improved balance control, and heightened levels of physical activity among stroke patients [37]. A crucial aspect of exergames, particularly relevant to stroke rehabilitation, is their ability to simulate repetitive, task-oriented movements that mirror real-life scenarios, significantly contributing to the process of neural reintegration and recovery [10]. Moreover, the increased engagement levels associated with exergames may potentially lead to better patient adherence to prescribed rehabilitation regimens, a challenge often encountered in traditional therapy methods [26].

The integration of technologies such as motion tracking, analytic dashboards for visualizing progression, and virtual reality alongside exergames' inherent capabilities for progress tracking and difficulty adaptation according to individual patient progress and needs presents a compelling avenue for exergames in a therapeutic environment. This combination is particularly potent in improving activities of daily living function after stroke by bridging clinic-centric therapeutic sessions with home-based exercises [10]. Given the progressive nature of technology and our deepening comprehension of stroke rehabilitation, the scope and application of exergames are predicted to expand in the foreseeable future.

The potential of exergames based on virtual reality for stroke rehabilitation has been underscored by a growing body of research [15]. As such, this technology has been introduced into the therapeutic landscape with promising results. Virtual Reality (VR) has been associated with beneficial patient outcomes across a range of long-term conditions, most notably in the domain of upper-limb stroke rehabilitation [7]. This technology has also been linked with more effective recovery processes [9]. Numerous systems have been developed specifically for upper-limb stroke rehabilitation [11], with others focusing on enhancing gait and balance [19]. However, it is noteworthy that, as of this writing, only one system has been specifically designed to focus on lower-limb stroke rehabilitation [12]. This underscores the need for further research and development in this area to exploit the potential of VR-based exergames more fully in comprehensive stroke rehabilitation.

Another potential and prolific exergame approach is "Strength for Task" training, also known as resistance exercise. It has emerged as a promising approach to stroke rehabilitation through the use of exergames [39]. The approach strategically combines strength-based exercises, which prime the brain for learning, with task-specific movements, thereby promoting neural plasticity. Neural plasticity, which involves forging new neural pathways or rebuilding dormant ones in the brain, facilitates the connection between cerebral activity and subsequent muscular movement. The relearning of these movements contributes to improved patient locomotion [39]. Priming, an integral part of this process, is achieved through muscle-strengthening exercises, typically utilizing weights or resistance bands and encouraging the patient to exert maximum effort. Such exertion stimulates corticomotor excitability, thereby readying the neural pathways in the brain. When this is promptly followed by task-specific training, the brain is better prepared to foster neural plasticity [28]. While the use of exergames in stroke rehabilitation is not entirely novel, there currently exists an opportunity for developing an exergame specifically designed to facilitate unsupervised "Strength for Task" training or VR-based solutions for a home-based rehabilitation setting. These forms of exergames could significantly enhance therapeutic outcomes, optimizing the recovery of bodily function post-stroke [13].

9.3.4 The AGE Framework in the Stroke Rehabilitation Design Space

The main design constraint for exergames targeting stroke rehabilitation is a utilitarian goal of utilizing movements for stroke rehabilitation while simultaneously providing an engaging experience for patients. This can be achieved through various different technological capabilities (some of which are presented briefly above). The requirement of the specific game genre is to eliminate any potential injuries that can arise during gameplay. The exergame design should emphasize safety and beneficial play. The design places a different emphasis on the AGE heuristics.

The main heuristic that needs to be prioritized is the **Error Prevention in Play** heuristic, ensuring safe participation for the intended target group. Specifically, the physical injuries that can arise need to be eliminated. Despite the characteristic appeal of the **Fair and Flexible Play** heuristic, when designing an exergame for stroke rehabilitation, this heuristic must be limited and restrained as flexibility in the participant usage might risk gaining additional injuries in the context of stroke rehabilitation due to the misuse of movements. Hence, incorporating safeguards and restrictions in the design becomes crucial to prevent incorrect or excessive use, thereby ensuring therapeutic effectiveness while minimizing potential risks.

The remaining two AGE design heuristics, namely **Logical Play** and **Adjustable and Equitable Play**, hold significant importance. Logical Play can support the patients in understanding the gameplay. This can, in turn, reduce the cognitive complexity of the gameplay and result in a more detailed focus on the movements performed. Furthermore, following the Logical Play heuristic can contribute to a more positive experience for the patients as it allows them to participate in the gameplay more easily. Adjustable and Equitable Play can also contribute to a more positive game experience through adding features that tailor and personalize the game. This heuristic could also be applied in further versions of the game, which incorporate multiplayer modes, requiring an understanding of equitable play.

In the context of our specific case depiction, the Logical Play and Adjustable and Equitable Play heuristics are uniquely situated on the frontier between the inner and outer realms of the design space. What this implies is that the design constraints we have identified bear a comparatively restricted influence on these heuristics compared to the heuristic of Error Prevention in Play. Therefore, the impacts that the Logical Play and Adjustable and Equitable Play heuristics exert are less pronounced compared to the heuristic of Error Prevention in Play. This can be clearly observed in Fig. 9.2, where the location of the four design heuristics in the exergame for stroke rehabilitation design space is graphically represented.

Though their placement may infer limited interaction with our current design constraints, it is essential to note that Logical Play and Adjustable and Equitable Play could become more pivotal under different design parameters, game categories, and over time. Therefore, while their influence may be limited in our current scenario, their potential for future impact should not be underestimated. For example, after ensuring that the heuristic of Error Prevention in Play has been addressed, more emphasis can be placed on adding design features that support the understanding of the game along with tailored and personalized features. Before the heuristic of Logical Play has fully been addressed, the patient can also utilize support from healthcare providers in terms of understanding the game.

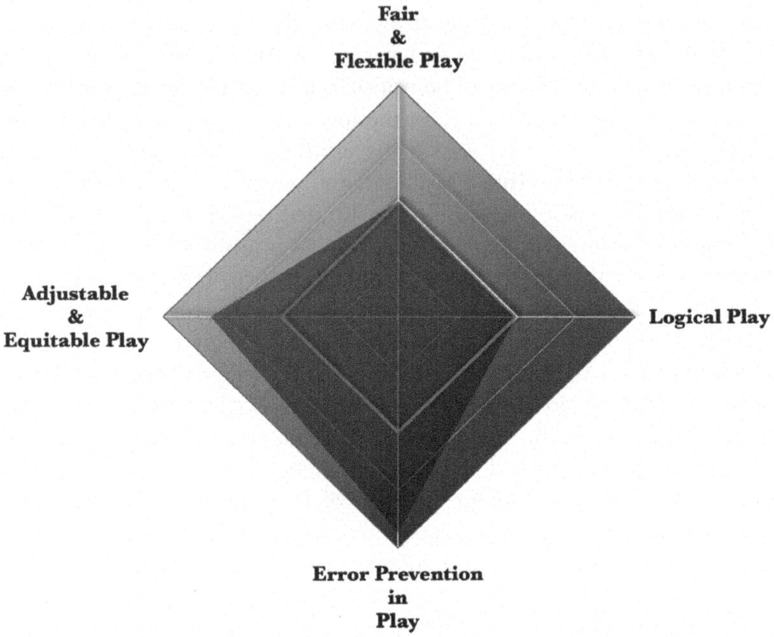

Fig. 9.2 The darkened segments of the AGE matrix display the directives and constraints for the AGE heuristics in a stroke rehabilitation exergame

9.4 Conclusion

Exergames offer a promising avenue for promoting health-related outcomes and generating enjoyable game experiences. While being considered as one overarching game category, exergames display large differences. Exergame designers have various different intentions behind developing their games. This can include everything from creating enjoyable game experiences to targeting more general and specific health-related outcomes. A common denominator for all exergames is, however, the use of movements as game controllers. Thus, all exergames contain a physical dimension in relation to the game experience. The physical dimension of exergames introduces complexity into the attainable exergame experience design space beyond that of non-movement-based games. In non-movement-based games, designers need to pay careful consideration to stakeholders and how to increase game experience attainability. The same holds true for exergames. However, the exergame experience needs to be constantly balanced with considerations of the movements utilized while playing and the various conditions and characteristics of the player's physical abilities. The Universal Design lens applied to the context of exergames must, therefore, include a consideration of the physical dimension of exergames as well. An attainable exergame experience cannot be achieved without considering the players' experiences and abilities in relation to the physical dimension. Applying the AGE framework to exergames, therefore, needs to include the perspective of movements. In the present chapter, we have discussed the relevance of the AGE heuristics in the context of exergames. Highlighting that while the heuristics offer unique perspectives that should be incorporated into the design in order to achieve an attainable game experience, their importance varies depending on the general design constraints of exergames and the specific design constraints related to different exergames. To illustrate this, the chapter has described a case of applying the AGE framework on exergames designed with the specific purpose of stroke rehabilitation patients.

References

1. Baranowski, T. (2017). Exergaming: Hope for future physical activity? or blight on mankind? *Journal of sport and health science, 6*(1), 44–46.
2. Barry, G., Galna, B., & Rochester, L. (2014). The role of exergaming in Parkinson's disease rehabilitation: A systematic review of the evidence. *Journal of neuroengineering and rehabilitation, 11*, 1–10.
3. Berglund, A., Jedel, I., Orädd, H., Fallström, J., & Berglund, E. (2023). Liopep: a gamified casual exergame application to help office workers not be active couch potatoes. In *IEEE 11th International Conference on Serious Games and Applications for Health, SeGAH*. IEEE.
4. Bianchi-Berthouze, N., Kim, W. W., & Patel, D. (2007). Does body movement engage you more in digital game play? and why?. In *Affective Computing and Intelligent Interaction: Second International Conference, ACII 2007 Lisbon, Portugal, September 12-14*, 2007 Proceedings 2 (pp. 102-113). Springer Berlin Heidelberg.
5. Bond, S., Laddu, D. R., Ozemek, C., Lavie, C. J., & Arena, R. (2021). Exergaming and virtual reality for health: Implications for cardiac rehabilitation. *Current Problems in Cardiology, 46*(3), 100472.
6. Born, F. (2022). Investigating the constructs that shape and enhance the experience of virtual reality exergames. https://doi.org/10.17185/duepublico/76109
7. de Bruin, E. D., Reve, E. V., & Murer, K. (2013). A randomized controlled pilot study assessing the feasibility of combined motor-cognitive training and its effect on gait characteristics in the elderly. *Clinical Rehabilitation, 27*(3), 215–225.
8. Chen, Y., Zhang, Y., Guo, Z., Bao, D., & Zhou, J. (2021). Comparison between the effects of exergame intervention and traditional physical training on improving balance and fall prevention in healthy older adults: A systematic review and meta-analysis. *Journal of Neuroengineering and Rehabilitation, 18*(1), 1–17.
9. Dean, C. M., Richards, C. L., & Malouin, F. (2000). Task-related circuit training improves performance of locomotor tasks in chronic stroke: A randomized, controlled pilot trial. *Archives of Physical Medicine and Rehabilitation, 81*(4), 409–417.
10. Donoso Brown, E. V., et al. (2014). Understanding upper extremity home programs and the use of gaming technology for persons after stroke. *Disability and Health Journal, 7*(4), 507–513.
11. Eliasson, A. C., Krumlinde-sundholm, L., Shaw, K., & Wang, C. (2005). Effects of constraint-induced movement therapy in young children with hemiplegic cerebral palsy: An adapted model. *Developmental Medicine and Child Neurology, 47*(4), 266–275.
12. Eng, J. J., & Tang, P. F. (2007). Gait training strategies to optimize walking ability in people with stroke: A synthesis of the evidence. *Expert Review of Neurotherapeutics, 7*(10), 1417–1436.
13. Fritz, S. L., Peters, D. M., Merlo, A. M., & Donley, J. (2013). Active video-gaming effects on balance and mobility in individuals with chronic stroke: A randomized controlled trial. *Topics in Stroke Rehabilitation., 20*(3), 218–225.

14. Gao, Z., Chen, S., Pasco, D., & Pope, Z. (2015). A meta-analysis of active video games on health outcomes among children and adolescents. *Obesity Reviews, 16*(9), 783–794.
15. Geijtenbeek, T., Steenbrink, F., Otten, B., Even-Zohar, O.: D-flow: Immersive virtual reality and real-time feedback for rehabilitation. In *Proceedings of the 10th International Conference on Virtual Reality Continuum and Its Applications in Industry, Hong Kong* (pp. 201–208). ACM
16. Göbel, S., Hardy, S., Wendel, V., Mehm, F., & Steinmetz, R. (2010, October). Serious games for health: personalized exergames. In *Proceedings of the 18th ACM international conference on Multimedia* (pp. 1663–1666).
17. Hamari, J., Koivisto, J., & Sarsa, H. (2014, January). Does gamification work?—A literature review of empirical studies on gamification. In *2014 47th Hawaii International Conference on System Sciences* (pp. 3025–3034). IEEE.
18. Hara, M., & Ovaska, S. (2014, October). Heuristics for motion-based control in games. In *Proceedings of the 8th Nordic Conference on Human-Computer Interaction: Fun, Fast, Foundational* (pp. 697–706).
19. Harley, L., Robertson, S., Gandy, M., Harbert, S., & Britton, D. (2011). The design of an interactive stroke rehabilitation gaming system. *Human-Computer Interaction Users and Application Part IV, 6764*, 167–173.
20. Harmonix Music Systems & RedOctane. (2005). *Guitar Hero* (Video game). RedOctane.
21. Huang, K., Zhao, Y., He, R., Zhong, T., Yang, H., Chen, Y., Ma, L., Jai, Y., & Chen, L. (2022). Exergame-based exercise training for depressive symptoms in adults: A systematic review and meta-analysis. *Psychology of Sport and Exercise* 102266.
22. Isbister, K., & Mueller, F. F. (2015). Guidelines for the design of movement-based games and their relevance to HCI. *Human–Computer Interaction, 30*(3–4), 366–399.
23. Ismail, N. A., Hashim, H. A., & Ahmad Yusof, H. (2022). Physical activity and exergames among older adults: A scoping review. *Games for Health Journal, 11*(1), 1–17.
24. Klimmt, C., Hartmann, T., & Frey, A. (2007). Effectance and control as determinants of video game enjoyment. *Cyberpsychology & Behavior, 10*(6), 845–848.
25. Kooiman, B., & Sheehan, D. D. (2015). Exergaming theories: A literature review. *International Journal of Game-Based Learning (IJGBL), 5*(4), 1–14.
26. Laver, K. E., et al. (2017). Virtual reality for stroke rehabilitation. *Cochrane Database of Systematic Reviews* (11).
27. Lee, S., Kim, W., Park, T., & Peng, W. (2017). The psychological effects of playing exergames: A systematic review. *Cyberpsychology, Behavior, and Social Networking, 20*(9), 513–532.
28. Martin, B., & Hanington, B .M. (2012). Universal methods of design: 100 ways to research complex problems, develop innovative ideas, and design effective solutions (207 p). Digital (Ed.), Rockport Publishers
29. McGloin, R., & Embacher, K. (2018). "Just like riding a bike": A model matching approach to predicting the enjoyment of a cycling exergame experience. *Media Psychology, 21*(3), 486–505.
30. Microsoft Corporation. (2010). *Microsoft Kinect for Xbox 360* [Hardware]. Microsoft.
31. Niantic, Inc. (2016). *Pokémon Go* (Mobile game). Niantic, Inc.
32. Nintendo. (2008). *Wii Fit* [Video game]. Nintendo.
33. Nintendo (2006). *Nintendo Wii* [Video game console]. Nintendo.
34. Pasco, D., Roure, C., Kermarrec, G., Pope, Z., & Gao, Z. (2017). The effects of a bike active video game on players' physical activity and motivation. *Journal of Sport and Health Science, 6*(1), 25–32.
35. Pesce, C. (2012). Shifting the focus from quantitative to qualitative exercise characteristics in exercise and cognition research. *Journal of Sport and Exercise Psychology, 34*(6), 766–786.
36. Roure, C., Pasco, D., Benoît, N., & Deldicque, L. (2020). Impact of a design-based bike exergame on young adults' physical activity metrics and situational interest. *Research Quarterly for Exercise and Sport, 91*(2), 309–315.

37. Saposnik, G., et al. (2010). Effectiveness of virtual reality using Wii gaming technology in stroke rehabilitation: A pilot randomized clinical trial and proof of principle. *Stroke, 41*(7), 1477–1484.
38. Sato, T., Shimizu, K., Shiko, Y., Kawasaki, Y., Orita, S., Inage, K., Shiga, Y., Suzuki, M., Sato, M., Enomoto, K., Takaoka, H., Mizuki, N., Kim, G., Hozumi, T., Tsuchiya, R., Otagiri, T., Mukaihata, T., Furuya, T., Maki, S., ... Eguchi, Y. (2021). Effects of nintendo ring fit adventure exergame on pain and psychological factors in patients with chronic low back pain. *Games Health Journal, 10*(3), 158–164.
39. Signal, N. E. J. (2014). Strength for task training: a novel intervention to improve locomotor ability following stroke [Internet] [Thesis]. Auckland University of Technology; 2014
40. Silpasuwanchai, C., & Ren, X. (2015). Designing concurrent full-body gestures for intense gameplay. *International Journal of Human-Computer Studies, 80*, 1–13.
41. Sinclair, J., Hingston, P., & Masek, M. (2007, December). Considerations for the design of exergames. In *Proceedings of the 5th International Conference on Computer Graphics and Interactive Techniques in Australia and Southeast Asia* (pp. 289–295).
42. Skalski, P., Tamborini, R., Shelton, A., Buncher, M., & Lindmark, P. (2011). Mapping the road to fun: Natural video game controllers, presence, and game enjoyment. *New Media & Society, 13*(2), 224–242.
43. Stanmore, E., Stubbs, B., Vancampfort, D., de Bruin, E. D., & Firth, J. (2017). The effect of active video games on cognitive functioning in clinical and non-clinical populations: A meta-analysis of randomized controlled trials. *Neuroscience & Biobehavioral Reviews, 78*, 34–43.
44. Subramanian, S., Skjæret-Maroni, N., & Dahl, Y. (2020). Systematic review of design guidelines for full-body interactive games. *Interacting with Computers, 32*(4), 367–406.
45. Sun, H. (2013). Impact of exergames on physical activity and motivation in elementary school students: A follow-up study. *Journal of Sport and Health Science, 2*(3), 138–145.
46. Sween, J., Wallington, S. F., Sheppard, V., Taylor, T., Llanos, A. A., & Adams-Campbell, L. L. (2014). The role of exergaming in improving physical activity: A review. *Journal of Physical Activity and Health, 11*(4), 864–870.
47. Ubisoft. (2009). *Just Dance* [Video game]. Ubisoft.
48. Vernadakis, N., Papastergiou, M., Zetou, E., & Antoniou, P. (2015). The impact of an exergame-based intervention on children's fundamental motor skills. *Computers & Education, 83*, 90–102.
49. Wiemeyer, J., Deutsch, J., Malone, L. A., Rowland, J. L., Swartz, M. C., Xiong, J., & Zhang, F. F. (2014). Recommendations for the optimal design of exergame interventions for persons with disabilities: challenges, best practices, and future research. *Games for Health Journal*.
50. Wüest, S., Van De Langenberg, R., & de Bruin, E. D. (2014). Design considerations for a theory-driven exergame-based rehabilitation program to improve walking of persons with stroke. *European Review of Aging and Physical Activity, 11*(2), 119–129.

Concluding Remarks

A Universal Design perspective on video games constitutes awareness. The diversity of the people interacting with your game needs to be understood in relation to the conditions they experience throughout their lives that arise in different contexts. Awareness also needs to be considered in choosing the manifold of options to include in the design and development stage to adhere to the diverse target population. Several barriers can surface between the player and the game, not only in terms of accessing the game but also in terms of attaining the in-game experience.

Barriers toward video game attainability can arise from more or less permanent conditions and situations. Overcoming these barriers through design can enable more people to access your game while simultaneously increasing the game experience for all. A loss of hearing could, for example, make subtitles a necessity for the person to follow the story in the game. At the same time, it could also benefit a person who is playing in a noisy environment, has problems with the speaker system in the game, or simply prefers interacting with the game through text instead of sound. Adding the accessibility feature of subtitles could, in that sense, enable both the person with a hearing loss to take part in the game but also allow the person without the hearing loss to experience the game in a specific context or based on their preferences. Choosing which design options to include in relation to the target player group of your game is thus tightly aligned with making the gaming experience beneficial for all; a cornerstone of the Universal Design concept.

Throughout the present book, we have aimed to open up your awareness of Universal Design in video games. Navigating which accessibility and game experience attainability options to add to a game requires a holistic view of the targeted players, stakeholders, and their experiences. With the attainable game experience (AGE) framework, we have introduced four game design heuristics accompanied by design constraints that highlight the heuristics' relative importance. The AGE framework provides a lens that broadens the view of inclusivity in video games and provides guidance on which aspects of your game can be adapted for higher game experience attainability. The AGE framework is supplemented with the AGE

A. Palmquist et al., *Universal Design in Video Games*, Human–Computer
Interaction Series, https://doi.org/10.1007/978-3-031-30595-5

methodology, underscoring the importance of understanding the stakeholders of your game and providing recommendations for gathering their diverse perspectives. While the AGE framework and methodology can be useful in terms of guiding video game design toward higher inclusivity and game experience attainability, it is not sufficient in itself to guarantee a successful universal game design.

At its core the game experience needs to be designed to be engaging in itself. This is a complex process, including the innovation of game designers and a continuous understanding of the player experience. Applying a Universal Design lens to a video game that does not produce the intended experience for reasons that go beyond inclusivity will do little for the success of a game. Instead, Universal Design applied with an in-depth understanding of the stakeholders and relevant adaptations toward attainability can allow for broader access to the engaging experience that the game already elicits to some players. The present book consequently does not provide guidance on successful game design but instead on how successful game design can be enhanced for all players, broadening the definition of what all players can entail.

Writing a book requires a trade-off between the breadth and depth of a specific topic. In our case, we have focused on the breadth of Universal Design in video games. Instead of providing concrete recommendations on which options to add to a specific type of video game, we have strived for a broader understanding of what Universal Design can encompass for video games. The book does not provide a comprehensive guide for how to design your game as universally as possible. Instead, it serves as a starting point for reflecting on which game experience attainability options you can include to make your game more universally designed. Therefore, the book's true potential lies in combination with other resources such as currently available game accessibility guidelines, consulting accessibility experts, and good practices for game design. As every game is unique, this cannot be done without consideration of the video game's characteristics and its stakeholders. Several trade-offs need to be made, balancing the needs of the stakeholders and the technological and financial resources available. Universal Design in video games requires effort and investment. However, it can also result in great rewards, including a more inclusive society and the financial gains associated with designing video games for all.

Index

A. Palmquist et al., *Universal Design in Video Games*, Human–Computer Interaction Series, https://doi.org/10.1007/978-3-031-30595-5

The manufacturer's authorised representative in the EU is Springer Nature Customer Service Centre GmbH, Europaplatz 3, 69115 Heidelberg, Germany. If you have any concerns regarding our products, please contact ProductSafety@springernature.com

Printed and bound by CPI Group (UK) Ltd, Croydon, CR0 4YY
01/10/2026
02225957-0009